Hiking Great Smoky Mountains National Park

HELP US KEEP THIS GUIDE UP TO DATE

Every effort has been made by the author and editors to make this guide as accurate and useful as possible. However, many things can change after a guide is published—trails are rerouted, regulations change, techniques evolve, facilities come under new management, and so on.

We would appreciate hearing from you concerning your experiences with this guide and how you feel it could be improved and kept up to date. While we may not be able to respond to all comments and suggestions, we'll take them to heart, and we'll also make certain to share them with the author. Please send your comments and suggestions to the following address:

Globe Pequot Press
Reader Response/Editorial Department
P.O. Box 480
Guilford, CT 06437

Or you may e-mail us at: editorial@GlobePequot.com

Thanks for your input, and happy trails!

Hiking Great Smoky Mountains National Park

Second Edition

Kevin Adams

FALCONGUIDES

GUILFORD, CONNECTICUT
HELENA, MONTANA
AN IMPRINT OF GLOBE PEQUOT PRESS

FALCONGUIDES®

FalconGuides is an imprint of Globe Pequot Press.
Falcon, FalconGuides, and Outfit Your Mind are registered trademarks of Morris Book Publishing, LLC.

All photographs by Kevin Adams

Text design: Sheryl P. Kober
Project Editor: Lynn Zelem
Layout: Justin Pospisil-Marciano
Maps: Jim Miller/Fennana Design © Morris Book Publishing, LLC

ISSN 1542-0477
ISBN 978-0-7627-7086-1

Printed in the United States of America

Contents

The Hikes

Northwest Section

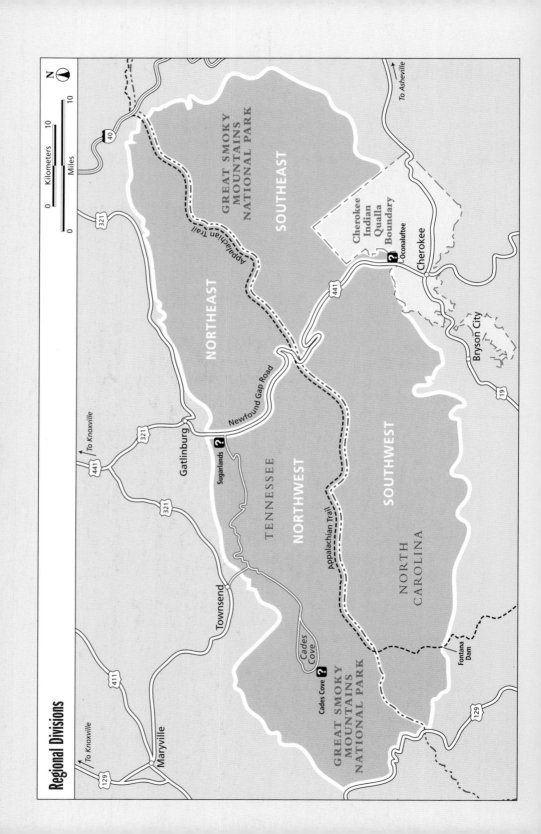

Regional Divisions

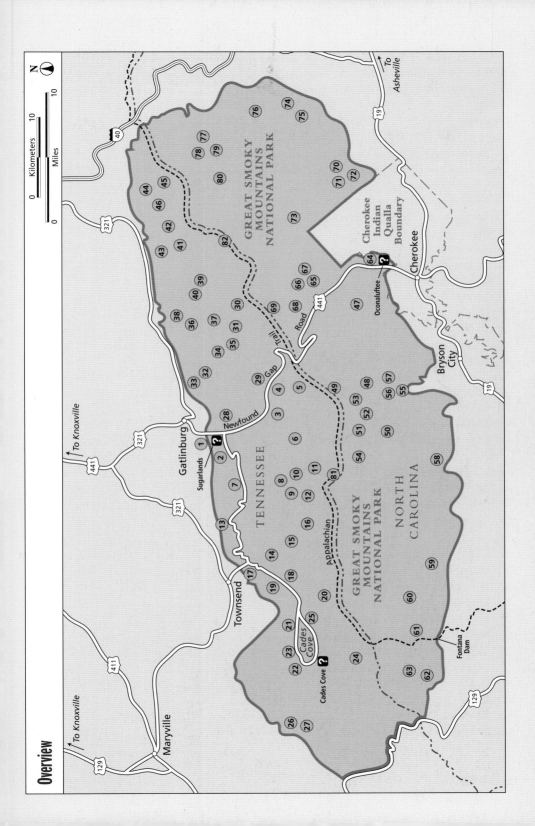

Overview

Southeast Section

Appalachian Trail

Acknowledgments

Great Smoky Mountains National Park as an ecosystem is the sum of many parts, each of which is vital to the whole. Similarly, as a national park, it exists because of the contributions from countless individuals, most of whom the average park visitor never encounters. The reason you are able to hike a trail in the Smokies without having to climb over fallen trees is because someone hiked the trail carrying a heavy saw and removed it for you. Despite operating on a shoestring budget, park employees and volunteers somehow are able to manage more than half a million acres for some ten million annual visitors.

In preparing this book I talked to dozens of these people—park rangers, interpretive volunteers, resource administrators, biologists, carpenters—even trash collectors. Each of them helped generously and with a smile. Just as they are vital to the Smokies, they were instrumental in helping me create this book. Thank you all. And thanks to everyone who works for the well-being of the Smokies.

I want to give a special thanks to my favorite trail companion: my lovely wife, Patricia. And to Titan, our crazy gray cat, for keeping my lap warm while I sat at the computer, even though he is a Fuzzy B.

◀ *White wake robin trillium (*Trillium erectum*).*

Introduction

We've always known that the Smokies are special. The Native Americans who took game here knew it. The early settlers who used the hollows to conceal their moonshine stills knew it. Even the loggers who stripped the mountainsides of their trees knew it. Today, millions of people discover, or rediscover, this special place every year.

You won't find the country's highest peaks here, nor its biggest waterfalls, widest rivers, or deepest canyons. No lakes, seashores, glaciers, volcanoes, or geysers exist within the boundary of Great Smoky Mountains National Park. They aren't needed here.

"The trees." That's the answer you often hear when asking first-time visitors what impresses them the most about the Smokies. Except for a few mountaintop balds and a few fields in lowland valleys, trees cover nearly the entire park. Living beneath all of these trees is an amazing variety of flora and fauna. Flowing underneath the trees are hundreds of miles of cascading streams, from tiny branches to small rivers.

An experience here is different from those in many other national parks. It is more intimate, more down-to-earth.

It is . . . great!

How to Use This Guide

The **Distance** heading gives the length of the hike, in miles, and the type of hike, as explained below. The mileages used in this book come from National Park Service information that is accurate and up-to-date as of this writing. The distances listed on the many trail signs and maps, however, are sometimes incorrect. (The Trails Illustrated maps and the official park trail map are generally up-to-date.) A **loop** hike starts and finishes at the same trailhead, with no (or very little) retracing of your steps. If you have to hike for some distance before beginning the loop part, it is a **lollipop** hike. A **reverse lollipop** is a loop hike with a tail along the loop, like the string on a Hershey's Kiss. On a **point-to-point** hike, you start at one location and end at another, without backtracking. Most point-to-point hikes require two vehicles (one left at each end of the trail) or a prearranged pickup or drop-off. One way to manage the logistical problems of shuttles is to arrange for another party to start at the other end of the trail. Trade keys when you meet that party on the trail, and each of you drive the other's vehicle home. Some point-to-point hikes make good **split-party** hikes. This is where your group drops you off and you hike back to meet them at the town or front-country campground where you're staying. On an **out-and-back** trip, you hike to a specific destination and then retrace your steps to the trailhead.

Hiking times are approximate and based on educated guesses. Everyone hikes at a different pace, and everyone spends a different amount of time smelling the roses along the way, so use the listed times with caution. As a rule, they are based on hiking a little over 2 mph, along with added time for enjoying the features along the hike.

Mount LeConte soars above Newfound Gap Road in this view from Chimney Tops.   **1**

(Experienced hikers can cover more ground than this on most trails in the Smokies.) Also in this heading is the manner in which most hikers will do the trip, from a day hike to backpacking trips of various lengths.

Difficulty ratings serve only as a general guide. What is difficult to one hiker may be easy to another. In this guidebook difficulty ratings do not take into account how long a route is, although generally the longer the hike, the more likely it is that it will be difficult. An **easy** hike is suitable for any hiker, including children and the elderly. Easy trails have no serious elevation gains or hazardous sections. Note, however, that couch potatoes may find the going tough on even the easy trails of the Smokies. **Moderate** hikes are for people who have some experience and at least an average fitness level. They may not be suitable for children or the elderly. The hike usually includes some hills and may include unbridged stream crossings. **Strenuous** hikes are only suitable for experienced hikers and those with an above-average fitness level. They can have substantial elevation gain and possibly some hazardous conditions. Some of the strenuous routes in this guide are crowded with hikers who probably should have chosen an easier trail. They crawl back to their cars and grumble about how rugged and inhospitable the park is.

Leashed dogs are permitted on only two trails in the park and bicycles on only four, all noted in the **Other trail users** heading. This heading is intended mainly to alert you to trails where horses are allowed. Trails that get a lot of horse traffic tend to be muddy and more eroded than hiker-only trails, and they suffer from the inevitable horse pies. However, you'll miss a lot of good hiking in the Smokies if you avoid horse trails. To make the experience more enjoyable, stop at a few of the horse pies and watch the dung beetles do their thing.

The **Maps** heading indicates on which of the U.S. Geological Survey topographical maps (USGS quad) the hike is located. These maps show incredible detail with landscape features and terrain. Unfortunately, many of them are horribly outdated regarding trail routes. In fact, they are so bad that you are advised against using them for that purpose. A number of the trails in this guidebook are not even shown on the USGS maps. Also included are the applicable Trails Illustrated maps, which are made of waterproof and tear-resistant plastic. Map #229 covers the entire park; Map #317 covers the eastern half of the park; Map #316 covers the western half of the park. These maps show contour lines and other features and are generally up-to-date. Another good map is the official park trail map, available for a small fee from park visitor centers and backcountry permit stations. It's smaller than the Trails Illustrated maps and serves well for a quick overview of all the trails in the park and for planning hikes. However, it is made of paper and is not well suited for trail use.

What It's Really Like

Prime season: Different seasons offer different experiences. In spring the park's famous ephemeral wildflowers bloom, with mid-April being about peak time. As the tree leaves start to come out, the wildflowers fade, but the vibrant hues from the emerging foliage create a show rivaling the autumn colors. Summer can have horrific traffic jams and the smog often severely restricts the distant views. But in summer the forest is ablaze with rhododendron blooms and the cold mountain streams provide a refreshing break for sweaty hikers. Autumn in the Smokies is unrivaled, with mid-October the normal peak for autumn leaf color. However, depending on the elevation, you can usually find good color throughout the month of October and even into November. October is insanely crowded, but most of the leaf peepers never stray far from their car so you can still find solitude on some of the trails. Winter is delightfully free of traffic jams and provides the clearest long-range views, but winter hiking in the Smokies requires extra planning.

Weather: Snow is common in the higher elevations from November through March, and you should also expect it in October and April. Spring is fickle, with warm sunny days changing to cold snowy ones in a heartbeat. Summer is hot and hazy, and afternoon thunderstorms are common. Autumn has wonderful weather, with a good number of warm blue-sky days and clear crisp nights.

Black bears: The Great Smokies have many black bears and seeing one is always a possibility—and a thrill. Keep that encounter safe by reading Make It a Safe Trip, below.

Bugs: Mosquitoes are typically not a problem in the Smokies since there is little standing water for them to breed. What *is* irritating are no-see-ums and blackflies. In warm weather they can drive you nuts. See Make It a Safe Trip for more information about nasty insects in the park.

Finding solitude: Some trails are overcrowded; others receive little use yet offer a hiking experience just as rewarding as the crowded trails. The Trail Finder lists some of the most popular trails. Avoiding hordes of people is simple: Don't hike the most popular trails except on winter weekdays, when your experience will range from seeing a few people to having the hike to yourself.

Thieves: Thieves may prowl the remote parking areas looking for vehicles left overnight or during the day. Even vehicles parked within plain sight of major roads have been broken into and vandalized. The hike descriptions alert you to places that have recurring problems, but you should be careful no matter where you leave your vehicle. Don't leave anything in sight and don't leave a note on the dashboard saying how long you're going to be out. Using a blanket or jacket to cover up stuff is like displaying a sign for thieves that you're hiding something valuable. Valuables are best left at home, or at least in your trunk.

Large furry things on the road: When hurrying to get to the trailhead in the early morning hours, or when feeling anxious while driving home in the evening, be especially watchful for white-tailed deer, elk, and other wildlife on the roadways. Hitting a deer will ruin your day—it's even harder on the animal.

Small flat things on the road: It's sad to see all the roadkill in a place such the Smokies—or anywhere, for that matter. Avoid adding to the flattened fauna by slowing down and watching the road. Box turtles and frogs like to come out after a rain in warm weather, and on a warm, wet night, the frogs are very active.

Water, water, everywhere: Water is everywhere in the Smokies, and nearly every drop of it started out as rain or condensation. You're likely to have to hike in rain no matter when you visit the park. In winter it can rain solid for days. Summer can bring a thunderstorm every afternoon for weeks. If hiking for more than a few hours, you should carry rain gear with you, regardless of the weather conditions when you set out.

Getting to the Park

It's estimated that two-thirds of the people in the United States are within a day's drive of the Smokies. The park is located on the North Carolina–Tennessee border, near the northern border of Georgia. The major interstate accesses are I-40 from the east and west, I-81 from the north, and I-75 from the north and south. Both I-40 and I-75 pass through Knoxville, Tennessee, just northwest of the park. Knoxville is the nearest major city. I-81 joins I-40 east of Knoxville. I-40 also passes through Asheville on the North Carolina side, about an hour from the park. A major access highway from the south is US 23 from Atlanta, which joins US 441 northeast of Atlanta. US 441 is the only transmountain highway in the Smokies, with a large network of smaller roads providing access from all directions. Study a road map to determine the best route from your location.

On your first Smokies trip, you'll likely enter the park at one of two main entrances: Cherokee, North Carolina, or Gatlinburg, Tennessee. Newfound Gap Road (US 441) connects the two towns, crossing over the Smokies' crest at Newfound Gap and essentially splitting the park in half. The main park visitor centers are located a short distance from each town: Oconaluftee Visitor Center for Cherokee, and Sugarlands Visitor Center for Gatlinburg. Two other visitor centers are located within park boundaries: a center located at the Cable Mill area in Cades Cove and one on Clingmans Dome. Numerous ranger stations and campgrounds provide additional sources of information throughout the park.

If you are flying to the park and renting a car, you will fly into either Knoxville, Tennessee, or Asheville, North Carolina. (Atlanta is an option as well, especially since many flights to Knoxville or Asheville will connect there.) Knoxville is a little closer and has a larger airport. If heading to the park's Gatlinburg entrance from Knoxville's McGhee Tyson Airport, you will take US 129 (Alcoa Highway) north to I-40 in the heart of Knoxville. Take I-40 east to TN 66 at exit 407 (you will see the signs for the park). Follow TN 66 south to Sevierville, where you'll pick up US 441 and follow it south through Pigeon Forge and into Gatlinburg.

If heading to the park's Townsend entrance in the western end of the park, take US 129 south from the Knoxville airport and pick up US 321/TN 73 in Maryville. Follow US 321 north to Townsend and continue straight instead of turning left to remain on US 321 (you will see the signs for the park). The Townsend entrance is becoming increasingly popular. It is the closest access to Cades Cove, one of the most popular locations in the park.

From Asheville's Regional Airport, you will take I-26 north to I-40 and head west on I-40 to US 23/74 at exit 27. US 23/74 is called Great Smoky Mountain Expressway and it offers numerous approaches to the park. Most visitors will follow one of the two main routes from the expressway: US 19 through Maggie Valley and into Cherokee or US 441 into Cherokee. All routes are well signed.

The 469-mile-long Blue Ridge Parkway terminates at Newfound Gap Road, between Cherokee and Oconaluftee Visitor Center.

If you don't already know something about the park, one of these accesses is likely to be your entry point. There are many additional vehicle entrances to the park, but a first-time visitor will want to drive the main roads initially to get a handle on the park before branching out.

Finally, a word of warning. First-time park visitors are often startled by the juxtaposition of the park and ultra-touristy Gatlinburg and Pigeon Forge (home to Dollywood), and to a slightly lesser extent, Cherokee. Although they don't exactly offer a wilderness experience, these towns do provide valuable services, including accommodations for those who aren't into camping or backpacking.

Supplies and Services

Unlike many other national parks, Great Smoky Mountains National Park does not have any public lodging, food, or fuel services within its borders. (LeConte Lodge on Mount LeConte is the only lodging exception, but you have to hike 5 miles to get there. The Cades Cove Campground store has basic food and camping supplies, but the store closes in winter.) The surrounding towns offer everything you need, but the services are seasonal at many places. The following closely surrounding towns have basic year-round services: Cherokee, Maggie Valley, Waynesville, and Bryson City in North Carolina; Gatlinburg, Pigeon Forge, and Townsend in Tennessee. Other small communities have gas stations and small stores that are open year-round, but most other services close for the winter. Many businesses close for the season even in some of the larger towns, such as Bryson City and Cherokee.

Other than Cades Cove, park front-country (vehicle) campgrounds offer minimal services, such as ice, firewood, and vending machines. Drink vending machines are available at Sugarlands and Oconaluftee Visitor Centers.

See appendix B for a list of commercial shuttle services.

The Trails

In the Smokies, unlike at some other parks, you can't just strike out and hike wherever you want. The rugged landscape and dense vegetation are not conducive to much off-trail hiking. Besides, doing so can harm the ecosystem, and with more than 800 miles of maintained trails in the park, it's just not necessary. You can have an intimate experience and see everything you'd want to see right from an official trail. Every hike in this guidebook uses only official trails. Some of the routes follow one trail only; others use a combination of several trails. One advantage to remaining on official park trails is that you don't have to worry too much about getting lost—as long as you carry a map showing the trails. Every trail junction is signed, and the park does a good job of keeping the signs up. (Bears sometimes chew them up and some of the older ones are rotting away.)

This guidebook includes all of the short self-guiding nature trails in the park, but it does not include any of the "Quiet Walkways." You'll see signs indicating these walkways along the main park roads. They have small parking areas so that only a few people can use the trails at a time. All of them are short and lead to some feature, such as a stream or an old homesite. Part of the charm of these paths is not knowing what's in store until you hike them. So no clues here. Discover them yourself.

In some areas of the park, particularly Sugarlands, Smokemont, Deep Creek, and Cades Cove, you may encounter wide, unsigned trails that obviously are being used regularly. These are usually bridle paths, and while they may be "official," they don't make the best hiking trails. Horses are allowed on many of the official hiking trails, but these unsigned bridle paths are intended primarily for horses. You can hike them if you want, but it is not recommended. Stick to the official hiking trails.

Everywhere in the park, you'll encounter unsigned side paths branching off from the official trails. Some of these paths are heavily traveled, while many of them are old trails that are mostly overgrown. Regardless of the condition, very few of these paths are maintained by the park, and hiking them is discouraged. Again, with over 800 miles of maintained and signed trails in the park, you can experience everything you want right from an official trail.

It is very important that you check ahead to make sure the trails for the hike you are planning are open. Trails may be closed temporarily for a number of reasons, including bear activity, storm damage, and maintenance.

Backcountry Campsites

The park is currently working on a new online system for managing backcountry camping. Permits and reservations will be required for all overnight stays and a small fee will be charged. All backcountry shelters and campsites will be rationed. The park hopes to have the new system implemented sometime in 2013. You should contact the park to find out if the system is in use before making your trip. The following information will apply until the new system is employed.

In the Smokies you must camp at a designated backcountry campsite unless you obtain a special cross-country permit, available only from designated park rangers. The rules for these permits are very strict and applications are not automatically approved. Unless you are working on a scientific research project or something similar, it is highly recommended that you stick to the main trails and campsites just like everyone else. (See The Trails, above.)

All backcountry campsites in the Smokies are numbered and all shelters are named. The sites have names too, but only the numbers are referred to on trail maps and when obtaining permits. All locations that provide backcountry permits have a map showing the location of sites and a listing of rationed sites. (Rationed sites require a reservation.) In addition, both the official park trail map and the Trails Illustrated maps list all of the backcountry campsites and shelters. While the list of rationed sites remains fairly constant, it can change in response to use patterns and bear activity.

All sites and shelters have a water source nearby, either a spring or a stream. Springs are not always dependable, and it's a good idea to check ahead before beginning an overnight trip in dry conditions. Rangers may not know whether a particular spring is dry, but they can give you a general idea of conditions.

Another consideration is that the park closes campsites occasionally due to bear activity or other reasons. The park posts these closings where permits are obtained, but you don't want to find out at the last minute that the site you've planned on is closed. Call the permit office at (865) 436-1231 to make sure your site is open before you head out.

At the time of this guide's publication, the following backcountry campsites are rationed and require a reservation in addition to a permit:

All shelters

9	Anthony Creek	47	Enloe Creek
10	Ledbetter Ridge	50	Lower Chasteen Creek
13	Sheep Pen Gap	55	Pole Road
17	Little Bottoms	57	Bryson Place
20	King Branch	60	Bumgardner Branch
21	Mile 53	61	Bald Creek
23	Camp Creek	71	CCC Camp
24	Rough Creek	83	Bone Valley
29	Otter Creek	84	Sugar Fork
36	Upper Walnut Bottom	85	Sawdust Pile
37	Lower Walnut Bottom	86	Proctor
38	Mount Sterling	90	Lost Cove
46	Estes Branch	113	Birch Spring Gap

Backcountry Permits

Read the opening paragraph of Backcountry Campsites, above, for information about the park's new permit system. The following information applies until the new system is implemented.

In Great Smoky Mountains National Park, you must have a permit for any overnight stay in the backcountry, regardless of whether the campsite is rationed. The Backcountry Camping Permit system is designed to protect the park's natural and cultural resources, as well as to provide the best backcountry experience for hikers.

See the introduction for Hikes 81 and 82 if you are doing a thru-hike of the Appalachian Trail.

Permits are free and can be obtained from Oconaluftee or Sugarlands Visitor Centers, ranger stations, most front-country campgrounds, and at some trail information boards. The permit is obtained through a self-registration process. If the site where you wish to camp is not rationed, simply read the instructions on the permit, fill it out, and place one copy in the permit box. If you choose a rationed site, you have to call the Backcountry Reservation Office to obtain a reservation. (Be prepared with alternative dates if you call at the last minute.) The Reservation Office will give you a number to write on your permit. The office is open seven days a week from 8 a.m. to 6 p.m. ET. Call (865) 436-1231 for reservations. The general backcountry information number is (865) 436-1297.

Backcountry Use Regulations

These regulations apply to *all* backcountry users, including Appalachian Trail thru-hikers.

In the Great Smokies, *do:*
- Have a permit to camp in the backcountry.
- Follow all instructions on the permit, and keep the permit in your possession while hiking.
- Camp only at designated campsites and shelters.
- Build fires only in established fire rings at designated campsites or shelters.
- Use only wood that is dead and down to build fires. Backpacking stoves are encouraged.
- Suspend your food and odorous items from the provided suspension cables.
- Carry out all trash. If you can pack it in, you can pack it out.
- Have a valid state fishing permit from either North Carolina or Tennessee if you fish in the park. A permit from either state allows you to fish anywhere in the park. Be sure to obtain specific fishing regulations from the park before you fish.

In the Great Smokies, *do not:*
- Feed, harass, or intentionally disturb wildlife.
- Cut, carve, or deface trees or buildings.
- Take non-service pets into the backcountry. (Non-service pets are allowed *only* on Oconaluftee River and Gatlinburg Trails.)
- Make campsite "improvements" such as fire rings, rock walls, or drainage trenches.
- Use a wheeled vehicle or cart on hiking trails. The exceptions for bicycles are Gatlinburg and Oconaluftee River Trails and the lower portions of Deep Creek

and Indian Creek Trails. The exceptions for wheeled carts are the lower sections of Hazel Creek, Forney Creek, and Noland Creek.

- Cut switchbacks.
- Wash dishes or bathe (with soap) in park streams.
- Pitch a tent at backcountry shelters. Appalachian Trail thru-hikers may camp outside shelters if there is no bunk space available. See the introduction for the Appalachian Trail at the beginning of Hikes 81 and 82.
- Dispose of human waste within 100 feet of a campsite or water source or within sight of a trail. You should bury feces in a 6-inch-deep hole.
- Gather ramps. The park no longer allows picking these onion-like plants.
- Stay more than one night in a row at a shelter or more than three consecutive nights at a campsite. (This may change with the new fee system.)

Leave No Trace

If you turned around and backtracked the hike you just made, would you see any evidence that you had been there? Did the animals and plants feel any effect from your visit?

Going into a national park such as Great Smoky Mountains National Park is like visiting a world-renowned museum. You wouldn't want to leave your mark on an art treasure, would you? If everybody going through the museum leaves one little mark, the piece of art will quickly be destroyed—and of what value is a big building full of trashed art? The same goes for an environment such as the Smokies, which is as magnificent as any masterpiece by any artist. If we all leave just one little mark on the landscape, the wilderness will soon be despoiled.

The park can accommodate human use if everyone behaves responsibly, but a few thoughtless or uninformed visitors can ruin it for everybody. All visitors have a responsibility to know and follow the rules of Leave No Trace hiking and camping. Today, most people want to walk softly, but some aren't aware that they have poor manners. Often their actions are dictated by the outdated habits of a previous generation of campers who cut green boughs for evening shelters, built campfires with fire rings, and dug trenches around tents. In the 1950s these "camping rules" may have been acceptable, but they leave long-lasting scars, and today such behavior is absolutely unacceptable. The wilderness is shrinking and the number of users is mushrooming. More and more camping areas show unsightly signs of heavy use.

A new code of ethics has grown out of the necessity of coping with the unending waves of people who want a rewarding wilderness experience. Today, we all must leave no clues that we have gone before. Canoeists can look behind their boat and see no trace of their passing. Hikers should have the same goal.

- Leave nothing, regardless of how small it is, along the trail or at the campsite. Pack out everything, including orange peels, cigarette butts, and gum wrappers. If possible, pick up trash that others leave behind.

- Follow the main trail. Avoid cutting switchbacks and walking on vegetation beside the trail.
- Do not deface any natural feature or any manmade structure by carving, marking, or destroying in any manner.
- Do not pick wildflowers or any plant. All living things in the park are protected by law.
- Camp only in designated campsites and only use existing campfire rings if you must build a fire. Camp stoves are recommended.

For more information about treading softy in the outdoors, visit the website for Leave No Trace Center for Outdoor Ethics at www.lnt.org.

Make It a Safe Trip

The Boy Scouts of America have been guided for decades by what is perhaps the best single piece of safety advice: "Be prepared!" It might seem a bit excessive to place so much emphasis on safety when hiking in a park whose trails are all signed and well maintained, but just ask the park rangers what they think about it. Their job is to find and rescue all the people who think nothing can happen to them.

- Tell somebody where you're going and when you plan to return. Pilots must file flight plans before every trip, and anybody venturing into the backcountry should do the same. File your "flight plan" with a friend or relative—or at the hotel desk—before taking off. (Don't leave your itinerary on the dashboard of your car. This only invites thievery.)
- Bring extra food and water.
- Bring warm clothing and raingear, no matter what the weather forecast is.
- Stay on the official park trails. On a regular trail in the Smokies, you, or someone who finds you in distress, is rarely more than a dozen or so miles from help, and usually much closer. If something happens to you while you are off-trail, the chances of rescuers finding you or of you getting help are greatly diminished.
- If you get lost, try not to panic. Yes, that's a trite statement. It's also sage advice. Unless you've done something really stupid like wander for miles off-trail before stopping to realize that you don't know where the heck you are, getting lost in the Smokies is not necessarily a big deal. Sit down and relax for a few minutes while you carefully check your map. Most important, as mentioned above, *do not leave the trail.* You are never truly lost while on an official park trail. Many tragedies have occurred in the Smokies because hikers became twisted around and thought they would be better off by leaving the trail. If you stay on the trail, the chances of meeting another hiker who can help you are much greater (it's probably impossible if you're off-trail). Also, if you don't make it back when you're supposed to and a search party is sent out, they will scan the trails first.

- Don't wait until you're confused before looking at your map. Follow the map as you go along so that you have a continual fix on your location.
- Keep your party together if you become lost.
- Physical conditioning is an important consideration. Being fit not only makes outdoor travel more fun, it also makes it safer.
- Check the weather forecast and keep an eye on cloud formations. You don't want to get caught in a lightning storm on a ridgeline or find yourself crossing a stream during a flash flood. Remember, though, that the weather in the Smokies can change very quickly and the forecasts are not always accurate.
- Don't eat wild plants unless you have positively identified them and then only eat the fruiting body. Don't destroy plants.
- Before you leave for the trailhead, find out as much as you can about the route, especially the potential hazards.
- Don't exhaust yourself or other members of your party by traveling too far or too fast. Let the slowest person set the pace.
- Stay clear of all wild animals.
- Take a first-aid and survival kit that includes at least basic supplies.
- Stay on the trail. Yes, it's worth repeating.

Lightning. The Smoky Mountains are prone to sudden thunderstorms, especially during summer. If you get caught by a lightning storm, you need to take special precautions.

- Lightning can travel far ahead of a storm and linger afterward. Take cover before the storm hits, and don't leave until you are sure it is safe.
- Don't try to make it back to your vehicle—it isn't worth the risk. Instead, seek shelter even if it's only a short way back to the trailhead. Lightning storms usually don't last long, and from a safe vantage point you might even enjoy the sights and sounds.
- Be especially careful not to get caught on a mountaintop or exposed ridge. Other bad places to be are under large, solitary trees, out in the open, or near water.
- Seek shelter in a low-lying area, ideally in a dense stand of small, uniformly sized trees.
- Stay away from anything that might attract lightning, such as metal tent poles, graphite fishing rods, or pack frames.
- Get in a crouch position, and place both feet firmly on the ground.
- Don't walk or huddle together with others. Instead, stay at least 50 feet apart so that if somebody is hit by lightning, others in your party can give first aid.
- If someone is struck by lighting and he or she is not breathing, prolonged CPR should be administered.

Hypothermia. Be aware of the dangers of hypothermia—a condition in which the body's internal temperature drops below normal. It can lead to mental and physical collapse—even death. It is among the more serious dangers for Smoky Mountain hikers.

Hypothermia is caused by exposure to cold and is aggravated by wetness, wind, and exhaustion. The moment you begin to lose heat faster than your body produces it, you're suffering from exposure. Your body starts involuntary exercises, such as shivering, to stay warm, and makes involuntary adjustments to preserve normal temperature in vital organs, restricting blood flow to the extremities. Both responses drain your energy reserves. The only way to stop the drain is to reduce the degree of exposure.

With full-blown hypothermia, as energy reserves are exhausted, cold reaches the brain, depriving you of good judgment and reasoning power. You won't be aware that this is happening. You lose control of your hands. Your internal temperature slides downward. Without treatment, this slide leads to stupor, collapse, and eventually death.

To defend against hypothermia, you need to stay dry. When clothes get wet, they lose about 90 percent of their insulating value. Wool loses relatively less heat, while cotton, down, and some synthetics lose more. Choose rain clothes that cover the head, neck, body, and legs and provide good protection against wind-driven rain. Most hypothermia cases develop in air temperatures between thirty and fifty degrees Fahrenheit, but hypothermia can develop in warmer temperatures.

If your party is exposed to wind, cold, and wetness, you should be on the lookout for hypothermia symptoms. Watch yourself and others for uncontrollable fits of shivering; vague, slow, slurred speech; memory lapses; incoherence; immobile or fumbling hands; frequent stumbling or a lurching gait; drowsiness (to sleep is to die); apparent exhaustion; and inability to get up after a rest. When a member of your party has hypothermia, he or she may deny any problem. Believe the symptoms, not the victim. Even mild symptoms demand treatment, as follows:

- Get the victim out of the wind and rain.
- Strip off all wet clothes.
- If the victim is only mildly impaired, give him or her warm drinks and then get the victim in warm clothes and a warm sleeping bag. Place well-wrapped water bottles filled with heated water close to the victim.
- If the victim is badly impaired, keep him or her awake. Put the victim in a sleeping bag with another person—both naked. If there are other people who can help, have them lie on the outside of the sleeping bag with the victim.
- Seek medical help as soon as it is safe to do so. Do not leave a hypothermic victim alone.

Heat exhaustion. Like hypothermia, heat-related illness is a serious concern and should not be taken lightly. It is caused by an insufficient supply of water to the body in hot temperatures. Victims can suffer from nausea, feeling dizzy or faint, headaches, vomiting, muscle cramps, behavior changes such as stumbling and disorientation, and a general feeling of weakness. If you see these symptoms in a person, you should immediately try to lower their body temperature. Get them out of the sun and have them drink lots of water. If you're near a creek or spring, get the water from the creek and constantly pour it over the victim's body. (Do not immerse the victim in the creek, as this may make the condition worse.) Find something to use as a fan to move air over the victim's body.

Seek medical help as soon as possible. Heat exhaustion can lead to heatstroke, a very serious medical emergency.

Bad bugs. Blackflies and no-see-ums are a major nuisance to summer hikers in the Smokies. The good news is that they just irritate you—they don't cause any real harm. Bees, on the other hand, do cause serious problems. Most bee stings in the park come from yellow jackets, which have a nasty habit of building their underground nests in the middle or the edge of hiking trails. If you're lucky enough to see the bees before you walk over them, just give them a wide berth and walk slowly around the nest. While yellow jackets are aggressive, they won't attack unless they feel threatened. If they fly around you while you walk by, don't swat at them. That will pretty much guarantee a sting.

If you are stung on your hand, remove your rings immediately, before any swelling occurs. For most people, one or two bee stings are not a serious issue, resulting only in temporary pain and minor swelling. However, multiple stings can be serious, even if you are not allergic to bee stings. If you experience symptoms other than local swelling and pain, such as difficulty in breathing or breaking out in welts, this is a serious issue. Take an antihistamine, such as Benadryl, and seek medical help immediately.

If you know you are allergic to bee stings, you should take precautions before hiking in the Smokies from spring through fall. Consult with a doctor about proper prevention measures and always have your bee-sting kit with you on the trail.

Bad plants. Many poisonous or obnoxious plants live in the Smokies, but only two are likely to cause any trouble for most hikers. The first is poison ivy. Poison ivy only grows in disturbed and usually open areas, but that still gives it a lot of real estate to thrive in the park. The plant is pervasive is some areas, particularly old homesites and along old roads. As with all safety concerns, the best treatment is prevention. Learn to identify the plant and just stay the heck away from it.

The other nasty plant in the Smokies is wood nettle. You might not be familiar with this plant, but the first time you brush against it while wearing shorts, you'll never forget it. Examine a wood nettle plant closely and you'll see thousands of tiny prickles all over the leaves and stem. They sting like fire when you brush against them, although the pain is fortunately short-lived. Wood nettle is very common and has a habit of growing along trails. Learn to identify it and, as with poison ivy, stay away from it.

Long, slithery animals. Two kinds of venomous snakes live in the Smokies: the northern copperhead and the timber rattlesnake. Both of them would prefer not to have an encounter with you just as much as you would prefer not to have an encounter with them. So, if you don't seek them out and if you don't do something stupid like stick your hands and feet where you can't see, you'll likely be just fine. If you happen across a snake on the trail, simply give it a wide berth and leave it be. Remember, *all* living things are protected in the park, whether or not they are potentially dangerous.

If a venomous snake bites you, do not apply a tourniquet and do not make any incisions. These outdated field treatments often do more harm than good. Instead, seek medical attention as soon as possible, *without* rushing. You should hike slowly, trying to keep the blood circulation down as much as possible. If you are with someone, send that person for help while you remain stationary. Try to remain calm. Many snakebites are dry, with no venom being injected.

Bad shoes and tree limbs. Perhaps the most common medical emergencies that befall hikers in the Smokies are leg and ankle injuries. When hikers don't pay attention to where they're going, they can step on a loose rock or stick and wham!—they're on the ground with a scraped knee or twisted ankle, or worse. A very common cause of hikers hitting the trail—literally—is stepping on wet, barkless water breaks on the trail. You know, those tree limbs running diagonally across the trail to divert water. Once the bark falls off, they are slick as ice when wet. Nearly all of these injuries can be prevented by following these two pieces of advice: Pay attention to where you're stepping and *don't wear sandals.*

Some people think that to "get back to nature" means it's obligatory to put on the Tevas or Keens. Sandals are perfectly fine in some situations, but hiking in the Smokies is not one of them. Sandals provide nearly zero ankle protection and they allow sticks and stones to get in and irritate your feet. The ones with open toes are particularly dangerous to wear on the rocky trails of the Smokies. Do your feet a favor and wear ankle-supporting hiking boots.

Bad water. Regardless of how "crystal clear" a stream or spring might appear, there is no guarantee that the water in the Smokies is safe to drink. You don't know what animal might have left its mark 5 minutes before you got there. All sorts of bacteria, viruses, and parasites could be in the water, including *Giardia lamblia,* a nasty little protozoan that causes severe abdominal cramps and diarrhea.

The best defense against illness is to bring all drinking water to a roiling boil for 1 minute. It is not necessary to boil the water for 5 or 10 minutes. Boiling water is impractical on many trips, so many people use pump-style water filters. Most of these types of filters will remove *Giardia* and bacteria, but most viruses are too small to filter. Iodine treatments are often impractical with the cold water temperatures of mountain springs. With very cold water, the time required for iodine to purify the water could be several hours, depending upon the concentration.

Don't fall in the water. If you do much hiking in the Smokies, sooner or later you're going to have to ford a stream. In winter and early spring, with water levels at their highest, many streams are too large to rock-hop and they must be waded. In summer, when streams are typically at their lowest levels, most creek crossings in the Smokies are rock-hoppable, but the conditions could change quickly if a thunderstorm moves through. During any time of year, prolonged or heavy rains can swell streams to unsafe levels.

Stream crossings in the Smokies are different from those at some other national parks. The creeks here are steep and rocky mountain streams. When the water is up, they can become raging torrents. If you fall in, the accepted practice of lying on your back and going downstream feet first until you can right yourself still applies, but it may be impossible to do so before you crash into a few dozen rocks and fallen trees. These aren't wide glacial or valley rivers we're talking about here: The streams here are full of rocks and downfall. The best advice, of course, is not to fall in.

A good idea is to practice. Most creek crossings have bridges or foot logs. Try fording the stream on the upstream side of the foot log, using it to keep your balance. You'll quickly learn how to read currents. Before attempting any ford, consider the following:

- Don't attempt a crossing if you feel unsafe. Never feel embarrassed by being cautious.
- Don't automatically cross at the trail. Search upstream and downstream for a better crossing.
- Loosen the belt straps on your backpack. It will help you maintain your balance as you cross and allow you to get out of the pack quickly if you fall.
- Streams in the Smokies are very cold. Don't attempt a long crossing in bare feet, even in summer, unless you have experience doing so. Your legs can numb and you can injure your feet on sharp rocks or sticks.
- Many hikers carry lightweight sandals, which work well as creek-crossing shoes and camp shoes. Keep in mind, however, that sandals provide no ankle protection. You need to be extremely careful crossing streams when you can't see the bottom.
- In winter even a short crossing can be dangerous. A good idea is to take off your socks and cross wearing just your boots. Once across, immediately dry your feet and put your socks and boots back on. You can dry your boots by the campfire that night.
- A walking stick can help you keep your balance, but rocky creek bottoms make it difficult to get a good purchase with one. Be sure to plant the stick firmly before taking your next step.

Be bear aware. Something happened on May 21, 2000, that had never before happened in the Smokies: A person was killed by a black bear. It is not known whether the victim did anything to provoke the attack. While such incidents are extremely rare—and there's no reason to panic about man-eating bears prowling the park—the case does underscore the need for all hikers to educate themselves about proper conduct in bear country.

The majority of bear attacks occur when a hiker surprises a bear. Therefore, it's vital to do everything possible to avoid these surprise meetings. Be alert at all times, keeping a watchful eye on the surroundings, not just the trail ahead of you. Stay on the trail, where there's less chance of a sudden encounter. Be especially watchful in summer when hiking near berry patches or black cherry trees. That clump of blueberries ahead might have a black bear in it. Make noise when you hike to alert the bears to your presence.

If you see a bear on the trail, freeze. Chances are, the bear doesn't give a hoot about you and will carry on with its business. Let it. A bear that snorts or paws the ground is just telling you that you are too close. Listen up. Don't get any closer, and if the bear is not moving away, slowly separate yourself from the bear. A bear that feels threatened might make a bluff charge. Stand your ground—don't run. It's tough to stand your ground against a charging bear, but that is exactly what you should do. No human can outrun a bear.

A bear that follows you but does not exhibit aggressive behavior, such as snorting, pawing, or bluff charging, may consider you a food source. Continue retreating and change directions. If the bear continues to follow, arm yourself with whatever you can, such as a knife or stick, and stand your ground. If you're with a group, huddle together to appear larger. Raise and spread your arms. Start yelling and throwing rocks. Don't throw food, as this will only encourage more behavior that is aggressive. As an absolute last resort, try throwing your entire pack at the bear. The time the bear spends investigating its contents may be just enough time for you to get away. If the bear ignores your pack, particularly if it has food in it, you might be in serious jeopardy. Hold tight to your knife or stick, and if the bear makes contact and continues attacking, fight back as aggressively as you can. Don't play dead; that seems only to work with grizzlies. Black bears usually bluff charge, but if they do make contact, they might consider you food.

Bears are attracted to campsites by the smell of food. Minimize those odors and you minimize bear encounters. Store all food and toiletry items in plastic bags when not in use, and don't cook in your tent. All shelters and campsites in the Smokies now have cable-hanging systems for suspending food. The safest approach is to suspend your entire pack, but if you are very careful with food odors, you can suspend just the food in a separate bag. All food, trash, toiletry items, lip balm, tobacco, etc., must be suspended. The use of these cable systems has greatly reduced bear encounters in the Smokies.

Trail Finder

Easy (E); Moderate (M); Strenuous (S)

Stream Hikes

5 Road Prong (E)
9 Cucumber Gap and Little River (M)
10 Little River (E)
11 Goshen Prong (M)
15 Indian Flats Falls (M)
22 Abrams Falls (M)
29 Alum Cave Bluffs (M)
34 Rainbow Falls (S)
39 Porters Creek (M)
41 Ramsey Cascades (M)
54 Silers Bald and Forney Creek (S)
59 Hazel Creek and Bone Valley (E)
60 Eagle Creek, Spence Field, and Hazel Creek (S)
67 Bradley Fork and Chasteen Creek (M)
68 Kephart Prong (E)
74 Boogerman (M)
78 Big Creek (E)

Hikes with Good Distant Views

21 Rich Mountain Loop (M)
24 Gregory Bald via Cades Cove (S)
29 Alum Cave Bluffs (M)
30 Charlies Bunion (M)
31 Mount LeConte via The Boulevard (S)
35 Mount LeConte via Rainbow Falls and Bull Head (S)
40 Brushy Mountain (M)
45 Mount Cammerer (S)
51 Clingmans Dome (S)
52 Andrews Bald (S)
54 Silers Bald and Forney Creek (S)
61 Shuckstack (S)

69 Charlies Bunion and Bradley Fork (S)
77 Mount Sterling (S)
79 Big Creek and Mount Sterling (S)
80 Big Creek Perimeter Loop (S)
81 Appalachian Trail West (S)
82 Appalachian Trail East (S)

Hikes with Big Trees

7 Laurel Falls and Cove Mountain (M)
20 Spence Field via Cades Cove (S)
24 Gregory Bald via Cades Cove (S)
34 Rainbow Falls (S)
35 Mount LeConte via Rainbow Falls and Bull Head (S)
39 Porters Creek (M)
41 Ramsey Cascades (M)
42 Albright Grove (M)
46 Maddron Bald and Hen Wallow Falls (S)
67 Bradley Fork and Chasteen Creek (M)
69 Charlies Bunion and Bradley Fork (S)
70 Hemphill Bald (M)
74 Boogerman (M)
75 Rough Fork and Caldwell Fork (M)
79 Big Creek and Mount Sterling (S)
80 Big Creek Perimeter Loop (S)

Wildflower Hikes

3 Cove Hardwoods Nature Trail (E)
15 Indian Flats Falls (M)
16 Lynn Camp Prong and Appalachian Trail (S)

Hikes to Avoid If You Don't Want to See Lots of People

Hikes to Avoid If You Don't Like Crossing Unbridged Streams

Hikes for People Training to Be Navy Seals

Hikes for People Training to Be Couch Potatoes

Hikes for People Who Like Cultural History

10 Little River (E)
13 Walker Sisters Home (M)
21 Rich Mountain Loop (M)
28 Sugarlands Valley Nature Trail (E)
43 Old Settlers Trail (M)
59 Hazel Creek and Bone Valley (E)
68 Kephart Prong (E)
75 Rough Fork and Caldwell Fork (M)
76 Little Cataloochee (M)

Waterfall Hikes

7 Laurel Falls and Cove Mountain (M)
14 Spruce Flats Falls (M)
15 Indian Flats Falls (M)
22 Abrams Falls (M)
34 Rainbow Falls (S)
36 Grotto Falls (M)
38 Baskins Creek Falls (S)
41 Ramsey Cascades (M)
55 Juney Whank Falls (M)
56 Deep Creek Loop (E)
78 Big Creek (E)

Geology Hikes

4 Chimney Tops (S)
29 Alum Cave Bluffs (M)
30 Charlies Bunion (M)

31 Mount LeConte via The Boulevard (S)
35 Mount LeConte via Rainbow Falls and Bull Head (S)
78 Big Creek (E)
81 Appalachian Trail West (S)
82 Appalachian Trail East (S)

The Author's Favorites

3 Cove Hardwoods Nature Trail (E)
5 Road Prong (E)
17 Chestnut Top Wildflowers (E)
24 Gregory Bald via Cades Cove (S)
29 Alum Cave Bluffs (M)
31 Mount LeConte via The Boulevard (S)
32 Noah "Bud" Ogle Nature Trail (E)
37 Mount LeConte via Trillium Gap (S)
39 Porters Creek (M)
41 Ramsey Cascades (M)
46 Maddron Bald and Hen Wallow Falls (S)
68 Kephart Prong (E)
69 Charlies Bunion and Bradley Fork (S)
73 Hyatt Ridge (M)
78 Big Creek (E)
79 Big Creek and Mount Sterling (S)

Map Legend

Transportation

≡40≡ Interstate Highway

≡488≡ US Highway

≡49≡ State Highway

Local Road

= = = = Unpaved Road

------ Featured Trail

------ Trail

▷1 → Hike Direction

Water Features

Body of Water

River/Creek

Waterfall

Land Management

— - — - State Line

National Park

Symbols

▲ Backcountry Campground

▲ Campground

— Dam

🗼 Fire Tower

❗ Gate

🅿 Parking

▲ Peak/Summit

🛆 Picnic Area

■ Point of Interest/Structure

🛈 Ranger Station

🚻 Restrooms

○ Town

① Trailhead

❓ Visitor Center

Northwest Section

*Mountain laurel (*Kalmia latifolia*).*

1 Gatlinburg Trail

This walk between Sugarlands Visitor Center and Gatlinburg is not for people look-ing for a wilderness experience in the Smokies. As a shuttle or out-and-back hike, there are better short hikes than this. However, it's a great split-party hike, especially if you're staying in Gatlinburg. Have your party drop you off at the visitor center and meet them back in town, or head out early in the morning and meet your party at the visitor center. The trail is popular among locals as a fitness and dog-walking path. It's one of only two trails in the park that allow dogs (on leash) and one of only four that allow bicycles. (Oconaluftee River Trail allows dogs and bikes; Deep Creek Trail and Indian Creek Trail allow bikes on their lower sections.) A highlight of the hike is the short side trip to Cataract Falls.

Start: Sugarlands Visitor Center
Distance: 3.8 miles out and back
Hiking time: About 2 hours—day hike
Difficulty: Easy
Trail surface: Concrete, asphalt, gravel, dirt, and a few yards of grass
Other trail users: Dogs, bicycles
Maps: Gatlinburg USGS quad; Trails Illustrated

#229 Great Smoky Mountains; Trails Illustrated #317 Clingmans Dome Cataloochee; Trails Illustrated #316 Cades Cove Elkmont
Other: The visitor center parking lot is huge but still fills up on summer and autumn weekends. Restrooms and drink vending machines are available at the center. The end of the hike has parking for a half-dozen vehicles only.

Finding the trailhead: The hike begins at Sugarlands Visitor Center, about 2 miles south of Gatlinburg along Newfound Gap Road. GPS: N35 41.148' / W83 32.214'
If doing this hike as a shuttle, you need to leave a vehicle at the Gatlinburg end of the trail, which is located on the short spur road turning west off Newfound Gap Road, a few hundred feet from Gatlinburg. GPS: N35 42.343' / W83 31.420'

The Hike

The hike begins on the concrete walkway in front of the restroom building. In 50 yards you come to the trailhead for Fighting Creek Nature Trail (Hike 2), turning to the left. Continue along the concrete path to the park headquarters building. Walk completely around the front and right side of the building to reach Park Headquar-ters Road at a small parking area. Turn left (west) and follow the road 100 yards to another park service road turning to the left. If taking the side trip to Cataract Falls described under Options, you want to take this road; otherwise, continue following Park Headquarters Road to where it ends at the park maintenance yard. Gatlinburg Trail leaves the road here, bypassing to the right of the maintenance area and follow-ing West Prong Little Pigeon River downstream.

Upon leaving the maintenance area, you are finally on a real trail, but this is no wilderness walk. On your way to Gatlinburg, you pass under the Gatlinburg Bypass

Cataract Falls.

road and closely parallel Newfound Gap Road for some distance. A few old home-sites, rock walls, and the crossing of West Prong Little Pigeon River will help keep your mind off asphalt for part of the hike.

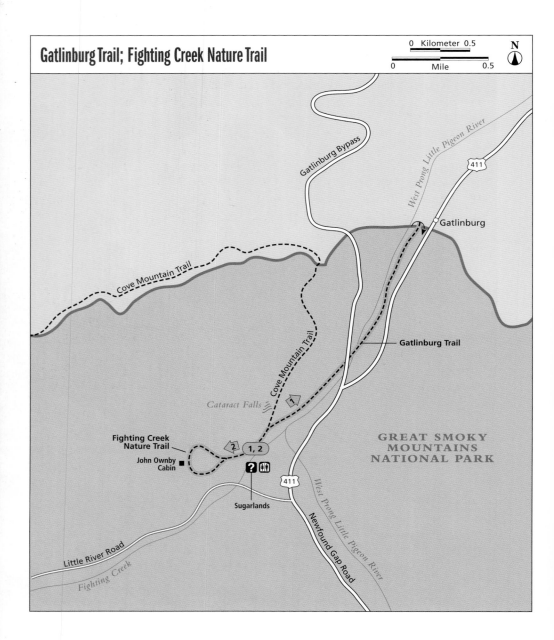

Gatlinburg Trail; Fighting Creek Nature Trail

Gatlinburg Trail ends on the short spur road off Newfound Gap Road at the park boundary. A left turn takes you into the concrete and asphalt jungle of Gatlinburg. A right turn takes you in a few yards to Newfound Gap Road, which leads back to the visitor center. For your safety, if you're doing this hike as an out-and-back hike, you'll want to backtrack on the trail rather than walking along this busy road.

Miles and Directions

0.0 Start between the restroom building and vending machines. Pass by Fighting Creek Nature trailhead in 50 yards and continue on the concrete path.

0.1 Walk in front of park headquarters building and around the right side to the small parking area at Park Headquarters Road. Turn left (west) and follow road.

0.2 A park service road turns to the left. The side trip to Cataract Falls begins here. Continue along the road you are on.

0.4 Road ends at a park maintenance area. Follow the trail that skirts around the right side, between the maintenance yard and West Prong Little Pigeon River.

0.8 Pass under the overpass of Gatlinburg Bypass road.

1.2 Cross West Prong Little Pigeon River on a substantial footbridge.

1.9 Park boundary at Gatlinburg. Return the way you came.

3.8 Arrive back at trailhead.

Options: The short side trip to Cataract Falls is highly recommended. At 0.2 mile into the hike, you come to a service road turning to the left. Follow this road 100 yards to the bridge over Fighting Creek. Immediately beyond the bridge, Cove Mountain Trail goes to the right and follows the creek downstream. Cataract Falls is located 0.1 mile along this trail.

You can combine this hike with all or part of Fighting Creek Nature Trail (Hike 2). Read the narrative for that hike to see how you can access Cataract Falls from it and eliminate the walk around the park headquarters building.

2 Fighting Creek Nature Trail

Fighting Creek Nature Trail provides a good introduction to the Smokies, especially for families and those who don't care to tackle the tough hikes. It's short, easy, crosses over streams, and features a cabin. A short side trip takes you to scenic Cataract Falls. Pick up the self-guiding leaflet at the trailhead and read about the way of life that existed here before the park was established.

(See map for Hike 1: Gatlinburg Trail.)

Start: Sugarlands Visitor Center
Distance: 1.1-mile lollipop
Hiking time: About 45 minutes—day hike
Difficulty: Easy
Trail surface: Packed dirt
Other trail users: Hikers only

Maps: Gatlinburg USGS quad; Trails Illustrated #229 Great Smoky Mountains; Trails Illustrated #317 Clingmans Dome Cataloochee; Trails Illustrated #316 Cades Cove Elkmont
Other: The visitor center parking lot is huge but still fills up on summer and autumn weekends. Restrooms and vending machines are available at the center.

Finding the trailhead: The hike begins at Sugarlands Visitor Center, about 2 miles south of Gatlinburg along Newfound Gap Road. GPS: N35 41.148' / W83 32.214'

The Hike

As with most of the self-guiding nature trails in the park, there's little danger of not finding your way along Fighting Creek Nature Trail. Follow the concrete walkway from the restroom building, and in 50 yards turn left at the sign for the nature trail. You'll cross a small stream and walk under a power line before coming to the footbridge over Fighting Creek. A gnarly old sycamore tree with three trunks grows beside the trail at the bridge.

After crossing the creek the nature trail loop goes left and straight ahead, while the path to Cataract Falls goes right and follows the creek downstream. You want to turn left and head upstream to follow the number sequence in the trail pamphlet. You'll pass under another power line and then go on a loose parallel of Little River Road all the way to the John Ownby Cabin. After exploring the cabin continue on the loop trail behind the upper corner of the cabin, near the chimney.

Miles and Directions

0.0 Start between the restroom building and vending machines. In 50 yards turn left onto Fighting Creek Nature Trail.

0.2 Three-way intersection just after crossing Fighting Creek. Turn left and follow the trail upstream. (Optional side trail to Cataract Falls goes to the right.)

0.5 John Ownby Cabin. Trail loops back from the upper (chimney) side of the cabin.

0.9 Arrive back at three-way intersection. Return the way you came if not hiking to Cataract Falls.

1.1 Arrive back at trailhead.

Options: For the short side trip to Cataract Falls, follow the obvious path downstream from the three-way intersection. After you pass under a road, climb the bank on the left to reach the trailhead for Cove Mountain Trail (N35 41.290' / W83 32.295'). Follow this trail downstream about 0.1 mile to the falls.

A VEIL OF WHITE

In the mid-1980s an April hike in the Smokies was much different than it is today. Back then the spring forest was a veil of white, created by countless flowering dogwood trees. Dogwood (*Cornus florida*) was among the most common understory trees in the park before an exotic fungus decimated the trees. First discovered in the park in 1988, the dogwood anthracnose fungus has since killed well over half of the park's dogwood trees, with over 90 percent mortality in the park's cove forests. Trees at low elevations and those that grow in the open, exposed to the sun, are less prone to attack from the fungus. You can see several dogwoods in the Sugarlands Visitor Center area, including some along Fighting Creek Nature Trail.

3 Cove Hardwoods Nature Trail

If you like wildflowers and scenic cove forests, it doesn't get much better than this. From early April until early May, wildflowers literally carpet the ground. You don't even have to hike the trail—the picnic area itself is a good viewing spot. During the peak bloom of fringed phacelia, the flowers literally cover the ground. Indeed, more than one visitor has driven quickly by and thought he or she was seeing a late snow. This is a self-guiding nature trail, so you might want to pick up a trail guide from the box at the trailhead. Return the guide after the hike, or drop 50 cents in the slot if you want to keep it.

Start: Chimneys Picnic Area
Distance: 1.0-mile lollipop
Hiking time: About 45 minutes—day hike
Difficulty: Moderate
Trail surface: Forest floor with some asphalt sections
Best season: Early spring for the wildflowers
Other trail users: Hikers and wildflower gawkers only

Maps: Mount LeConte USGS quad; Trails Illustrated #229 Great Smoky Mountains; Trails Illustrated #317 Clingmans Dome Cataloochee; Trails Illustrated #316 Cades Cove Elkmont
Other: The parking area has room for several vehicles. A restroom building sits down the bank on the opposite side of the road.

Finding the trailhead: Drive 4.5 miles south on Newfound Gap Road from Sugarlands Visitor Center and turn right (east) into Chimneys Picnic Area. If coming from Newfound Gap, drive north (toward Gatlinburg) 12.8 miles and turn left into the picnic area. Park in the first parking area on the right (GPS: N35 38.175' / W83 29.508'). The picnic area is closed and gated from sunset to sunrise. If you want to take some early-morning photographs, you have to park at the gate and walk the extra distance. Do not block the gate.

The Hike

Start by climbing the steps up the bank on the west end of the parking area and passing by the old amphitheater. The trail soon forks. You can go either way, as it's a loop, but if you're following the trail guide, you need to go to the right. It's mostly an easy hike over packed ground and through a few small streams, but there are a few steep grades, some covered in asphalt to prevent erosion. Resist the urge to leave the trail, especially while the wildflowers are blooming. Trampling is a concern here, and it's unnecessary since you can see every species of wildflower from the trail.

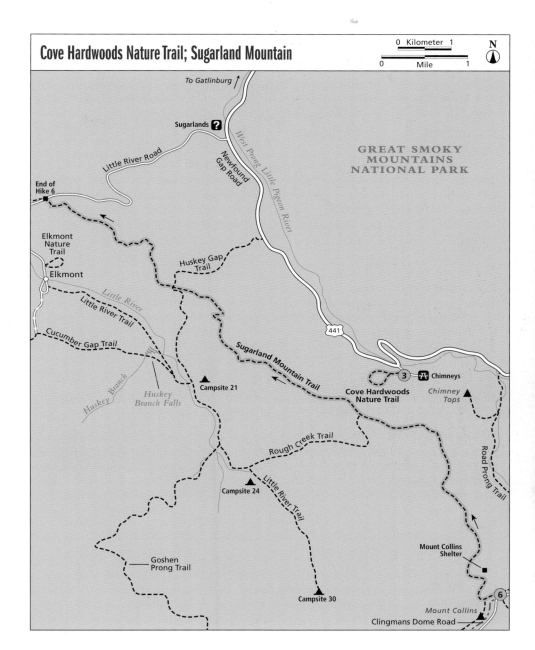

0 Kilometer 1

0 Mile 1

N

To Gatlinburg

Sugarlands ?

West Prong Little Pigeon River

GREAT SMOKY
MOUNTAINS
NATIONAL PARK

Little River Road

Newfound
Gap Road

End of
Hike 6

Elkmont
Nature
Trail

Huskey Gap
Trail

Elkmont

Little River

Little River Trail

441

Cucumber Gap Trail

Sugarland Mountain Trail

3 ⛺ Chimneys

Huskey Branch

Campsite 21

Cove Hardwoods
Nature Trail

*Chimney
Tops*

*Huskey
Branch Falls*

Rough Creek Trail

Road Prong Trail

Campsite 24

Little River Trail

Goshen
Prong Trail

Mount Collins
Shelter

6

Campsite 30

Mount Collins

Clingmans Dome Road

Miles and Directions

0.0 Start from the west end of the parking area.

0.1 Trail forks. Turn right to follow the interpretive markers in the trail guide.

0.9 Return to fork and follow the trail back the way you came.

1.0 Arrive back at trailhead.

4 Chimney Tops

This hike offers cascading streams, wildflowers, scenic forest views, rugged rock outcrops, and unparalleled vistas. Access to the trailhead is easy, and the hike is relatively short. What it doesn't offer, though, is solitude. You're going to have company, so prepare your mind for it.

Start: Chimney Tops trailhead on Newfound Gap Road

Distance: 4.0 miles out and back

Hiking time: About 3.5 hours—day hike

Difficulty: Strenuous, due to steep trail and rock scrambling

Trail surface: Packed dirt and rocks

Other trail users: Hikers only

Maps: Mount LeConte USGS quad; Trails Illustrated #229 Great Smoky Mountains; Trails Illustrated #317 Clingmans Dome Cataloochee

Special considerations: Hike to Chimney Tops on a weekend or during the summer or fall season and you can expect to rub shoulders with other hikers the entire way. The steep trail seems to deter no one, even those who shouldn't attempt such a difficult and potentially dangerous trek. Scrambling up the peaks requires using both hands and feet, so make sure you can strap everything to your back or waist if you bring it. Once on the summit, pay particular attention to where you step. The slightest distraction can cause disastrous results. Do not let kids run free on this hike. Be extremely careful if hiking in winter, as snow and ice make the Chimney Tops' summit too dangerous to climb.

Other: The parking lots can handle several vehicles, but they fill up quickly anytime other than winter weekdays. Restrooms are available 2.4 miles north of the trailhead at Chimneys Picnic Area.

Finding the trailhead: Chimney Tops parking area is located on Newfound Gap Road, 5.9 miles north of Newfound Gap and 6.8 miles south of Sugarlands Visitor Center (GPS: N35 38.088' / W83 28.219'). Don't confuse Chimney Tops with Chimneys Picnic Area, which is located 2.4 miles north of the trailhead.

The Hike

Begin from the main parking area at the sign and descend to the bridge over Walker Camp Prong. Cascades, pools, and huge boulders (many good for sunning) make this spot extremely popular. Look downstream to see the confluence with Road Prong. You'll cross that stream very shortly. Where the two creeks join, the waterway becomes West Prong Little Pigeon River. After the first crossing of Road Prong, the trail swings around to the left.

The trail now climbs noticeably, crosses Road Prong for a second time, and continues ascending to the third and final crossing. Just beyond that crossing, in an area known as Beech Flats, the trail swings around to the right, while Road Prong Trail continues following the creek upstream (see Hike 5). Go right here, remaining on the wide and well-graded Chimney Tops Trail. A moderate ascent leads to a metal culvert across the trail. Stop here and rest; you'll need it. The next several hundred yards climb

Spring view along Chimney Tops Trail.

extremely steeply up the drainage, with no switchbacks to lessen the grade. You do make one switchback later on, but by that time you'll have put most of the steep part behind you. After that switchback the grade moderates and even descends a short distance before leveling out somewhat on a narrow ridge. A short walk (*scramble* is a better term, what with all the roots and rocks) along this ridge leads to the base of the Chimneys.

Now comes the difficult part of the hike—yep, worse than that steep climb you just made up the ravine. A sign here warns you to go no farther. You should take heed. You can scramble up the rocky ridge directly in front of you, but do not continue around toward the right. This route is closed due to heavy erosion helped by hikers, and it can be very dangerous. If you do make the climb straight ahead, you'll need to use both hands and feet to make it to the top.

Your reward at the summit is one of the finest panoramic views in the park. To the northeast, in bold relief, stands the imposing massif of Mount LeConte. To the right of LeConte extends the narrow ridgeline called The Boulevard. To the southeast towers Mount Mingus, which you may have noticed from a clearing back down the trail, and to the right of Mingus is the Road Prong drainage. If you follow the ridge leading down the left side of Mount Mingus, you'll see "the Loop" on Newfound Gap Road, although vegetation hides most of it in summer. Toward the west are the steep slopes of Sugarland Mountain, of which the ridgeline forming the Chimney Tops is a spur. To the northwest lies the West Prong Little Pigeon River drainage leading into Sugarlands, with Cove Mountain in the distance.

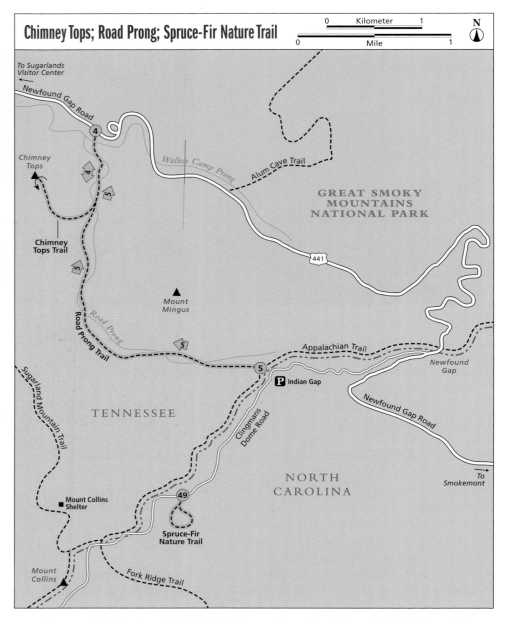

0   Kilometer   1

0   Mile   1

N

To Sugarlands
Visitor Center

Newfound Gap Road

Chimney
Tops

Walker Camp Prong

Alum Cave Trail

GREAT SMOKY
MOUNTAINS
NATIONAL PARK

441

Chimney
Tops Trail

Mount
Mingus

Road Prong

Road Prong Trail

Appalachian Trail

Newfound
Gap

5

Indian Gap

Newfound Gap Road

Sugarland Mountain Trail

TENNESSEE

Clingmans Dome Road

NORTH
CAROLINA

To
Smokemont

Mount Collins
Shelter

49

Spruce-Fir
Nature Trail

Mount
Collins

Fork Ridge Trail

At your feet is the jagged, slatelike Anakeesta Formation. The rock is difficult and dangerous to walk on, so be careful. The juncos and red squirrels don't have a problem with it, though, and you're sure to get a scolding from a squirrel if you spend much time reflecting up here. Their constant chatter seems to say, "Why don't you feed me? Don't you see how cute I am?" You can tell them that the park strictly forbids you to feed any wildlife.

From the summit of Chimney tops, retrace your steps to the trailhead.

Miles and Directions

0.0 Start from the parking area at the signpost.

0.1 Cross Walker Camp Prong on a long footbridge.

0.2 First bridge over Road Prong. After crossing turn to the left and remain on the main trail.

0.4 Second bridge over Road Prong.

0.8 Third bridge over Road Prong.

0.9 Junction with Road Prong Trail, which goes straight ahead and continues following the creek upstream. You want to go to the right and remain on the wide Chimney Tops Trail.

2.0 Arrive at Chimney Tops. Return the way you came.

4.0 Arrive back at trailhead.

Option: Hike 5 follows Road Prong Trail to Beech Flats and then continues on Chimney Tops Trail to the parking area. A side trip to Chimney Tops from that hike lets you do both hikes in the same trip. This works well as a shuttle hike, with a vehicle left at the lower parking area.

ANAKEESTA

The jagged rock you scramble up to reach the peak of Chimney Tops is part of the Anakeesta Formation, a type of metamorphic rock composed primarily of slate. Anakeesta comprises much of the rugged central crest of the Smokies, including Mount LeConte, Charlies Bunion, and Clingmans Dome. It only takes a casual glance to see that Anakeesta rock is highly susceptible to weathering, easily breaking apart along its cleavages due to freezing and thawing of water. Arch Rock, along Alum Cave Trail (Hike 29), likely formed from such action.

5 Road Prong

The easy hike along Road Prong of West Prong Little Pigeon River offers a little something of everything the Smokies is famous for except grand vistas, and if you take the side trip to the Chimneys, you'll get that too. The best part is that you'll have most of this hike to yourself, since few people hike the 2.4-mile section from Indian Gap to Chimney Tops Trail.

(See map for Hike 4: Chimney Tops.)

Start: Road Prong trailhead on Clingmans Dome Road
Distance: 3.3 miles point to point
Hiking time: About 2 hours–day hike
Difficulty: Easy, due to downhill grade the entire way
Trail surface: Rocks and boot-packed dirt
Best season: Spring for the wildflowers
Other trail users: Hikers only
Maps: Clingmans Dome and Mount LeConte USGS quads; Trails Illustrated #229 Great

Smoky Mountains; Trails Illustrated #317 Clingmans Dome Cataloochee
Special considerations: Clingmans Dome Road is closed to vehicles Dec 1–Mar 31. During this time you can hike along the road or take the Appalachian Trail. The AT roughly parallels the road from Newfound Gap and passes through Indian Gap.
Other: There is usually ample parking at the trailhead. Restrooms are available at Newfound Gap and at the Clingmans Dome parking area at the end of the road.

Finding the trailhead: At Newfound Gap turn west on Clingmans Dome Road and drive 1.2 miles to the Indian Gap Parking Area on the north side (GPS: N35 36.567' / W83 26.797'). If doing this hike as a shuttle, you need to leave a vehicle at Chimney Tops trailhead on Newfound Gap Road, 5.9 miles north of Newfound Gap or 6.8 miles south of Sugarlands Visitor Center (GPS: N35 38.088' / W83 28.219').

The maps show Indian Gap being located about 0.75 mile to the east; the gap at the parking area is unnamed. All Smokies publications list the gap at the trailhead as Indian Gap, however.

The Hike

Start from the middle of the parking area, immediately cross the Appalachian Trail, and then head down the Road Prong drainage. The first section is steep and rocky. If it's raining, you'll think you're walking through a creek bed. There are a few more short stretches like this, but mostly this is an easy downhill stroll. Spruce, fir (near the beginning), buckeye, and birch trees anchor the lush forest.

You soon come to the first creek crossing—no problem at this stage. Look for coneflower and jewelweed in summer. A few yards from the crossing, you have to walk through the creek bed for several yards, and shortly afterward you come to a massive landslide area. Watch the trout swimming in the pool above the debris dam. They're lucky to be where they are. When you cross the creek just below the huge

Road Prong. ▶

debris pile, notice that the stream is orange from the iron leachate released from the slide. Enough of this nasty stuff can make a creek inhospitable to aquatic creatures. Notice also the heavy siltation in the creek.

From the base of the debris dam, you go through a stretch where there is no real trail and you have to cross the stream a few times and walk through the streambed. Keep working your way downstream and you'll come to the obvious resumption of a legitimate trail. From this point, an up-and-down stretch takes you away from the stream. As you begin descending again to the creek, notice the forest to the right. You'd think you were in a Pacific Northwest rain forest, with thick moss and ferns covering every inch of ground. The trail descends steeply to the creek near the top of a small and beautiful waterfall, sometimes called "Talking Falls." Continue down the trail a bit to a short scramble path leading to the base of the falls. In summer it's difficult to resist jumping into the large, deep pool at the base of the falls. Below the falls the creek continues as a series of small falls and cascades, but there is no good way to view any of them.

Just before crossing the creek again, you pass by a large, narrow, sharp-pointed rock on the left that looks like an ax head stuck in the ground. This is Standing Rock, and the crossing just below it is Standing Rock Ford. A new footbridge here makes this an easy crossing—a good thing, since it used to be dangerous in high water. Downstream is a small cascading waterfall informally named "Trickling Falls," but like the cascades above the ford, there's no good way to access the creek for a good view.

Below the ford, the trail looks as though it might have been a road at one time. It was, as the trail follows the old Oconaluftee Turnpike, which served for many years as the main route from Cherokee, North Carolina, to Sevierville, Tennessee. When the park was established and a new road was built over the mountains, the new highway crossed the mountains a mile east of Indian Gap at the "new-found" gap.

Now you pass through a relatively flat area known as Beech Flats, and at 2.4 miles you reach the junction with Chimney Tops Trail. Straight ahead, Chimney Tops Trail continues down the Road Prong drainage, and to the left it ascends 1.1 miles to Chimney Tops. If going left to the Chimneys, which is highly recommended, turn to Hike 4. If continuing straight, descend and quickly cross Road Prong again on a wide, sturdy footbridge. Continue descending along the creek and make two more crossings, both on footbridges. The bridges make perfect platforms for composing photographs of the cascading stream.

Shortly after the third footbridge over Road Prong, the trail crosses Walker Camp Prong on a long footbridge. Just downstream from the crossing, Walker Camp Prong joins Road Prong to form West Prong Little Pigeon River. The picturesque setting, with cascades and large rocks, and the proximity to the parking area make this spot extremely popular on sunny days. The Chimney Tops trailhead parking area is a short distance farther up the bank.

Miles and Directions

0.0 Start from the west end of the parking area and cross over the Appalachian Trail onto Road Prong Trail.

0.8 Pass by a landslide.

2.4 Junction with Chimney Tops Trail at Beech Flats. Go to the right and continue following the creek downstream.

3.3 Chimney Tops trailhead on Newfound Gap Road.

Options: You can do this hike in the opposite direction, but it would be uphill all the way. Hike it in the direction outlined here and you'll have enough energy to take the side trip to Chimney Tops and experience its grand views.

SLITHERY, SLIMY CRITTERS

The Smokies have been called the Salamander Capital of the World, with thirty species known to occur here—more than 6 percent of the world's salamander species. The smallest adults measure a little over an inch long. The largest, called the hellbender, can grow to well over 2 feet long! One species, Jordan's red-cheeked salamander, occurs nowhere else in the world. A salamander you often encounter while hiking in the Smokies on a wet day is the eastern red-spotted newt. In its juvenile (eft) stage, it is bright reddish orange with small black circles running down each side of its back. If you spend much time hiking in the Smokies, you'll certainly see this little guy crawling across the trail.

A great location to search for hidden salamanders is at wet trail crossings, such as on Road Prong Trail, particularly the upper elevations. Turn over a few rocks in the wet areas and you're sure to find some. It's best not to pick them up, but if you must, make sure to wet your hands before you handle them so you don't dry out their skin, which could harm them. And make sure you carefully put the salamanders and the rocks back in place.

6 Sugarland Mountain

It's almost unheard of that you can hike more than 12 miles in the Smokies without having to do much climbing, but that's exactly the situation here. By starting on the main Smokies crest, it's pretty much downhill all the way except for a moderate stretch toward the end. Along the way you drop more than 3,500 feet in elevation and pass through several forest types—spruce fir at the highest elevation, and then high-elevation birch, hemlock, northern hardwood, and pine. Some of the trees at the upper end are quite impressive. This is one of the better hikes in the book for showing the diversity of forests of the Smokies.

(See map for Hike 3: Cove Hardwoods Nature Trail.)

Start: Fork Ridge trailhead on Clingmans Dome Road
Distance: 12.3 miles point to point
Hiking time: About 6 hours—day hike
Difficulty: Easy, due to downhill grade most of the way
Trail surface: Forested trail
Other trail users: Hikers only
Maps: Clingmans Dome, Mount LeConte, and Gatlinburg USGS quads; Trails Illustrated #229 Great Smoky Mountains; Trails Illustrated #317 Clingmans Dome Cataloochee (only shows upper portion of hike); Trails Illustrated #316 Cades Cove Elkmont (only shows lower portion of hike)
Special considerations: Clingmans Dome Road is closed to vehicles Dec 1–Mar 31. The only dependable water source on this hike is a tiny spring near the start.
Other: There's room for only a few vehicles, but that's usually not a problem. Restrooms are available at Newfound Gap and at the end of Clingmans Dome Road, 3.4 miles farther west.

Finding the trailhead: From Newfound Gap, drive 3.5 miles west on Clingmans Dome Road and park on the left (south) side of the road at the Fork Ridge trailhead (GPS: N35 35.424' / W83 28.167'). You need to leave a vehicle at the lower trailhead. From Sugarlands Visitor Center, drive 3.7 miles west on Little River Road to the trailhead at Fighting Creek Gap (GPS: N35 40.310' / W83 34.831').

The Hike

Begin by crossing Clingmans Dome Road and taking the connector path that leads a few hundred feet to the Appalachian Trail. Turn left (west), and hike 0.3 mile to the junction with Sugarland Mountain Trail, on the right. Head north on Sugarland Mountain Trail, and at 0.3 mile from the Appalachian Trail, you pass a side path on the right that leads to Mount Collins Shelter. This is the closest shelter to a road in the park and consequently receives a lot of use. A few hundred yards farther from the side path, the trail passes a tiny spring—a water source for the shelter and the only dependable water along this entire hike. Along this stretch you pass several impressive birch trees, some with good-size spruces growing out of limb crotches high above the ground.

The good views soon appear and continue intermittently all the way to the junction with Rough Creek Trail. Off to the right, toward the northeast and northwest, you can see Mount LeConte, the Chimneys, Gatlinburg, and Pigeon Forge. Off to the left are Goshen Ridge and the Little River drainage. Beyond Rough Creek Trail the best views end and the forest changes from old growth to second growth.

At 8.3 miles you find yourself standing near what used to be Campsite #21. The campsite is now located near the junction of Huskey Gap Trail and Little River Trail. When you look around and realize that you're standing in the middle of the upper drainage of Big Medicine Branch, you can understand why the park relocated the campsite. Pitch a tent here and a heavy storm could wash you and your tent down the mountain.

Cross over Huskey Gap Trail at 9.3 miles and about 0.5 mile farther, look toward the east for an overgrown view of Mount LeConte. The trail passes through some pine stands killed by southern pine beetles and reaches Mids Gap at about 11 miles. An unmaintained side path to the left leads to Mids Branch. Just past the gap you begin the longest uphill stretch of the hike, at nearly 0.5 mile long. Next, you begin the descent to Fighting Creek Gap, the steepest grade of the hike. There's considerable tree blowdown along this stretch, evidence of the thin soil layer on these steep hillsides.

Fighting Creek Gap is also the trailhead for the insanely popular Laurel Falls Trail (Hike 7), so expect to reacquaint yourself with people when you finish the hike.

Miles and Directions

0.0 Start on the Appalachian Trail connector path located on the opposite side of the road from the parking area.

0.1 Turn left (west) on the Appalachian Trail.

0.4 Turn right (north) on Sugarland Mountain Trail.

0.7 Side path on the right leads to Mount Collins Shelter.

5.2 Junction with Rough Creek Trail coming up from the left. Continue straight on Sugarland Mountain Trail.

9.3 Huskey Gap and junction with Huskey Gap Trail. Continue straight on Sugarland Mountain Trail.

12.3 Arrive at Fighting Creek Gap.

Options: There are two other possible endings for this hike. From Huskey Gap, at the 9.3-mile point, you can take the Huskey Gap Trail in either direction. A right (northeast) turn takes you to Newfound Gap Road in 2.0 miles, and a left (southwest) takes you to Little River Trail in 2.1 miles, where you would turn right and follow Little River downstream 2.7 miles to the trailhead near Elkmont Campground. The latter option works well as a split-party hike if you're staying at the campground. Have your party drop you off at the upper trailhead and you can meet them back at the campground later in the day.

FOREST DIVERSITY

More than fifty detailed forest types occur in the Smokies. From these, botanists have categorized fifteen general forest types. The best way to see the most forest diversity on one hike is to start at the high elevations and hike to the lowlands, as on the Sugarland Mountain hike. You'll begin in the spruce-fir forest and, depending on the hike, pass through half a dozen or more forest types on the way down. A great reference for learning about the forests of the Smokies is *The Forests of Great Smoky Mountains National Park* by Dan Williams, available from park visitor centers.

A lush cove hardwood forest in the Smokies.

7 Laurel Falls and Cove Mountain

This is a Jekyll and Hyde hike. The first 1.3 miles to Laurel Falls are possibly the most popular hike in the park and is insanely crowded. You might have the remaining 2.7 miles to Cove Mountain all to yourself, as nearly everyone stops at the falls. They don't know what they're missing, as this section passes through a scenic old-growth forest carpeted in spring with abundant wildflowers.

Start: Fighting Creek Gap on Little River Road

Distance: 8.0 miles out and back (2.6 miles out and back if only hiking to the falls)

Hiking time: About 4 hours–day hike

Difficulty: Moderate, with some long easy stretches. If you're pushing a baby stroller, the final 0.25 mile to the falls is a little rough.

Trail surface: Paved path and forest trail

Best seasons: Winter to avoid the crowds, spring for the wildflowers

Other trail users: Hikers and baby strollers only

Maps: Gatlinburg USGS quad; Trails Illustrated #229 Great Smoky Mountains; Trails Illustrated #316 Cades Cove Elkmont

Special considerations: The only way to avoid a billion people on the first 1.3 miles to Laurel Falls is to hike first thing in the morning or on a cold, miserable day during winter.

Other: Two large parking lots line each side of Fighting Creek Gap, but they are usually full by midmorning except in winter. Restrooms are available at Sugarlands Visitor Center.

Finding the trailhead: From Sugarlands Visitor Center, drive 3.7 miles west on Little River Road to the trailhead at Fighting Creek Gap (GPS: N35 40.310' / W83 34.831'). Laurel Falls Trail begins on the north side of the road, opposite Sugarland Mountain Trail, which is on the south side.

The Hike

Begin on the north side of the parking area at the obvious trailhead. The first 1.3 miles to Laurel Falls is paved and mostly easy, although it's an uphill grade most of the way. This part of the trail is also a self-guided nature trail, with a brochure available at the trailhead to teach you about the forest. Even if you don't see anyone on the trail (unlikely), there always seems to be people at the falls—wading, sitting, climbing (discouraged), picnicking, and photographing. An unsightly concrete bridge extends partly across the pool and presents a challenge to photographers not wanting any man-made elements in their images, but you can crop it out if you're careful.

Beyond the falls, you're hiking on a legitimate trail (no pavement) and you're probably all alone. About 0.2 mile from the falls, a sharp switchback brings you back toward the creek and then a broad swing around a ridge puts you on a parallel course along Jay Bird Branch—out of sight in the drainage below, but within earshot. As you climb along the north side of the ridge, you pass through an old-growth forest

Laurel Falls.

of incredible beauty. Large trees of several species grow here, including basswood, buckeye, and some huge yellow poplars (tulip trees). In early spring wildflowers cover the forest floor; later in the season mushrooms are abundant. Sadly, many of the big eastern hemlocks in this forest have died from the adelgid infestation. (See the sidebar for Hike 36.)

The trail leaves the big trees and ascends gradually to the junction with Little Greenbrier Trail on the left (west), which leads 4.3 miles to Wear Cove Gap. Your hike continues straight on Laurel Falls Trail, climbing moderately on the flanks of Cove Mountain to the junction with Cove Mountain Trail on a ridge. A service road for the fire tower is just ahead. To the right (east), Cove Mountain Trail leads 8.4 miles to the park headquarters. To the left (west), a short walk takes you to a small clearing on the summit of Cove Mountain and the fire tower.

No good views greet the hiker on the Cove Mountain summit, since an air-quality monitoring station now occupies the fire tower above the first few flights. The other side of the clearing affords a meager view down a power-line clearing toward Wear Cove.

Miles and Directions

0.0 Start on Laurel Falls Trail on the north side of the road.

1.3 Arrive at Laurel Falls.

3.1 Junction with Little Greenbrier Trail coming in from the left (west). Continue north on Laurel Falls Trail.

Laurel Falls and Cove Mountain; Walker Sisters Home

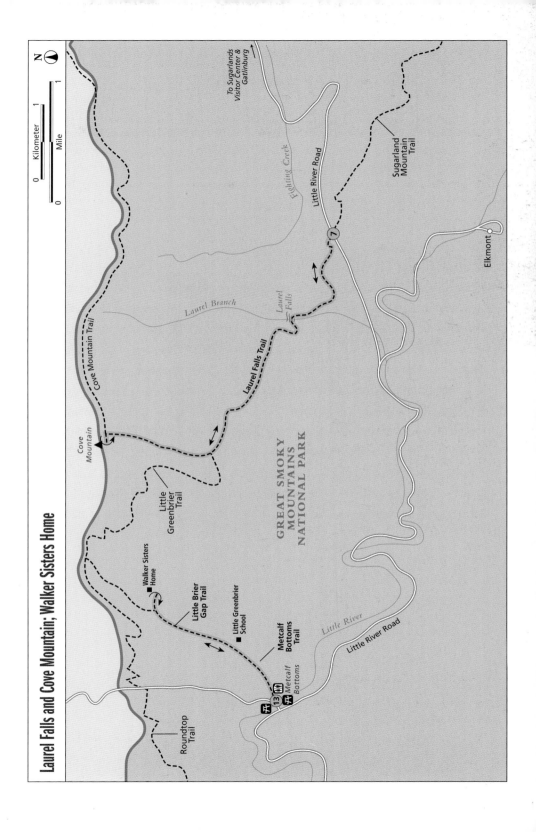

3.9 Junction with Cove Mountain Trail on the ridge. Turn left (west) and follow the old roadbed.

4.0 Arrive at the summit of Cove Mountain. Return the way you came.

8.0 Arrive back at trailhead.

Options: With a second vehicle or prearranged shuttle service, you have two options that allow you to avoid backtracking. You could hike back down to the junction with Little Greenbrier Trail and follow it to Wear Gap, or you could hike along the ridge from Cove Mountain to the park headquarters near Gatlinburg. Before choosing this option, however, note that when hiking Cove Mountain Trail, you often are within sight of the development surrounding Gatlinburg.

WONDERFUL WATERFALLS

With more than 2,100 miles of streams and an average rainfall exceeding 85 inches in the higher elevations, it's surprising that the Smokies do not have a large number of significant waterfalls. Waterfalls in the park tend to be small and not very high, and if they are high, they are on very small streams. Look to the topography for an explanation. Most of the streams in the park start out as springs in the higher elevations and they flow steeply to the lowlands. By the time they gain sufficient size to create significant waterfalls, they have already left the steep mountain slopes and no longer flow over topography that forms big waterfalls. You'll find countless cascades here, and a few dozen small and medium falls. Some of these are very scenic and extremely popular, such as Laurel Falls, Rainbow Falls, and Grotto Falls. However, if you want to see the big thundering kinds of waterfalls, you need to head west from the Smokies to Tennessee's Cumberland Plateau or head east to North Carolina's Blue Ridge Escarpment region.

8 Elkmont Nature Trail

This self-guiding nature trail makes a great short day hike for families staying at Elkmont Campground. Grab a copy of the brochure (50 cents to keep) before starting the hike and use it to help interpret the features encountered along the way.

Start: Elkmont Nature trailhead near Elkmont Campground
Distance: 1.0-mile loop
Hiking time: About 30 minutes—day hike
Difficulty: Easy
Trail surface: Forest trail
Other trail users: Hikers only

Maps: Gatlinburg USGS quad; Trails Illustrated #229 Great Smoky Mountains; Trails Illustrated #316 Cades Cove Elkmont
Other: The parking lot is small but rarely fills. Restrooms are available at Elkmont Campground.

Finding the trailhead: Drive 4.8 miles west on Little River Road from Sugarlands Visitor Center and turn left at the sign for Elkmont Campground. Drive 1.4 miles and turn left just before the campground entrance station. Drive 0.3 mile to the parking area for the Elkmont Self-Guiding Nature Trail, on the left. GPS: N35 39.456' / W83 34.831'

The Hike

This nature trail begins at the south corner of the parking lot. Cross Mids Branch on an asphalt-filled I-beam and wind your way up an old railroad line. Cross an old capped-off spring and then pass around a meadow at an old homeplace. Cross the branch again and climb a south-facing slope, passing through a neat rhododendron and mountain laurel tunnel. A series of short switchbacks brings you back to the trailhead.

Miles and Directions

0.0 Start from the south corner of the parking lot at the sign.
0.5 Pass around a meadow at an old homeplace.
1.0 Arrive back at the parking lot.

IVY

Among the most common understory shrubs in the park, mountain laurel (*Kalmia latifolia*) embellishes the forest in a veil of pink during May and June. Called "ivy" by the locals, it often grows in impenetrable thickets on the dry, south-facing slopes in the park. Many park trails, including Elkmont Nature Trail, were built by carving tunnels through these thickets.

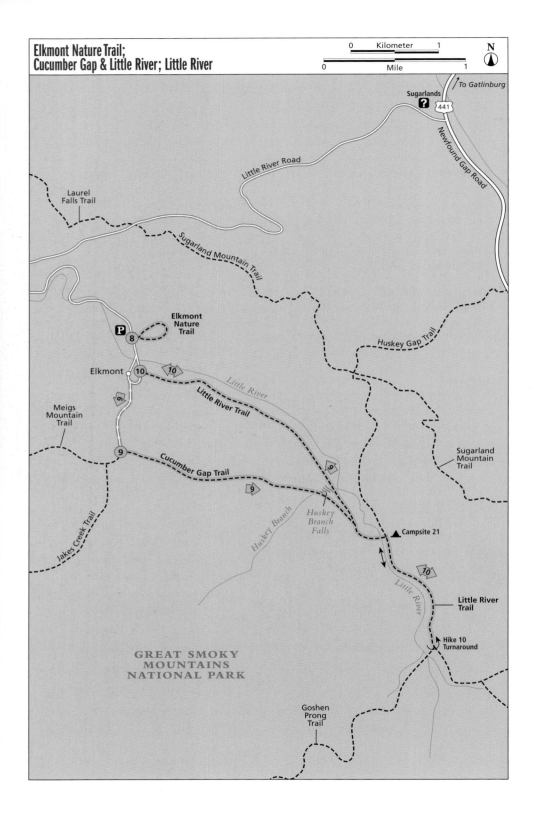

Elkmont Nature Trail;
Cucumber Gap & Little River; Little River

0   Kilometer   1
0   Mile   1

N

To Gatlinburg

Sugarlands
?
441

Newfound Gap Road

Little River Road

Laurel
Falls Trail

Sugarland Mountain Trail

Huskey Gap Trail

Elkmont
Nature
Trail

P
8

Little River

Elkmont
10
10

9

Little River Trail

Meigs
Mountain
Trail

Sugarland
Mountain
Trail

9

Cucumber Gap Trail

9

9

Huskey Branch

Huskey
Branch
Falls

Campsite 21

Jakes Creek Trail

Little River

10

Little River
Trail

Hike 10
Turnaround

GREAT SMOKY
MOUNTAINS
NATIONAL PARK

Goshen
Prong
Trail

9 Cucumber Gap and Little River

If you're looking for an easy, relatively short, and interesting loop hike, it doesn't get much better than this. It makes a wonderful day hike if you're staying at Elkmont Campground—you don't even have to drive to the trailhead, since the campground is so close. A little over 2 miles of this hike are along Little River on Little River Trail, covered in more detail in Hike 10. Read that hike description as well as this one for a better understanding of this section of the park.

(See map for Hike 8: Elkmont Nature Trail.)

Start: Jakes Creek trailhead near Elkmont Campground
Distance: 5.5-mile loop
Hiking time: About 2.5 hours—day hike
Difficulty: Half moderate, half easy
Trail surface: Forest trail and an old gravel railroad bed
Best seasons: Spring for the wildflowers, Oct for autumn foliage

Other trail users: First 0.3 mile open to equestrians; remaining portion is for hikers only
Maps: Gatlinburg USGS quad; Trails Illustrated #229 Great Smoky Mountains; Trails Illustrated #316 Cades Cove Elkmont
Other: A large paved parking lot is at the trailhead, but it can fill on weekends and anytime during the summer or autumn. Restrooms are available at the campground.

Finding the trailhead: The trailhead is located in the Elkmont section of the park, near Elkmont Campground. Drive 4.8 miles west on Little River Road from Sugarlands Visitor Center and turn left at the sign for the campground. Drive 1.4 miles and turn left just before the campground entrance station. Drive 1.1 miles to the gate, passing by the trailhead for Little River Trail (Hike 10) along the way. A paved parking area lies to the right of the gate. GPS: N35 39.129' / W83 34.893'

The Hike

Walk up the gravel road past the gate on Jakes Creek Trail. Climb fairly steeply to the junction with Cucumber Gap Trail, cutting sharply back to the left (east). Take Cucumber Gap Trail and make a long, gradual ascent through second-growth yellow poplar (tulip tree) and abundant spring wildflowers to Cucumber Gap. Beyond the gap the forest changes to hemlocks (dead ones), with a dense rhododendron understory. After easily crossing Huskey Branch in a pleasant setting, you soon reach the junction with Little River Trail—a wide, gravel road on which you could drive a Winnebago most of the way.

Turn left (north) on Little River Trail. Soon after you first see Little River, you cross Huskey Branch once more, this time right over Huskey Branch Falls. The portion of the falls above the trail is especially photogenic on overcast days with diffused lighting. Huskey Branch continues falling under the bridge and into a deep pool in Little River.

Historic vacation cottage in Elkmont.

From here, you follow closely along Little River the remaining 2.0 miles to the paved road. Turn left onto the road and follow it 0.5 mile back to the trailhead.

Miles and Directions

0.0   Start at the gate on Jakes Creek Trail.

0.3   Make a sharp left (southeast) turn onto Cucumber Gap Trail.

2.7   Cucumber Gap Trail ends at Little River Trail. Turn left (north).

5.0   Junction with the paved road at Little River trailhead. Turn left and follow the road back.

5.5   Arrive back at trailhead.

HISTORIC ELKMONT

First-time visitors to the Elkmont section of the park all ask the same question: What's the deal with all the dilapidated houses? The structures are vacation cottages built in the early 1900s before the park was established. While most everyone else had to leave when the park moved in, the owners of these cabins successfully lobbied to retain use of their properties. Many of these leases, which were renewed several times, remained in effect until the early 1990s. The final one expired in 2001. The park had originally planned to remove all of the structures and allow the land to revert to its natural state, but Elkmont was placed on the National Register of Historic Places as a historic district, requiring a change of plans. In 2009, after much public input, the park service confirmed a plan to restore and preserve about one-fourth of the Elkmont cottages, as well as the old Appalachian Clubhouse. The clubhouse renovation is complete and the building is available for rent as a day-use facility.

10 Little River

On this hike you can devote half an hour, half a day, or half a week if you choose to camp. You can amble along the flat trail as far as you like, and when you've had enough, turn around and amble back. It's a creek walk, a forest walk, and a history lesson all in one. During early April you'll see dwarf irises, trilliums, and numerous other wildflowers. During October Little River Trail becomes a riot of color and is one of the finer autumn forest walks in the Smokies. At any time of year—from a half hour before sunrise until a half hour after sunset—you can dip a fly into the river and try your hand at the large brown and rainbow trout.

Little River Trail follows an old logging grade used by Little River Lumber Company to extract the virgin timber before the park was established, and even afterward. The company agreed to sell their lands only if they could continue logging for an additional five years, which they did. All along the hike, you see evidence of the logging operations—a railroad rail here, a steel cable over there. The forest has recovered nicely, but you'll see no old growth on this hike.

(See map for Hike 8: Elkmont Nature Trail.)

Start: Little River trailhead near Elkmont Campground
Distance: 7.6 miles out and back (or whatever distance you choose)
Hiking time: About 3.5 hours—day hike, with options for camping
Difficulty: Easy
Trail surface: Old railroad bed
Best seasons: Spring for the wildflowers, Oct for autumn foliage

Other trail users: Hikers only
Maps: Gatlinburg and Silers Bald USGS quads; Trails Illustrated #229 Great Smoky Mountains; Trails Illustrated #317 Clingmans Dome Cataloochee (upper portion only); Trails Illustrated #316 Cades Cove Elkmont
Other: Several parking spaces are available at the trailhead parking lot, but they fill up on most days. From spring through fall, if you don't get here early, you might have to park some distance from the gate and walk. Restrooms are available at the campground.

Finding the trailhead: The trailhead is located in the Elkmont section of the park, near the Elkmont Campground. Drive 4.8 miles west on Little River Road from Sugarlands Visitor Center and turn left at the sign for the campground. Drive 1.4 miles and turn left just before the campground entrance station. Drive 0.6 mile to a fork in the road and the parking area on the left. Little River Trail starts at the gate on the left road fork. GPS: N35 39.205' / W83 34.792'

The Hike

Begin on the roadbed beyond the gate on the upper end of the parking area. For the first 0.2 mile, you pass by old vacation homes and through the site for the Smokies' famous synchronous fireflies. (See the sidebars for this hike and Hike 9.)

Fireflies light up the forest in this multiple exposure.

Once you leave the cabins behind, you'll enjoy an easy walk along Little River, sometimes kissing it, sometimes out of sight of it, but always close to it. About a mile from the end of the hike, the old railroad grade becomes more trail-like but still easy to hike. The junction with Goshen Prong Trail at mile 3.7 is the farthest point to which most day hikers care to venture, but you should continue at least another 0.1 mile on Goshen Prong Trail to the bridge over Little River to enjoy the scenic crossing. Hike 11 crosses this bridge on its way down from Clingmans Dome.

Miles and Directions

0.0 Start at the east end of the parking area at the gate.

0.1 Pass by old vacation cabins and the location for the synchronous fireflies.

2.0 Cross over Huskey Branch Falls.

2.3 Junction with Cucumber Gap Trail, coming in from the right. Continue straight on the wide Little River Trail.

2.7 Junction with Huskey Gap Trail on the left, soon after crossing Little River on a footbridge. Stay to the right on Little River Trail, following the river upstream.

3.7 Trail forks just after the bridge over Lost Creek. Take the right fork onto Goshen Prong Trail, heading southwest.

3.8 Bridge over Little River. Return the way you came.

7.6 Arrive back at trailhead.

Options: You can continue on Little River Trail an additional 2.5 miles from the junction with Goshen Prong Trail, passing the popular Campsite 24 and proceeding to Campsite 30, at trail's end.

A couple of hiking possibilities exist using Little River Trail as a base. See Hike 9 for a good day-hike loop. A good overnight loop would be to hike Little River Trail to Campsite 24 or 30 and spend the first night. The next day follow Rough Creek Trail up to Sugarland Mountain Trail. Go north on it to Huskey Gap Trail and then back to Little River Trail. You could spend a second night at Campsite 21 near the junction of Huskey Gap Trail and Little River Trail for a leisurely trip, or hike all the way back on the second day. Total round-trip mileage, if staying the first night at Campsite 24, is 16.2 miles.

FLASHES IN THE NIGHT

As you walk the first mile or so along Little River Trail, you pass through habitat for one of the Smokies' most interesting—and now famous—inhabitants. *Photinus carolinus* is a species of firefly—"lightning bug" for most Southerners—that lives all across the East. However, here in Elkmont it does something very special. Groups of male fireflies of this species sometimes flash in unison. One moment the forest will be dark—save for a few flashes from fireflies of different species—and in the next few moments, it will be filled with hundreds of flashes going off at the same time. The critters no doubt have been doing this for a long time, but it was only first documented here in 1993, the first authenticated existence of synchronous flashing in North America.

As it turns out, synchronous flashing is not all that rare and can be observed at many locations in the southern Appalachians and elsewhere, including other areas of the park. But for observers, Elkmont is where it all began and witnessing the phenomenon has become an incredibly popular event. Park visitors from all over the country walk the short distance along Little River Trail to see the show. The event has become so popular that the park closes Elkmont to personal vehicles for a ten-day period in June when the fireflies are at their best. If you want to see them then, you need to make reservations to park at Sugarlands Visitor Center and then ride the trolley to Elkmont. A small fee is charged.

11 Goshen Prong

Beginning on the Smokies' highest mountain, traversing the crest line along the Appalachian Trail, following a sizable stream from its source, and ending with a historical walk along one of the park's major rivers, this hike encompasses just about everything the park is famous for and passes through a rich diversity of plants.

Start: Forney Ridge Parking Area on Clingmans Dome

Distance: 13.9 miles point to point

Hiking time: About 7 hours—day hike or overnighter

Difficulty: Moderate, with the final 4.0 miles easy

Trail surface: Very rocky sections, forested trail, old railroad bed

Best seasons: Spring for the wildflowers, Oct for autumn foliage

Other trail users: Hikers only

Maps: Clingmans Dome, Silers Bald, and Gatlinburg USGS quads; Trails Illustrated #229

Great Smoky Mountains; Trails Illustrated #317 Clingmans Dome Cataloochee (upper portion only); Trails Illustrated #316 Cades Cove Elkmont

Special considerations: Clingmans Dome Road is closed Dec 1–Mar 31. After heavy rains 2 crossings of Fish Camp Prong may be tricky.

Other: The parking area at the beginning is huge but still fills up on weekends and any day during summer and autumn. Pit toilets are located at the parking area. A visitor center is located near the start of the paved trail to the Clingmans Dome Tower.

Finding the trailhead: At Newfound Gap turn west onto Clingmans Dome Road and follow it 7.0 miles to its end at Forney Ridge Parking Area. The trail begins on the extreme western end of the parking lot. GPS: N35 33.409' / W83 29.772'

You need to leave a vehicle at the lower trailhead. Drive 4.8 miles west on Little River Road from Sugarlands Visitor Center and turn left at the sign for Elkmont Campground. Drive 1.4 miles and turn left just before the campground entrance station. Drive 0.6 mile to a fork in the road and the parking area on the left. GPS: N35 39.205' / W83 34.792'

The Hike

You have a decision to make at the beginning of this hike. You can take the paved path to Clingmans Dome Tower on the mountain's summit and pick up the Appalachian Trail (AT) from there, or you can bypass the tower (and the crowds) by taking Clingmans Dome Bypass Trail. If you've never seen the view from the observation tower, by all means, go for that route—you need to see it at least once. But if you've "been there, done that," you might want to get away from the pavement—and the crowds—as quickly as possible. For the tower route, see Hike 51.

For the "I'm sick of crowds route," turn left (west) off the paved tower path at the western end of the parking area. Forney Ridge Trail leads about 0.2 mile to the junction with Clingmans Dome Bypass Trail, which takes off to the right (north) from the junction. The 0.5-mile moderate climb from here to the AT is very rocky and

A hiker enjoys the view from the Goshen Prong Trail footbridge over Little River.

depressing as it passes through a forest devastated by the balsam woolly adelgid and air pollution (See the sidebar for Hike 49). A positive aspect of this section is that a large number of small trees have grown back.

▶ **The elaborate footbridge carrying Goshen Prong Trail over Little River is amusingly nicknamed the Goshen Gate Bridge.**

Once at the AT, turn left (west), but take time to admire the view off the north side of the trail toward Mount LeConte. The 1.9 miles of the AT to Goshen Prong Trail are relatively easy and provide numerous open vistas. At a nondescript junction Goshen Prong Trail turns off to the right (north) and begins a rocky and steep course down the upper drainage of Goshen Prong. A birch forest with scattered red spruce soon replaces the spruce forest of the ridgeline. Farther down you find beech trees, and hemlocks (now dead) replace the spruce. The trail gradient has moderated considerably.

Look out to the right for a rock overhang with a small fissure cave. A few hundred yards farther, the trail crosses an unnamed side branch below a scenic cascade over mossy, stratified rock. Soon you cross another side stream (both easily rock-hopped) and begin a noisy parallel of the cascading Goshen Prong. Along a stretch where the trail swings away from the creek, look for old logging relics. The path you're on follows the old logging railroad line, so you might spot a railroad rail or a steel cable. Once back alongside the creek, you have to cross a small landslide on the bank. The park has installed steel cables to make it safer to negotiate the landslide when the rocks are wet or icy.

A few hundred yards farther, where Goshen Prong joins Fish Camp Prong, the trail passes Campsite 23, popular with fishers. (Fishing is prohibited in all waters upstream of the creek junction.) The campsite sits on the right, a few hundred feet off the trail. Fish Camp Prong, which you now follow, splits below the campsite and forms an island. You must cross the creek first to get onto the island and then again on the other end. Both crossings are a little tricky in high water, but usually they are an easy rock-hop.

For the remainder of the hike on Goshen Prong Trail, you keep close company with Fish Camp Prong. The creek (more like a little river at this point) spills, churns, cascades, and slides all the way to its junction with Little River. Photographers will want to linger along this stretch. Near the end of Goshen Prong Trail, you swing away from the creek a bit and cross Little River on a long steel footbridge. Upstream, Split Branch joins Little River. Downstream is the mouth of Fish Camp Prong.

If you can pull yourself away from the views at the bridge, continue a few hundred yards to the junction with Little River Trail. To the right, it's 0.5 mile to Campsite 24. To the left, Little River Trail follows Little River 3.7 miles to the trailhead near Elkmont Campground. At 1.0 mile from the Goshen Prong Trail junction, Huskey Gap Trail bears off to the right. Stay to the left on Little River Trail and soon cross the river on a wide bridge. About 0.75 mile farther you cross Huskey Branch at Huskey Branch Falls. Continue following Little River downstream to the trailhead.

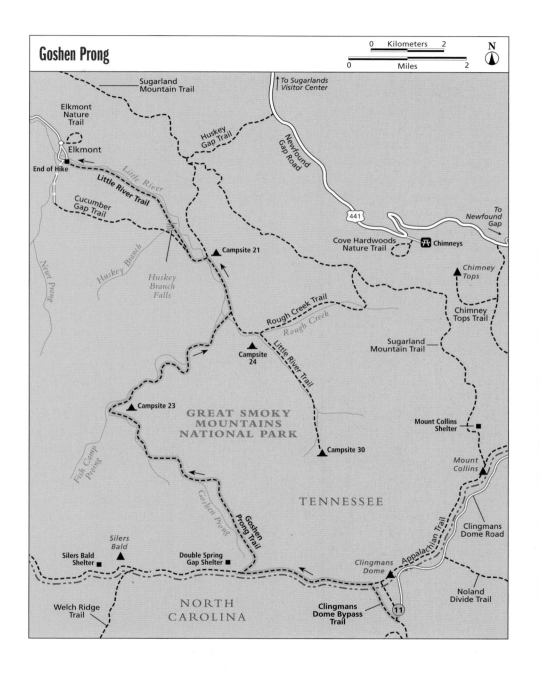

Goshen Prong

0 Kilometers 2
0 Miles 2

N

Sugarland Mountain Trail

Elkmont Nature Trail

↑ To Sugarlands Visitor Center

Huskey Gap Trail

Newfound Gap Road

Elkmont

End of Hike

Little River

Little River Trail

Cucumber Gap Trail

441

To Newfound Gap

Huskey Branch

Newt Prong

Huskey Branch Falls

Campsite 21

Cove Hardwoods Nature Trail

Chimneys

Chimney Tops

Chimney Tops Trail

Rough Creek Trail

Rough Creek

Little River Trail

Sugarland Mountain Trail

Campsite 24

Campsite 23

GREAT SMOKY MOUNTAINS NATIONAL PARK

Mount Collins Shelter

Campsite 30

Mount Collins

Clingmans Dome Road

Fish Camp Prong

TENNESSEE

Goshen Prong

Silers Bald

Silers Bald Shelter

Double Spring Gap Shelter

Goshen Prong Trail

Appalachian Trail

Clingmans Dome

Clingmans Dome Bypass Trail

Noland Divide Trail

Welch Ridge Trail

NORTH CAROLINA

11

Miles and Directions

0.0   Start from the western end of the parking area on Forney Ridge Trail.

0.2   Forney Ridge Trail cuts back to the left. Turn to the right (north) on Clingmans Dome Bypass Trail.

0.7   Junction with the Appalachian Trail. A right turn takes you to Clingmans Dome Tower. Turn left (west) on the Appalachian Trail.

2.6   Turn right (north) onto Goshen Prong Trail.

7.0   Campsite 23.

10.1   Bridge over Little River.

10.2   Reach the end of Goshen Prong Trail. Turn left (north) on Little River Trail.

11.2   Huskey Gap Trail bears off to the right. Continue on Little River Trail.

11.6   Cucumber Gap Trail bears off to the left. Continue on Little River Trail.

11.9   Cross over Huskey Branch Falls.

13.9   Arrive at Little River trailhead.

12 Jakes Creek and Lynn Camp Prong

With picturesque streams, views, wildflowers, a scenic waterfall, and some fun ridge walking, this hike makes a good option for those looking for a long day hike or an easy overnighter. Another plus is that it isn't very crowded, although you probably won't have the entire hike to yourself except in the dead of winter.

Start: Jakes Creek trailhead near Elkmont Campground
Distance: 16.9-mile lollipop
Hiking time: About 9 hours—day hike, overnighter, or 2-nighter
Difficulty: Strenuous, due to steep grades and a creek wade
Trail surface: Forest trails with rocks and roots
Other trail users: Equestrians
Maps: Gatlinburg, Silers Bald, and Thunderhead Mountain USGS quads; Trails Illustrated #229 Great Smoky Mountains; Trails Illustrated

#316 Cades Cove Elkmont
Special considerations: The Lynn Camp Prong crossing is rock-hoppable only after a prolonged dry spell. Come prepared to wade. The small spring at Campsite 26 may dry up during prolonged dry periods. The closest water is about 0.5 mile down Lynn Camp Prong Trail.
Other: A large paved parking lot is at the trailhead, but it can fill on weekends and anytime during the summer or autumn. Restrooms are available at the campground.

Finding the trailhead: The trailhead is located in the Elkmont section of the park, near Elkmont Campground. Drive 4.8 miles west on Little River Road from Sugarlands Visitor Center and turn left at the sign for the campground. Drive 1.4 miles and turn left just before the campground entrance station. Drive 1.1 miles to the gate, passing by the trailhead for Little River Trail (Hike 10) along the way. A paved parking area lies to the right of the gate. This is the same trailhead as for Hike 9. GPS: N35 39.129' / W83 34.893'

The Hike

Walk up the gravel road past the gate on Jakes Creek Trail. Climb fairly steeply to the junction with Cucumber Gap Trail, cutting sharply back to the left (east). Continue straight ahead on Jakes Creek Trail, following an old logging grade. Descend slightly a few hundred feet to the junction with Meigs Mountain Trail on the right. Stay on Jakes Creek Trail and hike through a characteristic second-growth yellow poplar (tulip tree) forest while making a steady ascent on a wide parallel of Jakes Creek. You meet up with the creek at an especially scenic cascade. Look for a steel cable sticking out of the side path leading down to the pool, a sign of bygone logging activity.

A short distance beyond the cascade, the graded roadbed ends at a crossing of Newt Prong. Look for an old railroad rail sticking out of the ground here, an even surer sign that logging once occurred in these woods. Cross the creek on a foot log and begin ascending alongside Jakes Creek. After a steep section, cross the creek on stepping stones (tricky in high water) and swing away from the creek on a level grade before climbing again after a switchback.

Pressing on, you pass Campsite 27 on the left, right beside the trail. The forest here is pleasant, but the campsite is not one of the best. The ground is bare and rooty, and it looks as though it could become a miserable collection of muddy runnels during a hard rain. Maybe that's why campers at this site tend to spread out through the woods—not the most environmentally sound practice.

It's a rooty climb, though not too steep, from the campsite to Jakes Gap. Four trails intersect here. Straight ahead, Panther Creek Trail descends to Lynn Camp Prong—you'll climb this trail later in the hike. To the right, an unmaintained and overgrown manway leads to the summit of Blanket Mountain. As with all unmaintained trails in the park, hiking this one is not recommended.

Turn left (south) on Miry Ridge Trail. Despite the unflattering name, this is a fine portion of the hike. As you climb moderately up the northwest slope of Dripping Spring Mountain, pay attention to the forest. When you swing around the ridge and begin skirting the southeast side, notice the difference in both the temperature and plant life. On the more south-facing slope, you pass through a long mountain laurel tunnel with a ground cover of galax, trailing arbutus, and wintergreen—all indicator plants of a dry environment. Soon you pass through another tunnel, this one created by rhododendron, and now you come out in a clearing just below the summit of Dripping Spring Mountain. There's a good view from here of Cold Spring Knob on the Smokies crest and of Mellinger Death Ridge straight ahead. A side path climbs to a higher vantage point on the summit of Dripping Spring Mountain, but the view from the main trail is perfectly fine.

Now you pass through another laurel tunnel and have a good walk along the contour line before descending easily through a dying hemlock forest to a saddle. A signpost here indicates that Campsite 26 lies off to the left (northeast) side of the saddle. The obvious side path leads a few hundred yards to the site, situated in a grove of silverbell, maple, and dead hemlock. (See the sidebar for Hike 36.)

A gentle walk takes you from the saddle to the junction with Lynn Camp Prong Trail. Turn right (southwest) and follow Lynn Camp Prong Trail down and away from the ridgeline. The next 2.2 miles are a cakewalk (in this direction)—not too steep, easy creek crossings, and downhill all the way. Watch for wildflowers along this stretch, but don't get so caught up in them that you overlook the wood nettle that's growing everywhere. You don't want to brush against that stuff (See Bad Plants in the introduction). The trail dumps out in a clearing on an old railroad bed. This is Campsite 28. Straight ahead is the horse-hitching rail, and to the right is the camping area, located on both sides of Buckeye Cove Branch.

To the left is the continuation of Lynn Camp Prong Trail, following the mostly level railroad bed 1.5 miles to the Greenbrier Ridge Trail and Middle Prong Trail junction. Greenbrier Ridge Trail turns left at the junction, while Middle Prong Trail (your route) turns right as a continuation of the railroad grade. The trail descends moderately now, making a left switchback and then a right switchback. In the outside curve of the second switchback, an obvious side path leads a few hundred feet to

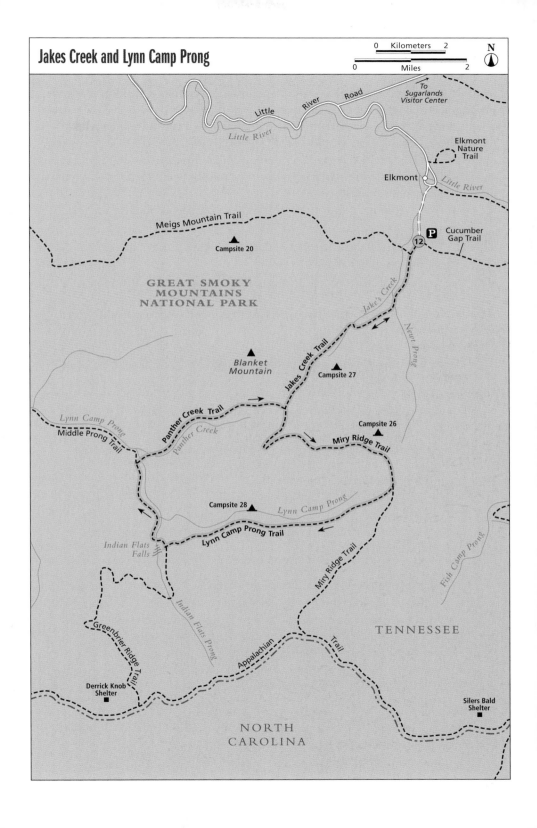

Jakes Creek and Lynn Camp Prong

Indian Flats Falls, a highly recommended side trip. Continuing down the trail, you make a few more switchbacks and cross Indian Flats Prong on a low bridge. From here, it's an easy 1.2-mile walk on the gradually descending railroad grade to the obvious junction with Panther Creek Trail.

Panther Creek Trail crosses Lynn Camp Prong immediately from the start. There's no bridge and it's a safe bet that you won't be able to rock-hop it. Once across, your reward is a long, rocky, and rooty haul up the Panther Creek drainage. You cross the creek many times and finally pull away for a final steep grind to Jakes Gap. Take a breather at the gap—you deserve it.

From Jakes Gap, retrace your steps on Jakes Creek Trail to complete the hike.

Miles and Directions

0.0 Start at the gate on Jakes Creek Trail.

0.3 Junction with Cucumber Gap Trail, which cuts back to the left. Continue straight ahead on Jakes Creek Trail.

0.4 Junction with Meigs Mountain Trail, on the right. Continue following Jakes Creek upstream on Jakes Creek Trail.

2.6 Campsite 27.

3.3 Reach Jakes Gap at junction with Miry Ridge Trail and Panther Creek Trail. Turn left (south) onto Miry Ridge Trail.

5.2 Campsite 26.

5.8 Turn right (southwest) onto Lynn Camp Prong Trail.

8.0 Campsite 28.

9.5 Junction with Middle Prong Trail and Greenbrier Ridge Trail. Turn right (north) on Middle Prong Trail.

9.7 Side path on the left leads to Indian Flats Falls.

11.3 Junction with Panther Creek Trail on the right. Wade across Lynn Camp Prong to start hiking on Panther Creek Trail.

13.6 Arrive back at Jakes Gap. Return to trailhead on Jakes Creek Trail the way you came.

16.9 Arrive back at trailhead.

Options: The hike passes three backcountry campsites, providing numerous possibilities for backpacking trips. For an overnighter, a good choice is Campsite 26. This gives you a tough 11.7-mile hike the next day, so you might want to push on to Campsite 28 and spend the night there. For two-night trips, there are two good options. One is to stay both nights at Campsite 27, using the second day to make a day-hike loop of the remainder of the hike. The other option is to stay the first night at Campsite 27 and the second night at Campsite 28.

13 Walker Sisters Home

History lovers will find this hike especially rewarding, as it passes by an old combination schoolhouse-church and ends at a particularly fine homesite featuring an old cabin, springhouse, and corncrib with overhanging eaves. And although you probably won't have it all to yourself unless you go in the dead of winter, you won't have to share the trail with hordes of hikers.

(See map for Hike 7: Laurel Falls and Cove Mountain.)

Start: Metcalf Bottoms trailhead near Metcalf Bottoms Picnic Area
Distance: 3.2 miles out and back
Hiking time: About 2 hours–day hike
Difficulty: Easy, with some moderate sections
Trail surface: Forest trail and old roadbed

Other trail users: Hikers only
Maps: Wear Cove USGS quad; Trails Illustrated #229 Great Smoky Mountains; Trails Illustrated #316 Cades Cove Elkmont
Other: There's usually room for a few vehicles along the road. Otherwise, you can park back at the picnic area. You pass restroom facilities as you drive through the picnic area.

Finding the trailhead: The trail begins from Metcalf Bottoms Picnic Area, located roughly halfway between Sugarlands Visitor Center and the Townsend Y on Little River Road. Turn into the picnic area and cross the bridge over Little River. The trail starts on the right side, immediately beyond the bridge on the upstream side of the creek. GPS: N35 40.751' / W83 38.844'

The Hike

Metcalf Bottoms Trail begins as a gravel road heading upstream. The trail soon swings away from Little River and climbs rather steeply, passing a water tower on the right and an old homesite across from the tower. After the climb the trail descends through a rhododendron tunnel to Little Brier Branch and follows the branch upstream, crossing it twice on foot logs, to the old Little Greenbrier School building.

If you make this hike from spring through fall, you might find cars at the school. A narrow, winding, gravel road leads to the school from the paved road between Metcalf Bottoms and Wear Cove. You can drive here too, and cut 1.2 miles off the hike, but hiking the Metcalf Bottoms Trail is the better option if you want to experience this part of the park fully. It's the only option during winter, when the road is closed.

After exploring the old schoolhouse, continue your hike on Little Brier Gap Trail. It begins beyond the gate on the gravel road above the cemetery. After about 0.75 mile of mostly easy walking, Little Brier Gap Trail continues straight ahead, while your hike swings around to the right and continues less than 0.25 mile to Walker Sisters Home. Here you find a springhouse, corncrib/gear shed, and the cabin where the five Walker sisters lived. When the park was established, the sisters adamantly opposed leaving their home. They agreed to a compromise that allowed them to live out their lives on the land with a "lifetime lease." The last sister died in 1964.

Miles and Directions

0.0 Start at the Metcalf Bottoms trailhead.

0.6 Reach Little Greenbrier School. Walk through the schoolyard, climb the bank beside the cemetery, and begin hiking on the gated road, which is Little Brier Gap Trail.

1.4 Little Brier Gap Trail continues straight ahead, while the old road swings sharply around to the right. Stay on the road.

1.6 Reach Walker Sisters Home. Return the way you came.

3.2 Arrive back at trailhead.

Options: Little Brier Gap Trail continues about 0.4 mile to Little Brier Gap and the junction with Little Greenbrier Trail. With a second vehicle left as a shuttle, you could go west from the gap to Wear Cove Road, a little more than a mile above Metcalf Bottoms Picnic Area, or head east and pick up Laurel Falls Trail and take it back to the trailhead on Little River Road.

READING THE WALLS

Early settlers never needed to open a window for ventilation. Many cabins didn't even have windows, but airflow was never a problem. With log walls and puncheon floors, the rooms were nowhere close to being airtight, even with mud chinking applied between the logs. To help stop the cold air from blowing in, many occupants wallpapered their walls with newspapers, using a paste made from flour and water. Look on the walls inside Walker Sisters Home and you'll see the remnants of their wallpapering.

14 Spruce Flats Falls

Although it's among the most scenic waterfalls in the park, Spruce Flats Falls is relatively unknown compared to the more popular falls such as Laurel Falls and Grotto Falls. The waterfall consists of several drops, with the main one about 40 feet high. There is another section above what you can see from the trail, but there is no good vantage point from which to view it safely. The hike may not be as well known or publicized as many others in the park, but it's no secret either. If you're after photos and you don't want people in them, you need to be here early in the morning.

Start: Parking area for the office of Great Smoky Mountains Institute at Tremont
Distance: 2.0 miles out and back
Hiking time: About 1.5 hours—day hike
Difficulty: Moderate
Trail surface: Dirt, rocks, and roots
Other trail users: Hikers only
Maps: Wear Cove USGS quad; Trails Illustrated #229 Great Smoky Mountains; Trails Illustrated #316 Cades Cove Elkmont
Other: The office for Great Smoky Mountains Institute at Tremont has several paved parking spots, but they can fill up quickly during the summer and fall busy season. If the office is open, you can obtain information and purchase park literature. The office has restrooms.

Finding the trailhead: The trail begins from Great Smoky Mountains Institute at Tremont, an environmental-education facility in the Tremont section of the park. To reach the institute, head southwest from the Townsend Y (junction of Little River Road and TN 73) toward Cades Cove. At 0.2 mile from the Y, Tremont Road turns to the left. Follow this road 2.0 miles to the institute, on the left. Turn into the complex, crossing over Middle Prong of Little River, and park at the office, the first building on the left. GPS: N35 38.486' / W83 41.371'

The Hike

The first part of this hike is a little confusing as it winds its way around the complex of buildings for Great Smoky Mountains Institute at Tremont. At the parking area look for the gravel road heading uphill, away from the office. The road is to the left of the paved road leading into the institute complex. Two hundred feet up the gravel road is the dormitory building. Walk to the left of the building to Lumber Ridge trailhead at the edge of the woods. Hike 100 feet on Lumber Ridge Trail and turn right on Buckeye Trail. Buckeye Trail passes behind the institute complex and in about 0.2 mile comes to a fork. A right turn at the fork goes downhill to the institute. You want to take the left fork, heading uphill. After a few yards turn left and follow the switchback to keep from bumping into the water tank. At the second switchback turn right and continue heading uphill. You'll soon gain the ridge and hike the rest of the way on a poorly graded, rocky, and rooty path. The path descends steeply on its final approach to the falls.

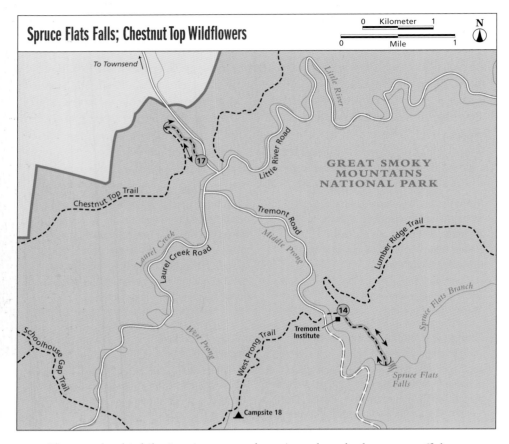

Spruce Flats Falls; Chestnut Top Wildflowers

If you make this hike in winter or early spring when the leaves are off the trees, you'll catch glimpses of Middle Prong below the trail and the gravel Tremont road running beside it. When you get to the falls, you may be surprised to discover that the waterfall is only a few hundred feet from the road. However, the road is on the other side of Middle Prong, which has no footbridge. The river is impossible to rock-hop and difficult—potentially dangerous—to wade.

Miles and Directions

0.0 Start on the gravel road leading uphill from the parking area, away from Middle Prong. Walk through the yard to the left of the dormitory and then hike 100 feet on the Lumber Ridge Trail, which is obvious.

0.1 Take Buckeye Trail, which turns to the right from Lumber Ridge Trail.

0.3 Trail forks, with the right fork leading downhill to the institute complex. Take the left fork, heading uphill.

1.0 Arrive at Spruce Flats Falls. Return the way you came.

2.0 Arrive back at trailhead.

Spruce Flats Falls.

HIKER'S BLOOMER

Among the earliest wildflowers to bloom in the Smokies—as early as late February—trailing arbutus (*Epigaea repens*) is a hiker's wildflower. It grows in dry forests, commonly along the upslope banks of hiking trails and dirt roads. It grows abundantly along the trail to Spruce Flats Falls, although to see its little pinkish-white flowers, you may have to move the leathery evergreen leaves out of the way.

15 Indian Flats Falls

The easy walk along Lynn Camp Prong is the quintessential Smokies stream hike. Many photographs taken along this stream show up on postcards or prints sold in area stores. In spring the trail sides explode with trilliums, dwarf irises, jacks-in-the pulpit, violets, anemones, and seemingly countless other wildflowers. In October the autumn foliage rivals any in the park. With the cascading Lynn Camp Prong as your escort and a scenic waterfall as your destination, this hike is a great one any time of year, not just in spring and fall.

Start: Middle Prong trailhead in the Tremont section of the park
Distance: 8.0 miles out and back
Hiking time: About 4 hours—day hike
Difficulty: Moderate
Trail surface: Old forest road
Best seasons: Spring for the wildflowers, Oct for autumn foliage
Other trail users: Equestrians
Maps: Thunderhead Mountain USGS quad; Trails Illustrated #229 Great Smoky Mountains; Trails Illustrated #316 Cades Cove Elkmont
Special considerations: The last 3.0 miles of

Tremont Road are closed in winter. An excellent option is to bring a bicycle for the closed road section and make this a hike-bike combination trip. Bicycles are not allowed on the hiking trail.
Other: Ample parking is usually available at the trailhead, but on busy weekends you may have to park some distance back from the gate. The closest restrooms are back at the Great Smoky Mountains Institute at Tremont office. If the institute is not open, the next closest facilities in the park are at Cades Cove Picnic Area. The town of Townsend has closer facilities.

Finding the trailhead: The hike begins at the end of Tremont Road. Head southwest from the Townsend Y (junction of Little River Road and TN 73) toward Cades Cove, and at 0.2 mile turn left onto Tremont Road. The road passes Great Smoky Mountains Institute at Tremont, located on the left at 2.0 miles, and then changes to gravel. Drive 3.0 miles on the gravel portion to the end of the road at a traffic circle. GPS: N35 37.113' / W83 40.188'

The Hike

The trail is a continuation of the gravel road and follows an old railroad grade built by Little River Lumber Company in the early twentieth century. After crossing Lynn Camp Prong on a sturdy bridge, stay to the left on the main gravel road. Unless you're like Forrest Gump and you don't mind stepping in horse pies, it's a good idea to keep an eye at your feet as well as the trail ahead. At about 0.5 mile the road makes a wide swing to the left at the largest set of cascades on Lynn Camp Prong. The trail continues alongside the creek and comes out near the top of the uppermost drop. Photographers really enjoy this stretch of the creek.

The road continues alongside the creek another 3.0 miles to a bridge over Indian Flats Prong, just above where that creek joins Lynn Camp Prong. (Back at the

Autumn along Lynn Camp Prong. ▶

Indian Flats Falls; Lynn Camp Prong and Appalachian Trail

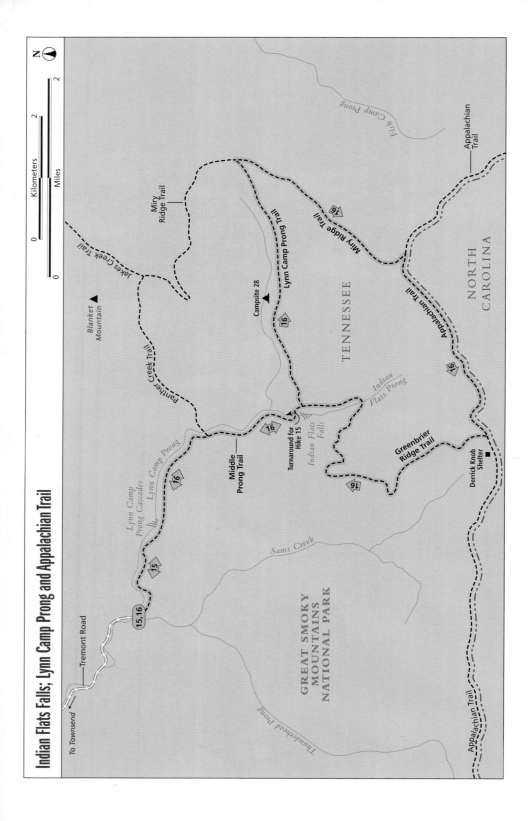

trailhead, Thunderhead Prong joins Lynn Camp Prong to form Middle Prong Little River.) Beyond the bridge, the grade increases. You make a couple of broad left-hand switchbacks and then a sharp right-hand switchback. Then you come to the first sharp left-hand switchback. Look here for an obvious side path to the right heading toward the creek. The path leads a few hundred feet over rocks and roots to the base of the uppermost drop of Indian Flats Falls.

The waterfall consists of four separate drops, each of them scenic and worthy of a photograph. However, only the uppermost fall is easily accessible. If you want to see the lower drops, you have to scramble down the makeshift paths, over and under rhododendron thickets. Resist the urge to do this, for both your safety and to keep from destroying the vegetation and soil along the creek bank.

Miles and Directions

0.0   Start behind the gate and cross Lynn Camp Prong on the bridge. Stay to the left beyond the bridge, on the main road.

0.5   Lynn Camp Prong Cascades.

2.3   Junction with Panther Creek Trail on the left. Continue straight on the main road.

3.5   Bridge over Indian Flats Prong.

3.9   Follow the obvious side path to Indian Flats Falls on the right.

4.0   Arrive at Indian Flats Falls. Return the way you came.

8.0   Arrive back at trailhead.

Options: Two other hikes in this book use portions of Middle Prong Trail and pass by Indian Flats Falls: Hike 12 and Hike 16.

FLOATING LOGS

About half a mile into Middle Prong Trail, you pass by a section of scenic cascades on Lynn Camp Prong. A short distance upstream is the site of an old logging splash dam. Middle Prong Trail follows the course of an old logging railroad, but before railroads were built, loggers sometimes floated logs out of the mountains. Of course, a stream like Lynn Camp Prong is hardly big enough to float a log, so the loggers built dams across the streams to build up a pond, into which they stored logs hauled in from the surrounding slopes. When the pond was full, the loggers opened a release gate and the flood of water and logs rushed downstream. Splash dams were used with limited success in the Smokies. The rough terrain was often not conducive to floating logs, even in a flood of water, and loggers often spent a great deal of time freeing log jams. Splash damming was extremely damaging to the streamside environment and some areas of the park still carry scars from the practice.

Autumn leaves collect in a pool along Lynn Camp Prong.

16 Lynn Camp Prong and Appalachian Trail

This hike provides a good opportunity to get deep into the Smokies without making an overly strenuous effort. You get to experience a few miles of the Smokies crest (without views, though), and after the first 4.0 miles, you have the hike pretty much to yourself. A couple of camping options allow you to do the hike as an overnighter or a lazy two-nighter. If you're up to it, the hike is doable as a long day hike.

(See map for Hike 15: Indian Flats Falls.)

Start: Middle Prong trailhead in the Tremont section of the park

Distance: 21.0-mile lollipop

Hiking time: About 12 hours—killer day hike, tough overnighter, or 2-nighter

Difficulty: Strenuous, due to length and some steep sections

Trail surface: Old forest road and forested trails

Best seasons: Spring for the wildflowers, Oct for autumn foliage

Other trail users: Equestrians permitted on first 7.8 miles

Maps: Thunderhead Mountain and Silers Bald USGS quads; Trails Illustrated #229 Great

Smoky Mountains; Trails Illustrated #316 Cades Cove Elkmont

Special considerations: The last 3.0 miles of Tremont Road are closed in winter, so you'll probably want to hike this one only from spring to fall. There are better winter trips than this one, with 6.0 additional miles of road walking required. After heavy rains an unbridged crossing of Indian Flats Prong could be a wade.

Other: Ample parking is usually available at the trailhead, but on busy weekends you may have to park a ways back from the gate. The closest restrooms are back at the Great Smoky Mountains Institute at Tremont office. If the institute is not open, the next closest facilities in the park are at Cades Cove Picnic Area. The town of Townsend has closer facilities.

Finding the trailhead: The hike begins at the end of Tremont Road. Head southwest from the Townsend Y (junction of Little River Road and TN 73) toward Cades Cove, and at 0.2 mile turn left onto Tremont Road. The road passes Great Smoky Mountains Institute at Tremont, located on the left at 2.0 miles, and then changes to gravel. Drive 3.0 miles on the gravel portion to the end of the road at a traffic circle. GPS: N35 37.113' / W83 40.188'

The Hike

The first 7.8 miles of this hike are also covered in Hikes 12 and 15. Refer to them for more details. The hike begins on Middle Prong Trail as a continuation of the gravel road behind the gate. Cross the creek on a footbridge and stay to the left after crossing to remain on the main road. Pass by the trailhead for Panther Creek Trail at 2.3 miles and at mile 3.5, cross Indian Flats Prong on a low bridge and begin climbing on switchbacks. At the second sharp switchback, an obvious side path on the right leads a few hundred feet to Indian Flats Falls. Plan to spend a little reflection time here.

Back on Middle Prong Trail, it's a short climb to the junction with Lynn Camp Prong Trail and Greenbrier Ridge Trail. You'll come back to this junction later in the hike. Now, you want to go left (north) on Lynn Camp Prong Trail. After an easy 1.5 miles, you arrive at Campsite 28, your first night's stay on a two-night backpack. Pressing on from the campsite, make a continuous 2.2-mile climb to the junction with Miry Ridge Trail on the ridgeline.

Turn right (south) on the ridge and follow Miry Ridge Trail 2.5 miles to the junction with the Appalachian Trail (AT). Although you climb to the crest of the Smokies along this ridge, the grade is not as steep as you might expect. A cool feature of this section is the gnarled trees covered in moss and lichens. Look for a large birch tree with a good-size rhododendron growing from a crotch in the tree more than 15 feet above the ground.

At the junction with the AT, turn right (west) and make the steepest climb of the hike up Cold Spring Knob. Now you get a real lesson in Smokies ridge walking. It's sort of like Smokies weather in the spring—if you don't like it right now, don't worry because it'll change real soon. Up and down you go until the final descent to the Greenbrier Ridge Trail junction. Derrick Knob Shelter is 0.3 mile farther along the AT. The shelter is your second night's stay on a two-night backpack.

If skipping the shelter, turn sharply right (northeast) and head down Greenbrier Ridge Trail. It's a nearly continuous descent of 4.2 miles back to the junction with Lynn Camp Prong Trail and Middle Prong Trail. You pass through a variable second-growth forest along the way and make two uncertain stream crossings. The first, on a tributary to Indian Flats Prong, is the easier and isn't a problem except in very high water. The second crossing is over Indian Flats Prong and requires careful negotiation in high water. After prolonged rains this crossing could be a wade. The creek here is very scenic, but try not to let that distract you on the crossing.

After the second creek crossing, it's less than 0.5 mile back to Middle Prong Trail. Retrace your steps on Middle Prong Trail to the trailhead.

Miles and Directions

0.0 Start behind the gate and cross Lynn Camp Prong on the bridge. Stay to the left beyond the bridge, on the main road.

0.5 Lynn Camp Prong Cascades.

2.3 Junction with Panther Creek Trail on the left. Continue straight on the main road.

3.5 Bridge over Indian Flats Prong.

3.9 Obvious side path to Indian Flats Falls is on the right.

4.1 Junction with Lynn Camp Prong and Greenbrier Ridge Trails. Turn left (north) onto Lynn Camp Prong Trail.

5.6 Campsite 28.

7.8 Junction with Miry Ridge Trail on the ridgeline. Turn right (south) onto it.

10.3 Turn right (south) onto Appalachian Trail.

12.7 Turn sharply right (northeast) onto Greenbrier Ridge Trail.

16.9 Arrive back at junction of Lynn Camp Prong, Middle Prong, and Greenbrier Ridge Trails. Follow Middle Prong Trail back to the trailhead.

21.0 Arrive back at trailhead.

Options: While it's possible for experienced hikers to do this trip in a day, it is not recommended. A better choice is to spend two nights, staying at Campsite 28 the first night and Derrick Knob Shelter on the second night. You could do the trip as an overnighter, staying the first night at site 28, but this leaves you with 15.4 miles on the second day with a heavy pack. You could spend the first night at Derrick Knob Shelter, but if you do that, you'll probably want to reverse the loop part of the route so it will be only 8.6 miles to the shelter instead of 13.0. If you do spend the night at Derrick Knob Shelter, the total mileage for this hike will be 21.6.

A CRUEL DEATH

At several points along Greenbrier Ridge Trail and Miry Ridge Trail are good views of Mellinger Death Ridge, which separates the Indian Flats Prong and Lynn Camp Prong drainages. The ridge is named for Jasper Mellinger, who met an unfortunate fate while hiking through the area. Accounts of the incident vary, but it generally goes that Mellinger stumbled into a bear trap that had been improperly set by two brothers. Unable to free himself, and without the trappers checking daily as they should have, Mellinger was close to death before the men found him. Fearing retribution, the brothers killed Mellinger and threw his body over a cliff so it would look like an accident. One brother took the secret to his grave; the other brother, on his death bed, admitted to the murder some thirty years later. Mellinger's remains were found and his identity confirmed by his pocket watch.

17 Chestnut Top Wildflowers

The first 0.5 mile of Chestnut Top Trail provides possibly the finest spring wildflower show of any trail in the Smokies of comparable distance. Considering that the Smokies have perhaps the greatest flowering display in the country, that's a bold statement. Hike the trail in the middle of April and see for yourself. There are trilliums, waterleaf, violets, dwarf iris, spring beauty, squawroot, anemone, toothwort, bloodroot, jack-in-the-pulpit, hepatica, false Solomon's seal, fire pink, cancer root, purple phacelia, wild ginger—and that's just a warm-up! The flowering display continues somewhat throughout the spring and summer and even into autumn, but try to make this hike in April if possible.

(See map for Hike 14: Spruce Flats Falls.)

Start: Chestnut Top trailhead at the Townsend Y
Distance: 1.0 mile out and back
Hiking time: About 45 minutes—day hike (allow more time to view the wildflowers)
Difficulty: Moderate
Trail surface: Forest trail
Best season: Apr for the wildflowers
Other trail users: Hikers only

Maps: Wear Cove USGS quad; Trails Illustrated #229 Great Smoky Mountains; Trails Illustrated #316 Cades Cove Elkmont
Other: The parking area is large, but if you hike this trail in summer or on a sunny weekend from spring through fall, you might not find an empty spot. The Y is an extremely popular swimming, sunning, and tubing spot. The nearest facilities are available in Townsend, a couple of miles north.

Finding the trailhead: The hike begins from TN 73 near the junction with Little River Road and Laurel Creek Road, known locally as the Townsend Y. A long, narrow parking area is on the river (north) side of the road (GPS: N35 39.643' / W83 42.540'). Look for a split-rail fence marking the trailhead on the south side, opposite Little River.

The Hike

Begin at the split-rail fence on the opposite side of the road from the parking area. The trail is a continuous moderate ascent for about 0.5 mile, at which point it leaves the northeast-facing slope and swings around to a south-facing slope. Turn around here if you came only for the wildflowers.

Miles and Directions

0.0 Start from the Chestnut Top trailhead at the split-rail fence.

0.5 The trail swings away from the northeast-facing slope. Return the way you came.

1.0 Arrive back at trailhead.

Option: With a second vehicle or a shuttle, you can hike all of Chestnut Top Trail to Schoolhouse Gap, 4.3 miles from the trailhead. At the gap you would pick up Schoolhouse Gap Trail and follow it 2.2 miles down to Laurel Creek Road, 3.6 miles from the Townsend Y.

*Bloodroot (*Sanguinaria canadensis*).*

18 Lead Cove and Finley Cane

This hike and the route described in Hike 19 don't offer anything remarkable as far as Smokies scenery goes, but they are unique in that they are moderate-length loop hikes that are easily accessible. That's a relatively rare thing in the park, and consequently these hikes are very popular choices. The first 1.8 miles of this hike are also popular as the first leg of a hike to Spence Field on the Smokies' crest line.

Start: Lead Cove trailhead on Laurel Creek Road
Distance: 7.1-mile loop
Hiking time: About 3 hours—day hike
Difficulty: Moderate
Trail surface: Forest trail
Other trail users: Equestrians
Maps: Thunderhead Mountain USGS quad; Trails Illustrated #229 Great Smoky Mountains;

Trails Illustrated #316 Cades Cove Elkmont
Other: The combination of a popular trailhead and limited parking might mean you have to park alongside the road during busy weekends. Be careful as traffic on Laurel Creek Road can be terrible. Restrooms and a camp store are available at the Cades Cove Campground, a few miles farther southwest from the trailhead.

Finding the trailhead: From the junction of Little River Road and TN 73 (Townsend Y), head south on Laurel Creek Road toward Cades Cove. At 5.6 miles there is a narrow parking area on both sides of the road. The hike starts on Lead Cove Trail, which begins on the south side of the road. GPS: N35 36.418' / W83 44.685'

The Hike

Both Finley Cane Trail and Lead Cove Trail start from the south side of the road. Take Lead Cove Trail, on the right. You soon meet up with Sugar Cove Prong on the left, which you cross a short distance later. The trail ascends—steeply in places—through second-growth mixed hardwoods. You pass an old homesite on the left, and at one point the forest opens up in a clearing with views of Turkeypen Ridge. Shortly beyond the clearing, Lead Cove Trail ends on a ridge at Bote Mountain Trail.

Turn left (north) and follow Bote Mountain Trail along the ridge. The ridge walk is an easy descent, with a few steep sections. Good views of Defeat Ridge are off the east side of the trail. In a few places you can look back to see Thunderhead Mountain and Rocky Top. After 2.5 miles along the ridge, the trail forks, with Bote Mountain Trail going right and continuing along the ridge and Finley Cane Trail heading left and away from the ridge. Take Finley Cane Trail back to the trailhead.

Finley Cane Trail descends gradually to the starting point on Laurel Creek Road through a scenic hardwood forest with spring wildflowers, rhododendron tunnels, and a patch of cane. About 0.25 mile from the road, you pass a limestone sinkhole on the right that looks like a filled-in mine shaft. Just beyond the sinkhole, the trail forks. The right fork is a connector to Turkeypen Ridge Trail at its junction with Crib

Lead Cove and Finley Cane; Turkeypen Ridge and Finley Cane; Spence Field via Cades Cove

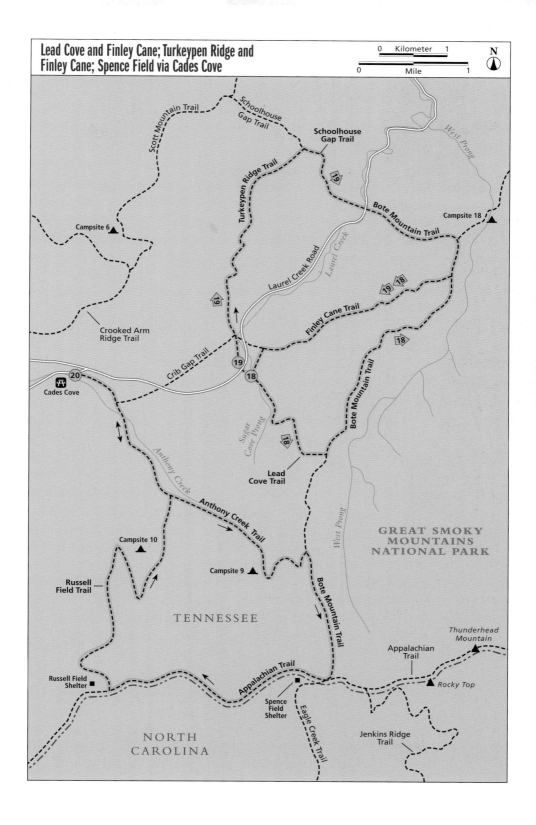

0 Kilometer 1

0 Mile 1

N

Scott Mountain Trail

Schoolhouse Gap Trail

Schoolhouse Gap Trail

West Prong

Turkeypen Ridge Trail

19

Bote Mountain Trail

Campsite 18

Campsite 6

Laurel Creek

19

Laurel Creek Road

Crooked Arm Ridge Trail

19 18

Finley Cane Trail

18

Crib Gap Trail

19

Bote Mountain Trail

18

20

Cades Cove

18

Sugar Cove Prong

Lead Cove Trail

Anthony Creek

Anthony Creek Trail

GREAT SMOKY MOUNTAINS NATIONAL PARK

West Prong

Campsite 10

Campsite 9

Russell Field Trail

TENNESSEE

Bote Mountain Trail

Thunderhead Mountain

Appalachian Trail

Russell Field Shelter

Appalachian Trail

Rocky Top

Spence Field Shelter

Eagle Creek Trail

NORTH CAROLINA

Jenkins Ridge Trail

Gap Trail, and it passes through a tunnel under Laurel Creek Road. The tunnel allows horses to cross the road safely. Taking the left fork, ascend slightly and cross Sugar Cove Prong before reaching the parking area.

Miles and Directions

0.0   Start on Lead Cove Trail on the south side of the road.

1.8   Junction with Bote Mountain Trail. Turn left (north) onto it.

4.3   Bote Mountain Trail forks to the right. Bear left (southwest) onto Finley Cane Trail.

7.1   Arrive back at trailhead.

Options: See Hike 19 for a description of two longer loop hikes involving the three trails hiked on this loop.

19 Turkeypen Ridge and Finley Cane

This hike and the route described in Hike 18 do not offer anything remarkable as far as Smokies scenery goes, but they are unique in that they are moderate-length loop hikes that are easily accessible. That's a relatively rare thing in the park, and consequently these hikes are very popular choices. The 1.1-mile section of this hike on Schoolhouse Gap Trail, from Dorsey Gap to Laurel Creek Road, is very popular, especially in the spring.

(See map for Hike 18: Lead Cove and Finley Cane.)

Start: Turkeypen Ridge trailhead on Laurel Creek Road
Distance: 9.0-mile loop
Hiking time: About 4 hours—day hike
Difficulty: Moderate
Trail surface: Forest trail and old forest roads
Other trail users: Equestrians
Maps: Wear Cove and Thunderhead Mountain USGS quads; Trails Illustrated #229 Great Smoky Mountains; Trails Illustrated #316

Cades Cove Elkmont
Special considerations: To complete the loop, you have to cross Laurel Creek Road twice. The road is often busy with vehicles (including monster motor homes) traveling to and from Cades Cove. Watch the kids.
Other: The combination of a popular trailhead and limited parking might mean you have to park alongside the road during busy weekends. Be careful as traffic on Laurel Creek Road can be terrible. Restrooms and a camp store are available at the Cades Cove Campground, a few miles farther southwest from the trailhead.

Finding the trailhead: From the junction of Little River Road and TN 73 (Townsend Y), head south on Laurel Creek Road toward Cades Cove. At 5.6 miles there is a narrow parking area on both sides of the road. The hike starts on Turkeypen Ridge Trail, on the north side of the road. GPS: N35 36.418' / W83 44.685'

The Hike

Begin hiking on Turkeypen Ridge Trail on the north side of the road. In spring you'll pass large patches of squawroot near the start of the hike. Squawroot is bear food in early spring, being one of the few edibles available for them at this time. After 0.2 mile Crib Gap Trail turns left and an unnamed path goes to the right. Continue straight ahead on Turkeypen Ridge Trail. Soon you cross Laurel Creek at a small rock overhang and begin a moderate ascent to a small gap. You might find the rusted remains of an old stove at the gap.

From the gap, the trail continues on an easy undulating course along the flanks of Turkeypen Ridge. You eventually cross over the ridge before descending to Schoolhouse Gap Trail at Dosey Gap. Turn right (east) on Schoolhouse Gap Trail and follow this old roadbed 1.1 miles to Laurel Creek Road. Along the way, you meet up with

Spence Branch and follow it downstream. In late summer look for cardinal flower, joe-pye weed, and ironweed growing along the creek.

At the road turn left and walk 100 yards along the path, then cross over the road to the trailhead for Bote Mountain Trail. Hike this trail 1.2 miles up an unnamed creek drainage to a saddle and junction with West Prong Trail, which comes in from the left (north). Go right (south), continuing on Bote Mountain Trail, and follow the dry ridge about 0.3 mile to the junction with Finley Cane Trail. The river you hear on the east side of the ridge is West Prong Little River. Finley Cane Trail, which you want to take, turns sharply right (west) and descends gradually through a scenic hardwood forest, spring wildflowers, rhododendron tunnels, and yes, a patch of cane, before reaching the starting point on Laurel Creek Road.

About 0.25 mile from the road, you pass a limestone sinkhole on the right that looks like a filled-in mine shaft. The trail forks just beyond the sinkhole. The right fork is a connector to Turkeypen Ridge Trail at its junction with Crib Gap Trail, and it passes through a tunnel under Laurel Creek Road. The tunnel allows horses to cross the road safely. Taking the left fork, ascend slightly and cross Sugar Cove Prong before reaching the parking area.

Miles and Directions

0.0   Start on the north side of the road on Turkeypen Ridge Trail.

0.2   Junction with Crib Gap Trail. Continue straight ahead on Turkeypen Ridge Trail.

3.6   Junction with Schoolhouse Gap Trail. Turn right (east) onto the old road.

4.7   Arrive at the parking area on Laurel Creek Road (GPS: N35 37.642' / W83 43.571'). Follow the road to the left for 100 yards, then cross the road and begin hiking on Bote Mountain Trail.

5.9   Junction with West Prong Trail. Stay to the right (south) on Bote Mountain Trail.

6.2   Junction with Finley Cane Trail. Turn sharply right (west) onto it.

9.0   Arrive back at trailhead.

Options: Since this loop crosses the road twice, you can hike in four different directions. None is any better than the others, so you might as well hike it in the direction described above.

You can leave out Finley Cane Trail from this hike and instead continue up Bote Mountain Trail and follow Lead Cove Trail back to the trailhead. This adds approximately 1.6 miles to the total distance. See Hike 18 for a description of a shorter loop using Lead Cove Trail, Bote Mountain Trail, and Finley Cane Trail.

20 Spence Field via Cades Cove

Anthony Creek cascading over mossy boulders, cove forests carpeted in spring wild-flowers, two Appalachian Trail shelters, big trees, great autumn foliage, and scenic Spence Field all conspire to make this a terrific hike during any time of year. It's a popular one too, with Spence Field being a favorite destination of backcountry hikers. Count on meeting lots of other hikers during the summer and on weekends any time of year.

(See map for Hike 18: Lead Cove and Finley Cane.)

Start: Anthony Creek trailhead in Cades Cove Picnic Area
Distance: 13.2-mile lollipop hike
Hiking time: About 7 hours—day hike, multiple options for camping
Difficulty: Strenuous
Trail surface: Boot-, horse-, and livestock-packed dirt, with lots of rocks and roots thrown in
Best seasons: Spring for the wildflowers, Oct for autumn foliage
Other trail users: Equestrians
Maps: Cades Cove and Thunderhead Mountain USGS quads; Trails Illustrated #229 Great Smoky Mountains; Trails Illustrated #316 Cades Cove Elkmont
Special considerations: Spence Field Shelter is among the most popular backcountry shelters in the park. Make reservations as early as possible if you plan to overnight there and be prepared with alternative dates. You might choose to stay at Russell Field Shelter instead. Campsite 9 is also very popular and requires a reservation. Both Russell Field Shelter and Campsite 10 also require a reservation, but they aren't quite as popular.
Other: Parking is very limited at the trailhead, but the parking lot at the start of Cades Cove Loop Road has plenty of spaces. Restrooms are at the picnic area. Basic supplies are available at the nearby campground store.

Finding the trailhead: The trail begins from Cades Cove Picnic Area, but there is no suitable hiker parking and the picnic area is gated at night. Park just outside the picnic area at the start of the one-way loop road for Cades Cove. To reach the parking area, drive 7.5 miles west on Laurel Creek Road from the Townsend Y (the junction of Little River Road and TN 73), and park in the large paved parking lot on the left, just after passing the road to the campground and just before you begin the loop road (GPS: N35 36.404' / W83 46.697'). To reach the trailhead, walk back to the road that leads to the campground. The picnic area entrance is directly across from it. Walk to the far end of the picnic area to a gated gravel road. A sign is here for Anthony Creek Trail. GPS: N35 36.296' / W83 46.199'

The mileages given are from the trailhead. The distance from the parking area to the trailhead is about 0.2 mile.

Foot log over Anthony Creek.

The Hike

The trail starts on an old roadbed and soon passes Crib Gap Trail, which is on the left. Remaining on the road, you pass through a horse camp, and a little later you cross Anthony Creek on a wide bridge. Soon you cross Anthony Creek again—this time on a foot log—and the grade increases. Make one more crossing of Anthony Creek on a wide footbridge, then cross Left Prong Anthony Creek on a foot log just before the junction with Russell Field Trail. You'll come down this trail later in the hike; now, you want to go to the left (east) and remain on Anthony Creek Trail. The forest through here is lovely, with big yellow poplars (tulip trees) and a lush understory of rhododendron. The eastern hemlocks are dead or dying, but the forest retains a scenic appearance.

Cross Anthony Creek a final time at an especially picturesque section of the forest and creek. Beyond the foot log, the trail ascends through an open cove forest carpeted with spring wildflowers, and it steepens on the approach to Campsite 9. Among the loveliest backcountry campsites in the park, site 9 sits beside the cascading Anthony Creek in an open forest. In spring wildflowers are everywhere and they make it very difficult to walk around without trampling them. In autumn the forest is ablaze with color. Shortly beyond the campsite the trail makes a sharp switchback to the left and leaves Anthony Creek behind. Continue climbing steeply and reach Bote Mountain Trail on the ridgeline.

Autumn along Anthony Creek Trail.

Turn right (south) onto Bote Mountain Trail. The first 0.3 mile or so is along an old roadbed ending at a turnaround. Much of the next couple of miles follows the ridge crest. In places the trail is very deeply rutted, with no good alternative other than plowing right through the trench—a miserable experience during a heavy rain. In pre-park days herders drove livestock to the high grassy balds to graze during the summer, with Bote Mountain Trail one of the routes they traveled. The countless grinding hooves helped create these deep gullies. Hiking boots and horse hooves continue the tradition.

Bote Mountain Trail becomes very rocky on its approach to the Appalachian Trail (AT) at Spence Field. About 0.25 mile from the AT, you enter a scenic birch forest, carpeted in spring with spring beauty. A huge yellow birch stands on the right side of the trail, and just beyond it the trail makes a switchback to the left before its final approach to Spence Field.

On reaching the AT, you can go left (east) and in a little over 2,000 miles arrive at Mount Katahdin, Maine. To continue the hike described here, you want to turn right (west), but you might want to take a short side trip to the left and hike up to the grassy knoll. Off to the right (south) on this knoll is a fine view into the Eagle Creek watershed. Despite all the reports about the "spectacular" views from Spence Field, this is probably the only good distant view you'll find up here. Make no mistake, Spence Field itself is spectacular—a somewhat open grassy bald with azaleas, mountain laurel, rhododendron, mountain ash, and numerous serviceberry trees growing with low, spreading branches. Historically, the views from the bald were open, but encroaching vegetation has closed them off. So, while the views *of* the bald are wonderful, the views *from* the bald are lacking.

After taking in the view from the knoll, head back west on the AT, and in a few hundred feet from the Bote Mountain Trail junction, come to the junction with Eagle Creek Trail on the left. A 0.2-mile walk down this trail takes you to Spence Field Shelter, a good choice for your home tonight if doing this trip as an overnighter. If staying at the shelter, you'll find water at a spring several hundred feet farther down on Eagle Creek Trail.

If continuing on the hike, keep heading west on the AT. The 2.6-mile stretch from Spence Field to the Russell Field Shelter is easy compared with the hike up to Spence Field and easy compared to most other sections of the AT in the Smokies. There are a few slight humps, but mostly it's a pleasant downhill grade. Russell Field Shelter sits at the junction with the AT and Russell Field Trail. The setting is attractive, and the rustic shelter, like most in the park, is charming.

Russell Field Trail leads directly in front of the shelter, heading north. On it, you quickly pass a spring (the shelter's water source), and at about 0.5 mile from the shelter, you pass through obvious remaining vestiges of Russell Field. This open grassy area is scenic, but the bald is now mostly overgrown and the views obscured. In pre-park days these open grassy fields extended back to the ridge at the shelter. Local farmers grazed their cattle here during the warm season, just as they did at Spence Field.

Autumn forest along Russell Field Trail. ▶

The next couple of miles from Russell Field are rather uneventful, first with some dry ridge walking along Ledbetter Ridge and then a steep descent down the flanks of the ridge toward Left Prong Anthony Creek. You'll first come to the right fork of Left Prong and follow it downstream through what once was a majestic old-growth forest. The next mile or so used to harbor one of the more remarkable hemlock forests in the park, with many huge trees. Now the hemlocks are nothing but skeletons and may be downfall by the time you see them. Some impressive trees of other species do grow here, and there are a few pockets of forest that haven't been affected visually by the death of the hemlocks, but hiking through here is a sad experience for anyone who loves old-growth forests and big trees. A patch of these big hemlocks used to shelter Campsite 10, which sits right beside the trail among a tangle of rhododendron. With the hemlocks dead and sunlight entering the forest floor, the site is now becoming a tangle of briars. (See the sidebar for Hike 36 for information about the hemlock deaths.)

A short distance beyond Campsite 10, you have to cross the right fork of Left Prong Anthony Creek. In normal flows this should be a fairly easy rock-hop, but after a heavy rain it could be a little tricky. About 0.1 mile farther down is a crossing over Left Prong Anthony Creek, this time on a foot log. Arrive back at the junction with Anthony Creek Trail at 0.9 mile from Campsite 10. Turn left (west) and follow the trail back the way you came.

Miles and Directions

0.0   Start from the Anthony Creek trailhead in Cades Cove Picnic Area.

0.2   Junction with Crib Gap Trail on the left. Continue straight ahead on the main path.

1.7   Junction with Russell Trail, coming in from the right (south). Go to the left (east) to remain on Anthony Creek Trail.

2.9   Pass by Campsite 9.

3.6   Junction with Bote Mountain Trail. Turn right (south) onto it.

5.3   Junction with the AT at Spence Field. Turn right (west) onto it.

5.4   Junction with Eagle Creek Trail coming in from the left. Spence Field Shelter is 0.2 mile down this trail. Continue straight (west) to remain on the AT and complete the hike.

8.0   Junction with Russell Field Trail at Russell Field Shelter. Turn right (north) on Russell Field Trail, walking directly in front of the shelter.

10.6 Pass by Campsite 10.

11.5 Return to junction with Anthony Creek Trail. Turn left (west) to finish the hike.

13.2 Arrive back at trailhead.

Options: With two shelters on the AT and a campsite on the way up and down, you could do this hike as one-nighter or a lazy two- to four-nighter. Most people opt for either a long day hike or an overnighter using Spence Field Shelter as the camp. A good number of people hike to Spence Field and return by the same route, but this shaves only 2.4 miles off the loop described here.

BALD IS BEAUTIFUL

Spence Field and Russell Field are, or were, grassy balds, two of a dozen or so in the Smokies and several dozen scattered across the southern Appalachians. Scientists don't know how the balds got here or even whether they are manmade or natural, although there seems to be a consensus that many of them were here before the arrival of Europeans.

The mountain oat grass on Smokies' balds served as prime grazing land. Farmers herded livestock to the meadows in spring and left them to graze through the summer. Bote Mountain Trail follows one route the herders used for getting their livestock to Spence Field. After the park was established in the 1930s, the balds were left to nature and woody vegetation slowly crept in. Some, like Russell Field, are now covered in trees and shrubs. Spence Field still has a few open areas and retains a semblance of what it once was, although trees now block most of the distant views. In the 1980s the park began clearing the encroaching vegetation on Gregory Bald and Andrews Bald, a task that continues today in an effort to maintain the balds to something resembling their pre-park status. And the scientists continue to search for answers for how the balds got here in the first place.

21 Rich Mountain Loop

A great attribute of this hike is that you get to experience some of the beauty of Cades Cove without having to encounter the crowds that always seem to occur on the 11.0-mile loop road through the cove. Except for a short stretch at John Oliver Cabin, you'll have this hike pretty much to yourself.

Start: Rich Mountain Loop trailhead
Distance: 8.6-mile lollipop
Hiking time: About 4 hours—day hike or overnighter
Difficulty: Moderate
Trail surface: Forest trail
Other trail users: Equestrians
Maps: Cades Cove and Kinzel Springs USGS
quads; Trails Illustrated #229 Great Smoky Mountains; Trails Illustrated #316 Cades Cove Elkmont
Other: The parking lot is huge, so you should have no problem finding a spot. Restroom facilities and basic supplies are available at the nearby campground store.

Finding the trailhead: Park in the large parking area at the entrance gate to Cades Cove. Reach the cove by driving 7.5 miles west on Laurel Creek Road from the Townsend Y (the junction of Little River Road and TN 73). The trail begins opposite the parking lot, just beyond the gate. GPS: N35 36.404' / W83 46.697'

The Hike

Begin by walking the Cades Cove Loop Road. Just beyond the gate, Rich Mountain Loop Trail enters the woods on the right (north) side. The 1.4-mile stretch to John Oliver Cabin is an easy undulating course along the edge of cleared fields and in open forests with many standing dead trees. This is a great place to look for pileated and other woodpeckers. Even if you don't see a pileated, there's a good chance you'll hear its junglelike call. About 0.5 mile into the hike, you pass Crooked Arm Ridge Trail. This is where you come out after completing the loop.

After exploring the 1820s homestead, leave the Cades Cove crowds behind and continue the trail to the north, behind the cabin. The trail soon meets up with Marthas Branch and starts climbing in earnest. Pass an old crumbled chimney on the right and cross over the branch several times before leaving the drainage to climb the flank of Cave Ridge. At mile 3.0 on the crest of the ridge, there is a great narrow-field view of Cades Cove. Below you is Sparks Lane, and far in the distance on the crest line are Spence Field, Russell Field, and Mollies Ridge.

From the overlook, it is 0.3 mile to the junction with Indian Grave Gap Trail. Turn right here and continue ascending the ridge for another 0.8 mile to the junction with Rich Mountain Trail in a small scenic saddle. Campsite 5 is located a few hundred feet down Rich Mountain Trail. At one time the Rich Mountain Shelter stood here, but all that remains now is the foundation. Water is available from a spring several hundred feet down the drainage.

Continuing along the ridge on Indian Grave Gap Trail, you come to a side trail on the left about 0.3 mile from the Rich Mountain Trail junction. You're on Cerulean Knob, the highest point on Rich Mountain. The side path leads 100 steep yards to the summit and the foundation remains of the old Rich Mountain Fire Tower. Views are not good—you might catch a few winter glimpses into Dry Valley to the north. Back on the main trail, continue heading east. After a short distance you get a great winter view into Dry Valley, much better than the one from Cerulean Knob.

Continue along Indian Grave Gap Trail until you come to a power-line clearing that is right before the junction with Scott Mountain Trail, which goes left, and Crooked Arm Ridge Trail. Crooked Arm Ridge Trail is a continuation of Indian Grave Gap Trail. A couple hundred yards down Scott Mountain Trail is Campsite 6 and a small spring. If doing this hike as an overnighter, you have the option of staying here or back at Campsite 5.

From the trail junction, continue straight ahead on Crooked Arm Ridge Trail. The trail descends steeply to Rich Mountain Loop Trail. Deep ruts and horse pies make this stretch an unpleasant hiking experience. However, several good leafy views into the cove make it bearable. About 0.25 mile before you reach Rich Mountain Loop Trail, you cross Crooked Arm Branch. Shortly below the crossing is a small cascade that is very scenic during a heavy rain. Most times, it's just a trickle.

Once back at Rich Mountain Trail, turn left and retrace your steps to the trailhead.

Miles and Directions

0.0 Start on Rich Mountain Loop Trail, which begins on the right (north) side of Cades Cove Loop Road, just beyond the entrance gate.

0.5 Crooked Arm Ridge Trail goes to the right. Continue on Rich Mountain Loop Trail.

1.4 Arrive at John Oliver Cabin. The trail continues behind the cabin, to the north.

3.3 Junction with Indian Grave Gap Trail. Turn right onto the trail and continue ascending the ridge.

4.1 Junction, left, with Rich Mountain Trail at Campsite 5. Continue on Indian Grave Gap Trail to the east.

5.9 Junction with Scott Mountain Trail, which goes to the left, and Crooked Arm Ridge Trail, which is a continuation of Indian Grave Gap Trail. You want to take Crooked Arm Ridge Trail.

8.1 Return to the junction with Rich Mountain Loop Trail. Turn left and retrace your steps back to the trailhead.

8.6 Arrive back at trailhead.

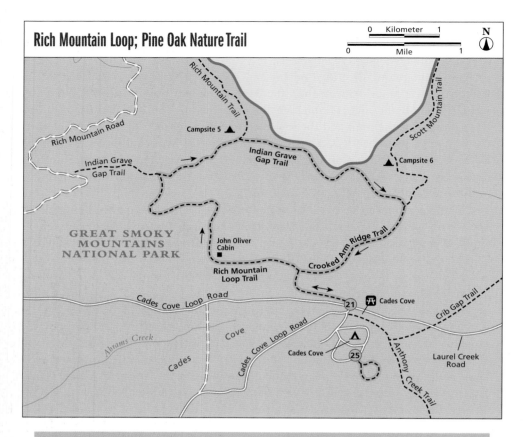

SMOKY BEARS

Great Smoky Mountains National Park is home to an estimated 1,500 black bears. A bear sighting is possible anywhere in the park, but Cades Cove offers perhaps the best possibility, especially in late summer and early autumn when the blackberries and wild cherries ripen. Make the sighting safe by reading Be Bear Aware in the introduction.

22 Abrams Falls

Abrams Falls is only about 20 feet high, but it has the greatest water volume of any major waterfall in the park, and also the largest plunge pool. The hike follows closely beside Abrams Creek nearly the entire way, adding to the scenic appeal. The trailhead is located about halfway around the 11.0-mile one-way loop road in Cades Cove. Cades Cove receives more visitors (more than two million annually) than all but ten of our national parks. You can expect lots of traffic on the drive to the trailhead as well as on the hike to the falls.

Start: Abrams Falls trailhead in Cades Cove
Distance: 5.0 miles out and back
Hiking time: About 3 hours—day hike
Difficulty: Moderate
Trail surface: Rocks and boot-packed dirt
Best season: Winter, to avoid the crowds
Other trail users: Hikers only
Maps: Cades Cove and Calderwood USGS quads; Trails Illustrated #229 Great Smoky Mountains; Trails Illustrated #316 Cades Cove Elkmont
Special considerations: To reach the trailhead, you have to drive the one-way loop road

around Cades Cove. The road is normally closed to motor vehicle traffic on Wed and Sat mornings until 10 a.m. from early May through Sept.
Other: Even when the large gravel parking area fills up, as it often does, there is plenty of parking in the fields along the gravel road. Of course, if the parking area is so full that you have to park in a field, you might want to reconsider this hike and choose a trail that offers more solitude. Pit toilets are available at the trailhead.

Finding the trailhead: Reach Cades Cove by driving 7.5 miles west on Laurel Creek Road from the Townsend Y (the junction of Little River Road and TN 73). From the start of the Cades Cove Loop Road, drive 4.9 miles and turn right onto the gravel side road. Continue 0.4 mile along this road to a large parking area. The trailhead for Abrams Falls is on the north end of the lot. GPS: N35 35.474' / W83 51.137'

The Hike

Several paths lead off in all directions after you enter the woods from the parking area, but it's obvious which route to take to the falls. And if you're unsure, just follow everyone else. Just before the information kiosk, the appropriately named Wet Bottom Trail goes to the right, serving primarily as an equestrian route. At the kiosk Rabbit Creek Trail goes to the left and in a few yards fords Mill Creek. You want to take Abrams Falls Trail and cross over Abrams Creek on the wide footbridge, and once across, turn left and follow the trail downstream. (The trail to the right leads 0.5 mile to Elijah Oliver Place.)

You'll follow Abrams Creek downstream all the way to the falls. Sometimes you'll be right beside it on a level course; other times you'll be high above and out of sight of the creek. Three times you'll climb up and around a ridge, then descend the other side and cross a side stream. The first stream you cross is Arbutus Branch, the second is Stony Branch, and the third is Wilson Branch, just before the falls.

As you hike around Arbutus Ridge, the second rise you climb, notice that the forest changes dramatically, a result of an EF4 tornado that struck the western end of the park in April 2011. Arbutus Ridge is named for trailing arbutus, an early-blooming wildflower that grows along the dry sections of the trail. Another early bloomer that you might spot is fringed polygala, or gay wings, a beautiful pink wildflower that is uncommon in the Smokies. A good place to look for it is on the upslope banks after you cross Stony Branch.

▶ Abrams Creek, Abrams Falls, Abrams Gap, and Abrams Ridge are named for Cherokee Chief Abraham, of the nearby village of Chilhowee, now under the waters of Chilhowee Lake. It is one of few Indian place names enduring in the park.

After the third ridge the trail swings sharply into the Wilson Branch drainage and crosses the creek on a foot log. A few yards farther, Abrams Falls Trail swings to the right and continues following the creek downstream. You want to turn left here, and cross Wilson Branch again on a foot log. Abrams Falls is a short walk ahead.

Abrams Creek channels into the far side of a rock ledge extending across the river to create Abrams Falls. You can walk below the ledge right to the edge of the falls, but don't climb on the mossy rocks, as they are very slippery. On a hot summer day, it's hard to resist a dip in the pool, but this is not recommended because of the strong currents. Several people have drowned here.

Miles and Directions

0.0 Start from the north end of the parking lot. Follow the path behind the information kiosk and cross Abrams Creek on the wide footbridge. Turn left after crossing and follow the trail downstream.

2.4 Cross Wilson Branch on a foot log. Continue a few yards and turn left to cross the branch again on another foot log.

2.5 Arrive at Abrams Falls. Return the way you came.

5.0 Arrive back at trailhead.

Options: See Hike 26 for a route to Abrams Falls that does not require driving the Cades Cove Loop Road.

Abrams Falls; Cooper Road and Rabbit Creek; Pine Mountain and Abrams Falls; Abrams Creek and Cooper Road

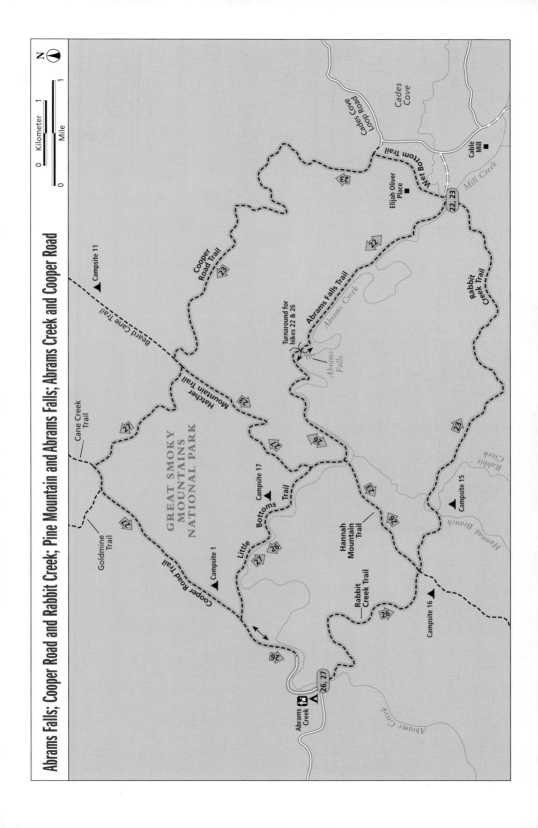

23 Cooper Road and Rabbit Creek

Although this hike begins from the most popular location in the park—Cades Cove—you'll have most of the trip to yourself. The extreme western end of the park sees far fewer hikers than other areas, but the rewards are just as good. There really isn't a preferred time of year to make this hike, but late May to early June is a good time. It's warm enough to make the creek wades bearable and the forest is ablaze in mountain laurel blooms. Winter has a special charm, but Abrams Creek can be impassable then.

(See map for Hike 22: Abrams Falls.)

Start: Abrams Falls trailhead in Cades Cove
Distance: 16.3-mile loop
Hiking time: About 9 hours—day hike, multiple options for camping
Difficulty: Moderate, with 3 difficult creek crossings
Trail surface: Old forest road and forest trails
Other trail users: Equestrians
Maps: Cades Cove, Kinzel Springs, Blockhouse, and Calderwood USGS quads; Trails Illustrated #229 Great Smoky Mountains; Trails Illustrated #316 Cades Cove Elkmont
Special considerations: To reach the trailhead, you have to drive the one-way loop road around Cades Cove. The road is normally closed to motor vehicle traffic on Wed and Sat mornings until 10 a.m. from early May through Sept.

There are 3 significant creek crossings on this hike. The first one, over Abrams Creek, is a definite wade and may be too dangerous to attempt in high water. The next one, over Rabbit Creek, could be a wade in very high water, and the last one, over Mill Creek, is a sure wade except in very low flows.

The small spring at Campsite 16 may dry up during prolonged dry spells.
Other: Even when the large gravel parking lot fills up, as it often does, there is plenty of parking in the fields along the gravel road. Pit toilets are available at the trailhead.

Finding the trailhead: Reach Cades Cove by driving 7.5 miles west on Laurel Creek Road from the Townsend Y (the junction of Little River Road and TN 73). From the start of the Cades Cove Loop Road, drive 4.9 miles and turn right onto the gravel side road. Continue 0.4 mile along this road to a large parking area. The trailhead is on the north end of the lot. GPS: N35 35.474' / W83 51.137'

The Hike

Start on Abrams Falls Trail like everyone else, but once you cross Abrams Creek on the footbridge, turn right at the sign for Elijah Oliver Place. An easy walk takes you to the cabin in 0.5 mile. This route bypasses the first section of Wet Bottom Trail, an appropriately named connector from the parking area to Cooper Road Trail that's used primarily for horses. After exploring the Elijah Oliver Cabin and outbuildings, continue on the dirt road leading from the cabin. Pass by a large barn on the left and then cross a small creek. Just past the creek crossing, take Wet Bottom Trail to the left and go 0.25 mile to Cooper Road Trail.

◀   *Early morning at Abrams Falls.*

A rainy day along Cooper Road Trail.

A right turn on Cooper Road Trail leads back to Cades Cove Loop Road in 0.2 mile. Your hike turns left (northwest) and follows the old road for 5.5 miles. It's typical Smokies hiking along this stretch, up over humps and ridges, down to cross small creeks and dry drainages. The road makes for good walking, with mostly moderate grades, though a few are a little steep. In summer look for cardinal flowers growing near the streams and yellow-fringed orchids along the side of the road.

At a small gap Hatcher Mountain Trail goes left, Beard Cane Trail goes right, and Cooper Road Trail continues straight ahead. If doing this hike as a two-night backpack, turn right (east) and Hike 1.0 mile on Beard Cane Trail to Campsite 11, a small, rarely used site. The next morning backtrack to this junction. If continuing on the hike, go left (west) on the Hatcher Mountain Trail. An EF4 tornado swept across the western end of the park in April 2011, causing extensive damage to many of the trails in the area. You'll see the effects from this tornado along several portions of the hike but in particular along Hatcher Mountain Trail.

After an easy climb from the gap, Hatcher Mountain Trail descends to cross two streams and ascends again to a ridgeline. From here, it's a long, easy ridgeline walk and descent to Abrams Creek. At 0.1 mile from the creek, Little Bottoms Trail comes in sharply from the right; continue straight to reach the creek.

The ford at Abrams Creek marks the junction of three trails: Hatcher Mountain Trail, which brought you here; Hannah Mountain Trail, which you now take; and Abrams Falls Trail, which leads 1.7 miles upstream to Abrams Falls. Abrams Falls is a highly recommended side trip, but on this hike you probably won't have time unless you're doing a two-night backpack.

Now you must wade across Abrams Creek. In summer slip off your boots and enjoy the invigorating water. In winter, or after prolonged rains, be very careful. The creek (actually a small river) can become a raging torrent during these times and crossing it might be extremely dangerous, or even impossible. Don't hesitate to turn back if you feel uncomfortable. If you do turn back, you can salvage the trip by taking Abrams Creek Trail back to the trailhead so that you don't have to backtrack.

After the crossing Hannah Mountain Trail climbs steeply for a short distance and then becomes a gentle ascent to a broad ridge. From the ridge to Scott Gap is easy walking along the contour line. At Scott Gap, Hannah Mountain Trail crosses Rabbit Creek Trail and continues 7.6 miles to Parson Branch Road. Rabbit Creek Trail goes to the right, heading to Abrams Creek Ranger Station; that leg and the section of Hannah Mountain Trail you just hiked are part of Hike 26. If doing an overnighter or two-night backpack, your home tonight is Campsite 16, a few hundred yards down the other side of the gap.

> ▶ Both Cooper Road Trail and Rabbit Creek Trail follow old access roads into Cades Cove. The Rabbit Creek route was never used extensively, but Cooper Road, built in the 1830s, served as the major commercial access into the cove. When you hike Cooper Road Trail, you are not viewing the cultural history of the Smokies— you are *walking* on it.

After admiring the large trees, including one huge yellow poplar, at the gap, turn left (east) on Rabbit Creek Trail and pass through a scenic forest with more large trees. About 0.75 mile from Scott Gap, steep banks squeeze the trail and you find yourself hiking in a small streambed through a narrow passage. Shortly beyond, you reach the crossing of Rabbit Creek, which is easily rock-hopped in low flows but a possible wade in higher water. Don't worry: Since you already made it across Abrams Creek to get to this point, you won't have a problem here. Beyond the crossing is Campsite 15, on the right. You could camp here on the second night of a two-night backpack instead of Campsite 16.

Now comes the hardest part of the hike, a mile-long, nearly continuous uphill grind along a spur to Andy McCully Ridge. Once on the ridge you have a few ups and downs typical of ridge hiking, and you might start to think this trail can't possibly go uphill anymore. The forest is an open mixture of pine and hardwoods, typical of the western end of the park.

Coon Butt marks the last of the climbing, except for a few slight swells. From here, the trail descends to cross More Licker Branch and then climbs over a small ridge before joining Victory Branch and following it downstream to Mill Creek. In the summer and fall dry season, you might be able to cross Mill Creek in high-top boots without getting your feet wet, but don't count on it. Usually this is a wet wade, but it's an easy one. Don't worry about cold feet: The trailhead and the heater in your car are just a few yards on the other side of the crossing.

Miles and Directions

0.0 Start from the north end of the parking lot. Follow the path behind the information kiosk and cross Abrams Creek on the wide footbridge. Turn right after crossing and follow the trail heading upstream.

0.5 Arrive at Elijah Oliver Place. Continue on the dirt road in front of the cabin.

0.8 Turn left on Wet Bottoms Trail just after crossing a small stream.

1.0 Junction with Cooper Road Trail. A right turn leads to the Cades Cove Loop Road. You want to turn left (northwest).

6.5 Junction with Hatcher Mountain Trail and Beard Cane Trail. Turn left (west) onto Hatcher Mountain Trail.

9.2 Junction with Little Bottoms Trail, coming in sharply from the right. Continue straight on Hatcher Mountain Trail.

9.3 Junction with Abrams Falls Trail and Hannah Mountain Trail at Abrams Creek ford. Wade Abrams Creek to begin hiking on Hannah Mountain Trail.

11.2 Turn left (east) onto Rabbit Creek Trail at Scott Gap. Campsite 16 is nearby.

12.2 Campsite 15.

16.3 Arrive back at trailhead, just after wading Mill Creek.

Options: The Abrams Creek area presents several possibilities for day-hike loops, as well as short or extended backpacking trips. The six backcountry campsites in the area provide many overnight options; study a trail map for possibilities. All the possible routes will combine trails described in Hikes 22, 23, 26, and 27.

24 Gregory Bald via Cades Cove

For every time of the year, there is a preferred hike in the Smokies. In the second half of June, this hike is the one. Excepting Roan Mountain (north of the park on the North Carolina–Tennessee border), there may be no finer destination in the entire southeastern United States than Gregory Bald during mid- to late June. Hundreds of azaleas grow on the bald, blooming in every imaginable color. You'll see whites, reds, yellows, oranges, and every shade in between—even stark fuchsias that look almost electrified, like wet finger paint.

Start: Gregory Ridge trailhead near Cades Cove

Distance: 11.4 miles out and back

Hiking time: About 6 hours—day hike or overnighter

Difficulty: Strenuous, due to steep grades

Trail surface: Forest trails and open grassy bald

Best season: Second half of June

Other trail users: Equestrians permitted on Gregory Bald; Gregory Ridge Trail is for hikers only

Maps: Cades Cove USGS quad; Trails Illus-trated #229 Great Smoky Mountains; Trails Illustrated #316 Cades Cove Elkmont

Special considerations: To reach the trailhead, you have to drive the one-way loop road around Cades Cove. The road is normally closed to motor vehicle traffic on Wed and Sat mornings until 10:00 a.m. from early May through Sept.

Other: Unless you get here early in the morn-ing, expect to find the traffic circle full and cars lined up along the road. Restroom facilities are located at the Cades Cove Visitor Center and Cable Mill area.

Finding the trailhead: Reach Cades Cove by driving 7.5 miles west on Laurel Creek Road from the Townsend Y (the junction of Little River Road and TN 73). From the start of the one-way Cades Cove Loop Road, drive 5.4 miles and turn right on Forge Creek Road, just past the large parking area for Cades Cove Visitor Center and Cable Mill. Follow the gravel road 2.2 miles to its end at a small traffic circle. Gregory Ridge Trail starts from the circle and is obvious. GPS: N35 33.750' / W83 50.750'

The Hike

Begin on Gregory Ridge Trail and climb over a short hump before leveling off to a crossing of Forge Creek on a foot log. Beyond the crossing, the trail soon passes through an old-growth forest entangled with rhododendron. The creek is nearby on the left, but you can only catch glimpses through the thick understory. Cross the creek again on a foot log and swing away from it a few hundred yards before making a third and final crossing. Just beyond this crossing, the trail passes through Campsite 12. The site doesn't offer a lot of privacy, although one tent site does sit off the trail a bit.

Continue past the campsite and begin climbing more steeply as you ascend the ridge on switchbacks. Notice the change in vegetation on the drier ridge. Below, the

Aerial view of Gregory Bald.

dominant understory was rhododendron. Here, on the drier ridge, you'll see mountain laurel, with a ground cover of galax and trailing arbutus. Pines are here too, as well as blueberries. Farther up, the vegetation changes again, and if hiking in April, you'll see spring wildflowers. There are a few good views, especially in winter with the leaves gone. From Campsite 12, it's uphill all the way until about 0.2 mile from Rich Gap, where the trail levels off.

At the gap you come to a four-way intersection. To the left, Gregory Bald Trail goes 2.1 miles to the Appalachian Trail on Doe Knob. Straight ahead is the path leading to Moore Spring, site of a former herder's cabin and, more recently, a backcountry shelter.

To reach Gregory Bald, turn right (west) on Gregory Bald Trail and follow the ridgeline, ascending first around a knoll, then leveling out before the final steep push to Gregory Bald.

If you can't make this hike when the azaleas bloom, that's OK. The views alone are more than worth the climb. Cades Cove sprawls out to the northeast; to the southwest lies Joyce Kilmer–Slickrock Wilderness in the Unicoi Mountains; due south is Fontana Lake, and between the lake and you stands Shuckstack Tower. Trees obscure the view to the west.

The hike as described here ends on the bald, but if you're doing this trip as an overnighter, continue on Gregory Bald Trail and descend 0.4 mile to Campsite 13, one of the finest in the Smokies. A large, grassy, and somewhat open clearing in a level swag provides several tent sites offering relative privacy. The site is rationed and usually full on weekends and on weekdays in June. If spending the night here, set your alarm

◄ *Cades Cove is hidden under a shroud of fog in this view from Gregory Bald.*

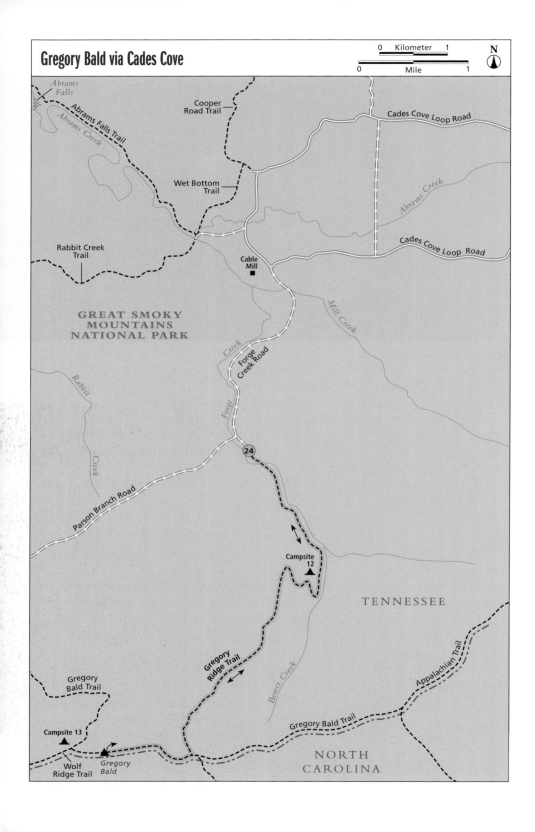

Gregory Bald via Cades Cove

0   Kilometer   1

0   Mile   1

N

Abrams
Falls

Cooper
Road Trail

Cades Cove Loop Road

Abrams Falls Trail

Abrams Creek

Wet Bottom
Trail

Abrams Creek

Rabbit Creek
Trail

Cades Cove Loop Road

Cable
Mill

GREAT SMOKY
MOUNTAINS
NATIONAL PARK

Mill Creek

Creek

Forge
Creek Road

Rabbit

Forge

Creek

24

Parson Branch Road

Campsite
12

TENNESSEE

Appalachian Trail

Gregory
Ridge Trail

Bower Creek

Gregory
Bald Trail

Gregory Bald Trail

Campsite 13

Wolf
Ridge Trail

Gregory
Bald

NORTH
CAROLINA

clock and hike back up on the bald for the sunrise. You'll have the bald and the show to yourself at this hour. In June there is also a good chance at spotting a whitetail deer fawn on the bald. You'll almost certainly see a few adults in early morning and evening.

Miles and Directions

0.0 Start on Gregory Ridge Trail from the upper south side of the traffic turnaround.

2.0 Campsite 12.

5.0 Arrive at Rich Gap. Turn right (west) onto Gregory Bald Trail.

5.7 Arrive at Gregory Bald. Explore the open bald and return the way you came.

11.4 Arrive back at trailhead.

Options: If you don't want to backtrack, you can take Gregory Bald Trail to the trailhead on Parson Branch Road and then walk along the road back to Forge Creek Road. The Gregory Bald section is 4.5 miles and the Parson Branch Road section about 5 miles. From Parson Branch Road to the traffic circle is only 0.1 mile. This makes for a loop hike of about 15.3 miles, which is doable as a long day hike. Or you could camp at Campsite 13 and finish the loop the next day. You can drive to the trailhead on Parson Branch Road, but the road is one-way from the cove and makes shuttling a hassle. Getting back to the cove requires a 2-hour drive from the Gregory Bald trailhead.

The azaleas are in full bloom on Gregory Bald.

25 Pine Oak Nature Trail

Cades Cove Nature Trail, which was located along Cades Cove Loop Road, is no longer an official park trail. In its place is Pine Oak Nature Trail, which is located near Cades Cove Campground. Although any hike is a good hike, the old nature trail wouldn't make anyone's short list for favorite hikes, so it's not a big loss. Pine Oak Nature Trail offers a better hiking experience and makes a great outing for those staying at the campground.

(See map for Hike 21: Rich Mountain Loop.)

Start: Cades Cove Campground
Distance: 0.8-mile loop
Hiking time: About 35 minutes
Difficulty: Moderate
Trail surface: Forest trail
Other trail users: Hikers only

Maps: Cades Cove USGS quad; Trails Illustrated #229 Great Smoky Mountains; Trails Illustrated #316 Cades Cove Elkmont
Other: The parking lot is large, but it can fill up on weekends and any day during summer and fall. Restrooms and a camp store are available here. The store closes in winter.

Finding the trailhead: The actual trailhead is located directly opposite site C16 in Cades Cove Campground, but if you are not a camper, you have to park in the parking lot across from Cades Cove Ranger Station. To reach it, drive 7.5 miles west on Laurel Creek Road from the Townsend Y (the junction of Little River Road and TN 73). Turn left at the sign for Cades Cove Campground and drive the short distance to the ranger station on the right and the large parking area across the street on the left. The amphitheater and camp store are beside the parking area. GPS: N35 36.178' / W83 46.587'

The Hike

Begin by walking through the campground to site C16, which is located along the east side of the perimeter road. It is less than 0.2 mile from the ranger station to the trailhead. The sign at the start says this is a 0.5-mile hike, but it is longer than that. About 100 feet from the start, you come to the loop portion, at which point you can go either way.

If hiking the loop in a clockwise direction, you pass through a pine forest, the lower portion of which is totally devoid of downfall—campers have snatched every stick for their campfires. The trail climbs steeply to cross over a dry ridge with chestnut oak, white pine, red maple, and mountain laurel. Before cresting the ridge, there is an open, narrow view toward Cades Cove, with Rich Mountain looming in the distance.

After leaving the ridge you descend steeply through a narrow ravine to the Cooper Branch drainage. The remainder of the hike is a pleasant stroll through a forest of oak, hickory, white pine, and rosebay rhododendron, crossing small branches on mossy foot logs.

Miles and Directions

0.0 After walking through the campground to site C16, begin the hike across the road at the trail sign. Walk 100 feet to a T junction. The loop begins here. To follow the hike description, turn left and follow the trail clockwise.

0.8 Arrive back at trailhead.

The Pine Oak Nature Trail provides the ideal habitat for many species of wildflowers, including the pink lady's slipper orchid.

26 Pine Mountain and Abrams Falls

The pine-oak woods in the western end of the park receive little visitation compared with the park's other regions. You'll have most of this hike to yourself, but expect lots of company at Abrams Falls.

(See map for Hike 22: Abrams Falls.)

Start: Parking area near Abrams Creek Ranger Station

Distance: 11.7-mile reverse lollipop

Hiking time: About 6 hours—day hike, over-nighter, or 2-nighter

Difficulty: Moderate, with a potentially difficult and dangerous creek wade

Trail surface: Old forest roads, gravel roads, and forest trails

Best season: Late May through early June is a great time to hike because of the mountain laurel bloom and because it is safer to wade Abrams Creek in warm weather.

Other trail users: Equestrians permitted on about half of the hike

Maps: Calderwood USGS quad; Trails Illustrated #229 Great Smoky Mountains; Trails Illustrated #316 Cades Cove Elkmont

Special considerations: An unbridged crossing over Abrams Creek cannot be rock-hopped, and in high water it might be too dangerous to wade. Little Bottoms Trail is not graded and is unsuitable for sandals or other shoes without ankle support. The small spring at Campsite 16 may dry up during prolonged dry spells.

Other: The parking area is in a large field, so all of the possible parking places rarely fill up. However, on summer weekends you might not get an easy spot to pull into. The campground has restroom facilities, but to use them you'd have to walk about 0.3 mile in the opposite direction from the trailhead.

Finding the trailhead: The trailhead parking area is in a field near Abrams Creek Ranger Station at the western end of the park. From the junction of Foothills Parkway and US 129 (approximately 22 miles south of Maryville, Tennessee, and 25 miles north of Fontana, North Carolina), go less than 0.1 mile south on US 129 and turn left on Happy Valley Road. Drive 5.7 miles on this road through Happy Valley and turn right at the sign for the campground and ranger station. Pass the ranger station at 0.6 mile; the parking area, located on both sides of the road, is a short distance farther. GPS: N35 36.557' / W83 56.110'

The Hike

From the parking area, walk back up the road and turn left onto Rabbit Creek Trail, located just beyond the ranger station. The trail leads a short distance to Abrams Creek and follows it downstream through lush spring wildflowers to a foot log below a ford. From the foot log, you have a fine view of Abrams Creek. Study the creek carefully here. If you'd feel uncomfortable wading this ford (which you might have to do anyway if heavy flooding has washed away the foot log), you need to reconsider making this hike, since the crossing later on has no foot log. While that crossing is much farther upstream—with a lower water flow—the ford here still provides a good indication of what you can expect.

Shortly beyond the crossing, the trail passes through a clearing with wild roses, daylilies, and daffodils, revealing that this was once a homesite. Here the trail begins climbing Pine Mountain. You get a few level spurts along the way, but this is mostly a long and sometimes steep haul up the mountain. A man-made flat pad in an outside bend marks the high point of the climb and the highest elevation of the entire hike at 2,064 feet. You can rest your lungs on the 0.5-mile descent to Scott Gap.

Scott Gap marks the intersection of Rabbit Creek Trail and Hannah Mountain Trail. Rabbit Creek Trail continues straight and reaches Cades Cove in another 5.1 miles, while a right turn on Hannah Mountain Trail takes you to Parson Branch Road. Campsite 16 lies on a bed of pine needles a few hundred feet down the west side of the gap. If you're making this hike as a leisurely two-night backpack, this will be your first night's stay.

Before leaving the gap, take time to admire the large trees here, including the massive yellow poplar (tulip tree). Now turn left (east) on Hannah Mountain Trail and enjoy one of the easiest stretches of trail in the park as you follow the contour line on a long hike over cushiony pine needles. At a broad ridge the trail begins a gradual descent to Abrams Creek, with only the last portion being steep. You must wade the creek to complete the hike, but don't hesitate to turn back if you feel uncomfortable.

Once on the far side, turn right on Abrams Falls Trail and follow it upstream 1.7 miles to Abrams Falls. After viewing the falls, backtrack to the trail junction and head downstream on Hatcher Mountain Trail. Soon the trail forks, with Hatcher Mountain Trail heading right and up the mountain, while Little Bottoms Trail (your route) goes left and downhill. Little Bottoms Trail is poorly graded in places, looking more like a spot on the hillside with the leaves raked away than it does a hiking trail. You definitely need ankle-supporting hiking boots on this trail.

About 0.7 mile from the Hatcher Mountain Trail junction is Campsite 17, one of the most pleasant sites in the Smokies. It sits on a large level bench above Abrams Creek in a forest of hemlock (now dead) and white pine. Pine needles cushion the tent pads and the sites are far enough apart to provide reasonable privacy. This is your second night's stay on a two-night backpack and if spending only one night, this might be a better choice than Campsite 16. For one thing, you have most of the hike behind you, and you can laze your way back to the car the next day. Site 17 is very popular and rationed, so you want to make reservations as early as possible.

Beyond the campsite the trail continues to follow Abrams Creek downstream before eventually pulling away and climbing steeply to a ridge. An even steeper descent takes you to Cooper Road Trail at Campsite 1. At only 1.3 easy miles from the trailhead, this site is often crowded, particularly with youth groups. A left turn onto Cooper Road Trail takes you to Abrams Creek Campground in 0.9 mile. Walk through the campground and along the gravel road back to the trailhead.

Miles and Directions

0.0 Start by walking along the road back toward the ranger station. Turn left onto Rabbit Creek Trail, just beyond the station.

0.1 Cross Abrams Creek on a foot log.

2.7 Reach Scott Gap and turn left (east) on Hannah Mountain Trail. Campsite 16 is nearby.

4.6 Wade Abrams Creek to the junction with Hatcher Mountain Trail and Abrams Falls Trail. Turn right and follow Abrams Falls Trail upstream to Abrams Falls.

6.3 Arrive at Abrams Falls. Backtrack to the ford.

8.0 Return to junction with Hatcher Mountain and Abrams Falls Trails at the creek ford. Follow Hatcher Mountain Trail downstream.

8.1 Hatcher Mountain Trail forks to the right and heads uphill. You want to take the left fork onto Little Bottoms Trail and descend.

8.8 Campsite 17.

10.4 Junction with Cooper Road Trail at Campsite 1. Turn left (southwest) and follow the road to Abrams Creek Campground.

11.3 End of Cooper Road Trail at Abrams Creek Campground. Walk through the campground on the gravel road.

11.7 Arrive back at parking area.

Options: You can shave 3.4 miles off the total distance by passing up the side trip to Abrams Falls. For an all-day loop or a one- to two-night backpacking trip, you can combine this hike with Hike 27. Camp the first or second night at Campsite 17, then backtrack to the junction with Hatcher Mountain Trail. Take Hatcher Mountain Trail to Cooper Road Trail and follow Cooper Road Trail back to the trailhead. See Hike 27 for more details.

27 Abrams Creek and Cooper Road

Cooper Road was once a major access route into Cades Cove. Its wide and relatively gentle grade makes it a popular trail for equestrians and hikers. While you're likely to encounter horses and a few hikers along portions of this hike, you'll probably have most of it to yourself.

(See map for Hike 22: Abrams Falls.)

Start: Parking area near Abrams Creek Ranger Station
Distance: 11.6-mile lollipop
Hiking time: About 6 hours—day hike, multiple options for camping
Difficulty: Moderate
Trail surface: Gravel roads, old forest roads, and forest trails
Best season: Late May through early June for the mountain laurel bloom
Other trail users: Equestrians permitted on most of the trails of this hike
Maps: Calderwood and Blockhouse USGS

quads; Trails Illustrated #229 Great Smoky Mountains; Trails Illustrated #316 Cades Cove Elkmont
Special considerations: Portions of this hike receive heavy horse traffic, so watch out for horse pies. You might stop at a few and observe the dung beetles. Little Bottoms Trail is not graded and is unsuitable for sneakers or sandals. You need ankle-supporting boots when hiking it.
Other: The parking area is in a large field, so all of the possible parking places rarely fill up. However, on summer weekends you might not get an easy spot to pull into. Restrooms are available in the campground.

Finding the trailhead: The trailhead parking area is in a field near the Abrams Creek Ranger Station at the western end of the park. From the junction of Foothills Parkway and US 129 (approximately 22 miles south of Maryville, Tennessee, and 25 miles north of Fontana, North Carolina), go less than 0.1 mile south on US 129 and turn left on Happy Valley Road. Drive 5.7 miles on this road through Happy Valley and turn right at the sign for the campground and ranger station. Pass the ranger station at 0.6 mile; the parking area, located on both sides of the road, is a short distance farther. GPS: N35 36.557' / W83 56.110'

The Hike

Walk along the gravel road to Abrams Creek Campground and take one of the forks through the campground to the other side. Cooper Road Trail begins here, beyond the gate. After 0.9 mile and two quick fords of Kingfisher Creek, arrive at the junction with Little Bottoms Trail on the right, just before Campsite 1. Take Little Bottoms Trail on an extremely steep climb up and over a ridge, eventually leveling out at Abrams Creek. If making this hike in the summer, you'll immediately notice, and appreciate, the lower temperature here at the creek compared to what it was back up on the ridge.

Now follow the poorly graded trail upstream along scenic Abrams Creek, arriving at Campsite 17 on the left. Camp here if making this trip as an overnighter. The site sits at a former homesite a few feet above Abrams Creek. It is large, with good privacy and a soft pine-needle ground cover. The site is especially popular among fishers.

Pressing on from Campsite 17—and watching your footing along the poor trail—you come to the junction with Hatcher Mountain Trail, cutting sharply left (northwest) and climbing the mountain. Continuing straight at this junction will take you in 1.8 miles to Abrams Falls, a highly recommended side trip. If skipping the falls, turn left onto Hatcher Mountain Trail. An EF4 tornado swept across the western end of the park in April 2011, causing extensive damage to many of the trails in the area. You'll see the effects from this tornado along several portions of the hike, but in particular along Hatcher Mountain Trail. Begin a long, moderate ascent through a forest of pine, sassafras, oak, and huckleberry. The trail now descends gradually and crosses a couple of branches before ascending again and making the final descent to the junction with Cooper Road Trail at a small gap.

To the right on Cooper Road Trail, it is 5.7 miles to Cades Cove. Straight ahead, Beard Cane Trail leads 4.2 miles to Ace Gap Trail. Your hike goes left (north) on Cooper Road Trail and follows an easy, mostly downhill route to Cane Gap. Look for pink lady's slipper orchids growing along this stretch in May and June.

At Cane Gap, Cane Creek Trail goes straight ahead, while Cooper Road Trail swings around to the left. Continuing on Cooper Road Trail, hike along a short level section before making a steep climb to the junction with Goldmine Trail, forking off to the right. Stay left (south) and enjoy a 1.6-mile downhill run to the junction with Little Bottoms Trail. Along the way you cross Kingfisher Creek and some of its tributaries.

From the trail junction with Little Bottoms Trail, retrace your steps to the trailhead.

Miles and Directions

0.0 Start on the gravel road leading to Abrams Creek Campground. Follow the road through the campground.

0.4 Cooper Road Trail, which is a continuation of the gravel road, begins at the gate on the far side of Abrams Creek Campground.

1.3 Junction with Little Bottoms Trail at Campsite 1. Turn northeast on Little Bottoms Trail.

2.9 Campsite 17.

3.6 Turn sharply back to the left (northwest) on Hatcher Mountain Trail.

6.4 At a small gap, turn left (north) on Cooper Road Trail.

8.1 Junction with Cane Creek Trail at Cane Gap. Swing to the left (south) to remain on Cooper Road Trail.

8.7 Junction with Goldmine Trail, turning to the right. Continue south on Cooper Road Trail.

10.3 Return to junction with Little Bottoms Trail. Follow Cooper Road Trail back to Abrams Creek Campground.

11.2 End of Cooper Road Trail at Abrams Creek Campground. Walk through the campground on the gravel road.

11.6 Arrive back at trailhead.

Options: The 3.6-mile round-trip side trip to Abrams Falls is highly recommended if you have the time and energy.

The Abrams Creek area presents several possibilities for day-hike loops, as well as short or extended backpacking trips. The six backcountry campsites in the area provide many overnight options; study a trail map for possibilities. All the possible routes will combine trails described in Hikes 22, 23, 26, and 27.

FEATHERED FRIENDS

Nearly 250 species of birds are documented in the Smokies, with about sixty being permanent residents and at least 110 breeding in the park. At least a dozen place names in the park are named after birds, including the appropriately named Kingfisher Creek, which you cross a few times on the Abrams Creek and Cooper Road hike. When you cross the creek, take a break and watch carefully: There's a chance you'll be rewarded with the sight of a belted kingfisher.

Northeast Section

A backpacker takes a breather under Alum Cave Bluffs.

Hiking to Mount LeConte

The Cascades have Mount Rainier, Yellowstone has Old Faithful, and Great Smoky Mountains National Park has Mount LeConte. At 6,593 feet LeConte is only the third-highest peak in the Smokies, behind Clingmans Dome and Mount Guyot, but in many people's minds, it's bigger than Everest. In 1924, when the U.S. government sent a party to study the possibility of creating a national park in the region, a local group of park supporters took them to LeConte. Of all the places in the Smokies from which they could choose, they knew that Mount LeConte would make the biggest impression. The mountain continues to impress.

Three hikes in this guidebook lead to the summit of LeConte: Hike 31, Hike 35, and Hike 37. All three are doable as day hikes, but you also have two options for staying overnight on the summit. Mount LeConte Shelter sits in an open field a few feet below High Top, the highest of LeConte's peaks. Its amenities are just like any other shelter in the park, except that no fires are allowed. (The sensitive environment on LeConte's summit is not conducive to the indiscriminate gathering and dragging of firewood that has occurred in the past.) Not too far from the shelter, but still on LeConte's summit, is LeConte Lodge. Hikers who don't know anything about LeConte's history are quite startled when they happen upon the lodge after making what they thought was a hike into the "wilderness." The lodge opened in the late 1920s and has been in operation ever since, albeit with many improvements along the way. There is no electricity or running water, but modern enhancements include flush toilets and gas heat.

Helicopters fly in supplies for the lodge at the start of the season. (The lodge closes in winter.) During the operating season llamas pack fresh food and clean laundry to the lodge. Passing the llama train on Trillium Gap Trail is a special treat for hikers. The meals rarely change. For dinner, it's soup and cornbread, stew beef, green beans, mashed potatoes (from a mix), spiced apples, peaches, and a cookie for dessert. Wine is available. For breakfast, it's pancakes, Canadian bacon, scratch biscuits, grits, and scrambled eggs. The lodge's famous hot chocolate is served anytime. LeConte Lodge also offers lunch service for day hikers, either as a sack lunch or a sit-down meal, the latter requiring a reservation.

After supper guests hike a short trail to Cliff Top to watch the sunset. Before breakfast a few guests hike out to Myrtle Point to watch the sunrise. Cliff Top is also the site of a number of weddings. Yep, more than one bride and groom have hiked up here with a minister and wedding party and exchanged vows on the rocks of Cliff Top.

Reservations for staying at the lodge are not only required but very hard to get. The number to call is (865) 429-5704. Visit the lodge website (www.lecontelodge .com) for full details.

The three hikes detailed in this guidebook use every trail that leads to LeConte's summit and cover the most popular and practical hike combinations. A few other options exist if taking advantage of a shuttle service or second vehicle. Study a trail map for possibilities.

Finally, a word of caution. You might think that a winter hike to LeConte would allow you to experience the mountain without encountering hordes of other hikers. You'd be right, but before you embark on such a trek, consider your abilities honestly. That sunny fifty-degree weather you leave in Gatlinburg can turn into a severe snowstorm on LeConte's summit. Also, the north-facing sections of the rocky trails keep a near-constant glaze of ice throughout winter, making hiking dangerous even when the weather is pleasant. Hiking to LeConte in winter can be a great experience—just make sure you fully prepare for it.

28 Sugarlands Valley Nature Trail

Physically challenged hikers will enjoy this chance to explore the Smokies away from the roads. The entire path is paved and nearly level. As a self-guiding nature trail, it has numbered features along the way, as well as tactile exhibits for the visually impaired. An interpretive leaflet (50 cents to keep) is available at the trailhead. Additionally, features along this trail have been recorded on audiotape. A copy of the tape and a tape player are available at Sugarlands Visitor Center. While the paved path, easy access, and proximity to the main park road might detract from a "wilderness" experience, this hike provides a wonderful opportunity for those wanting a short, easy hike.

Start: Sugarlands Valley Nature trailhead near Sugarlands Visitor Center
Distance: 0.5-mile loop
Hiking time: About 20 minutes—day hike
Difficulty: Easy
Trail surface: Paved trail
Other trail users: Hikers, wheelchairs, baby strollers
Maps: Gatlinburg USGS quad; Trails Illustrated #229 Great Smoky Mountains; Trails Illustrated #317 Clingmans Dome Cataloochee; Trails Illustrated #316 Cades Cove Elkmont
Special considerations: This is the only trail in the park that is easy for people in wheelchairs.
Other: The parking lot is small but rarely fills. Restrooms are available at Sugarlands Visitor Center.

Finding the trailhead: Drive 0.4 mile south of Sugarlands Visitor Center on Newfound Gap Road. The paved parking area is on the left (east) side of the road. The trail is signed and obvious. GPS: N35 40.778' / W83 31.877'

The Hike

It's impossible to lose your way on this hike—just follow the pavement. The trail passes by a couple of chimneys, a stone wall, and other signs of human activity in pre-park times. An average hiker can complete the walk easily in 20 minutes, but what's the hurry? This hike has a lot to offer those who slow down and take the time to absorb it.

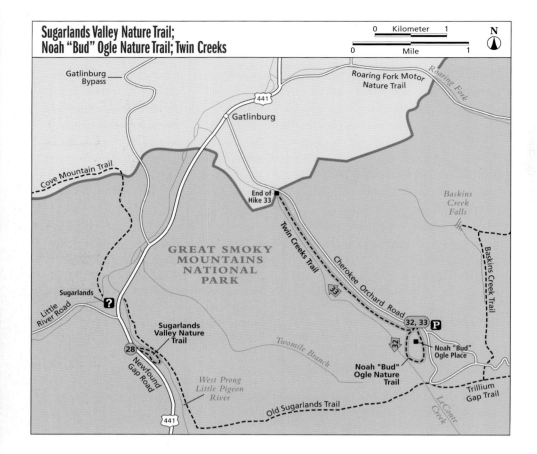

Miles and Directions

0.0   Start from the obvious trailhead at the parking area.

0.5   Arrive back at trailhead.

29 Alum Cave Bluffs

It doesn't get much better than this! Every able person who visits the Smokies is encouraged to make this hike at least once, even if you can't stand a crowd. If continuing the 2.7 miles from the bluffs to Mount LeConte, this hike would rank high among the best in the park. Even if you stop at the bluffs and backtrack as outlined in this hike, it's still hard to beat. Of course, there always seems to be a downside. Any day between spring and fall and on weekends during the winter, you can expect to encounter a few billion people on this hike.

Start: Alum Cave trailhead on Newfound Gap Road
Distance: 4.6 miles out and back
Hiking time: About 3 hours—day hike
Difficulty: Moderate, with some short steep sections
Trail surface: Boot-packed trail covered in rocks and roots
Other trail users: Hikers only
Maps: Mount LeConte USGS quad; Trails

Illustrated #229 Great Smoky Mountains; Trails Illustrated #317 Clingmans Dome Cataloochee; Trails Illustrated #316 Cades Cove Elkmont
Other: Even though Alum Cave trailhead has more parking places than most other trails in the park, it also fills up faster than most. Show up at noon and you'll be looking for a spot along the road, some distance from the trailhead. Pit toilets are located at the northern parking area.

Finding the trailhead: On Newfound Gap Road, drive 4.2 miles north of Newfound Gap or 8.5 miles south of Sugarlands Visitor Center. There are two large parking lots on the north side of the road. GPS: N35 37.757' / W83 27.077'

The Hike

An obvious path begins from the east corner of the northern (lower) parking area and from the west corner of the southern (upper) parking area. In a few yards you cross Walker Camp Prong and a short distance farther Alum Cave Creek, both on sturdy bridges. Now you hike on a gentle uphill course alongside the creek and through an old-growth forest. Some of the big hemlocks are still living as of early 2012. (See the sidebar for Hike 36.) The creek bed looks different from most other creeks in the Smokies, and it is. The steep slopes of the Alum Cave Creek drainage make it especially prone to flooding, and the regular torrents keep the streambed scoured clean of moss, ferns, and the usual undergrowth seen along other Smoky Mountain waterways.

After making a few crossings of Alum Cave Creek on sturdy foot logs, you cross Styx Branch a couple of times on foot logs, probably not realizing that Alum Cave Creek had forked off eastward toward the slopes of Anakeesta Knob. At mile 1.4 you cross Styx Branch just below the entrance into Arch Rock, one of the most interesting geological features in the park. The trail climbs through an opening, an "arch" in

View from underneath Alum Cave Bluffs.

the Anakeesta Formation. It's not an arch like those in Arches National Park or those in the valley and ridge provinces of Tennessee and Kentucky. In simplistic terms, those arches formed by erosion from running water. Here, in the Anakeesta Formation, holes in the rock are likely caused from the expansion and crumbling caused by millions of years of freezing and thawing.

Beyond Arch Rock you cross Styx Branch for the final time on a foot log and then swing around a broad ridge to cross another stream. Just before the trail makes a sharp right turn to head up the drainage for the creek, look to the left to see a large yellow birch tree with several other species growing out of its trunk. There's a rhododendron, a mountain laurel, some small spruces, and a good-size birch growing as a separate tree.

The trail climbs steeply now, and soon you get a profile view of Little Duck Hawk Ridge. Farther up, at an especially scenic vista called Inspiration Point, you get another good view of the ridge. See if you can find both arches in the ridge. In summer one of them may be hard to spot.

From Inspiration Point, you have a short ascent to the bluffs. It's not a cave, as the name suggests, but rather an overhanging rock ledge. However, this isn't your average rock overhang. *Andy Griffith Show* fans may recall a popular line of Barney's when they see the bluff for the first time. "It's big, *really* big." It's geologically unique, too. The bluffs create a very dry environment below the overhang, which is responsible for the thick, flour-like powder you walk through. Several very rare minerals have been discovered here, some not known to occur anywhere else in the world. What isn't here, though, is a lot of alum. In pre-park days several attempts were made to

Alum Cave Bluffs; Charlies Bunion; Mt. LeConte via The Boulevard

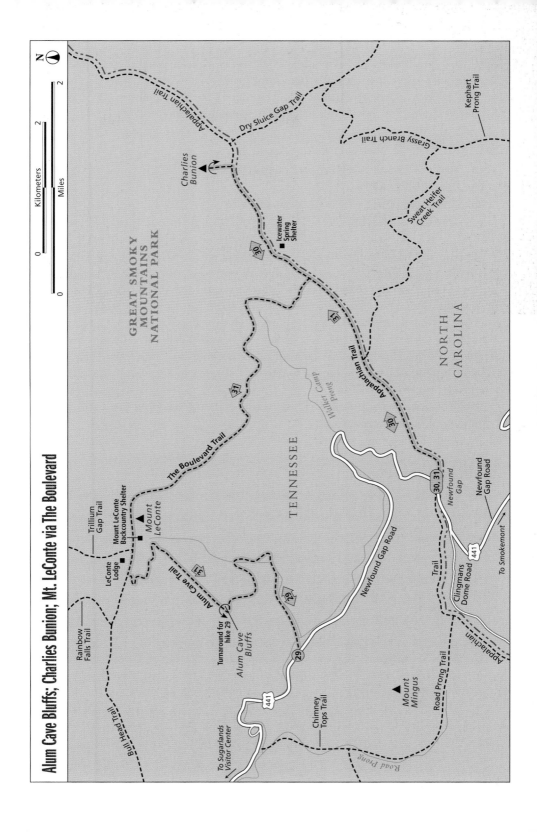

mine the bluffs for various minerals. The full extent of those mining operations isn't known, but none of them had any significant success.

The bluffs mark the end of this hike, but Alum Cave Trail continues 2.7 miles to Mount LeConte. See the options below if choosing to continue.

Miles and Directions

0.0   Start from the north side of the parking area at the trail sign.

1.4   Hike through Arch Rock.

2.3   Arrive at Alum Cave Bluffs. Return the way you came.

4.6   Arrive back at trailhead.

Options: Many people hike Alum Cave Trail all the way to Mount LeConte and back as a day hike, including a lot of overweight and out-of-shape people huffing and puffing up the trail. There seems to be a mystique about having "made it" to LeConte. Here are a couple of options that allow you to see LeConte's summit without backtracking. Arrange for a shuttle and start at Newfound Gap, returning along Alum Cave Trail (see Hike 31), or have the shuttle take you to the Grotto Falls trailhead and hike up Trillium Gap Trail to the summit and return on Alum Cave Trail. Hike 35 outlines a third route to Mount LeConte via Rainbow Falls Trail and a return by Bull Head Trail.

Before hiking to the summit, be sure to read "Hiking to Mount LeConte" at the beginning of the Northeast section.

BLUFFING BIRDS

Alum Cave Bluffs is home not only to uncommon minerals but uncommon birds as well. Ravens and peregrine falcons make homes on the bluffs. Ravens are relatively frequent at many high-elevation sites in the southern Appalachians, particularly around rocky bluffs like Alum Cave. Peregrine falcons are another story. Between 1984 and 1986 the park service released thirteen young peregrines in the park. In 1997 a pair of peregrines raised three chicks in a nest near Alum Cave Bluffs, the first recorded nesting of peregrines in the park since 1942. Today, the bluffs continue to support the only verified peregrine nesting site in the Smokies, although nesting is also suspected on Greenbrier Pinnacle.

30 Charlies Bunion

Nearly everyone who visits the Smokies spends a little time at Newfound Gap, where this hike begins. Unless you just like hanging out in crowds, you'll want to park and hit the trail quickly. However, don't expect to get away from everyone on this hike. Charlies Bunion is a classic Smokies hike and can be crowded any time of year except winter. Winter hiking along this trail is very rewarding, with great vistas and the opportunity for seeing interesting ice formations. However, only experienced hikers should attempt it in winter. Regardless of when you make the hike, the views from Charlies Bunion are spectacular.

(See map for Hike 29: Alum Cave Bluffs.)

Start: Newfound Gap
Distance: 8.2 miles out and back
Hiking time: About 5 hours—day hike or overnighter
Difficulty: Moderate, with some difficult rocky sections
Trail surface: Forest trail with *lots* of rocks
Other trail users: Hikers only
Maps: Clingmans Dome, Mount LeConte, and Mount Guyot USGS quads; Trails Illustrated #229 Great Smoky Mountains; Trails Illustrated #317 Clingmans Dome Cataloochee
Special considerations: It is common for snow and ice to cover the trail in winter. Charlies Bunion has dangerous drop-offs.
Other: Newfound Gap has a very large parking lot, but it can fill up on weekends or any day during the summer and autumn season. Restrooms are available here.

Finding the trailhead: The trailhead is located at Newfound Gap Overlook on the Smokies crest. Drive 15.5 miles north on Newfound Gap Road from Oconaluftee Visitor Center or 12.7 miles south from Sugarlands Visitor Center. The trailhead is on the northeast end of the parking lot, between the paved path leading to the restrooms and the Rockefeller Memorial. GPS: N35 36.669' / W83.25.495'

The Hike

Begin hiking the Appalachian Trail (AT) from the northeast corner of the parking area. The trail starts out level and wide, but you soon begin a 1.5-mile steady ascent to a grassy knoll. You're walking through a high-elevation spruce–fir forest, with occasional openings providing vistas of Mount LeConte to the north. In late April and early May, spring beauty and trout lily cover the ground.

From the knoll, descend 0.2 mile to a gap and the junction with Sweat Heifer Creek Trail at a huge gnarled birch tree. The gap is a good spot for a breather. Walk a few hundred feet on Sweat Heifer Creek Trail to a grove of young American beech trees. Beech bark disease killed all the mature trees, and the trunks have now fallen, leaving an open view over the young trees. Although the view of a healthy mature beech forest would be much preferred, the lack of tall trees provides great views into the Oconaluftee River watershed.

View from Charlies Bunion.

Back on the AT, head east and begin a steep ascent. You soon pass an open view into North Carolina, taking in Clingmans Dome, Newfound Gap Road, and a glimpse of Bryson City, similar to the view back at the beech trees. At 2.7 miles you reach the junction with The Boulevard Trail. The Boulevard Trail forks left (north) and leads to Mount LeConte.

For a terrific (though difficult) side trip, go about 0.1 mile on The Boulevard Trail and look for a side path to the right. There may be a sign for "the Jumpoff" marking the spot. It is at a wide spot in the trail created from an uprooted tree on the left. The path climbs the bank on the right over rocks and roots. The rugged path leads about 0.5 mile to an overlook that provides a great view of Charlies Bunion.

Now back on the AT at the junction with The Boulevard Trail, continue heading northeast on the AT. After 0.3 mile a short side path on the right leads to Icewater Spring Shelter, situated in an open grassy area with good views. You'll probably see other day hikers here, posing for pictures in front of the shelter.

Just beyond the shelter, the trail passes literally over Icewater Spring. A rusty old pipe provides a drop so that you can fill a water bottle, but there's something unappealing about drinking water that comes out of a heavily trodden trail. (Be sure to treat all drinking water in the Smokies, no matter the source.)

Beyond the spring it's an easy hike of about a mile to the side trail for Charlies Bunion, on the left. There's no marker for the side trail, but don't worry, you can't miss it. Charlies Bunion stands out like few other landmarks in the park. The bare, jagged cliffs remind you more of the young Rockies than the old, worn Appalachians. The views are spectacular. To the west is the Jumpoff; to the northwest is the unmistakable Mount LeConte; and to the northeast is Greenbrier Pinnacle. You'll want to spend some time here, but take extra precautions. Many people have fallen while climbing on the rocks.

The side path circles the knoll and comes back to the AT. Turn right (west) and backtrack to the trailhead.

Miles and Directions

0.0 Start on the AT on the northeast end of the parking lot.

1.7 Sweat Heifer Creek Trail comes in from the right. Continue heading east on the AT.

2.7 The Boulevard Trail forks to the left (north). (See hike text for a side trip from here.) Continue northeast on the AT.

3.0 Short side path on the right leads to Icewater Spring Shelter.

4.0 Path on the left leads to Charlies Bunion.

4.1 Arrive at Charlies Bunion. Return the way you came.

8.2 Arrive back at trailhead.

Option: You can do this hike as an overnighter by staying at Icewater Spring Shelter. This provides you with the opportunity to view the sunset from Charlies Bunion, an experience few people have.

CHARLIE'S WHAT?

A visitor to Charlies Bunion in the early 1920s would have seen a much different site than what we see today. The bare jagged rocks would have been covered in dense vegetation, barely revealing the precipitous nature of the mountain peak. In 1925 a horrific forest fire swept up from the Kephart Prong drainage and consumed the vegetation on the mountain. Four years later a heavy storm hit the mountain, and without any vegetation to secure the spoil, the downpour scoured the soil from the rocks. A group of hikers visited the mountain soon afterward—among them Horace Kephart, for whom nearby Mount Kephart is named, and one Charlie Conner. As the story goes, Kephart likened the exposed jagged rocks to Charlie Conner's bunion, hence the name Charlies Bunion.

31 Mount LeConte via The Boulevard

If you have to choose only one hike in the Smokies, this would be a good choice. It gives you nearly everything the park is famous for, and by starting at an elevation of 5,046 feet and ending at close to 3,800 feet, it's not overly strenuous. You're going to get a good workout to be sure, but at least you won't think you're in boot camp. Before making this hike, be sure to read "Hiking to Mount LeConte" at the beginning of the Northeast section.

(See map for Hike 29: Alum Cave Bluffs.)

Start: Newfound Gap
Distance: 13.2 miles point to point
Hiking time: About 7 hours—day hike or overnighter
Difficulty: Strenuous
Trail surface: Forest trail with *lots* of rocks, some sections over solid rock
Other trail users: Hikers only
Maps: Clingmans Dome and Mount LeConte USGS quads; Trails Illustrated #229 Great Smoky Mountains; Trails Illustrated #317 Clingmans Dome Cataloochee
Special considerations: Some of the qualities that make this hike so appealing—precipitous drop-offs and paths carved out of solid rock—also make it very dangerous, especially with snow or ice on the trail. This is a hike for surefooted hikers wearing ankle-supporting hiking boots. Leave the sandals in the car. Only experienced and well-prepared hikers should attempt this hike in winter. You might start out at Newfound Gap in flurries, only to find yourself wading in a foot of snow on Mount LeConte.

If you wish to spend the night at LeConte Lodge on Mount LeConte's summit, you'll need to make reservations well ahead of time. The back-country shelter on Mount LeConte also requires reservations, as do all other shelters in the park.
Other: Newfound Gap has a very large parking lot, but it can fill up on weekends or any day during the summer and autumn season. Restrooms are available here.

Finding the trailhead: The trailhead is located at Newfound Gap Overlook on the Smokies crest. Drive 15.5 miles north on Newfound Gap Road from Oconaluftee Visitor Center or 12.7 miles south from Sugarlands Visitor Center. The trailhead is on the northeast end of the parking lot, between the paved path leading to the restrooms and the Rockefeller Memorial. GPS: N35 36.669' / W83.25.495'

You'll need to leave a vehicle at the Alum Cave trailhead, where this hike ends. On Newfound Gap Road, drive 4.2 miles north of Newfound Gap or 8.5 miles south of Sugarlands Visitor Center. There are two large parking lots on the north side of the road. GPS: N35 37.757' / W83 27.077'

The Hike

Begin hiking the Appalachian Trail (AT) from the northeast corner of the parking area. The trail starts out level and wide, but you soon begin a 1.5-mile steady ascent to a grassy knoll. You're walking through high-elevation spruce-fir forest, with occasional openings providing vistas of Mount LeConte to the north. In late April and early May, spring beauty and trout lily cover the ground.

Fog enshrouds a landslide along The Boulevard Trail.

From the knoll, descend 0.2 mile to a gap and the junction with Sweat Heifer Creek Trail at a huge, gnarled birch tree. The gap is a good spot for a breather. Walk a few hundred feet on Sweat Heifer Creek Trail to a grove of young American beech trees. Beech bark disease killed all the mature trees, and the trunks have now fallen, leaving an open view over the young trees. Although the view of a healthy mature beech forest would be much preferred, the lack of tall trees provides great views into the Oconaluftee River watershed.

Back on the AT, head east and begin a steep ascent. You soon pass an open view into North Carolina, taking in Clingmans Dome, Newfound Gap Road, and a glimpse of Bryson City. At 2.7 miles you reach the junction with The Boulevard Trail forking to the left (north). Leave the AT here and follow The Boulevard Trail about 0.1 mile to a side path on the right for the Jumpoff. There may be a sign here. It is at a wide spot in the trail created from an uprooted tree on the left. The path goes to the right and climbs the bank on rocks and roots. The rugged path leads about 0.5 mile to an overlook that provides a great view of Charlies Bunion. If planning to overnight on Mount LeConte, this side trip is highly recommended. If you're doing this trip as a day hike, you may not want to take the extra time.

From the side path, The Boulevard Trail ascends a bit and then begins a long, fairly steep descent along the northwest flank of Mount Kephart, crossing over the upper reaches of Walker Camp Prong and finally reaching a narrow ridgeline. This is The Boulevard, and you follow it all the way to Mount LeConte. Along the ridge are occasional open views to the right (north) into the Porters Creek watershed and leafy peeks left (south) into the Walker Camp Prong watershed. At your feet Rugel's ragwort, found only in the Smokies, grows abundantly along the trail in many places. Look for the foliage in spring and the nodding yellow flowers in summer.

At about 2.5 miles from the AT, you swing sharply around to the right over Anakeesta Ridge. Look down at your feet. That gray slatelike rock you're standing on is the Anakeesta Formation. Its type and orientation are responsible for the incredible geologic features encountered along this hike. You can see how easily this rock might fracture and break apart. Later on this hike you'll see the effects of such fracturing.

Descend from the ridgeline to the remnants of a small landslide and look back behind you to see the summit of Anakeesta Knob and Anakeesta Ridge extending from it. Now go on an undulating course and come to a sharp left swing around a ridge, with open views to the north. You're now ascending the flanks of Myrtle Point and you pass massive cliffs with sand myrtle clinging in cracks.

At this point you must cross the remnants of a massive landslide. What a horrific sight this must have been while the landslide was occurring. You'll see several more landslide scars on the remainder of the hike, but few places in the Smokies allow you to experience one of these scars as intimately as this one does. A steel cable helps with the footing on the path through the slide and is a necessity with ice or snow on the trail. Beyond the slide you make a sharp left turn and come to a very dangerous section of trail. Back at the slide, at least you could see the danger and act accordingly. Here, a thin veil of vegetation hides the sheer vertical drops created by landslides.

Soon the excitement and exhilaration of the hike turn to depression as you near LeConte's highest peak, High Top, and pass through its graveyard of fir trees. Every mature tree is dead, with many still standing as ghostly skeletons, while others lie in a jumbled tangle like chopsticks. (See the sidebar for Hike 49 for a description of what's going on.) In recent years many young fir trees have grown back and somewhat lessen the visual disturbance.

The Boulevard Trail runs through a lush spruce-fir forest.

After passing through a thick growth of young fir trees, a side path to Myrtle Point cuts back to the left. (If you're overnighting on LeConte, you'll want to hike back out to Myrtle in the morning to view the sunrise.) Just beyond the side path, you cross the highest point on Mount LeConte at 6,593 feet and the second-highest point reached by maintained trail in the Smokies. Clingmans Dome, at 6,643 feet, is a mere 50 feet higher, but some people want Mount LeConte to be the highest mountain in the park. Look over to the left on High Top's summit. That pile of rocks looks very out of place, doesn't it? It's a lighthearted attempt by some people to make Mount LeConte higher than Clingmans Dome. They have a long way to go.

After topping out on High Top, you pass the best view so far, toward Newfound Gap and Clingmans Dome. The parking area where you began this hike is clearly visible behind Anakeesta Ridge. Shortly beyond the vista is Mount LeConte Backcountry Shelter, one of only three shelters not located near the AT (Kephart and Laurel Gap are the other two). Just beyond the shelter you pass a side path to Cliff Top on the left and then come to the three-way trail junction near LeConte Lodge. (Cliff Top is where you'll watch the sunset if overnighting on LeConte.)

Trillium Gap Trail goes right (northeast) and Rainbows Falls Trail continues straight ahead. The Boulevard Trail officially ends here. The scattered collection of buildings making up LeConte Lodge lies just beyond the trail junction. Trillium Gap Trail takes you behind the lodge and to the spring. Rainbow Falls Trail, which continues this hike, brings you past the front of the lodge a short distance farther to the junction with Alum Cave Trail, on the left (west).

Alum Cave Trail starts out level, but that quickly changes as the trail swings around to the east and skirts beneath the sheer cliffs of Cliff Top. Steel cables serve as helpful handholds with the wet rocks and are crucial when there's ice on the trail. The 2.5 miles of descent between here and Alum Cave Bluffs are steep and rocky, with several stretches of trail carved out of solid rock. Along the way are a number of landslide scars and several good views. At one point along this stretch, you come to an ingenious solution to navigating a steep, rocky slope. The trail engineers angled a large, long tree trunk down the slope and sawed steps into it. Tar and gravel give traction to the steps. Farther down, the trail actually ascends a bit, and where it swings to the left and begins descending again, a side path leads a few feet to a view point known as Gracies Pulpit, which gives a somewhat open view of Mount LeConte.

From Gracies Pulpit, the trail descends a rock slope very steeply and soon comes to Alum Cave Bluffs. Walk under the bluffs and continue descending. At 0.9 mile from the bluffs, you hike *through* Arch Rock. It's not an arch like those in Arches National Park or those in the valley and ridge provinces of Tennessee and Kentucky. In simplistic terms, those arches were formed by erosion from running water. Here, in the Anakeesta Formation, holes in the rock are caused by the expansion and crumbling resulting from millions of years of freezing and thawing.

After passing through Arch Rock, you cross Styx Branch on a footbridge and have an easy 1.4-mile walk to Alum Cave trailhead. Along the way you make several creek

Sunrise illuminates a landslide along The Boulevard Trail. Steel cables provide handholds in icy conditions.

crossings, first of Styx Branch and then Alum Cave Creek, and you pass through a scenic old-growth forest. Some of the old hemlock trees in this section are still alive as of early 2012. (See the sidebar for Hike 36.)

Miles and Directions

0.0 Start on the AT on the northeast end of the parking lot.

1.7 Sweat Heifer Creek Trail comes in from the right. Continue heading east on the AT.

2.7 Bear to the left (north) on The Boulevard Trail.

2.8 A side path on the right leads 0.5 mile to the Jumpoff.

7.6 Just before the highest point on Mount LeConte's summit, a side path on the left leads to Myrtle Point.

7.9 Arrive at Mount LeConte Backcountry Shelter.

8.1 Junction with Trillium Gap Trail and Rainbow Falls Trail. LeConte Lodge is immediately beyond the junction. Continue straight ahead on Rainbow Falls Trail.

8.2 Turn left (west) on Alum Cave Trail.

10.9 Pass under Alum Cave Bluffs.

11.8 Hike though Arch Rock.

13.2 Arrive at Alum Cave trailhead.

32 Noah "Bud" Ogle Nature Trail

As a self-guiding nature trail, this hike doesn't get a lot of attention from the "hard-core" hiking crowd. Nature trails are for tourists, some might say. That's a shame because this is one of the best hikes in the park for its length. In early spring wild-flowers are abundant. The trail passes by the cascading LeConte Creek and the Ogle Tub Mill. Beyond the mill the trail passes through a forest set amidst a jumble of huge, mossy boulders. Finally, there's the Ogle Place itself, a restored cabin and barn open for exploring. Those hard-core hikers don't know what they're missing.

(See map for Hike 28: Sugarlands Valley Nature Trail.)

Start: Parking area for Noah "Bud" Ogle Place on Cherokee Orchard Road
Distance: 0.8-mile loop
Hiking time: About 30 minutes–day hike
Difficulty: Easy
Trail surface: Forest trail with lots of rocks

Best season: Spring for the wildflowers
Other trail users: Hikers only
Maps: Mount LeConte USGS quad; Trails Illustrated #229 Great Smoky Mountains; Trails Illustrated #317 Clingmans Dome Cataloochee; Trails Illustrated #316 Cades Cove Elkmont
Other: Ample parking is available at the cabin, but there are no facilities.

Finding the trailhead: From US 441 in Gatlinburg, turn at traffic light #8 onto Historic Nature Trail-Airport Road and drive 0.6 mile to a confusing intersection. Stay to the right and continue straight ahead. You soon enter the park on Cherokee Orchard Road. Reach Noah "Bud" Ogle Place on the right, 2.6 miles from traffic light #8. The parking area is on the right, just before the cabin. The nature trail starts behind the cabin. GPS: N35 41.005' / W83 29.412'

The Hike

Begin the hike by exploring the old Ogle farm. The nature trail begins behind the cabin and crosses a couple of small streams. At 0.3 mile you come to the trailhead for Twin Creeks Trail (Hike 33) on the right. Continue straight ahead and pass by mossy rock walls. You'll soon come to the Ogle tub mill beside the cascading LeConte Creek. Walk along the creek a short distance before turning away and climbing up the bank. Now you pass through a scenic forest where the ground is literally covered in a jumble of boulders. At some places rock and trail are the same, but there is no danger of losing the path. Trail signs mark all of the turns, and if the signs are missing, just follow the rocks with no moss on them. Once through the boulder field, you cross a number of branchlets, some on picturesque foot logs, and arrive back at the Ogle barn.

Tub mill along Noah "Bud" Ogle Nature Trail.

Miles and Directions

0.0 Begin from the parking area and walk behind the cabin to start the trail.

0.3 Twin Creeks Trail (Hike 33) goes to the right. Continue straight ahead.

0.8 Arrive back at the Ogle Place.

GRIST FOR THE MILL

In the 1800s and into the early 1900s, the Smokies were home to hundreds of gristmills. Some fourteen operated on LeConte Creek alone. Only four mills remain in the park today. Ogle Mill on LeConte Creek and Reagan Mill on nearby Roaring Fork are tub mills. Water from the flume is directed onto a small wooden water wheel (turbine) that turns horizontally, like a roulette wheel, and has angled blades that catch the water. A vertical shaft rises from the water wheel and powers the millstone housed above. Mingus Mill, near Oconaluftee Visitor Center, is a cast-iron turbine mill, which is similar to the tub mill but with a metal turbine. Cable Mill, in Cades Cove, is a classic overshot gristmill. In the overshot design, water from the flume pours over a waterwheel that turns vertically, like a Ferris wheel, with the water catching in little buckets that pivot as the wheel rotates.

33 Twin Creeks

While there's no such thing as a bad hike in the Smokies, this one isn't one of the best. The forest here is scraggly and seems to be struggling to recover from years of pre-park farming and clearing. Poison ivy covers the trail sides, and you're within earshot (sometimes eyesight) of a paved road the entire way. That said, one attribute of this hike makes it worth including in this guidebook. It makes a great split-party hike. Go with the family to visit Noah "Bud" Ogle Place, maybe hiking the nature trail, and then let them go back to the hotel in Gatlinburg while you laze your way back on foot. The trail ends at the common boundary between the park and Gatlinburg.

(See map for Hike 28: Sugarlands Valley Nature Trail.)

Start: Parking area for Noah "Bud" Ogle Place on Cherokee Orchard Road
Distance: 2.4 miles point to point
Hiking time: About 1.5 hours—day hike
Difficulty: Easy
Trail surface: Forest trail
Other trail users: Hikers only
Maps: Mount LeConte and Gatlinburg USGS quads; Trails Illustrated #229 Great Smoky Mountains; Trails Illustrated #317 Clingmans Dome Cataloochee; Trails Illustrated #316 Cades Cove Elkmont
Other: Ample parking is available at the cabin, but there are no facilities.
Special considerations: Poison ivy grows abundantly along the entire route. Make sure the kids (and their parents) know how to identify it before making this hike.

Finding the trailhead: From US 441 in Gatlinburg, turn at traffic light #8 onto Historic Nature Trail–Airport Road and drive 0.6 mile to a confusing intersection. Stay to the right and continue straight ahead. You soon enter the park on Cherokee Orchard Road. Reach Noah "Bud" Ogle Place on the right, 2.6 miles from traffic light #8. The parking area is on the right, just before the cabin. The nature trail starts behind the cabin. GPS: N35 41.005' / W83 29.412'

The Hike

Begin the hike by exploring the old Ogle farm, and then start hiking Noah "Bud" Ogle Nature Trail, which begins behind the cabin. At 0.3 mile turn right (north) on Twin Creeks Trail. Descend gently, passing by rock walls, boxwood shrubs, and other signs of early settlement. About a mile into the hike, you pass through a rock wall and then have to cross a paved road. (The road leads to Twin Creeks Science and Education Facility.)

Soon you'll cross a small creek branch at the junction with Grassy Branch Trail. That trail and a few others weave through the mountains between here and the park entrance on Newfound Gap Road. These trails are open to the public, but their primary use is for equestrians.

From the creek crossing, it's a short walk to the end of the trail on Cherokee Orchard Road. A right turn takes you back to Noah "Bud" Ogle Place in 1.75 miles. A left turn takes you into the asphalt and concrete morass of Gatlinburg.

Miles and Directions

0.0 Begin from the parking area and walk behind the cabin to start the trail.

0.3 Turn right (north) on Twin Creeks Trail.

1.0 Junction with paved road that leads to Twin Creeks facility. Cross over the road and continue on Twin Creeks Trail.

2.4 End of Twin Creeks Trail on Cherokee Orchard Road at the park boundary.

DISCOVERING LIFE

The paved road you cross over on the Twin Creeks hike leads to the park's Twin Creeks Science and Education Facility. The facility is the heart and brain for scientific research in the park. A fascinating project under way in the park at the time of this writing is the All Taxa Biodiversity Inventory (ATBI), conducted by Discover Life in America (DLIA), a nonprofit organization based in the park. ATBI is a concentrated effort to identify and record every single species living within Great Smoky Mountains National Park, with the exception of bacteria. DLIA funds and coordinates the project, bringing in scientists from all over the world who are experts in their fields.

Scientists estimate that there are some 100,000 living organisms in the park, not including bacteria. As of early 2012 the ATBI checklist includes just under 18,000 species. An exciting aspect of the inventory is all the new discoveries being made. More than 7,000 species on the list are new to the park, and an astonishing 922 are new to science. That's right: Researchers have so far found 922 species no one knew existed in the world! We don't need to go to the tropical rainforests or the depths of the oceans to discover new life. ATBI shows just how little we know about our own backyard.

The objective of the ATBI project is not just in creating a checklist. As DLIA states, "It is a complex and living database of species locations, habitats, genetic diversity, population density, symbiotic relationships, and predator-prey interactions. It is a cooperative effort between expert scientists specializing in all different forms of life. It is a way to discover new species in need of protection, to identify new threats in time to act, and to understand how to protect a complex and valuable ecosystem like the Smoky Mountains."

As you probably noticed on the sign as you drove to the trailhead, Twin Creeks Science and Education Facility is not open to the public, so cross the road and continue on your hike. However, you can do so with the knowledge that some pretty amazing things are going on just a short distance up that road.

34 Rainbow Falls

At Rainbow Falls, LeConte Creek spills over a hanging ledge some 80 feet to the rocks below. Much of the water changes to mist before it reaches bottom, and from the proper angle on a sunny day, you can see rainbows in the mist. In winter, after prolonged cold spells, the waterfall can freeze from bottom to top. Although seeing it requires a difficult and fairly long round-trip hike, Rainbow Falls is among the more popular destinations in the park. Expect to have some company on this hike at any time of year.

Start: Rainbow Falls trailhead on Cherokee Orchard Road

Distance: 5.4 miles out and back

Hiking time: About 3.5 hours—day hike

Difficulty: Strenuous, due to steep grades and rocky trail

Trail surface: Forest trail covered with more rocks than you can imagine

Best season: Spring for the wildflowers

Other trail users: Hikers only

Maps: Mount LeConte USGS quad; Trails Illustrated #229 Great Smoky Mountains; Trails Illustrated #317 Clingmans Dome Cataloochee; Trails Illustrated #316 Cades Cove

Elkmont (shows the trailhead only)

Special considerations: Climbing the rocks at the waterfall can be dangerous. Also, pay careful attention if you visit the falls in cold weather and scramble up under the ledge. Icicles form on the overhanging rocks and constantly break off, hitting the ground like missiles. The trail is very rocky and unsuitable for sandals.

Other: Although there's room for several vehicles, the parking area fills quickly. Additional parking is available 0.1 mile farther on Cherokee Orchard Road. Pit toilets are available at the main parking area.

Finding the trailhead: From US 441 in Gatlinburg, turn at traffic light #8 onto Historic Nature Trail–Airport Road and drive 0.6 mile to a confusing intersection. Stay to the right and continue straight ahead. You soon enter the park on Cherokee Orchard Road. Reach the parking area for Rainbow Falls Trail and Bull Head Trail at 3.3 miles from traffic light #8 (GPS: N35 40.551' / W83 29.147'). Rainbow Falls Trail begins from the western end of the parking area.

The Hike

Begin on Rainbow Falls Trail at the western end of the main parking area. In a few hundred feet, you cross Trillium Gap Trail and begin climbing alongside LeConte Creek on a rocky path. The steady ascent continues all the way to the falls, and so do the rocks. You might be tempted to rename this trail the "Rocky Falls Trail" before you finish. LeConte Creek keeps close company most of the way. Only at a few places does the trail get out of earshot of the creek.

After a mile or so, the trail swings away and comes to a sharp right-hand switchback. In winter there's a view back toward Gatlinburg. You can see the Gatlinburg Space Needle and the Park Vista Hotel. Work your way back toward the creek and come to a high overlook at a left-hand turn in the trail. There's a perfect sitting rock

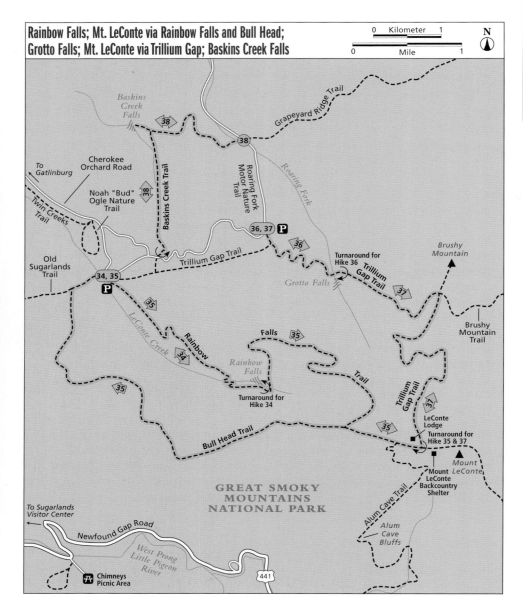

here at a silverbell tree. From here, the trail makes a quick swing away from the
creek, then returns to parallel it on a high bench before making the first crossing on
a foot log.

Now the big trees start to appear. There are several large hemlocks and a huge
cherry tree with the top blown out. Unfortunately, on an early 2012 hike, only one
of the old hemlocks was alive. (See the sidebar for Hike 36.) After crossing a couple
of side streams, one below a small waterfall, you cross LeConte Creek on another foot

log. From this crossing, Rainbow Falls is visible high above. Continue up the trail to a final crossing below the falls.

Although the view from the foot log is great, many hikers scramble up the rocks to get closer and to find different vantage points for photographs. Exercise extreme caution if you do this.

Miles and Directions

0.0 Start from the western end of the parking area on the obvious trail.

0.1 Cross Trillium Gap Trail.

2.7 Arrive at Rainbow Falls. Return the way you came.

5.4 Arrive back at trailhead.

Option: Rainbow Falls Trail continues from the waterfall to Mount LeConte's summit, but most hikers turn around at the falls. Hike 35 passes by Rainbow Falls on its way to LeConte's summit. To plan a Mount LeConte excursion, see "Hiking to Mount LeConte" at the beginning of the Northeast section.

Rainbow Falls.

35 Mount LeConte via Rainbow Falls and Bull Head

The only way to hike to Mount LeConte and return to your car without backtracking or long road walking is by utilizing Rainbow Falls Trail and Bull Head Trail. The first 2.7 miles to Rainbow Falls, detailed in Hike 34, is always crowded. Most people turn around at the falls, so the rest of the hike will be much less crowded.

(See map for Hike 34: Rainbow Falls.)

Start: Rainbow Falls trailhead on Cherokee Orchard Road
Distance: 13.6-mile loop
Hiking time: About 8 hours—day hike or overnighter
Difficulty: Strenuous, due to steep grades and rocky trail
Trail surface: Forest trail with lots of rocks
Other trail users: Hikers only
Maps: Mount LeConte USGS quad; Trails Illustrated #229 Great Smoky Mountains; Trails Illustrated #317 Clingmans Dome Cataloochee; Trails Illustrated #316 Cades Cove Elkmont (only shows the trailhead and the lower portion of Bullhead Trail)
Special considerations: A good portion of this hike is very rocky and unsuitable for sandals.

If hiking in winter or early spring, make sure you prepare for cold weather at the higher elevations. You could start out from the trailhead with temperatures in the forties or fifties Fahrenheit and find yourself hiking in a blizzard on LeConte's summit.

If you wish to spend the night at LeConte Lodge on Mount LeConte's summit, you'll need to make reservations well ahead of time. The backcountry shelter on Mount LeConte also requires reservations, as do all other shelters in the park. Read "Hiking to Mount LeConte" at the beginning of the Northeast section.
Other: Although there's room for several vehicles, the parking area fills quickly. Additional parking is available 0.1 mile farther on Cherokee Orchard Road. Pit toilets are available at the main parking area.

Finding the trailhead: From US 441 in Gatlinburg, turn at traffic light #8 onto Historic Nature Trail-Airport Road and drive 0.6 mile to a confusing intersection. Stay to the right and continue straight ahead. You soon enter the park on Cherokee Orchard Road. Reach the parking area for Rainbow Falls Trail and Bull Head Trail at 3.3 miles from traffic light #8 (GPS: N35 40.551' / W83 29.147'). Rainbow Falls Trail begins from the western end of the parking area.

The Hike

Begin on Rainbow Falls Trail at the western end of the main parking area. In a few hundred feet you cross Trillium Gap Trail and begin climbing alongside LeConte Creek on a rocky path. The steady ascent continues all the way to the falls, and so do the rocks. You might be tempted to rename this trail the "Rocky Falls Trail" before you finish. LeConte Creek keeps close company most of the way. Only at a few places does the trail get out of earshot of the creek.

After a mile or so, the trail swings away and comes to a sharp right switchback. In winter there's a view back toward Gatlinburg. You can see the Gatlinburg Space

Needle and the Park Vista Hotel. Work your way back toward the creek and come to a high overlook at a left-hand turn in the trail. There's a perfect sitting rock here at a silverbell tree. From here, the trail makes a quick swing away from the creek, then returns to parallel it on a high bench before making the first crossing on a foot log.

Now the big trees start to appear. There are several large hemlocks and a huge cherry tree with the top blown out. Unfortunately, on an early 2012 hike, only one of the old hemlocks was alive. (See the sidebar for Hike 36.) After crossing a couple of side streams, one below a small waterfall, you cross LeConte Creek on another foot log. From this crossing, Rainbow Falls is visible high above. Continue up the trail to a crossing below the falls.

From Rainbow Falls, the trail swings away from LeConte Creek and crosses a side stream twice before working back to the creek. This is the final crossing of LeConte Creek. There's no foot log, but you don't need one here. Often the creek runs underground, making this is a dry crossing.

Now you leave the creek and begin a long ascent on switchbacks that takes you to Rocky Spur, the prominent ridge separating the LeConte Creek and Roaring Fork watersheds. As you cross the ridgeline, look to the left and you might catch a glimpse of Gatlinburg. It's better, though, to pay attention to the trail and its many nuances. Notice the difference, for instance, in the vegetation now that you've rounded the ridge to the north-facing slope. Here are hemlocks and rhododendron, and the forest is darker, cooler, and wetter. Back on the south-facing slope, you passed through mountain laurel, with a ground cover of galax and trailing arbutus growing along the trail.

Continue on the north side of Rocky Spur for about a mile, make a switchback, and continue a short distance before rounding back to the south side. Look up ahead at that mountaintop. That's Cliff Top, where you'll want to watch the sunset if staying overnight on LeConte's summit. Pressing on, a side path turns off to the left and rejoins the main trail a few yards ahead. By now your energy is likely sapped and exploring this side trail to the top of Rocky Spur is probably not an appealing thought. Don't worry, you didn't miss very much.

Soon the trail swings around to the right and begins skirting Mount LeConte's summit. Cross the trickling headwaters of LeConte Creek (oops, that previous crossing wasn't the final one after all) and look north for great views of Rocky Spur, which you just ascended. To the west is an open view of Gatlinburg and its Space Needle.

Now you come to the junction with Bull Head Trail, coming in from the right. From here, it's a little more than a half a mile on a very rocky course to LeConte Lodge. At the lodge pat yourself on the back. You've made a near-continuous climb from the parking area on a long, difficult, rocky trail. Tomorrow, or in a little while if you are doing this hike in one day, you'll head back down Rainbow Falls Trail and turn west on Bull Head Trail. Fill up your water bottle before you start, though. Bull Head Trail is dry as a bone.

Now on Bull Head Trail heading west, two things immediately come to mind. First, this trail is not nearly as steep as Rainbow Falls Trail, and second, it's not nearly as rocky. The steepness increases later on, but you can enjoy a long stretch of easy hiking. This section of trail is great for viewing summer wildflowers. Farther down, it's better for spring wildflowers.

As the trail approaches Balsam Point, it switches to the south side of the ridge and begins descending much more steeply. It continues to do so until reaching a flat spot on the ridge leading to Bull Head. Just before here, you pass through what must be the longest rhododendron and mountain laurel tunnel in the park. On the ridge is the "Pulpit"—a stack of rocks made by the crews who built this trail. There's a fair view off the north side, but it's not as good as the views you had farther back up the trail.

Now enjoy a surprisingly long and level stretch. As you turn toward the south, look back up the trail to see Balsam Point far above that rhododendron tunnel you just passed through. Now the trail descends through a stand of pines killed by the southern pine beetle, a native insect. The vegetation here is indicative of the dry southern exposure: galax, wintergreen, trailing arbutus, and mountain laurel.

The trail swings around to a northern exposure and the vegetation changes instantly. Here it's cool and moist. Moss covers the rocks, and rhododendrons grow densely among the trees. This is a terrific spot to see spring wildflowers. Farther down, you pass two huge rock overhangs, one right after the other. They project completely over the trail and would provide great protection during a storm. Trouble is, there's never one of these things around when you need it.

The trail starts a serious descent now and continues that way to the junction with Old Sugarlands Trail. A left turn here takes you to Newfound Gap Road near Sugarlands Visitor Center. You want to go right and enjoy the easy 0.4-mile walk along the old road back to the trailhead.

Miles and Directions

0.0 Start from the western end of the parking area on the obvious trail.

0.1 Cross Trillium Gap Trail.

2.7 Arrive at Rainbow Falls. Continue on Rainbow Falls Trail.

6.1 Junction with Bull Head Trail, coming in from the right. Continue on Rainbow Falls Trail.

6.6 Junction with Alum Cave Trail, coming in from the right. Continue straight ahead a short distance to the lodge.

6.7 Arrive at LeConte Lodge and the junction with Trillium Gap Trail and The Boulevard Trail. After exploring the summit area, backtrack to junction with Bull Head Trail.

7.3 Return to junction with Bull Head Trail and turn left (west) on it.

13.2 Junction with Old Sugarlands Trail. Turn right (east) and follow the old roadbed back to the trailhead.

13.6 Arrive back at trailhead.

Options: For other ideas and to help plan a Mount LeConte excursion, see "Hiking to Mount LeConte" at the beginning of the Northeast section.

36 Grotto Falls

Grotto Falls is appropriately named. Roaring Fork spills from an overhanging ledge some 20 feet into a small pool, creating a dry space behind the falls for the trail to pass. The waterfall is lovely and makes a terrific photo subject. Postcard racks in Gatlinburg hold many different scenes of the falls. The hike to Grotto Falls is among the most popular in the park. Expect lots of company and get to the trailhead early if you want a parking space.

(See map for Hike 34: Rainbow Falls.)

Start: Parking area on Roaring Fork Motor Nature Trail
Distance: 2.6 miles out and back
Hiking time: About 2 hours—day hike
Difficulty: Moderate
Trail surface: Boot-, horse-, and llama-packed dirt
Other trail users: Equestrians (llamas use this trail as a route to supply LeConte Lodge)
Maps: Mount LeConte USGS quad; Trails Illustrated #229 Great Smoky Mountains; Trails Illustrated #317 Clingmans Dome Cataloochee
Special considerations: The access road

(Roaring Fork Motor Nature Trail) is closed Dec 1–Mar 31. An alternate winter access to Grotto Falls is to hike Trillium Gap Trail from the Rainbow Falls parking lot, but that access makes the hike 2.3 miles farther one-way, or 4.6 miles round-trip.
Other: The parking area holds several cars, but it fills up quickly on most days. When full, people park all along the road past the parking area, sometimes as far as 0.25 mile away. It isn't safe to park alongside this road and it damages the environment, so try to get here early for a suitable parking space. Pit toilets are available at the parking area.

Finding the trailhead: From US 441 in Gatlinburg, turn at traffic light #8 onto Historic Nature Trail–Airport Road and drive 0.6 mile to a confusing intersection. Stay to the right and continue straight ahead. You soon enter the park on Cherokee Orchard Road. At 3.6 miles from traffic light #8, you come to Roaring Fork Motor Nature Trail on the right. This one-way road passes old home-sites and several trailheads before looping back to Gatlinburg. At 1.7 miles from the start of the motor nature trail, you come to the parking area on the left for Grotto Falls. The trail begins across the road, at the far end of the parking area. GPS: N35 40.811' / W83 27.766'

The Hike

Start on the path from the parking area and hike a little more than 0.1 mile to join Trillium Gap Trail. Trillium Gap Trail leads to the summit of Mount LeConte, 6.6 miles and nearly 4,000 vertical feet from here. Don't worry: This hike barely makes a dent in either the elevation or total distance of the trail.

Continue straight ahead and climb moderately on hard-packed dirt all the way to the falls. Along the way you pass through a once-impressive old-growth hemlock forest. Now the huge hemlock trees that anchor this forest are dead or dying. (See the Hemlock Horror sidebar.) In and out you weave until finally rounding a ridge

Trillium Gap Trail passes behind Grotto Falls, giving hikers a unique view.

into the Roaring Fork drainage. From here, a short and level path takes you to Grotto Falls. The trail passes behind the waterfall, giving you an interesting perspective and a great photo op.

Miles and Directions

0.0   Start from the north end of the parking area on the obvious trail.

0.1   Trillium Gap Trail comes in from the right and goes straight ahead. Continue straight and follow Trillium Gap Trail to the falls.

1.3   Arrive at Grotto Falls. Return the way you came.

2.6   Arrive back at trailhead.

Option: Trillium Gap Trail continues from Grotto Falls to the summit of Mount LeConte. See Hike 37 for details. Also see "Hiking to Mount LeConte" at the beginning of the Northeast section.

HEMLOCK HORROR

In 2002 a park trail worker noticed a white cottony substance on the underside of a hemlock branch. This was the first documented sighting of the hemlock woolly adelgid (HWA) in the Smokies. First discovered in the East in the 1950s near Richmond, Virginia, the HWA spread across the state and in the late 1980s began attacking the hemlocks in Shenandoah National Park. Today, nearly every hemlock in that park is dead, as are most hemlocks all across the state.

In the Smokies researchers began combating the HWA soon after its discovery, using a variety of measures such as sprayed foliar treatments, systemic insecticides, and released predator beetles. This effort continues, but it may be too late for most of the park. Concentrated efforts in old-growth Hemlock Conservation Areas have been promising, but it takes five to ten years for biological controls like predator beetles to become established. No one anticipated just how quickly the HWA would spread across the park, or the entire southern Appalachian region for that matter. Today, the entire park is infested and most of the hemlocks are either already dead or will die soon.

The loss is incalculable, both from an aesthetic and an ecological standpoint. Eastern hemlock trees are among the most common trees in the park, as well as the oldest and largest. Hemlocks were not valued as a timber tree, so early loggers left a lot of them standing. Even in the second-growth forests of the Smokies, you could find giant hemlocks. In addition, more than 800 acres of old-growth hemlock forests occur in the Smokies, plus an additional 90,000 acres of younger hemlock forests of 75 to 100 years in age. For many people, these hemlock groves are, or were, the most beautiful and enchanting places in the park.

From an ecological standpoint, the loss of the hemlock trees and forests is frightening. Hemlocks serve an essential role in the ecosystem. With their large evergreen canopies, hemlock trees shade the forest floor, creating a microclimate that allows certain organisms to thrive. Streams that are shaded by hemlocks have lower water temperatures, which is vital to trout and some invertebrate species. Hemlock trees are also important for migrating birds. Some species of warblers nest almost exclusively in hemlocks. Researchers are studying these and other issues in an effort to understand the implications from the loss of the trees and to learn how to deal with them, but no one knows for sure what the impact will be.

When the chestnut blight wiped out American chestnut trees, oaks and hickories assumed a dominant role in the forest, and while they could not fully replace the chestnut's role, they were able to mitigate it. Acorns and hickory nuts became the primary food for bears and some other animals in place of chestnuts. With hemlocks, it's a different situation. No other tree can fill the ecological niche of the hemlock. Scientists don't know exactly what is going to happen, but what is certain is that the forest ecosystem of the Smokies, and all over the southern Appalachians, is going to change.

As of early 2012 the HWA infestation has killed hemlocks trees all over the park, and you will see the effects on nearly every trail, although there are still a few areas that seem to be doing OK. On some hikes, where the trail passes through old-growth hemlock groves or past the hemlock giants of the park, the scene is aesthetically horrific and redefines the nature of the hike.

It is too late to save most of the hemlock forests of the Smokies. We can only hope that we learn something positive from this episode. When the next alien pest begins attacking our native trees, as one surely will, let's hope that we will be better prepared and that we act quickly enough to thwart it.

37 Mount LeConte via Trillium Gap

For a trip to Mount LeConte, both this route and the route described in Hike 35 feature wildflowers, a scenic waterfall, and views. You can't go wrong with either hike. A feature of this hike is that it is wetter for much of the route, crossing numerous stream branches, and it is rife with verdancy. Hike 35 is dry along most of the upper portion of the hike. Another feature of Trillium Gap Trail is that it is the route used by the llama train to supply LeConte Lodge.

(See map for Hike 34: Rainbow Falls.)

Start: Parking area on Roaring Fork Motor Nature Trail
Distance: 13.4 miles out and back
Hiking time: About 8 hours—day hike or overnighter
Difficulty: Strenuous
Trail surface: Rocky forest trail
Best season: Spring for the wildflowers
Other trail users: Equestrians; llamas use this trail as a route to supply LeConte Lodge
Maps: Mount LeConte USGS quad; Trails Illustrated #229 Great Smoky Mountains; Trails Illustrated #317 Clingmans Dome Cataloochee
Special considerations: The access road (Roaring Fork Motor Nature Trail) is closed Dec 1–Mar 31. An alternate winter access route is to hike Trillium Gap Trail from the Rainbow Falls parking lot, but that access makes the hike 2.3 miles farther one-way, or 4.6 miles round-trip.

If you wish to spend the night at LeConte Lodge on Mount LeConte's summit, you'll need to make reservations well ahead of time. The backcountry shelter on Mount LeConte also requires reservations, as do all other shelters in the park. Read "Hiking to Mount LeConte" at the beginning of the Northeast section.

Other: The parking area holds several cars, but it fills up quickly on most days. When full, people park all along the road past the parking area, sometimes as far as 0.25 mile away. It isn't safe to park alongside this road and it damages the environment, so try to get here early for a suitable parking space. Pit toilets are available at the parking area.

Finding the trailhead: From US 441 in Gatlinburg, turn at traffic light #8 onto Historic Nature Trail-Airport Road and drive 0.6 mile to a confusing intersection. Stay to the right and continue straight ahead. You soon enter the park on Cherokee Orchard Road. At 3.6 miles from traffic light #8, you come to Roaring Fork Motor Nature Trail on the right. This one-way road passes old home-sites and several trailheads before looping back to Gatlinburg. At 1.7 miles from the start of the motor nature trail, you come to the large parking area on the left for Grotto Falls. The trail begins across the road, at the far end of the parking area. GPS: N35 40.811' / W83 27.766'

The Hike

Start on the path from the parking area and hike a little more than 0.1 mile to join Trillium Gap Trail. Continue straight ahead and climb moderately on hard-packed dirt all the way to the falls. Along the way you pass through a once-impressive old-growth hemlock forest. Now the huge hemlock trees that anchor this forest are dead

A llama train carrying supplies to LeConte Lodge passes behind Grotto Falls.

or dying. (See the sidebar for Hike 36.) In and out you weave until finally rounding a ridge into the Roaring Fork drainage. From here, a short and level path takes you to Grotto Falls. The trail passes behind the waterfall, giving you an interesting perspective and a great photo op.

Beyond the falls the trail is a little steeper and rockier, but it remains a pleasant hike through lush forest. You cross a couple of small streams, but you might want to hold off on filling your water bottle from them. The llamas have a habit of using the creeks as their restroom facilities. You should treat all water in the Smokies, but after you see an entire llama train doing their business in one of these creeks, filtering and boiling just doesn't seem to be adequate! There are several springs farther up, the last one on LeConte's summit. And there is treated drinking water from a pump at LeConte Lodge.

When you start to see grassy patches along the trail, you know you're nearing Trillium Gap. This is a typical beech gap, covered in dense grass and dominated by American beech trees. In early spring, spring beauty carpets the ground with so many blossoms that it looks like freshly fallen snow. Brushy Mountain Trail intersects at the gap, having climbed up the opposite side, and it continues on the left (north) to the summit of Brushy Mountain. If you have time, perhaps on the hike back down, the short side trip to Brushy is highly recommended (see Hike 40).

Water, rocks, and verdancy characterize the remaining 3.6 miles to LeConte's summit. The trail is steep and rocky, but the luxuriant vegetation takes your mind off the climb. Mosses, lichens, ferns, wildflowers, shrubs, and trees cover every square inch of ground except the rocky trail under your feet. You cross several creek branches, one below a postcard scene of a tiny waterfall flowing through mossy rocks. When you come to a sharp left-hand switchback after swinging around a broad ridge, look out over the drainage and see if you can see Twin Falls. The two falls are on small branches in the upper reaches of Roaring Fork. When the leaves are out, you probably won't see anything.

When you enter a fir tunnel, you're getting close to the trail's end. Soon you pass a horse-hitching rack on the right and then a spring on the left. LeConte Lodge is on the right, and the junction with The Boulevard Trail and Rainbow Falls Trail is just ahead.

Miles and Directions

0.0 Start from the north end of the parking area on the obvious trail.

0.1 Trillium Gap Trail comes in from the right and goes straight ahead. Continue straight and follow Trillium Gap Trail to the falls.

1.3 Walk behind Grotto Falls.

3.1 Junction with Brushy Mountain Trail at Trillium Gap. Side trip to Brushy Mountain summit is to the left (north) for 0.4 mile. To continue the hike to Mount LeConte, turn right (south) and remain on Trillium Gap Trail.

6.7 Arrive at LeConte Lodge on Mount LeConte summit. Return the way you came.

13.4 Arrive back at trailhead.

Option: You can turn this hike into a loop by utilizing the 2.3-mile section of Trillium Gap Trail between the Rainbow Falls parking area and the Grotto Falls parking area. You could hike to Mount LeConte via Trillium Gap Trail and return via either Rainbow Falls Trail or Bullhead Trail. See Hike 35 for details about these two trails.

THAT SURE IS A FUNNY-LOOKING HORSE

For a special treat when hiking Trillium Gap Trail to Mount LeConte, time your trip to coincide with the llama schedule. Every week, in season, a llama train heads up the trail early in the morning to supply LeConte Lodge with fresh food, clean laundry, and other necessities. They return by the same trail later in the day. The schedule may vary, but it's usually Monday, Wednesday, and Friday. You can find the current year's schedule on the lodge's website at www.lecontelodge.com. If you're spending the night on Mount LeConte, you can schedule to return on the day the llamas head up the mountain. That way, you're sure not to miss them.

38 Baskins Creek Falls

Considering the popularity of the Roaring Fork area and the short hike to Baskins Creek Falls, it's surprising that relatively few people make this hike. The waterfall is picturesque and well worth the difficult scramble required to reach the base. It's about 30 feet high and, interestingly, is located on Falls Branch and not Baskins Creek. Falls Branch joins Baskins Creek a short distance downstream.

(See map for Hike 34: Rainbow Falls.)

Start: Baskins Creek trailhead on Roaring Fork Motor Nature Trail
Distance: 6.0 miles out and back (3.2 miles if hiking only to falls and back)
Hiking time: About 3 hours—day hike
Difficulty: Strenuous, due to steep scramble path at falls
Trail surface: Forest trail
Other trail users: Hikers only
Maps: Mount LeConte USGS quad; Trails

Illustrated #229 Great Smoky Mountains; Trails Illustrated #317 Clingmans Dome Cataloochee
Special considerations: The access road (Roaring Fork Motor Nature Trail) is closed Dec 1–Mar 31. However, the ending trailhead is located close to the start of the motor nature trail.

One creek crossing on this hike could be a little tricky in very wet weather.
Other: The small parking area can fill up on weekends or anytime during the busy season. There are no facilities.

Finding the trailhead: From US 441 in Gatlinburg, turn at traffic light #8 onto Historic Nature Trail–Airport Road and drive 0.6 mile to a confusing intersection. Stay to the right and continue straight ahead. You soon enter the park on Cherokee Orchard Road. At 3.6 miles from traffic light #8, you come to Roaring Fork Motor Nature Trail on the right. This one-way road passes old home-sites and several trailheads before looping back to Gatlinburg. At 2.8 miles from the start of the motor nature trail, you come to a small parking area on the left, just before the Jim Bales Place. The obvious trail begins from the middle of the parking area. GPS: N35 41.649' / W83 27.984'

If doing this hike as a split-party hike or if starting from the other end as described in the Options, you'll find the ending trailhead on Roaring Fork Motor Nature Trail at 0.2 mile from the entrance gate. (You drive by it on the way to the start of the hike.) The trail crosses the road here; you want to hike on the left (north side). GPS: N35 40.663' / W83 28.716'

The Hike

Begin on the obvious path leading from the parking area. The trail passes a cemetery at the start of the hike before climbing to a ridgeline. After a short run on the ridge, you descend steeply to Baskins Creek. Don't take the side trail that forks right and heads downstream. Instead, cross the creek (tricky in high water) and make a short, steep climb over a small ridge. On the ridge crest, look out to the right to see the remains of an old chimney.

In summer cardinal flower grows in a tiny meadow below the ridge. Just beyond the meadow, on the right, is a side path leading to the waterfall. There may be a sign here indicating the falls, but the path is obvious. The side path leads about 0.3 mile to the base of the falls, passing an old homesite on the right and finally descending very steeply down the cliff at the falls.

Back on the main trail, to continue the hike, turn right and begin a gradual ascent. You'll soon pass another side path on the right, this one leading to Baskins Cemetery. Pressing on, the trail climbs steeply for a good distance, finally topping out on a ridge with winter views toward Gatlinburg. From here, you have a rather easy walk through a pleasant hardwood forest to the road. The trail crosses the road here and continues a few yards to its official terminus on Trillium Gap Trail.

Miles and Directions

0.0 Start on the obvious path from the middle of the parking area.

1.3 Obvious side path on the right leads to Baskins Creek Falls.

1.6 Arrive at base of waterfall. Return to main trail.

1.9 Turn right on main trail to continue hike.

3.3 End of hike at Roaring Fork Motor Nature Trail. Return the way you came.

6.0 Arrive back at trailhead.

Options: You can do this hike as a shuttle, but with less than 3 miles to get back to the trailhead, it might not be worth the hassle of bringing two cars. A better option might be a split-party hike. Have your group drop you off at trail's end, and hike it in reverse, meeting back up with them at the other end.

39 Porters Creek

It would be hard to pick a better spring hike in the Smokies than this one. For wild-flower lovers, this is about as good as it gets. Although most people do this trip as a day hike, if you're planning to spend a lot of time studying or photographing the wildflowers, a great option is to spend the night at Campsite 31 and backtrack the following day.

(See map with Hike 40: Brushy Mountain.)

Start: Porters Creek trailhead in the Greenbrier section of the park
Distance: 7.2 miles out and back
Hiking time: About 4 hours—day hike or overnighter
Difficulty: Moderate
Trail surface: Forest trail and old forest road
Best season: Spring for the wildflowers

Other trail users: Equestrians are permitted on the first mile
Maps: Mount LeConte and Mount Guyot USGS quads; Trails Illustrated #229 Great Smoky Mountains; Trails Illustrated #317 Clingmans Dome Cataloochee
Other: There's room for several vehicles scattered along the traffic loop, but there are no facilities. Pit toilets are available at the picnic areas on the gravel road leading to the trailhead.

Finding the trailhead: From US 441 in Gatlinburg, turn at traffic light #3 and drive east on US 321. At 5.9 miles turn right (south) onto Greenbrier Road. This road follows scenic Middle Prong of Little Pigeon River, changing to gravel just past the ranger station. Drive slowly, and watch for pedestrians in summer. At 3.1 miles the road to the Ramsey Cascades trailhead (Hike 41) turns left. Stay straight and continue another 0.9 mile to a traffic loop. Park at the far end of the loop, at the road gate. The trail is a continuation of the gravel road. GPS: N35 41.811' / W83 23.292'

The Hike

Start up the gravel road and soon come to a great view of Porters Creek at a washout. A little farther along you begin noticing relics of life before the park was established, such as rock walls and old homesites. Cross a small creek branch on a bridge and pass a nice patch of crested dwarf iris, just up the hill. An old cemetery lies to the right, and just beyond it is an old rusty vehicle sitting 100 feet into the woods. The road soon crosses a larger stream, this one with the option of wading the ford or crossing on a foot log. Kids love this one.

At 1.0 mile you reach the old traffic turnaround and the junction of three trails. On the far left, heading south along Porters Creek, is Porters Creek Trail. To the far right (west end) is a side trail leading a short distance to a historic farm site. (For a description of the site, see Hike 40.) In the middle of the two is the trailhead for Brushy Mountain Trail.

Continue on Porters Creek Trail and after 0.5 mile cross Porters Creek on two foot logs. If hiking in spring, you'll start to see what all the fuss is about as soon

*Large-flowered trillium (*Trillium grandiflorum*) carpets the mountainsides surrounding Fern Branch Falls.*

as you cross the creek. You'll see fringed phacelia, bishop's cap, several trillium and violet species, mayapple, blue cohosh, geranium, Fraser's sedge, toothwort, phlox—and countless more. Less than 0.5 mile farther, as if the wildflowers were not enough, you cross Fern Branch at the base of Fern Branch Falls. This surprisingly high waterfall tumbles over mossy rocks and logs.

Beyond the waterfall the wildflower displays continue, with the species variety depending upon the angle of the slope to the sun and the surrounding vegetation. At 3.6 miles the official trail ends at Campsite 31, a lovely site situated on a bank above Porters Creek. Some trail narratives state that Porters Creek Trail continues as an unmaintained route from Campsite 31 all the way to the Appalachian Trail at Dry Sluice Gap, 2,000 feet higher. It is not recommended that you hike on any unmaintained trails in the Smokies, but particular caution is advised for this one. The trail peters out in a short distance, and then you're facing a full mile of very steep rock scrambling.

Miles and Directions

0.0   Start at gate on the south end of the parking area.
1.0   Junction with Brushy Mountain Trail (center) and the side trail to the historic farm site (right). Stay to the left and continue following Porters Creek Trail upstream.
1.5   Cross Porters Creek.
1.8   Pass below Fern Branch Falls.
3.6   Arrive at Campsite 31. Return the way you came.
7.2   Arrive back at trailhead.

Option: The short side trip to the historic farm site (see Hike 40) is highly recommended.

40 Brushy Mountain

A fine outing featuring historic structures and ruins, wildflowers, and great views, the hike to Brushy Mountain is a gem of the Smokies. If you hike in April, expect lots of company along the first mile from folks hiking to see the wildflowers along Porters Creek (see Hike 39). Once you start on the Brushy Mountain Trail portion, you'll have most of the hike to yourself.

Start: Porters Creek trailhead in the Greenbrier section of the park
Distance: 11.8 miles out and back
Hiking time: About 6 hours—day hike
Difficulty: Moderate
Trail surface: Old forest road and forest trails
Best seasons: June for mountain laurel bloom, Aug for blueberries
Other trail users: Most of the hike is open to equestrians

Maps: Mount LeConte USGS quad; Trails Illustrated #229 Great Smoky Mountains; Trails Illustrated #317 Clingmans Dome Cataloochee
Other: There's room for several vehicles scattered along the traffic loop, but there are no facilities. Pit toilets are available at the picnic areas on the gravel road leading to the trailhead.

Finding the trailhead: From US 441 in Gatlinburg, turn at traffic light #3 and drive east on US 321. At 5.9 miles turn right (south) onto Greenbrier Road. This road follows scenic Middle Prong of Little Pigeon River, changing to gravel just past the ranger station. Drive slowly and watch for pedestrians in summer. At 3.1 miles the road to the Ramsey Cascades trailhead (Hike 41) turns left. Stay straight and continue another 0.9 mile to a traffic loop. Park at the far end of the loop, at the road gate. The trail is a continuation of the gravel road. GPS: N35 41.811' / W83 23.292'

The Hike

Start up the gravel road and soon come to a great view of Porters Creek at a washout. A little farther along you begin noticing relics of life before the park was established, such as rock walls and old homesites. Cross a small creek branch on a bridge and pass a nice patch of crested dwarf iris, just up the hill. An old cemetery lies to the right, and just beyond it is an old rusty vehicle sitting 100 feet into the woods. The road soon crosses a larger stream, this one with the option of wading the ford or crossing on a foot log. Kids love this one.

At 1.0 mile you reach the old traffic turnaround in an area known as Porters Flat. Three trails lead from here: On the far left, heading south along Porters Creek, is Porters Creek Trail; to the far right (west end) is a side trail leading a short distance to a historic farm site; and in the middle of the two is the trailhead for Brushy Mountain Trail.

The side trip to the farm site is recommended. The reconstructed buildings accurately represent structures that were common in pre-park days. There's a cantilevered barn, springhouse, and cabin. Smoky Mountains Hiking Club used the cabin as a hiking base camp for many years, but camping is now prohibited.

After exploring the farm site, take Brushy Mountain Trail and ascend past rock walls and other artifacts of early settlement, and cross a few small creek branches. The grade is easy at first but soon picks up and stays moderate the rest of the way.

Long Branch flows down the north side of a ridge and you get within earshot of it before turning to remain on the south side. Just beyond here is Fittified Spring, about 100 feet off the left side of the trail on a faint and easily missed path. Supposedly, an earthquake in 1916 caused this spring to flow intermittently, or in "fits." With summer vegetation, you might pass right by the spring and never see it.

If you're making this hike in late May or June when the mountain laurel blooms, the laurel tunnels up ahead are a highlight of the trip. Farther up on a rocky ridge, the trail opens up to a nice view. Now you enter a once-scenic forest with good-size hemlocks (now dead) and cross several small creek branches. One particularly scenic pool on Trillium Branch looks as though it could harbor a good-size brook trout. A good distance farther up, you cross Trillium Branch again. This time the creek creates a postcard-worthy scene as it slides and tumbles over mossy rocks.

Trillium Gap is a short distance from this last creek crossing. At the gap Trillium Gap Trail goes straight ahead down the other side to Grotto Falls and then Roaring Fork Motor Nature Trail. To the left it goes to Mount LeConte. Your hike goes right (north) on a deeply rutted trail and passes through a rhododendron tunnel, then a mountain laurel tunnel. The tunnels soon open up to great views of Mount LeConte behind you and the Porters Creek watershed to the right. Continue along the trail to a fork. The right fork leads a few feet to a restricted view toward the east. The left fork leads a few yards to a near-180-degree view toward the north. From that view, straight ahead (north) and below is the imposing Mount Winnesoka, to the right is Greenbrier Pinnacle, and to the left is Gatlinburg and the ever-present Space Needle. To the northeast, English Mountain looms in the distance. On a clear, smog-free day (a rare occurrence in the summer Smokies), you can see Pigeon Forge and Douglas Lake far to the northwest.

Brushy Mountain itself is worth the hike even if the views aren't clear. On its summit is a heath bald, with mountain laurel, Catawba rhododendron, sand myrtle, wintergreen, blueberry, and huckleberry—all shrubs or ground-cover plants.

After soaking up the views from Brushy Mountain's summit, return to the trailhead the way you came, or return to Trillium Gap and then head to Mount LeConte or Grotto Falls if doing one of those options.

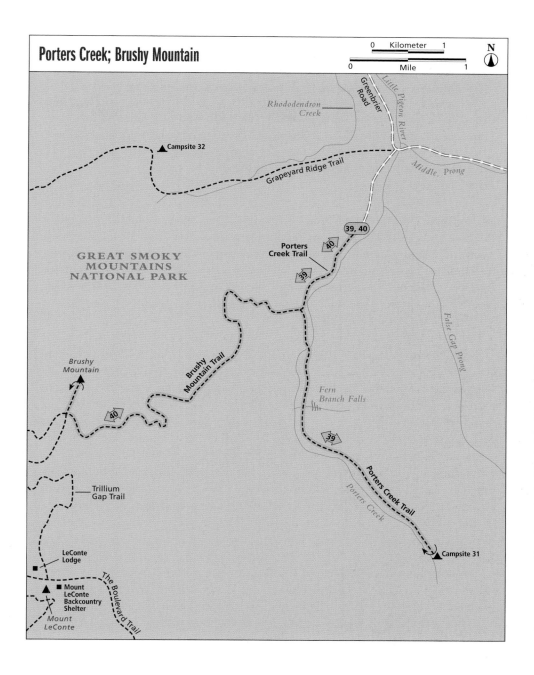

Porters Creek; Brushy Mountain

0 Kilometer 1

0 Mile 1

N

Little Pigeon River

Rhododendron Creek

Greenbrier Road

Middle Prong

Campsite 32

Grapeyard Ridge Trail

GREAT SMOKY MOUNTAINS NATIONAL PARK

39, 40

Porters Creek Trail

40

39

Brushy Mountain

Brushy Mountain Trail

False Gap Prong

Fern Branch Falls

40

39

Porters Creek Trail

Porters Creek

Trillium Gap Trail

LeConte Lodge

Mount LeConte Backcountry Shelter

Mount LeConte

The Boulevard Trail

Campsite 31

Miles and Directions

0.0 Start at the gate on the south end of the parking area.

1.0 Reach the junction with Brushy Mountain Trail (center) and the side trail to the historic farm site (right). Porters Creek Trail goes to the left (south) along the stream. After exploring the old farm site, return to this junction and take Brushy Mountain Trail, heading west.

5.5 Junction with Trillium Gap Trail at Trillium Gap. Turn right (north) to remain on Brushy Mountain Trail.

5.9 Arrive at the summit of Brushy Mountain. Return the way you came.

11.8 Arrive back at trailhead.

Options: With a second vehicle or shuttle, an excellent choice is to combine this hike with Hike 37. Leave a vehicle at the trailhead for Hike 37 and when you return to Trillium Gap from Brushy Mountain's summit, finish the hike by following Trillium Gap Trail to the west, passing by Grotto Falls along the way. Another option is to hike to Mount LeConte, following Trillium Gap Trail south from Trillium Gap.

41 Ramsey Cascades

Ramsey Cascades Trail provides an exceptional Smokies experience and is a good choice if you have only one day to hike in the park. The hike features abundant spring wildflowers, scenic old-growth forests, and the ever-present cascading streams. Ramsey Cascades is among the highest of the park's major waterfalls, and for some, the prettiest. Most literature lists the falls at 90 feet, but 60 feet is probably more accurate.

Start: Ramsey Cascades trailhead
Distance: 8.0 miles out and back
Hiking time: About 5.5 hours—day hike
Difficulty: Moderate, with a few steep sections
Trail surface: Little rocks, big rocks, roots, and a little dirt
Best season: Spring for the wildflowers
Other trail users: Hikers only
Maps: Mount Guyot USGS quad; Trails Illustrated #229 Great Smoky Mountains; Trails Illustrated #317 Clingmans Dome Cataloochee
Special considerations: It is tempting to climb the ledges that make up Ramsey Cascades; however, it is very dangerous to do so. A sign at the falls lists the number of people killed here.
Other: The trailhead has room for several cars, but there are no facilities. Pit toilets are available at the picnic areas on Greenbrier Road.

Finding the trailhead: From US 441 in Gatlinburg, turn at traffic light #3 and drive east on US 321. At 5.9 miles turn right (south) onto Greenbrier Road. This road follows scenic Middle Prong of Little Pigeon River, changing to gravel just past the ranger station. Drive slowly and watch for pedestrians in summer. At 3.1 miles the road to the Ramsey Cascades trailhead turns left and crosses Porters Creek. Drive 1.5 miles along this road to the trailhead parking area. GPS: N35 42.167' / W83 21.481'

The Hike

The trail, which is a continuation of the gravel road, begins east of the parking area. If you make this trek in April, the first thing you notice is a large patch of crested dwarf iris right beside the trail on the left. You then cross Little Laurel Branch on a culvert and immediately afterward cross Middle Prong of Little Pigeon River on a long footbridge. The bridge provides a great view of the cascading stream.

For the next 0.5 mile beyond the bridge, you pass through a terrific spring wildflower display. Showy orchis, creeping phlox, yellow trillium, wild geranium, and many other species grow here. The hiking is easy as the trail follows an old jeep road with only moderate grades. At 1.5 miles the jeep trail ends at a turnaround on the banks of Ramsey Prong, just before it enters Middle Prong. The old Greenbrier Pinnacle Trail cuts sharply to the left (north) just before the road ends. That trail leads to the sight of a former fire tower on the pinnacle, but the park no longer maintains the path. Ramsey Cascades Trail continues on the far side of the turnaround and follows Ramsey Prong upstream (east) through a dense understory of rhododendron.

Ramsey Cascades; Old Settlers Trail

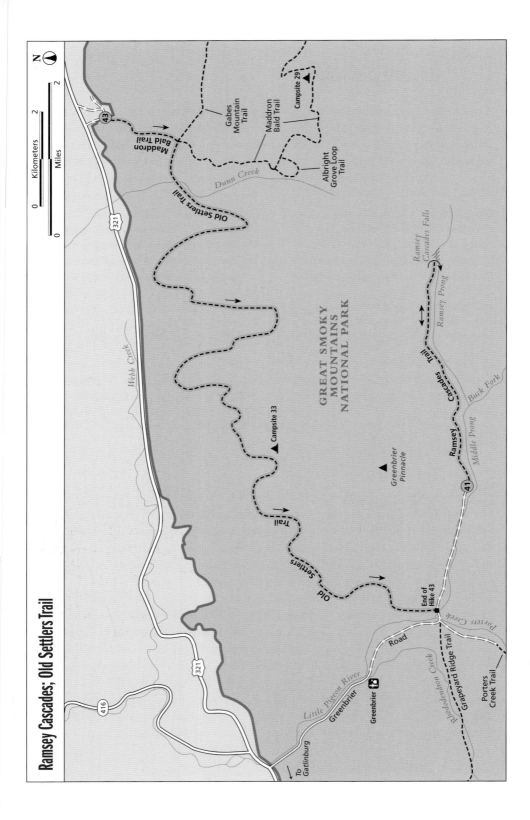

To Gatlinburg

416

321

Webb Creek

321

Little Pigeon River

Greenbrier

Greenbrier

Greenbrier Road

Rhododendron Creek

Grapeyard Ridge Trail

Porters Creek Trail

Porters Creek

End of Hike 43

41

Middle Prong

Buck Fork

Ramsey Cascades Trail

Ramsey Prong

Ramsey Cascades Falls

Old Settlers Trail

Old Settlers Trail

Greenbrier Pinnacle

Campsite 33

Campsite 29

Dunn Creek

Maddron Bald Trail

Maddron Bald Trail

Gabes Mountain Trail

Albright Grove Loop Trail

43

321

GREAT SMOKY MOUNTAINS NATIONAL PARK

N

0   2   Kilometers

0   2   Miles

You are now hiking on a bona fide Smokies trail, complete with slippery roots, rocks, and dense forest. At about 2.1 miles, a side stream crosses the trail and the forest opens up to a photogenic view of a rhododendron-framed cascade on Ramsey Prong. Just past this view, the trail crosses Ramsey Prong on an asphalt-covered foot log. Beyond the crossing the trail turns left and follows Ramsey Prong closely upstream. Many large hemlock skeletons stand along the trail, if they haven't yet toppled in a storm. At 2.6 miles you pass between two huge yellow poplars (tulip trees) and enter an enchanted cove forest with big trees and carpets of wildflowers. Moss and ferns cover everything in sight. Another yellow poplar, a massive one, is just ahead on the left.

After a steep section and several rock steps, the trail crosses Ramsey Prong for the last time at 2.9 miles. Leave the creek and rock-hop a side stream twice within a few hundred yards. The next 0.5 mile passes through a very scenic old-growth forest. As you near the falls, the trail approaches Ramsey Prong and the sound of crashing water makes you think you've arrived at the waterfall. It's only a tease, though, as the most difficult part of the hike is still to come. The next 0.3 mile is a continuous scramble over rocks and roots. You come to a side stream that enters Ramsey Prong just below the falls. Rock-hop the stream and scramble a few feet up to the base of the waterfall.

Miles and Directions

0.0   Start from the upper end of the parking area. The trail is a continuation of the road.

1.5   Old jeep road ends at a turnaround. The trail continues from the upper end.

4.0   Arrive at Ramsey Cascades. Return the way you came.

8.0   Arrive back at trailhead.

TOMATO OR TOMAHTO?

You might notice that *Ramsey* Cascades is spelled *Ramsay* Cascades on the USGS quad. It's not unusual for there to be more than one spelling of place names in the park. (In one nearby example, *Greenbrier* is often spelled *Greenbriar*.) In 2002 the U.S. Board on Geographic Names officially changed the name Ramsay to Ramsey. The name change reflects the correct spelling of its namesake, James Ramsey and his family, who settled in the area in the 1800s.

42 Albright Grove

Although the superlative scenic and ecological attributes of the Albright Grove hike are dulled by the devastating death of the eastern hemlock trees (see the sidebar for Hike 36), this hike remains a crown jewel in the Smokies. If you like big trees and lush forests, you'll love this hike. And if you don't like crowded trails, you'll like it even better. Relatively few people visit this remote section of the park.

Start: Maddron Bald trailhead in the Cosby section of the park
Distance: 6.8-mile lollipop (with a really long stick)
Hiking time: About 4 hours
Difficulty: Moderate
Trail surface: Old gravel road and rocky forest trails
Best season: Spring for the wildflowers
Other trail users: Hikers only
Maps: Jones Cove and Mount Guyot USGS quads; Trails Illustrated #229 Great Smoky Mountains; Trails Illustrated #317 Clingmans Dome Cataloochee
Special considerations: The trailhead may not be a safe place to leave your car. In the past, several vehicles have been stolen or vandalized. While such activity has subsided, you are still taking a chance parking here especially if leaving your vehicle overnight.
Other: There is room for only a few vehicles, but that's usually only a problem on summer weekends. Service stations and convenience stores are scattered along US 321.

Finding the trailhead: From US 441 in Gatlinburg, turn at traffic light #3 and head east on US 321. Drive 15.5 miles and turn right onto Baxter Road. (Baxter Road is about 0.1 mile beyond Yogi Bear's Jellystone Park Campground.) Stay on the paved Baxter Road for 0.3 mile and turn sharply right onto a gravel road. Go a few hundred feet to a gated dirt road on the left. Park here, but don't block the gate. GPS: N35 46.167' / W83 16.012'

The Hike

Begin at the gate on Maddron Bald Trail, an old wagon road, and climb moderately about 0.7 mile to the one-room Willis Baxter Cabin on the right. Continue climbing beyond the cabin, and at 1.2 miles you reach the junction with Old Settlers Trail on the right (Hike 43) and Gabes Mountain Trail on the left (Hike 46). Continue straight ahead on the old roadbed. About a mile farther the wagon road ends at an old traffic circle and the path becomes a real hiking trail.

For the remainder of the hike, you pass through an exceptional old-growth forest, with big yellow poplars (tulip trees), buckeyes, maples, silverbells, and other trees. Some of the largest and most common trees here are the eastern hemlocks. As of early 2012 many of the hemlocks are still alive, but the adelgid has killed most of them (see the sidebar for Hike 36).

About 0.5 mile from the old road turnaround, you cross the cascading Indian Camp Creek on a sturdy foot log, and in another 0.1 mile you come to the lower end

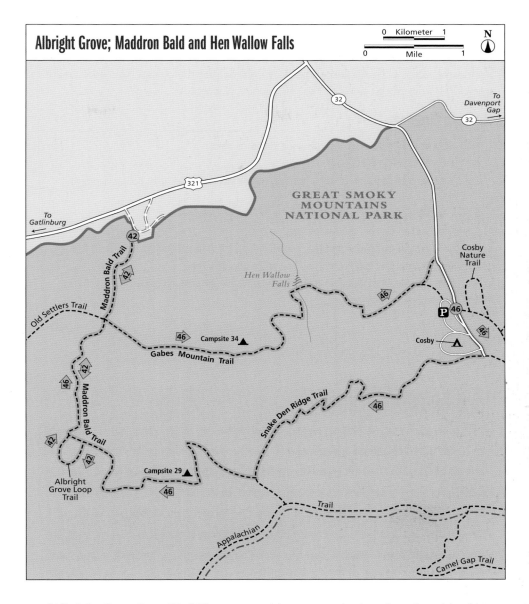

Albright Grove; Maddron Bald and Hen Wallow Falls

To Davenport Gap

To Gatlinburg

GREAT SMOKY MOUNTAINS NATIONAL PARK

Hen Wallow Falls

Cosby Nature Trail

Old Settlers Trail

Maddron Bald Trail

Campsite 34

Gabes Mountain Trail

Cosby

Snake Den Ridge Trail

Maddron Bald Trail

Campsite 29

Albright Grove Loop Trail

Appalachian Trail

Camel Gap Trail

of Albright Grove Loop Trail. You can go either way at the junction, since it's a loop hike. If going left and hiking the loop clockwise, remain on Maddron Bald Trail and ascend another 0.3 mile to the upper junction with Albright Grove Loop Trail. Turn right and follow the trail back to the lower junction.

Albright Grove is considered by many to be the finest old-growth forest in the park. However, the forest has changed dramatically in the past decade. Most of the huge hemlocks have died and the resultant sunlight reaching the forest floor has enabled weedy vegetation to gain a foothold. Also, two of the big yellow poplars are now dead, although an enormous one still remains. The 0.9-mile stretch between the end of the old road and the upper junction with the loop trail is in many ways just as impressive as the 0.7-mile loop trail. However, despite the change, this hike remains one of the finest forest hikes in the southern Appalachians.

Miles and Directions

0.0   Start at the gate and walk south along the gravel road.

0.7   Pass by Willis Baxter Cabin.

1.2   Junction with Old Settlers Trail (right) and Gabes Mountain Trail (left). Continue straight ahead.

2.3   Old road ends and real trail begins.

2.8   Cross Indian Camp Creek on foot log.

2.9   Lower junction with Albright Grove Loop Trail. Turn left to remain on Maddron Bald Trail.

3.2   Turn right onto Albright Grove Loop Trail at the upper junction.

3.9   Return to Maddron Bald Trail. Return to the trailhead the way you came.

6.8   Arrive back at trailhead.

Options: Hike 46, a one- to two-night backpacking trip, passes Albright Grove Loop Trail and other old-growth stands.

OLD-GROWTH GRANDEUR

Before the park was established, loggers had entered every major watershed of the Smokies. Some of the operations were enormous, even by today's standards. It's safe to say that without the park, the only old-growth forest remaining in the Smokies today would be in very small, isolated pockets. When the last logger pulled out in 1938, some 20 percent—100,000 acres—of old-growth forest remained. It is by far the largest tract of relatively undisturbed forest in the East. Albright Grove is one of the best locations in the park to see big trees, but a forest doesn't have to have big trees to qualify as old growth. For instance, in areas with harsh growing conditions, such as on exposed ridges and mountaintops, trees can be stunted and appear young, even though the forest ecosystem there may be very old and undisturbed. Of course, most visitors to the park would rather see big trees than stunted ones. See the Trail Finder in the introduction for a list of hikes other than Albright Grove where you can see some giants.

43 Old Settlers Trail

This hike isn't for everyone. In summer it's hot, buggy, overgrown, and infested with poison ivy. The views aren't good and the forest is mostly second growth. It's long and tiring, though only a few sections are steep. But if you're a history buff, this trail was made especially for you. Old Settlers Trail passes by (and through) more evidence of early-settlement history than does any other trail in the park. There are old rock walls, cemeteries, chimneys, wagon traces, rotting structures, and pieces of old stoves and dishes scattered about. Some of the stone walls are remarkable, as though the builders were trying to show off instead of just clearing a plot for planting or clearing a roadbed.

Old Settlers Trail is an assemblage of old paths and wagon roads, with many side paths leading off of it. A few of these side paths connect the trail with US 321, creating the possibility of breaking this hike into smaller segments. However, the trailheads on US 321 are not marked and it's frustrating trying to find them and then to find a safe place to park. The best bet is to stick with the hike as presented here and stay on the main trail. The side paths on this hike are too numerous to list. In most cases it is obvious which route is the main trail. Trail signs mark all questionable junctions.

(See map for Hike 41: Ramsey Cascades.)

Start: Maddron Bald trailhead
Distance: 17.0 miles point to point
Hiking time: About 9 hours—day hike or overnighter
Difficulty: Moderate
Trail surface: Old wagon roads and forest trails
Best season: Winter or early spring before the poison ivy comes out
Other trail users: Hikers only
Maps: Jones Cove, Mount Guyot, and Mount LeConte USGS quads; Trails Illustrated #229 Great Smoky Mountains; Trails Illustrated #317 Clingmans Dome Cataloochee
Special considerations: Poison ivy is abundant along most of this hike. Consider making

this hike in winter, when the leaves are gone. Wintertime also better reveals the rock walls, cemeteries, and other artifacts of early settlement.

You need a shuttle to make this hike. If you use 2 vehicles, note that the trailhead off US 321 may not be a safe place to leave your car. In the past, several vehicles have been stolen or vandalized. While such activity has subsided, you still take a chance parking here. The best option is to leave your vehicle at the Greenbrier trailhead and have a shuttle bring you to the trailhead off US 321.
Other: Both trailheads hold only a few vehicles, but that shouldn't be a problem. Neither trailhead has facilities of any kind.

Finding the trailhead: The hike ends at Old Settlers trailhead in the Greenbrier section of the park. You need to leave a vehicle here and drive to the starting trailhead or arrange for a shuttle service to pick you up here. To get here from US 441 in Gatlinburg, turn at traffic light #3 and drive east on US 321. At 5.9 miles turn right (south) onto Greenbrier Road. This road follows scenic Middle Prong of Little Pigeon River, changing to gravel just past the ranger station. Drive slowly, and watch for pedestrians in summer. At 3.1 miles the road to Ramsey Cascades trailhead turns left and immediately crosses Porters Creek. Take this road and cross three bridges in the first 0.1 mile. Park just beyond the third bridge, on the left. GPS: N35 42.467' / W83 22.794'

To get to the start of the hike, go back to US 321 and turn right. Drive 9.6 miles from the Greenbrier entrance (15.5 miles from Gatlinburg) and turn right onto Baxter Road. (Baxter Road is about 0.1 mile beyond Yogi Bear's Jellystone Park Campground.) Stay on the paved Baxter Road for 0.3 mile and turn sharply right onto a gravel road. Go a few hundred feet to a gated dirt road on the left. Park here, but don't block the gate. GPS: N35 46.167' / W83 16.012'

The Hike

Begin on the Maddron Bald Trail, which starts as an old wagon road, and climb moderately for about 0.7 mile to the one-room Willis Baxter Cabin on the right. Beyond the cabin the ascent continues, and at 1.2 miles you reach the junction with Gabes Mountain Trail on the left and Old Settlers Trail on the right. Maddron Bald Trail continues straight ahead, but you want to turn right (north) onto Old Settlers Trail. You'll stay on the trail for the rest of the hike.

Descend through a hemlock forest to pick up an old wagon road—a common theme on this hike. Look closely here and from now on for evidence of pre-park settlement. There are some old metal pieces (a stove?) on the left and remnants from a chimney on the right. A side path leads from the chimney to a cemetery that has only slabs of rock as headstones. Now cross a small creek branch and shortly afterward cross Indian Camp Creek on a sturdy foot log. Next comes a rock-hop of Dunn Creek, which could be tricky in high water. Notice the fine rock wall on the left just beyond the crossing. Now begin a long, gradual ascent up a small drainage and swing around sharply to the right on a switchback. Now it's a climb up and around Snag Mountain (look for mountain laurel blooms in June) and a descent to a small tributary of Webb Creek. An old homesite sits on the left, just beyond the creek. Pick up an old wagon road and follow it down a small ridge to another crossing of the tributary.

You soon meet up with Webb Creek and follow alongside it. There are rock walls everywhere—to the right, across the creek, and even one across the trail that you have to walk through. Where the trail crosses the creek, a sign says that the T. McCarter Barn is 600 feet to the right. The side path leads to a left turn onto an old road that leads to the barn. Behind the barn, another path leads several yards to the foundation remains of a homesite and a standing springhouse. Be careful: The path is overgrown with poison ivy. You're not far from US 321 at this point and you can hear the traffic.

Back on the main trail, cross Webb Creek and pass an impressive rock wall on the left that's nearly 6 feet high. The best rock wall of the entire hike (and probably in all the park) is just ahead. The wall is 5 feet high, 3 feet thick, and about 100 yards long. No stone seems out of place, as though they were placed according to a computer-generated master plan.

Now cross several small creek branches and come to Texas Creek, where the trail joins an old roadbed and heads upstream. (A side path at this point follows the creek

Numerous rock walls are found along Old Settlers Trail.

downstream to US 321.) About a quarter mile upstream, you pass a homesite on the left with two chimney remains and some rotten timber lying in one corner. Now climb—steeply in places—high into the Texas Creek drainage, crossing several feeder streams and finally crossing Texas Creek before swinging out of the drainage. The trail then climbs to a ridge and descends through a scenic forest with some good-size eastern hemlocks and yellow poplars (tulip trees). In this forest you'll find the greatest concentration of fallen American chestnut trees you'll likely see anywhere in the park. Soon the downfall will include the hemlocks, after dying from the hemlock wooly adelgid infestation. (See the sidebar for Hike 36.)

After crossing Tumbling Creek you quickly climb over a ridge and descend steeply to pick up an old roadbed along Noisy Creek. Soon you cross the creek twice in quick succession and a third time a little farther down. After the third crossing the trail continues to follow the roadbed along the creek to a fork. The path on the right follows the creek downstream to US 321, while your trail turns left and heads away from the creek.

Pass more rock walls and a chimney on the left, and then swing around into the Ramsey Creek drainage and follow that creek upstream, crossing it five times and passing two chimneys. After the fifth crossing the trail begins a brutal climb—the steepest of the hike—and passes a chimney on the left. After moderating the ascent and rounding a broad ridge, the trail descends through a dry forest of pines (killed by southern pine beetles), oaks, sourwood, and mountain laurel to a crossing of Redwine Creek.

Just beyond the creek crossing lies Campsite 33, situated directly on top of an old homesite. You can pitch your tent in the former living room. Rocks from the crumbling chimney have been commandeered for the fire ring and as chairs. Park rules strictly forbid such activity, so don't contribute.

Shortly beyond the campsite, the trail swings left around a ridge, while another path goes right and follows the ridge. Staying left on the main trail, you pass more rock walls and then a chimney right beside the trail. Just past the chimney, the trail crosses an old roadbed. About 25 yards to the left sits an old log structure without a roof. A right turn on the roadbed leads to US 321. You want to go straight and descend to cross Timothy Creek.

Shortly beyond the creek crossing, the trail descends steeply for a short distance before moderating and following a drainage downstream. As the grade begins to level out, an obvious path goes to the right, but you need to stay to the left as the sign indicates. Shortly beyond here, the terrain flattens and you experience the rare occurrence of a totally level hike in the Smokies. This was prime bottomland for early settlers.

Once through the bottomland, the trail ascends alongside Soak Ash Creek and follows it high into the drainage, crossing it a few times and passing another homesite. Finally, the trail leaves the drainage and goes on a long gradual climb to cross Copeland Divide. In doing so, you climb some, level some, descend some, and cross Snakefeeder Branch. But mostly you climb.

Once over Copeland Divide you descend to pick up the Little Bird Branch drainage, eventually crossing the branch and following it downstream before swinging away, crossing an unnamed branch, and then arriving at Bird Branch. Cross Bird Branch and enjoy the level 0.3-mile final push to the trailhead.

Miles and Directions

0.0 Start on Maddron Bald Trail, the signed and obvious roadbed leading from the parking area.

1.2 Junction with Old Settlers Trail and Gabes Mountain Trail. Turn right (north) onto Old Settlers Trail.

10.4 Campsite 33.

17.0 Trailhead on Ramsey Cascades Road.

44 Cosby Nature Trail

Cosby Self-Guiding Nature Trail makes a great outing for families staying at the nearby campground, but it's also worth driving here just for the hike. The trail passes through a splendid forest with many large trees. In spring wildflowers carpet the ground. Use the trail brochure to learn some of the history and nature at the numbered posts.

Start: Cosby Campground
Distance: 1.0-mile loop
Hiking time: About 45 minutes
Difficulty: Easy
Trail surface: Forest trail
Best season: Spring for the wildflowers
Other trail users: Hikers only
Maps: Hartford USGS quad; Trails Illustrated #229 Great Smoky Mountains; Trails Illustrated #317 Clingmans Dome Cataloochee

Other: The parking lot holds only a few vehicles, but you shouldn't have a problem. If it's full, you can park at the hiker parking lot behind the campground registration building, which is where you want to park for any extended hiking in the area. Restrooms are available at the picnic area.

Finding the trailhead: From the US 321 and TN 32 junction in Cosby, drive 1.2 miles and turn right at the sign for Cosby Campground. Follow this road 2.2 miles (passing by the trailhead for Hikes 45 and 46) to the parking lot on the left at the campground amphitheater. The signed and obvious trail begins from the parking lot. GPS: N35 45.245' / W83 12.419'

The Hike

Start from the parking lot and in a few feet meet Low Gap Trail. Low Gap Trail starts at the hiker parking area behind the campground registration building and creates part of the loop for the nature trail on its way to the Appalachian Trail. Turn right, but do not take the immediate side path that leads down to Cosby Creek. Continue straight, and in a short distance, another path turns to the left. Take this path and wind through a scenic forest and over numerous foot logs. You come back to Low Gap Trail a short distance above where you broke off from it. Turn right, cross Cosby Creek on a foot log, and then come to a side path cutting sharply left that leads to the road. Stay to the right and hike a short distance back to the trailhead.

Miles and Directions

0.0 Start on the obvious path from the parking lot. In a few feet turn right on Low Gap Trail and pass by a side path on the left.

0.1 Look for a signed path on the left for the nature trail.

0.8 The nature trail returns to Low Gap Trail. Turn right on it.

1.0 Arrive back at trailhead.

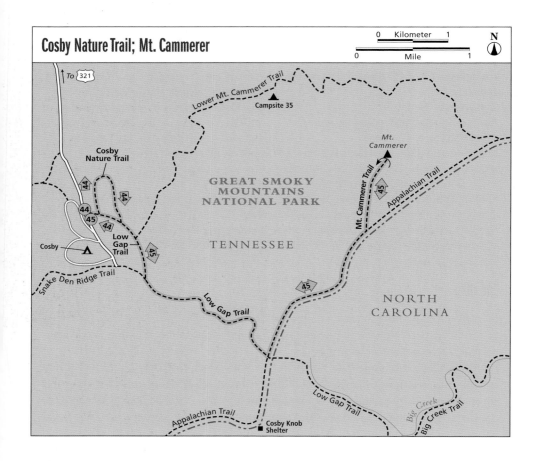

Cosby Nature Trail; Mt. Cammerer

45 Mount Cammerer

This hike provides the shortest route to the Mount Cammerer Lookout on the rocky summit of Mount Cammerer. The Civilian Conservation Corps built the fire lookout in the 1930s, using the same design as the lookouts on the treeless and rocky mountains of the western states. After falling in disrepair the lookout was restored in 1995 and it is now open for hikers to enjoy, although it is again in need of some repair. The panoramic view from the lookout is spectacular at any time, but if you can make this hike in October when the autumn foliage peaks, you'll have a hard time pulling yourself away.

(See map for Hike 44: Cosby Nature Trail.)

Start: Low Gap trailhead at the entrance to Cosby Campground
Distance: 11.2 miles out and back
Hiking time: About 7 hours—day hike
Difficulty: Strenuous, due to steep grade
Trail surface: Rocks, roots, and a little dirt
Best seasons: Spring for the wildflowers, Oct for autumn foliage

Other trail users: Equestrians
Maps: Hartford and Luftee Knob USGS quads; Trails Illustrated #229 Great Smoky Mountains; Trails Illustrated #317 Clingmans Dome Cataloochee
Other: The hiker parking lot is plenty large enough most of the time. If it's full, picnic area parking is right behind it. Restrooms are available at the picnic area.

Finding the trailhead: From the US 321 and TN 32 junction in Cosby, drive 1.2 miles and turn right at the sign for Cosby Campground. Follow this road 2.1 miles to the campground registration building. Drive past the building and turn left to loop back to the hiker parking area. Low Gap Trail starts on the south end of the parking area. GPS: N35 45.353' / W83 12.496'

The Hike

Low Gap Trail begins from the hiker parking area and soon passes behind the campground amphitheater and the trailhead for Cosby Nature Trail. Pay attention to the trail signs through here, because a number of paths lead off from the main trail. At 0.4 mile you come to what looks like an old traffic turnaround. A right turn here takes you over a ford of Cosby Creek and to the campground. Don't turn right; go to the left for a few yards to the junction with Lower Mount Cammerer Trail. Turn right (south) at this junction to stay on Low Gap Trail.

At 0.8 mile you come to a T junction, with the path on the right leading back to the campground. You want to go to the left and follow Cosby Creek upstream. The forest to this point is very scenic, with many large trees and a carpet of spring wildflowers. As of early 2012, even some of the eastern hemlocks seem to be doing OK here (see the sidebar for Hike 36).

Mount Cammerer Lookout.

The next 2.1 miles is a steady uphill grind over rocks and roots to Low Gap on the Appalachian Trail (AT). At Low Gap turn left (north) on the AT and continue the steady climb for about a mile before leveling out on an easier grade. At 2.1 miles from Low Gap, you reach the junction with Mount Cammerer Trail. The AT goes to the right and descends, while you want to go left (straight ahead, actually) and continue following the ridgeline. After hiking 0.5 mile on Mount Cammerer Trail, you come to a horse-hitching rack. The trail continues behind a No Horses sign another 0.1 mile to the lookout. (As rough as the trail is, you have to feel sorry for any horse that makes it to the rack!)

After resting and soaking up the views from the lookout, retrace your steps to the trailhead.

Miles and Directions

0.0   Begin hiking south on Low Gap Trail.

0.1   Pass behind the campground amphitheater at the trailhead for Cosby Self-Guiding Nature Trail. Continue straight ahead and cross a branch. The nature trail turns to the left. Continue straight on the main path.

0.3   Trail forks. Take the left fork and cross small branch and a short distance farther cross Cosby Creek.

0.4   Come to a T intersection. Turn left (away from the creek) and in 100 feet come to junction with Lower Mount Cammerer Trail, which continues straight ahead. Turn right (south) to continue on Low Gap Trail.

0.8 T intersection at Cosby Creek. Turn left and follow the trail upstream.

2.9 Junction with the AT. Turn left (north).

5.0 Junction with Mount Cammerer Trail. AT veers to the right and goes downhill. Continue straight ahead on Mount Cammerer Trail.

5.6 Arrive at Mount Cammerer Lookout. Return the way you came.

11.2 Arrive back at trailhead.

Options: The described hike is the shortest route to the lookout. A longer route that does not require backtracking uses Lower Mount Cammerer Trail. You take it at the junction with Low Gap Trail near Cosby Campground and hike about 7.5 miles to the AT. A right turn on the AT takes you to the Mount Cammerer Trail in 2.3 miles. Complete the loop by taking the AT down to Low Gap Trail and then following it back to the trailhead. Total round-trip mileage for this option is about 18.7 miles. That's tough for a day hike. You could overnight at Campsite 35 on Lower Mount Cammerer Trail to break up the hike, but the extra weight from camping gear makes the hike just as difficult to do in two days as in one day unencumbered. Don't be tempted to spend the night at Mount Cammerer Lookout. This is strictly prohibited. You will see the damage from campers and others who have misused this historic lookout.

Another route to Mount Cammerer is from Davenport Gap. You hike 5.3 tough miles on the AT to the Mount Cammerer Trail junction. This route is more strenuous, and it may not be safe to leave a vehicle at Davenport Gap. For a day hike, the route presented here is the best option.

Hike 80 also passes Mount Cammerer on its route.

TOWER OR LOOKOUT?

At one time ten fire towers existed within the boundaries of Great Smoky Mountains National Park. Only four remain. Three of those, Cove Mountain, Mount Sterling, and Shuckstack, are all of the same design—60-foot steel towers with an enclosed cabin at the top. These are referred to as "fire towers." The fourth, Mount Cammerer, is of a totally different design and is usually called a "lookout." Generally, the term "tower" refers to an observation structure that rises high above the landscape, often built to rise above the trees, while a "lookout" refers to a structure that is at or near ground level.

Mount Cammerer Lookout is believed to be the only one of its kind in the East. When you see the view from it, you won't care whether it's a lookout, a tower, or just an overlook. You can go inside, but the view is not good through the stained and scratched windows. The wraparound deck allows you to experience the views without obstruction.

46 Maddron Bald and Hen Wallow Falls

For people who like trees, this may be the best backpacking trip in the park. Much of the hike passes through old-growth forest, including what many people believe to be the finest "virgin" woods in the park, at Albright Grove. Throw in a high and pretty waterfall, abundant spring wildflowers, and a heath bald, and you have a grand adventure ahead of you.

(See map for Hike 42: Albright Grove.)

Start: Snake Den Ridge trailhead at Cosby Campground
Distance: 18.1-mile loop
Hiking time: About 10 hours—tough day hike, overnighter, or 2-nighter
Difficulty: Strenuous
Trail surface: Forest trails and old forest road
Best season: Spring for the wildflowers
Other trail users: The first 4.9 miles is open to equestrians; the remainder of the hike is for hikers only.

Maps: Hartford, Luftee Knob, Mount Guyot, and Jones Cove USGS quads; Trails Illustrated #229 Great Smoky Mountains; Trails Illustrated #317 Clingmans Dome Cataloochee

Other: The hiker parking lot is plenty large enough most of the time. If it's full, picnic area parking is right behind it. Restrooms are available at the picnic area.

Finding the trailhead: From the US 321 and TN 32 junction in Cosby, drive 1.2 miles and turn right at the sign for Cosby Campground. Follow this road 2.1 miles to the campground registration building. Drive past the building and turn left to loop back to the hiker parking area (GPS: N35 45.353' / W83 12.496'). The hike begins by following the road into the campground.

The Hike

From the parking area, walk through the campground to Campsite B51. Snake Den Ridge Trail enters the forest directly opposite the campsite and climbs gradually along an old roadbed. Soon you pass Cosby Horse Trail, which comes in from the left. The horse trail serves as a connector to Low Gap Trail. Stay to the right and continue climbing along the old roadbed. You soon pass an old graveyard on the right and shortly afterward reach an old turnaround. A side path on the right leads a few feet to a concrete slab and an overlook of Rock Creek. Look for clumps of showy orchis in April.

A few feet from the side path, Snake Den Ridge Trail continues past three boulders on the right and is now a bona fide trail. Hike through a scenic forest of hemlock and basswood with an understory of rhododendron, and soon cross Rock Creek on a foot log. The forest continues to be picturesque, with good-size trees, although many of the large hemlocks are dead. There's yellow poplar (tulip tree), silverbell, and maple. Spring wildflowers carpet the ground.

Maddron Bald Trail foot log over Indian Camp Creek.

About a mile above the Rock Creek crossing, you come to a crossing of Inadu Creek above a small waterfall. Inadu means "snake" in Cherokee, and it's one of the few Native American names retained in the park. As you leave the creek and begin ascending the ridge, the vegetation changes to plants more adapted to a drier environment—pine, galax, trailing arbutus, and mountain laurel. Climbing on, you pass through a moist cove with numerous painted trilliums in spring. Beyond here, you climb a short knife ridge with nearly 360-degree views. Mount Cammerer is prominent in the view toward the east. Soon you enter a darker, cooler forest and begin to see red spruce. As you climb higher, you pass through a ground cover of spring beauty with patches of trout lily, both blooming in April.

The junction with Maddron Bald Trail is not far ahead. From the junction, Snake Den Ridge Trail continues another 0.7 mile to the Appalachian Trail (AT), but your hike turns right (west) and follows Maddron Bald Trail. Enjoy the first significant downhill section of the hike as you travel through a dark spruce forest to Maddron Bald. Although the vegetation on the bald restricts the vistas somewhat, the views are great to the south and west.

Descending from the bald, you pass through a hemlock forest and then arrive at Campsite 29 beside Otter Creek. This is your first night's stay on a two-night backpack or your only stay on an overnighter. The site sits in a mossy boulder field—not the best terrain for camping, but pleasant enough. It isn't private, since the trail encircles the site, but it's far enough from any trailhead that you're not likely to have any walk-by traffic unless you hang out at the site in the middle of the day.

Pressing on from the campsite, the trail weaves a bit and then swings around a ridge separating the Otter Creek and Copperhead Branch drainages. An obvious side path on the right leads a few yards to a wonderful view. You soon cross Copperhead Branch and then Indian Camp Creek at a photogenic cascade amongst huge, mossy boulders. Farther down you cross a side branch, and then cross Indian Camp Creek again. Fifty yards farther, cross Copperhead Branch once again. Now you pass between two giant hemlock trees, one on each side of the trail, and soon begin a high parallel course above Otter Creek.

Here you pass what must be the oddest-looking stump in the Smokies. It's huge— so huge that four people could pack themselves into the hollow center. It has several rhododendron trees growing all over it and a hemlock or two. Shortly beyond the stump, you cross Indian Camp Creek once more and arrive at the upper junction with Albright Grove Loop Trail. It's 0.3 mile from here on Maddron Bald Trail to the lower junction with Albright Grove Loop Trail, but this hike turns left and follows Albright Grove Loop Trail for 0.7 mile through the old-growth forest (The destination for Hike 42 is Albright Grove.)

Rejoin Maddron Bald Trail at the lower end of Albright Grove Loop Trail, and in 0.1 mile you cross Indian Camp Creek for the final time, on a foot log. For the next 0.5 mile, the trail passes through an old-growth forest featuring several large trees. You exit the old growth onto an old roadbed and follow it down to the junction with Old Settlers Trail and Gabes Mountain Trail in a small clearing.

Your hike follows the Gabes Mountain Trail to the right (south) and begins climbing again, though not too steeply. For the next 1.8 miles, you cross over small creek branches and hike through a beautiful forest with yellow poplar, buckeye, beech, Fraser magnolia, and silverbell. At your feet are numerous species of spring wildflowers, and you pass huge American chestnut stumps.

Campsite 34 is situated right beside Greenbrier Creek. The forest here is pleasantly open, and the tent sites have a little more privacy than Campsite 29. This is your home on the second night of a two-night backpack.

For the most part, you're finished climbing once you leave Campsite 34. There's some gradual ascending, but nothing significant. The forest remains outstanding, and there are scenic stream crossings.

At the third crossing of Lower Falling Branch, you can't help but realize that you're looking out over the top of Hen Wallow Falls. Hiking in this direction, you might be tempted to try a scramble down the bank for a close view, but save your energy. A short distance farther a side path to the left leads safely (but steeply) to the base of the falls. Lower Falling Branch at this point is a continuous set of cascades and drops. The side path comes out at the base of the uppermost drop, which is about 50 feet high. No path leads to views of the lower drops, and any attempt to get down there would risk life and limb.

Back on the main trail, you can take heart that the huffing and puffing is all behind you. Except for a few minor humps, it's downhill from here. As you near the end, the trail forks, with the left fork leading 0.3 mile to the picnic area and the right fork going 0.3 mile to the campground at site A44. Take the left fork and come out on Cosby Road. Turn right and follow the road back to the parking area.

Miles and Directions

0.0   Start by walking along the road into the Cosby Campground and follow the campsite markers to site B51.

0.3   Snake Den Ridge Trail begins on the right side of the road, directly opposite campsite B51.

4.9   Turn right (west) onto Maddron Bald Trail.

6.5   Campsite 29.

9.0   Come to the upper junction with Albright Grove Trail. Turn left onto it.

9.7   Come to the lower junction of Albright Grove Trail with Maddron Bald Trail. Continue straight ahead on Maddron Bald Trail.

10.3   Trail begins following old roadbed.

11.4   Junction with Old Settlers and Gabes Mountain Trails. Turn right (south) on Gabes Mountain Trail.

13.2   Campsite 34.

15.9   Side path on the left leads to Hen Wallow Falls.

18.0   Junction with Cosby Road. Turn right and walk on the road back to parking area.

18.1   Arrive back at parking area.

A HELL OF A PLACE

Maddron Bald is a lot different from some other balds in the Smokies, such as Gregory Bald and Andrews Bald. Those are grassy balds, characterized by a ground cover of mountain oat grass, a few shrubs such as blueberry, azalea, a few Catawba rhododendron, and several different species of herbs. Grassy balds are mostly open. Maddron Bald, on the other hand, is totally grown over. Maddron is a heath bald, characterized by a dense covering of shrubs in the heath family, such as Catawba rhododendron, Carolina rhododendron, mountain laurel, and sand myrtle. Like the grassy balds, large trees don't grow on heath balds, and from a distance, they appear smooth, giving them the local name of laurel slicks.

Standing in the middle of Maddron Bald, however, it's plain to see that a heath bald is anything but slick. Just imagine how difficult it would be to walk through one without a trail. This trait has led to another local name for heath balds: laurel hells. More than 400 heath balds occur in the Smokies, ranging from tiny patches to over 50 acres in size. Some of the more notable ones accessed by hikes in this guidebook include the summit of Brushy Mountain (Hike 40) and areas on the summit of Mount LeConte and its access trails (Hikes 31, 35, and 37). You can also view a large number of heath balds from the higher elevations of Newfound Gap Road.

Southwest Section

Mingus Mill.

47 Mingus Mill and Newton Bald

Don't worry about all the people you see in the trailhead parking lot. They're here to see Mingus Mill, a restored late nineteenth-century gristmill. You'll have the hike to yourself. You can explore the mill before you hike or, since it is so close to the parking area, save it for another day when you have more time. The mill still operates using the originally installed water-powered mechanism. Hours may vary, but generally, the mill opens daily in summer and on weekends in spring and fall.

This hike is a good day hike for campers staying at Smokemont Campground. Arrange for a shuttle to the trailhead, make the hike, and walk back to the campground in time for dinner.

Start: Mingus Creek trailhead at Mingus Mill parking area
Distance: 11.4 miles point to point
Hiking time: About 6 hours—day hike or overnighter
Difficulty: Moderate
Trail surface: Gravel road and forest trails
Other trail users: Equestrians permitted on most of the route
Maps: Smokemont USGS quad; Trails Illustrated #229 Great Smoky Mountains; Trails Illustrated #317 Clingmans Dome Cataloochee
Special considerations: You might be tempted to turn this hike into a loop by walking 2.8 miles along Newfound Gap Road, but this is very dangerous. In many places there isn't much of a shoulder and the heavy traffic is looking out for scenery, not you. It would be a nightmare of a walk.

A park firing range is located near the start of the hike. When the range is in use, the trail could be closed temporarily.

Other: The Mingus Mill parking area fills up on weekends, but if you get there by midmorning, you should be OK. Restrooms are available at the trailhead.

Finding the trailhead: From Oconaluftee Visitor Center, drive 0.4 mile south on Newfound Gap Road and turn left at the sign for Mingus Mill. Reach the parking area immediately (GPS: N35 31.248' / W83 18.553'). The road ends beyond the parking area at a turnaround, and the trail begins as a continuation of the road.

If leaving a second vehicle at hike's end, go to the trailhead for Newton Bald Trail, located about 2.8 miles farther north on the west side of Newfound Gap Road, just across from the entrance to Smokemont Campground (GPS: N35 33.159' / W83 18.583'). There are pullouts on each side of the road. Also, a hiker parking area is located on the right, just after crossing the river on the way to the campground.

The Hike

From the grounds of Mingus Mill, you can follow the raceway to Mingus Creek and cross over to get on Mingus Creek Trail, but this could be a wet crossing in high water. The parking area for the mill marks the official start of Mingus Creek Trail and this hike. Take the gravel road that begins from the turnaround and follow it along

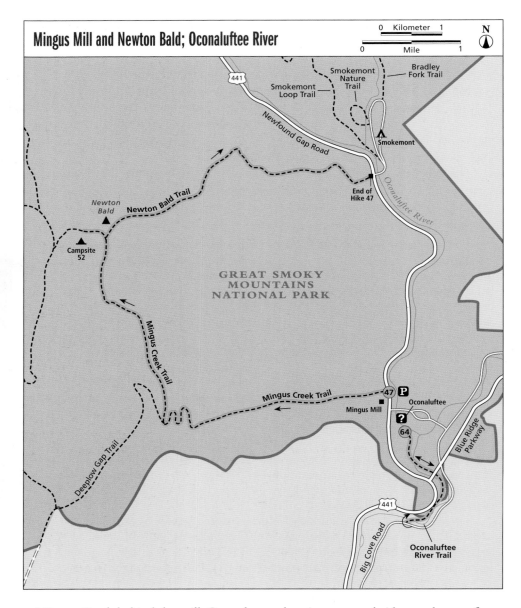

0 Kilometer 1

0 Mile 1

N

441

Smokemont
Nature
Trail

Smokemont
Loop Trail

Bradley
Fork Trail

Newfound Gap Road

Smokemont

Oconaluftee River

Newton
Bald

Newton Bald Trail

End of
Hike 47

Campsite
52

GREAT SMOKY
MOUNTAINS
NATIONAL PARK

Mingus Creek Trail

Mingus Creek Trail

47 P

Oconaluftee

Mingus Mill

?

64

Blue Ridge Parkway

Deeplow Gap Trail

441

Big Cove Road

Oconaluftee
River Trail

Mingus Creek behind the mill. Cross the creek twice on auto bridges and pass a firing range. (If the range is in use, the trail may be closed temporarily.) Continue on the service road, ascending gradually, and cross the creek once more just before passing an old water plant with an ugly metal building.

The service road ends here and the trail becomes rocky. Soon you cross Madcap Branch on a foot log and come to a fork. A right turn takes you to an old cemetery. Your hike goes to the left and follows Madcap Branch upstream. (Pay attention at the fork, as the most trodden path goes to the right and there may not be a sign.) After rock-hopping the branch and then a feeder, you start to climb. Look for large patches of sharp-lobed hepatica along the trail. The wildflower is unusual in that its distinctive three-lobed leaves remain throughout the winter. The trail continues on a long and sometimes steep ascent, crossing Madcap Branch or its branchlets many times before swinging away and climbing the ridge on switchbacks.

At a small gap in the ridgetop, Deeplow Gap Trail goes straight ahead and down the other side. Your hike goes right and follows up the ridgeline. It starts out surprisingly level and then begins climbing—moderately at first, but with a few steep stretches later on. Occasional views are off both sides of the trail. After following on or near the ridgeline for nearly 3 miles, you arrive at Newton Bald and the junction with Newton Bald Trail. Newton Bald is no longer a bald. Trees completely cover the summit and it's hard to tell that it was once open.

Turn left (north) onto Newton Bald Trail and hike an easy 0.3 mile to Campsite 52, straddling a small saddle. The trail passes right through the tiny site. Water is available from a very small spring 75 yards down the northeast side. If you're doing this hike as an overnighter, this is home for tonight.

Backtrack to the junction with Mingus Creek Trail, but stay on Newton Bald Trail. You now have a 5.0-mile near-continuous and sometimes steep descent to Newfound Gap Road. Look out for wildflowers in spring; this trail is a good one for them. About 0.25 mile before reaching the road, you pass a bridle path on the right, and a short distance farther there's another horse trail on the right. Stay to the left at both junctions.

Miles and Directions

0.0 Start on Mingus Creek Trail, which begins at the gravel road leading from the far end of the parking area.

1.3 A right fork leads to a cemetery. Go to the left to remain on Mingus Creek Trail.

2.9 Junction with Deeplow Gap Trail, which goes straight ahead. Turn right to remain on Mingus Creek Trail.

5.8 Junction with Newton Bald Trail on Newton Bald. Turn left (north) and walk along the ridge.

6.1 Arrive at Campsite 52. Backtrack to junction with Mingus Creek Trail.

6.4 Return to junction with Newton Bald and Mingus Creek Trails. Go to the left on Newton Bald Trail.

11.4 End of hike at Newfound Gap Road.

48 Deep Creek

The Deep Creek that most people see is more like a little river, but then most people never venture as far into the headwaters as you will on this hike. Actually, you *start* on the headwaters and follow the creek downstream, watching it grow by the mile. By the time it reaches the Deep Creek Campground area, it's a major stream, though not any deeper than other park streams. If you like streams, wildflowers, lush forests, and a hike long enough to make you feel that you've accomplished something, this is about as good as it gets in the Smokies.

Start: Deep Creek trailhead on Newfound Gap Road

Distance: 14.2 miles point to point

Hiking time: About 7 hours, with multiple options for camping

Difficulty: Moderate

Trail surface: Forest trail and old forest road

Best season: Spring for the wildflowers

Other trail users: Lower portion of trail is open to equestrians

Maps: Clingmans Dome and Bryson City USGS quads; Trails Illustrated #229 Great Smoky Mountains; Trails Illustrated #317 Clingmans Dome Cataloochee

Special considerations: In wet weather some of the creek crossings could be a little tricky and might require wading. Creek crossings aside, this isn't the most pleasant trail to hike in the rain. The upper section is heavily overgrown with dog hobble. The wet foliage constantly brushing against you is very irritating.

Other: The parking area at the actual trailhead has room only for a few vehicles. A larger parking area is located 0.1 mile south. There are no facilities, but there are restrooms at Newfound Gap, 1.7 miles to the north.

Finding the trailhead: For the beginning trailhead, from Oconaluftee Visitor Center drive 13.9 miles north on Newfound Gap Road to a small parking area on the left (west) side of the road (GPS: N35 35.960' / W83 25.353'). This is 1.7 miles south of Newfound Gap. Deep Creek Trail begins from the pullout and is obvious. If this parking area is full, there is another parking space located 0.1 mile to the south.

The ending trailhead is located near Deep Creek Campground. Follow the signs to the campground from downtown Bryson City. As you enter the park, continue on the paved road past the campground entrance and the picnic area to where the road ends at a large parking area on the left. GPS: N35 27.877' / W83 26.051'

The Hike

Descend from the trailhead on switchbacks through a lush scenic forest and cross several small branches. Wildflowers abound in the wet spots. Lettuce saxifrage grows here—look for its blooms in May and June and its distinctive lance-shaped, coarsely toothed leaves throughout the summer. At about 1.5 miles you enter a boggy and surprisingly flat cove. Passing through the cove, you cross several branches and then meet up with Deep Creek. Swing away from the creek and go on a long stretch where you parallel the creek high on the bank. Dog hobble threatens to take over the trail through here and continues to be a nuisance for several more miles.

Continue downstream, sometimes close by the creek, sometimes high above it. At 3.9 miles you come to the first of eight backcountry campsites on Deep Creek Trail. This one is Campsite 53. The site is not very pleasant—a cleared-out spot in a briar patch with the trail passing right through it. Fork Ridge Trail turns off to the right here, crossing Deep Creek without benefit of a foot log.

Continuing on Deep Creek Trail, you follow along the creek closely but without many good views of it through the dense dog hobble and rhododendron. Come to Cherry Creek and make

Tom Branch Falls drops directly into Deep Creek.

a tricky rock-hop in normal flows or a wade in high water. Once across Cherry Creek climb up and away from Deep Creek then back down to it. Here the trail and creek are the same for several yards, and in very high water this stretch could be dicey. Look for a fallen hemlock by the creek that has several small trees growing from its trunk. There are birches, rhododendron . . . at least a half-dozen species.

Now leave the creek a bit and pass through a forest with some impressive yellow poplars (tulip trees). The hemlocks here were once impressive but are now skeletons. On returning to the creek, the ground is wet and boggy and you cross over two out-of-character corrugated metal pipes. Beyond the pipes the trail turns left and goes through a rerouted section that avoids even more boggy ground.

At about 6.5 miles you cross two creeks in quick succession (the first crossing of Nettle Creek might be tricky) and arrive at Campsite 54, just after the crossings. It's another small site, but it's much more attractive than Campsite 53. Less than a mile farther, you come to Campsite 55, a horse camp, on the left. Just beyond the campsite, Pole Road Creek Trail turns off to the right and crosses Deep Creep on two foot logs on its way to Upper Sassafras Gap on Noland Divide. Stay straight on Deep Creek Trail.

After a short up-and-down segment, you pass right through Campsite 56, a very small site in a hemlock grove. Soon the trail swings away from the creek and climbs a little to Campsite 57 at the junction with Martins Gap Trail. Campsite 57 is named Bryson Place and is the site of Horace Kephart's last permanent camp in the Smokies.

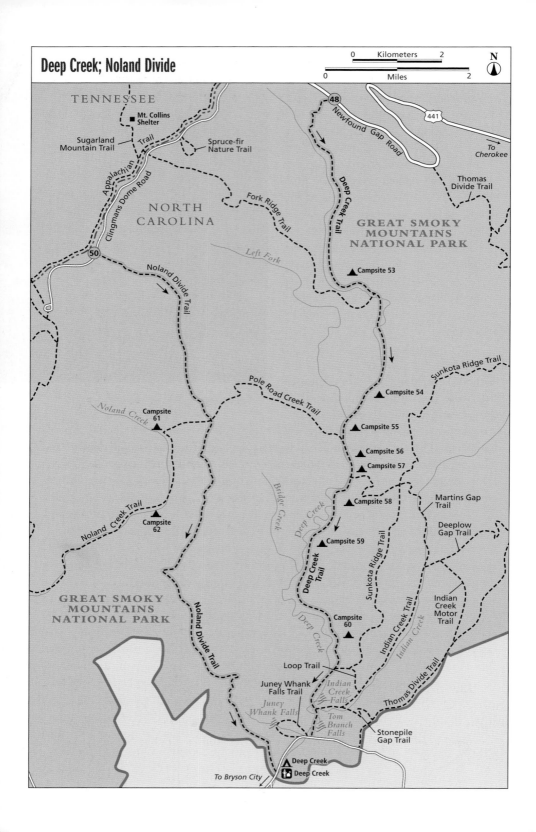

Deep Creek; Noland Divide

Kilometers 0 — 2
Miles 0 — 2

N

TENNESSEE

Mt. Collins Shelter

Sugarland Mountain Trail

Appalachian Trail

Spruce-fir Nature Trail

NORTH CAROLINA

Clingmans Dome Road

Fork Ridge Trail

Left Fork

Deep Creek Trail

Newfound Gap Road

48

441

To Cherokee

Thomas Divide Trail

GREAT SMOKY MOUNTAINS NATIONAL PARK

Campsite 53

50

Noland Divide Trail

Sunkota Ridge Trail

Noland Creek

Campsite 61

Pole Road Creek Trail

Campsite 54

Campsite 55

Campsite 56

Campsite 57

Noland Creek Trail

Campsite 62

Bridge Creek

Deep Creek

Campsite 58

Martins Gap Trail

Deeplow Gap Trail

GREAT SMOKY MOUNTAINS NATIONAL PARK

Campsite 59

Deep Creek Trail

Sunkota Ridge Trail

Indian Creek Trail

Indian Creek Motor Trail

Noland Divide Trail

Deep Creek

Campsite 60

Loop Trail

Juney Whank Falls Trail

Juney Whank Falls

Indian Creek Falls

Indian Creek

Thomas Divide Trail

Tom Branch Falls

Stonepile Gap Trail

Deep Creek

Deep Creek

To Bryson City

A few hundred feet off the right side of the trail lies a millstone and plaque honoring Kephart, placed in 1931 by the Horace Kephart Boy Scout Troop. (See the sidebar for Hike 68 for more about Kephart.) This isn't the best campsite. It's open and on a slope—and it's a horse camp. If here in May, look around the horse-hitching area for pink lady's slipper orchids. Martins Gap Trail goes to the left, between the campsite and hitching area. Again, stay on Deep Creek Trail.

Reach Campsite 58 in another 0.6 mile. It offers no privacy, but its setting right beside Deep Creek makes it appealing. Beyond the campsite the trail does a typical up-and-down routine. On the down side you come to Campsite 59, also beside Deep Creek. It has no privacy either, although a screen of dog hobble offers a little isolation. From here you go on a roller-coaster ride of ups and downs and then make a long, somewhat steep climb, the longest climb of the hike. After the climb an even longer descent takes you to Campsite 60, the prettiest one of all. It sits off the trail enough for a little privacy and has a ground cover of soft pine needles.

Cross Bumgardner Branch on a foot log just past the campsite, make a final climb, then descend to the old road turnaround. From here it's an easy 2.1-mile walk along the old roadbed to the trailhead.

Miles and Directions

0.0 Start on Deep Creek Trail from the parking area.

3.9 Campsite 53. Fork Ridge Trail turns to the right here and crosses Deep Creek. Continue following Deep Creel Trail downstream.

6.5 Campsite 54.

7.4 Campsite 55. A short distance beyond the campsite, Pole Road Creek Trail turns to the right and crosses Deep Creek. Continue following Deep Creel Trail downstream.

7.6 Campsite 56.

8.1 Campsite 57 and junction with Martins Gap Trail, which goes to the left. Continue following Deep Creek Trail downstream.

8.7 Campsite 58.

9.1 Campsite 59.

11.6 Campsite 60.

12.5 Junction with Loop Trail on the left. Continue following Deep Creel Trail downstream.

13.5 Junction with Indian Creek Trail on the left. Indian Creek Falls is a short distance up Indian Creek Trail. Continue following Deep Creel Trail downstream.

14.0 Pass by Tom Branch Falls, to the left, on the other side of Deep Creek.

14.2 End of hike at the lower trailhead.

Options: With eight campsites and five intersecting trails (each offering other hike possibilities), it's hard to decide how to plan a hike. If doing an overnighter, you might want to stay at Campsite 56, which is about halfway into the hike. On a lazy two-night backpack, a good choice is to camp at Campsite 54 the first night and #60 on the second.

49 Spruce-Fir Nature Trail

This hike is included in this guidebook only because the book features *all* of the park's self-guiding nature trails. The nature trails provide great opportunities to learn about the park ecosystem without investing a lot of effort. However, Spruce-Fir Nature Trail provides little more than a case of depression. Not too many years ago, you could hike a few dozen yards away from the road along this trail and feel as though you were in the middle of a wilderness. It was dark, cool, dense, and mysterious. Today, it's open, hot, weedy, and depressing. The large fir trees are dead and many of the spruces uprooted. Briers invade the open areas. This is a common scene in spruce-fir forests today. For an explanation of what's to blame for this destruction, see the sidebar.

A positive aspect of this hike is that it is one of the best places in the park to see Clinton's lily, a high-elevation plant with greenish-yellow bell-like flowers and distinctive elliptical basal leaves. Dense patches of the wildflower, which blooms in May, occur along this trail. Also, a number of young fir trees have grown back, helping to lessen the bleak nature of the hike.

(See map for Hike 4: Chimney Tops.)

Start: Spruce-Fir Nature trailhead on Clingmans Dome Road
Distance: 0.5-mile lollipop
Hiking time: About 20 minutes—day hike
Difficulty: Easy (Ignore the sign that says there are steep, 12 percent grades on this trail. This is an easy walk in the park.)
Trail surface: Forest trail, overlaid with wood planks for much of the way

Other trail users: Hikers only
Maps: Clingmans Dome USGS quad; Trails Illustrated #229 Great Smoky Mountains; Trails Illustrated #317 Clingmans Dome Cataloochee
Special considerations: Clingmans Dome Road is closed Dec 1–Mar 31.
Other: The pullout is small, but finding space is rarely a problem. If it is full, there is another pullout less than 0.1 mile farther up the road. Restrooms are available at the Forney Ridge Parking Area on Clingmans Dome.

Finding the trailhead: At Newfound Gap turn west onto Clingmans Dome Road and drive 2.6 miles to the small pullout on the left (east) side of the road. The trail begins at the interpretive sign. Interpretive brochures (50 cents to keep) are available from the trailhead. GPS: N35 35.742' / W83 27.529'

The Hike

The trail begins from the northernmost parking area and is easily followed. There are no distinctive landmarks along the way. Use the trail brochure for more detail on the dynamics and demise of the spruce-fir forest.

0.0 Start from the parking area at the trail sign. Walk 75 yards to the T junction. Go right or left to hike the loop.

0.5 Return to the T junction and retrace your steps to the trailhead.

Option: Perhaps the best option is to skip this hike entirely. Drive on up to Clingmans Dome and do Hike 51 instead. You'll see the same heartbreak of dead trees on that hike (more, actually), but at least you'll have distant views as a redeeming quality.

SOMETHING'S NOT RIGHT

You can't help but notice that something's not right in the highest elevations of the Smokies. All of the big trees are dead. Some stand like skeletons in a graveyard, but most have fallen. Many are uprooted and lying on the ground like pickup sticks. These are—or were—Fraser firs, the dominant tree species at elevations above 6,000 feet. Between 5,000 and 6,000 feet, the firs mix with red spruce. The culprit usually cited is the nonnative insect balsam woolly adelgid, *Adelges piceae*. Introduced from Europe in the early 1900s, the adelgid, which feeds on Fraser firs, reached the Smokies in the late 1950s. For decades there was no critical cause for alarm, but that changed dramatically in the 1980s when trees began dying at an alarming rate all over the southern Appalachians.

So what's the problem? As with most things related to ecosystem health, a combination of factors is to blame. A major contributing factor is pollution in the form of acid rain and ozone. The acidity level of the rain and fog on Clingmans Dome and other high-elevation mountains is extreme, somewhere between 2.5 and 3.5 pH. Acid rain and ozone weaken the tree's root system to the point that the tree cannot fight off normal stresses such as drought, extreme winds, and native pests. And with something as abominable as the non-native balsam woolly adelgid in the mix, the trees don't stand a chance. Young Fraser firs are abundant, as they are not attacked by the adelgid until they reach maturity, but the pest has killed most of the mature trees.

The natural environment isn't the only thing in danger up here. People breathe the same air that the trees do. The park constantly monitors ozone and issues warnings when the concentrations reach unsafe levels. During the summer, ozone concentrations regularly exceed the safety standards for public health and vegetation tolerance.

50 Noland Divide

Few other hikes in the Smokies offer the diversity of forest types that this one does. Starting at 5,929 feet and ending at just under 1,800 feet, the hike is roughly equivalent (ecologically) to driving from Canada to North Carolina. The hike also offers a diversity in the weather. From fall through spring the temperature can be in the fifties Fahrenheit at the lower trailhead while it's snowing at the upper. This hike isn't for everyone, though. You don't see a creek until a short distance from the end and there is only one completely clear view along the entire length.

(See map for Hike 48: Deep Creek.)

Start: Noland Divide trailhead on Clingmans Dome Road
Distance: 11.6 miles point to point
Hiking time: About 6 hours—day hike
Difficulty: Easy due to downhill grade most of the way, but with a few moderate sections
Trail surface: Forest trail
Other trail users: Equestrians
Maps: Clingmans Dome and Bryson City USGS quads; Trails Illustrated #229 Great Smoky Mountains; Trails Illustrated #317 Clingmans Dome Cataloochee
Special considerations: Clingmans Dome Road is normally closed Dec 1–Mar 31. There are no water sources for the majority of this hike.
Other: There is limited parking at the pullout, but it usually isn't a problem. Restrooms are located 1.5 miles farther on Clingmans Dome Road. The trailhead at the terminus is very large, but it can get crowded with horse trailers. Restrooms are available at Deep Creek Picnic Area, which is located at the trail terminus.

Finding the trailhead: To reach the upper trailhead and the start of the hike as described, drive 5.5 miles west of Newfound Gap on Clingmans Dome Road to the small pullout on the left (GPS: N35 34.037' / W83 28.907'). Noland Divide Trail begins beyond the gate.

To reach the lower trailhead at the end of the hike, follow the signs from downtown Bryson City to Deep Creek Campground. As you enter the park, continue to the campground entrance on the right. Directly across the road on the left is the trailhead at a large gravel parking area. GPS: N35 27.569' / W83 26.308'

The Hike

The first 0.5 mile descends on a service road and passes by an acid-precipitation monitoring tower. Just beyond the tower the footpath leads off to the left (southeast) and the grade lessens considerably. For many hikers, this segment is the best part of the hike. It passes through one of the most scenic spruce-fir (mostly spruce) forests in the park. Since it's not a pure stand of fir, you don't feel as though you're in a tree graveyard like you do up on Clingmans Dome. In April and early May, the ground is alive with spring beauty and trout lily. Patches of Clinton's lily bloom in May, and bluets bloom throughout the warm season. Also along this stretch are some impressive yellow birch trees, including one of the largest in the park.

Noland Divide Trail passes through a rhododendron tunnel.

When you leave the ridgetop and begin skirting the west side of Roundtop Knob, you leave the spruce forest behind and enter a forest of oak, beech, hemlock, and maple. From this point on, the forest is more open, and with the leaves off the trees, there are skimpy views in places. Continue descending, passing through rhododendron and mountain laurel tunnels, and reach Upper Sassafras Gap at mile 3.7. At the gap Pole Road Creek Trail heads down the left side of the ridge to Deep Creek; on the right Noland Creek Trail descends very steeply to Campsite 61. You want to go straight and stay on the ridge.

Now begin an ascent through a burned area. A large fire in November 2001 scorched this forest and you'll pass through several more burned areas on the remainder of the hike. After more than a decade, the forest has recovered well, but if you pay careful attention, you'll see evidence of the fires, such as a little more weedy growth along the trail than usual. A long, gradual descent takes you to Lower Sassafras Gap. Look for rhododendron growing here with impressively thick trunks.

Now you begin climbing again—not too steeply but long and continuously. You go around several knobs before leveling out on a ridge. After a mostly level walk along the ridge, you begin climbing again around the southeast side of Coburn Knob. After passing over a broad ridge, you come to a small spring gurgling right on the trail at about mile 6.7. This is the only water source along the trail so far, but don't count on it being more than a damp spot for most of year.

Just beyond the spring the trail makes a sharp switchback to the left and from here on it's all downhill except for a few quick ups and some level stretches. At mile

8.1 the trail veers left to skirt a small rocky ridge, while a side path goes straight for a few yards to an opening on the top of the ridge. This is Lonesome Pine Overlook, but don't look for a solitary pine up here. Pines and mountain laurel cover the ridge. The view south toward Bryson City is spectacular. You're probably happy to get a good view finally. For such a long ridge walk, the views to here are disappointing—practically nonexistent when the leaves are out. Look down to the left from the overlook. That narrow ridge (Beaugard Ridge) is the one you descend to the trailhead.

Now on Beaugard Ridge, enjoy a few more views. Here you can see farther to the west and off the left side of the trail back toward the Smokies crest. Descend a steep section on switchbacks and begin a long continuous descent. In places, you pass through great spring wildflower habitat. Complementing the flowers is a small waterfall that you cross in its middle. Just past the falls, on the right bank, is a large patch of speckled wood lily. Look for its white flowers in May and its distinctive dark blue fruit in August. Other wildflowers along this segment include Vasey's trillium, bloodroot, wild geranium, Solomon's seal, and spiderwort.

Farther down you pass through a drier area that has yellow-eyed grass, trailing arbutus, mountain laurel, and a few flame azaleas. Finally, after the long downhill stretch, you meet up with Deep Creek Horse Trail and a foot log crossing Durham Branch. A few yards farther is the parking area.

Miles and Directions

0.0 Start from the pullout on Noland Divide Trail, which begins as an old roadbed.

0.5 Shortly beyond a monitoring station, the road makes a sharp swing to the right. Leave the road here on the footpath that goes straight ahead (southeast).

3.7 Reach Upper Sassafras Gap and the junction with Pole Road Creek Trail and Noland Creek Trail. Continue following the ridgeline south on Noland Divide Trail.

8.1 A short spur path on the right leads to Lonesome Pine Overlook.

11.6 Arrive at lower trailhead.

51 Clingmans Dome

Hiking to the top of the highest mountain in the park (6,643 feet) and the third highest in the East (Mount Mitchell is first at 6,684 feet, Mount Craig is second at 6,647 feet) is bittersweet. On one hand, there can be great distant views and you get to experience the extremes of life at this elevation—wind, rain, snow, fog, cold. It's not uncommon to leave Gatlinburg in sunshine and 55-degree temperatures and find it snowing on Clingmans Dome. On the other hand, you experience the extremes of humankind's negative influence on the environment—smog, introduced pests, crowds, and bulldozed mountainsides. Clingmans Dome is an outdoor classroom and everyone should study here at least once.

Start: Forney Ridge Parking Area for Clingmans Dome
Distance: 1.5-mile loop
Hiking time: About 2 hours–day hike
Difficulty: Strenuous, due to steep path
Trail surface: Paved path and rocky trail
Other trail users: Hikers only
Maps: Clingmans Dome and Silers Bald USGS quads; Trails Illustrated #229 Great Smoky Mountains; Trails Illustrated #317 Clingmans

Dome Cataloochee; Trails Illustrated #316 Cades Cove Elkmont
Special considerations: You have to make this hike early in the morning to avoid the crowds. Clingmans Dome Road is closed Dec 1–Mar 31.
Other: The parking lot is huge, but it's often not big enough to accommodate weekend traffic. Pit toilets are located at the parking area. A new visitor center is located near the start of the hike.

Finding the trailhead: At Newfound Gap turn west onto Clingmans Dome Road and drive 7.0 miles to the Forney Ridge Parking Area at the end. The paved trail begins on the far western end of the parking area. GPS: N35 33.409' / W83 29.772'

The Hike

Begin the hike on the paved path at the western end of the parking area. After you pass the visitor center, the grade becomes very steep, with numerous benches providing rest stops. The distant views are good, but the forest all around you is very depressing from the death of the Fraser firs (See the sidebar for Hike 49). Just before the path levels off, a short connector to the Appalachian Trail (AT) turns off to the left. Continue on the paved path a short distance to the tower. A long circular ramp leads to an observation deck, some 50 feet above the ground.

Not too many years ago, the view from the deck was limited, with Fraser firs blocking much of the panorama. But today, with the trees dead and fallen, the view is open all around. Today, air pollution limits the views. The winter months provide the clearest views, but since Clingmans Dome Road is closed from December to March, November is the best month. When the view up here is good, it's *really* good.

Clingmans Dome; Andrews Bald; Forney Ridge and Noland Divide; Silers Bald and Forney Creek

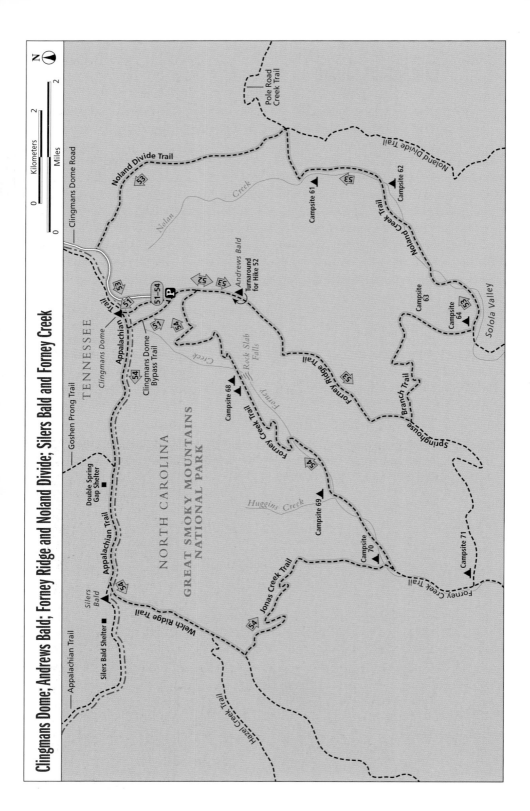

As you head back down, turn right onto the connector path you passed on the way up and follow it a few yards to the AT. Turn left (west) and find yourself alone. Few persons leave the paved path, so you might have the rest of the hike to yourself. Follow the AT for 0.3 mile to the junction with Clingmans Dome Bypass Trail. There are views along the way, but you already had the best possible views back up on the tower.

Turn left (southeast) on Clingmans Dome Bypass Trail. On a clear day you can see the Forney Ridge Parking Area up ahead. The 0.5-mile moderate descent from here to the junction with Forney Ridge Trail is very rocky and passes through a skeleton Fraser fir forest. A positive aspect is that a large number of small trees have grown back beside the trail, so parts of this section aren't as depressing as what you experienced on the paved path.

The junction with Forney Ridge Trail is a fork. The right fork leads down and eventually to Andrews Bald. You want to go left and make the 0.2-mile climb back to the parking area.

Miles and Directions

0.0 Start from the far western end of the parking area on the paved path.

0.5 Arrive at Clingmans Dome Observation Tower and the junction with the AT. Climb the tower and then hike west on the AT.

0.8 Turn left (southeast) onto Clingmans Dome Bypass Trail.

1.3 Bear left onto Forney Ridge Trail.

1.5 Arrive back at Forney Ridge Parking Area.

SOARING CONCRETE

First-time visitors to Clingmans Dome are often startled after hiking to the summit and seeing the observation tower. A circular 375-foot-long concrete ramp leads to an observation deck around 50 feet high. The juxtaposition of the

A backpacker pauses along the ramp to Clingmans Dome Tower.

concrete structure with Clingmans Dome summit is not unlike that of Gatlinburg with the park boundary. Completed in 1959, the tower replaced an earlier structure built by the Civilian Conservation Corps in the 1930s. That tower, made of wood, soon deteriorated. When the plans for the new tower were released, opinions were strong on both sides. Some thought the new structure was perfectly suited for the mountain, while others thought a concrete tower had no place there. The two sides are still arguing.

52 Andrews Bald

On the open and grassy Andrews Bald grow flame azaleas and Catawba rhododendron, both peaking their blooms sometime around mid- to late June. If you've been to Gregory Bald (Hikes 24 and 63), you might be a little disappointed in Andrews. Andrews Bald is like a smaller cousin to Gregory—fewer azaleas, restricted views, and with more encroaching vegetation. But don't let that stop you from coming. This is one of the finest day hikes in the park. On a clear day the views east into the Noland Creek watershed and southwest toward Fontana Lake are superb. And the azalea show on Andrews is the finest in the park except for Gregory.

(See map for Hike 51: Clingmans Dome)

Start: Forney Ridge Parking Area for Clingmans Dome

Distance: 3.6 miles out and back

Hiking time: About 3 hours—day hike

Difficulty: Strenuous, due to very rocky trail

Trail surface: Rocks—lots of them

Best season: Second half of June for azalea and rhododendron bloom

Other trail users: Hikers only

Maps: Clingmans Dome USGS quad; Trails Illustrated #229 Great Smoky Mountains; Trails Illustrated #317 Clingmans Dome

Cataloochee; Trails Illustrated #316 Cades Cove Elkmont

Special considerations: Clingmans Dome Road is closed Dec 1–Mar 31. This hike is extremely popular, especially in June when the azaleas bloom. A great option for avoiding the crowds is to arrive at the Forney Ridge Parking Area early and watch the sunrise from the parking lot. After sunrise you can hike to Andrews Bald before most people are stirring.

Other: The parking lot is huge, but it's often not big enough to accommodate weekend traffic. Flush toilets are located at the parking area. A visitor center is located near the start of the hike.

Finding the trailhead: At Newfound Gap turn west onto Clingmans Dome Road and drive 7.0 miles to the Forney Ridge Parking Area at the end. Forney Ridge Trail begins on the far western end of the parking area. The paved path to Clingmans Dome Tower goes to the right, while Forney Ridge Trail drops down off of it to the left. GPS: N35 33.409' / W83 29.772'

The Hike

You'll follow Forney Ridge Trail all the way to Andrews Bald. The first 0.2 mile is a steep descent to the junction with Clingmans Dome Bypass Trail. You need to cut sharply back to the left (south) to remain on Forney Ridge Trail. In the past, heavy rains (common here) turned this rocky trail into a creek bed, but new trail construction has made this situation much better.

Descend for a little more than a mile and in a small clearing reach the junction with Forney Creek Trail on the right. Stay straight (south) on Forney Ridge Trail. The forest here is darker and denser than you see in many other spruce-fir areas. The

Early morning view from Andrews Bald.

mature Fraser firs are dead, but there are more young trees here than in some places. The forest here provides a hint at what once covered these mountaintops. After a moderate ascent you exit the woods and descend to the bald.

Miles and Directions

0.0 Start from the western end of the parking area on Forney Ridge Trail.

0.2 At the junction with Clingmans Dome Bypass Trail, turn sharply back to the left (south) to remain on Forney Ridge Trail.

1.1 Junction with Forney Creek Trail on the right. Continue straight (south) on Forney Ridge Trail.

1.8 Arrive at Andrews Bald. Return the way you came.

3.6 Arrive back at Forney Ridge Parking Area.

Option: The hike to Andrews Bald is the first 1.8 miles of Hike 53, so you can do both of these hikes on the same trip.

53 Forney Ridge and Noland Divide

This trip encompasses what most people look for in a Smokies adventure: high-elevation views, old-growth forests, cascading streams, wildflowers, and a challenging hike. On the latter point, if you're attempting this hike in one day, plan to start early and drag in late. Plan also to be a tired puppy by the end of the day. The first 1.8 miles of this hike to Andrews Bald is the same route as in Hike 52.

(See map for Hike 51: Clingmans Dome)

Start: Forney Ridge Parking Area on Clingmans Dome

Distance: 18.4-mile loop

Hiking time: About 10 hours—killer day hike or overnighter

Difficulty: Strenuous, due to steep grades, rocky trails, and creek crossings

Trail surface: Forest trails, some very rocky, and a section of paved road walking

Best season: Second half of June for azalea and rhododendron bloom on Andrews Bald

Other trail users: The 2.8-mile section on Springhouse Branch Trail is open to equestrians; the rest is for hikers only

Maps: Clingmans Dome, Silers Bald, Noland Creek, and Bryson City USGS quads; Trails Illustrated #229 Great Smoky Mountains; Trails Illustrated #317 Clingmans Dome Cataloochee; Trails Illustrated #316 Cades Cove Elkmont (only shows western half of hike)

Special considerations: Clingmans Dome Road is closed Dec 1–Mar 31. The first 1.8 miles of this hike to Andrews Bald is extremely popular, especially in June when the azaleas bloom. A great option for avoiding the crowds is to arrive at the Forney Ridge Parking Area early and watch the sunrise from the parking lot. After sunrise you can hike to Andrews Bald before most people are stirring.

You must make at least one crossing of Noland Creek without a foot log or bridge. Count on it being a wade—after heavy rains it can be dangerous or impassable.

To complete this loop without benefit of a shuttle, you must walk the final 1.5 miles along Clingmans Dome Road, being very cautious to stay out of traffic by walking on the road shoulder.

Other: The parking lot is huge, but it's often not big enough to accommodate weekend traffic. Pit toilets are located at the parking area. A new visitor center is located near the start of the hike.

Finding the trailhead: At Newfound Gap turn west onto Clingmans Dome Road and drive 7.0 miles to the Forney Ridge Parking Area at the end. Forney Ridge Trail begins on the far western end of the parking area. The paved path to Clingmans Dome Tower goes to the right, while Forney Ridge Trail drops down off of it to the left. GPS: N35 33.409' / W83 29.772'

The Hike

Take Forney Ridge Trail and descend steeply for 0.2 mile to the junction with Clingmans Dome Bypass Trail. You need to cut sharply back to the left (south) to remain on Forney Ridge Trail. In the past, heavy rains (common here) turned this rocky trail into a creek bed, but new trail construction has made this situation much better.

Descend for a little more than a mile and in a small clearing reach the junction with Forney Creek Trail on the right. Stay straight (south) on Forney Ridge Trail. The forest here is darker and denser than you see in many other spruce-fir areas. The mature Fraser firs are dead, but there are more young trees here than in some places. The forest here provides a hint at what once covered these mountaintops. After a moderate ascent you exit the woods and descend to Andrews Bald.

The many paths spreading out over the bald are confusing. Just keep heading down to the lower end until you see the sign marking the trail's exit from the bald. Pass a hog exclosure on the right after leaving the bald. The trail is steep, rocky, and full of puddles when it's raining. Pass through a delightful rocky area with lush moss, ferns, lichens, and many wildflower species.

Here the footing changes from rocks to dirt and is fairly level, with even a few uphill sections. In places, briars overgrow the trail. After rounding over a ridge, you start a long and sometimes steep descent to Board Camp Gap at mile 5.6. Forney Ridge Trail ends here and Springhouse Branch Trail takes over. You want to go sharply left (northeast) on Springhouse Branch Trail.

For a while, you follow the contour line, and then you swing around a ridge and descend to the Springhouse Branch drainage, where you cross several branches in quick succession. The forest through here is old growth and this is great wildflower habitat. In spring this area is a highlight of the hike. The last and largest stream in the immediate vicinity is Springhouse Branch. After crossing it you descend somewhat steeply for about 0.75 mile to Mill Creek and cross it on a mossy foot log. Just before the crossing there's an old rock wall on the left, and just after, the remains of an old stone chimney. This place was obviously once someone's home.

The next 0.75 mile or so is on a loose parallel of Mill Creek, all the way to Solola Valley and Campsite 64. The valley saw heavy settlement before the park was established and even had its own post office. Today, all that remains are scattered foundations, clearings, broken artifacts, and such. Campsite 64 is a horse camp, and although its setting at the confluence of Mill Creek with Noland Creek is pleasant enough, the site is not the best for backpackers. It's badly worn and receives heavy horse use. If you're doing this hike as an overnighter, you might want to continue to the next site.

At Campsite 64 is the junction with Noland Creek Trail, which follows Noland Creek 4.1 miles downstream to Lakeshore Drive. Your hike goes east on Noland Creek Trail and follows the creek upstream. A short way upstream you cross the creek on a narrow foot log, and after ascending beside the creek, you cross it again. Come to Campsite 63 at mile 9.8 (1.4 miles from Campsite 64). The site is small and right beside the trail, but it's more appealing than site 64. This is a good place for an overnighter.

Continuing on, you soon cross the creek a third time on another foot log, and the trail then becomes steeper and rockier. The fourth creek crossing is a wade. Next, you come to Campsite 62, situated beside Noland Creek. Pressing on, you rock-hop a side stream and right afterward come to the final crossing of Noland Creek. It's a tough rock-hop, and in high water, it might not be safe even to wade across.

After hiking a segment away from the creek and making a couple of tributary crossings, arrive at Campsite 61, a small rationed site situated beside Noland Creek. Shortly beyond the campsite, the trail makes a sharp right switchback and begins a brutal ascent to Upper Sassafras Gap on Noland Divide. Noland Divide Trail intersects here. Turn left (northwest) on it and follow the ridgeline 3.7 miles to Clingmans Dome Road. Half a mile before reaching the paved road, the trail exits onto a gravel road, just below a tower used for monitoring acid precipitation. Follow the gravel road uphill to Clingmans Dome Road. (Hike 50 follows the route from Clingmans Dome Road to Sassafras Gap. Refer to it for a little more detail about this segment.)

Once on the paved road, turn left and walk the remaining 1.5 miles to the parking area, being very cautious to stay out of traffic by walking on the road shoulder.

Miles and Directions

0.0   Start from the western end of the parking area on Forney Ridge Trail.

0.2   At the junction with Clingmans Dome Bypass Trail, turn sharply back to the left (south) to remain on Forney Ridge Trail.

1.1   Junction with Forney Creek Trail on the right. Continue straight (south) on Forney Ridge Trail.

1.8   Arrive at Andrews Bald. Walk to the lower end of the bald and find the sign indicating that Forney Ridge Trail continues south.

5.6   At Board Camp Gap turn sharply left (northeast) onto Springhouse Branch Trail.

8.4   Junction with Noland Creek Trail at Campsite 64. Turn left (east), following the trail upstream.

9.8   Campsite 63.

11.0   Campsite 62.

12.6   Campsite 61.

13.2   Junction with Noland Divide and Pole Road Creek Trails at Upper Sassafras Gap. Turn left (northwest) onto Noland Divide Trail.

16.4   Junction with service road. Noland Divide Trail follows the road straight ahead, heading uphill.

16.9   Arrive at Clingmans Dome Road. Turn left and follow the road back to the parking area. Be very cautious along the road.

18.4   Arrive at Forney Ridge Parking Area.

Options: Several trails provide access to the Forney Creek and Noland Creek watersheds and the adjacent ridges. Experienced backpackers can plan extended trips using Clingmans Dome as a starting point. The Silers Bald and Forney Creek hike (Hike 54) outlines one such route. This is tough country. Don't plan to hike many miles each day, particularly on the way back up to Clingmans Dome.

54 Silers Bald and Forney Creek

It would be hard to pick a better two-night backpack than this one. You get to sleep in a backcountry shelter (everyone needs to experience it at least once) and at a backcountry campsite. You have good high-elevation views, and you pass through scenic forests. Finally, you experience a Smokies trademark: powerful cascading creeks that you have to figure out how to cross. That said, this hike isn't for everyone. It's very strenuous and the high-elevation forest destruction at the start is depressing.

(See map for Hike 51: Clingmans Dome)

Start: Forney Ridge Parking Area on Clingmans Dome
Distance: 20.4-mile loop
Hiking time: About 12 hours—killer day hike, overnighter, or 2-nighter
Difficulty: Strenuous, due to steep grades, rocky trails, and creek crossings
Trail surface: Forest trails, some very rocky, and old railroad grades
Other trail users: About half of the route is open to equestrians
Maps: Clingmans Dome and Silers Bald USGS quads; Trails Illustrated #229 Great Smoky Mountains; Trails Illustrated #317 Clingmans Dome Cataloochee (only shows the eastern half of the hike); Trails Illustrated #316 Cades Cove Elkmont

Special considerations: Clingmans Dome Road is closed Dec 1–Mar 31. Several unbridged creek crossings might be a little tricky even in low water, and in high water they are dangerous or impassable. Do not make this hike after prolonged rains.

Read the introduction to the Appalachian Trail chapter at the beginning of Hikes 81 and 82 before making this hike. It contains important information about when and how to plan your trip. Silers Bald Shelter, your first night's stay on a 2-night backpack, is one of the most popular shelters in the park. Make reservations early, no matter the season.

Other: The parking lot is huge, but it's often not big enough to accommodate weekend traffic. Pit toilets are located at the parking area. A visitor center is located near the start of the hike.

Finding the trailhead: At Newfound Gap turn west onto Clingmans Dome Road and drive 7.0 miles to the Forney Ridge Parking Area at the end. Forney Ridge Trail begins on the far western end of the parking area. The paved path to Clingmans Dome Tower goes to the right, while Forney Ridge Trail drops down off of it to the left. GPS: N35 33.409' / 83 29.772'

The Hike

You can take the paved path to Clingmans Dome Tower and pick up the Appalachian Trail (AT) from there or bypass the tower (and the crowds) by taking Clingmans Dome Bypass Trail. (For the tower route, see Hike 51.) This hike description takes you on the bypass route, beginning on Forney Ridge Trail.

At the beginning of the paved path leading to Clingmans Dome Tower, Forney Ridge Trail drops down to the left. Follow it 0.2 mile and turn right (actually straight) onto Clingmans Dome Bypass Trail. This rocky trail climbs moderately for 0.5 mile to the AT, just west of the Clingmans Dome summit.

At the AT turn left (west), but take time to admire the view off the north side of the trail toward Mount LeConte. The next 2.5 miles on the AT to Double Spring Gap Shelter are relatively easy and provide numerous open vistas. About 0.6 mile before reaching the shelter, you pass the junction with Goshen Prong Trail (Hike 11).

As its name suggests, Double Spring Gap has two springs, one on each side of the gap and only a few yards from the shelter. If you're getting water, the spring on the south side is much better, as the northern spring seeps through a boggy area. If you can't get reservations at Silers Bald Shelter, you could spend the night here instead.

Pressing on from the gap, the AT goes on its typical roller-coaster grade through a forest of beech, buckeye, and mountain ash. At one point the trail comes to an open grassy spot with fair views toward High Rocks. At this point you come to The Narrows—a knife-edge ridge with good views off both sides. The trail soon forks at the junction with Welch Ridge Trail, going left. You'll take Welch Ridge eventually, but if you're planning to spend the night at Silers Bald Shelter, or you just want to see Silers Bald, you need to go to the right and stay on the AT. A 0.2-mile steep climb brings you to the 5,607-foot summit of Silers Bald at a small clearing. There's only one fair view from the clearing, a look back toward Clingmans Dome. On a sunny day you can see the light reflecting from the cars at the Forney Ridge Parking Area. An obvious path leads north from the summit a few hundred feet to a rock outcrop with wonderful open views to the north, as well as leafy views to the east and west.

From the summit, descend on the AT to Silers Bald Shelter. The shelter has an overhanging green roof, benches, and skylights. If the weather is clear, you can take in a show after dinner. Hike back up on Silers Bald and watch the sunset from the rock outcrop.

From the shelter, backtrack to Welch Ridge Trail and enjoy the easiest part of the hike for the next 2.5 miles, although parts of the trail are heavily overgrown. Stay straight (south) at the Hazel Creek Trail junction, and in another 0.8 mile reach the junction with Jonas Creek Trail, cutting sharply left (east).

On Jonas Creek Trail you descend more than 2,000 feet in 4.1 miles—not an extreme descent, but keep in mind that every step down has to be made up, and that includes all the down steps you've already made from Clingmans Dome. During the descent you pass through a very scenic forest, though none of it is old growth. You also have to cross Jonas Creek five times without benefit of foot logs. In normal flows this isn't much of a problem. Just watch out for slick and wobbly rocks. In high water it could get a little dicey, especially with a heavy pack.

Reach Campsite 70 at the junction of Jonas and Forney Creeks. It's a large, unattractive site that gets a lot of horse use. Pass through the campsite and cross Forney Creek on a foot log. The old railroad grade on the far side is Forney Creek Trail. Turn left (north) onto it, and begin your climb back up the mountain.

Campsite 69, a good choice for your second night's camp (or only night's camp on an overnighter), is 1.4 miles ahead. To get there, you must cross several small side streams on old rotten bridge supports and cross Forney Creek three times. In normal flows you might be able to rock-hop the crossings and keep your feet dry. Be careful: Some of the rocks are very slick. If the water is very high, you might not be able to cross at all. The thought of backtracking from here is not amusing, so plan this trip carefully.

Arrive at Campsite 69 a few hundred feet beyond the third crossing. There are tent sites on the right between the trail and Forney Creek, or maybe you'll get lucky and the secluded spot on the left will be open. It sits beside Huggins Creek. Many old logging artifacts are scattered about the site. In fact, all along Forney Creek Trail you can see traces of logging history. Before the park was established, most of the Forney Creek watershed was logged to within a short distance of Clingmans Dome.

Rock Slab Falls.

Shortly beyond the campsite, you have to cross Forney Creek once more. This crossing is a little easier than the previous ones. The next 3.6 miles to Campsite 68 follow Forney Creek upstream, sometimes close, sometimes a little distance away. You cross numerous side streams and small ravines by way of rotten bridge supports, many of them studded with nails. You have to cross Forney Creek once more during this stretch, but it's the easiest crossing of all.

Campsite 68 has an upper (68a) and a lower (68b) site. The lower section, which you reach first, is a very small, open site, situated by Forney Creek. It may not have a signpost designating it, but don't worry about being confused about just where this site is. It's not one of the more attractive campsites in park—definitely not a place to spend much time contemplating nature.

The trail climbs extremely steeply beyond Campsite 68b and comes to an old railroad rail across the trail. Look in the creek below to see the wheels and axle of an old railroad car. Just beyond here you come to Rock Slab Falls—a long, high, sliding cascade on Forney Creek. Notice the crisscrossing quartz veins across the falls. The waterfall marks Campsite 68a. The location is very scenic, but it's small, and you may not find a tent spot.

From Rock Slab Falls, the trail makes a few switchbacks and creek crossings and becomes a real trail—a real steep trail. When you come to the upper reaches of Forney Creek, you actually walk in the streambed a few feet before you switchback to the left and away from the creek. The trail continues climbing steeply and becomes rocky, and you enter a dark forest of spruce, rhododendron, and birch. As you climb higher you begin to see young Fraser firs. With a heavy pack, this stretch is a killer.

Finally, you come to the ridgeline and the junction with Forney Ridge Trail. Don't celebrate just yet: You still have more than a mile of rocky climbing to go. Turn left (north) on Forney Ridge Trail and continue busting your lungs for 0.9 mile to the junction with Clingmans Dome Bypass Trail. Turn sharply right here, staying on Forney Ridge Trail, and climb 0.2 mile to the parking area.

Now you can celebrate!

Miles and Directions

0.0 Start from the western end of the parking area on Forney Ridge Trail.

0.2 Bear to the right (north) onto Clingmans Dome Bypass Trail.

0.7 Junction with AT. Turn left (west) on the AT.

2.6 Junction with Goshen Prong Trail on the right. Continue heading west on the AT.

3.2 Double Spring Gap Shelter.

4.5 Junction with Welch Ridge Trail, forking to the left. If camping at Silers Bald Shelter, continue heading west on the AT.

4.7 Silers Bald.

4.9 Silers Bald Shelter. Return to the junction with Welch Ridge Trail.

5.3 Turn sharply back to the right (south) on Welch Ridge Trail.

7.0 Junction with Hazel Creek Trail on the right. Continue straight (south) on Welch Ridge Trail.

7.8 Turn sharply to the left (east) onto Jonas Creek Trail.

11.9 Just beyond Campsite 70, turn left (north) onto Forney Creek Trail.

13.3 Campsite 69.

16.9 Campsite 68b.

17.3 Rock Slab Falls and Campsite 68a.

19.3 Turn left (north) on Forney Ridge Trail.

20.2 Arrive back at junction with Clingmans Dome Bypass Trail. Turn sharply to the right and return to the parking area.

20.4 Arrive back at parking area.

Options: Fit and experienced hikers can make this trip as a day hike, but it isn't recommended. Even as a two-night backpack, that last day out is tough. You can extend the hike to three nights by staying the first night at Silers Bald Shelter, the second night at Campsite 70, and the third night at Campsite 68a. However, this means staying the second night at a less-than-desirable campsite. As an overnighter, you can save weight by staying at either Double Spring Gap Shelter or Silers Bald Shelter and not carrying a tent. But you'd still have a brutal second day. The best option is to go for the two-night backpack.

55 Juney Whank Falls

As waterfalls go, Juney Whank Falls isn't anything to get excited about. However, the trail is short and if you're in the Deep Creek area for another hike, it's easy to include this one as well.

Start: Parking area for Deep Creek Trail near Deep Creek Campground
Distance: 0.7-mile loop
Hiking time: About 45 minutes—day hike
Difficulty: Moderate
Trail surface: Packed dirt
Other trail users: Equestrians
Maps: Bryson City USGS quad; Trails Illus-trated #229 Great Smoky Mountains; Trails Illustrated #317 Clingmans Dome Cataloochee
Other: If you get here in the middle of a summer weekday, you probably won't find a parking space in the paved lot. On a weekend you can forget it. Few other places in the park are as crowded. Restrooms are available at the picnic areas.

Finding the trailhead: Downtown Bryson City has many signs that direct you to Deep Creek Campground. As you enter the park, continue on the paved road past the campground entrance and the picnic areas to where the road ends at a turnaround. A paved parking area is on the left. The trail begins from the upper end of the parking area at the sign for Juney Whank Falls. GPS: N35 27.877' / W83 26.051'

The Hike

Don't worry about the crowds you see at the parking area. They're all headed up Deep Creek Trail, and except for a short segment at the end, you might have this hike to yourself.

The trail follows Juney Whank Branch upstream a short distance, then swings to the left and away from the creek, climbing to a junction with a bridle path coming in from the left. Stay to the right and continue climbing up the old roadbed. Climb moderately for about 0.2 mile to an obvious path on the right leading to the base of the waterfall.

From the falls, you can backtrack or continue up the bank to rejoin the bridle path (it circles around the top of the falls). Turn right and go 50 feet, then bear to the right off of the horse trail onto an obvious path. This path leads about 0.2 mile through a deep gully to Deep Creek Trail, where a right turn takes you back to the parking area.

Miles and Directions

0.0 Start from the upper (north) end of the parking area at the sign for Juney Whank Falls.

0.1 Bridle path comes in from the left. Stay to the right, heading uphill.

0.3 Turn right on the obvious path and descend about 75 yards to the waterfall. Continue following the path on the other side of the footbridge.

0.4 Rejoin the bridle path, which circles around the top of the waterfall. Turn right and go 50 feet to a fork. Turn right at the fork and descend.

0.6 Turn right at junction with Deep Creek Trail.

0.7 Arrive back at parking area.

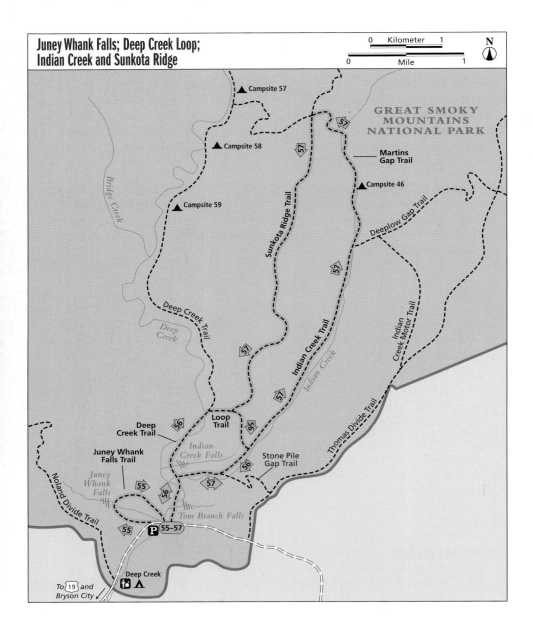

Juney Whank Falls; Deep Creek Loop; Indian Creek and Sunkota Ridge

56 Deep Creek Loop

This is an exceptional and relatively short hike that offers something interesting at any time of year. In autumn the colorful foliage is superb. From late autumn through early spring, the lack of foliage exposes Tom Branch Falls, among the more picturesque waterfalls in the park. Wildflowers grow in profusion in the spring. In summer? Ah, summer. In warm weather the first 0.7 mile of this hike is possibly the most popular walk in the entire park. You'll see countless people, young and old, hiking along the easy roadbed to Indian Creek Falls. Many of them carry inner tubes to float Deep Creek back to the parking area. You can't miss the roadside rental businesses vying for your attention as you approach the park's entrance. Bicycles are allowed along the first couple of miles of Deep Creek Trail and the lower section of Indian Creek Trail. So in summer you're likely to encounter backpackers, day hikers, fishers, tubers, baby strollers, scooters, and bicyclists.

(See map for Hike 55: Juney Whank Falls.)

Start: Parking area for Deep Creek Trail near Deep Creek Campground
Distance: 4.4-mile lollipop
Hiking time: About 2.5 hours—day hike
Difficulty: Easy
Trail surface: Old forest roads and forest trails
Other trail users: Equestrians and bicyclists (bicycles allowed only on the Deep Creek Trail and Indian Creek Trail portion; equestrians not allowed on the lower section of Deep Creek Trail)

Maps: Bryson City USGS quad; Trails Illustrated #229 Great Smoky Mountains; Trails Illustrated #317 Clingmans Dome Cataloochee
Other: If you get here in the middle of a summer weekday, you probably won't find a parking space in the paved lot. On a weekend you can forget it. Few other places in the park are as crowded. Restrooms are available at the picnic areas.

Finding the trailhead: Downtown Bryson City has many signs that direct you to Deep Creek Campground. As you enter the park, continue on the paved road past the campground entrance and the picnic areas to where the road ends at a turnaround. A paved parking area is on the left. The trail begins from the upper end of the parking area as a continuation of the road. GPS: N35 27.877' / W83 26.051'

The Hike

Start up the gravel road that continues from the road turnaround. In 0.2 mile you pass Tom Branch Falls on the right, dropping directly into Deep Creek on the opposite side. Only when the leaves are off the trees can you see much of this high waterfall. Soon you cross Deep Creek on an auto bridge and reach the junction with Indian Creek Trail on the right, just before Deep Creek Trail crosses Indian Creek. Turn onto Indian Creek Trail and follow it upstream. In a few hundred feet, you pass Indian Creek Falls—a long, steep, sliding cascade. You can see it from the trail or take a side path to the base for a closer view.

Continue on Indian Creek Trail—an old roadbed—and pass Stone Pile Gap Trail on the right, 0.5 mile from Deep Creek. Less than 0.25 mile farther, you come to Loop Trail on the left (west). Follow Loop Trail up a small drainage, pass by the lower end of Sunkota Ridge Trail, and then descend to Deep Creek Trail. Turn left, cross Deep Creek on a bridge, and follow the trail downstream. Cross Deep Creek once more before reaching the Indian Creek junction.

From the junction with Indian Creek Trail, retrace your steps to the parking area.

Miles and Directions

0.0 Start from the north end of the parking area on Deep Creek Trail as a continuation of the road.

0.2 Tom Branch Falls drops into opposite side of Deep Creek.

0.7 Turn right onto Indian Creek Trail.

0.8 Side path on the left leads a short distance to Indian Creek Falls.

1.2 Junction with Stone Pile Gap Trail on the right. Continue straight on the old roadbed.

1.5 Turn left (west) onto Loop Trail.

2.0 Junction with Sunkota Ridge Trail on the right. Continue on Loop Trail.

2.7 Junction with Deep Creek Trail. Turn left and follow Deep Creek downstream.

3.7 Return to junction with Indian Creek Trail. Retrace your steps to the trailhead.

4.4 Arrive back at trailhead.

Options: Indian Creek and Sunkota Ridge (Hike 57) is a longer loop hike that includes the lower section of this hike. Several other loop options exist in the Deep Creek area. Study a trail map for possibilities.

57 Indian Creek and Sunkota Ridge

If Hike 56 is not quite enough to get your heart pumping, this hike is just the ticket. It has everything that Hike 56 offers, and adds the ability to get farther back into the mountains and away from the crowds. It's among the finest moderate-length day hikes in the park. Before you make the trip, you should read the narrative for Hike 56 as it contains important information that pertains to the lower section of this hike.

(See map for Hike 55: Juney Whank Falls.)

Start: Parking area for Deep Creek Trail near Deep Creek Campground
Distance: 11.6-mile lollipop
Hiking time: About 6 hours—day hike, with overnight options
Difficulty: Moderate
Trail surface: Old forest roads and forest trails
Other trail users: Equestrians and bicyclists (bicycles allowed only on the Deep Creek Trail and Indian Creek Trail portion; equestrians not allowed on the lower section of Deep Creek Trail)

Maps: Bryson City and Clingmans Dome USGS quads; Trails Illustrated #229 Great Smoky Mountains; Trails Illustrated #317 Clingmans Dome Cataloochee
Other: If you get here in the middle of a summer weekday, you probably won't find a parking space in the paved lot. On a weekend you can forget it. Few other places in the park are as crowded. Restrooms are available at the picnic areas.

Finding the trailhead: Downtown Bryson City has many signs that direct you to Deep Creek Campground. As you enter the park, continue on the paved road past the campground entrance and the picnic areas to where the road ends at a turnaround. A paved parking area is on the left. The trail begins from the upper end of the parking area as a continuation of the road. GPS: N35 27.877' / W83 26.051'

The Hike

Start up the gravel road that continues from the road turnaround. In 0.2 mile you pass Tom Branch Falls on the right, dropping directly into Deep Creek on the opposite side. Only when the leaves are off the trees can you see much of this high waterfall. Soon you cross Deep Creek on an auto bridge and reach the junction with Indian Creek Trail on the right, just before Deep Creek Trail crosses Indian Creek. Turn onto Indian Creek Trail and follow it upstream. In a few hundred feet, you pass Indian Creek Falls—a long, steep, sliding cascade. You can see it from the trail or take a side path to the base for a closer view.

Continue on Indian Creek Trail—an old roadbed—and pass Stone Pile Gap Trail on the right, 0.5 mile from Deep Creek. Less than 0.25 mile farther, you come to Loop Trail on the left (west). You'll come down that trail to this point later in the hike. Now, you want to continue straight on the old roadbed of Indian Creek Trail. You'll pass old homesites and cross the creek a few times on bridges. Come to the junction with Deeplow Gap Trail at mile 3.6. Stay on the roadbed and cross Indian Creek two more times, at which point the road becomes overgrown and seems more like a trail. Cross the creek once more and make a short, moderate climb to the old road turnaround and the junction with Martins Gap Trail, just after crossing Estes Branch at Campsite 46. There's nowhere to go at the junction but straight ahead.

Now you're on a real trail, and you soon cross Indian Creek on foot logs twice more in quick succession. Farther ahead you cross the creek for the final time and begin a continuous moderate climb to Sunkota Ridge at Martins Gap. Martins Gap Trail crosses over the ridge and descends to Deep Creek. Your route goes to the left and follows the ridgeline on Sunkota Ridge Trail. You have a short climb over a small knoll at first and then a longer ascent. After topping out on the ascent, it's mostly downhill all the way to the junction with Loop Trail. In winter there are decent views from the ridgeline.

At Loop Trail turn left (east) and descend along a small, narrow ravine back to the junction of Indian Creek Trail and Loop Trail. From the junction, retrace your steps to the trailhead.

Miles and Directions

0.0 Start from the north end of the parking area on Deep Creek Trail as a continuation of the road.

0.2 Tom Branch Falls drops into opposite side of Deep Creek.

0.7 Turn right onto Indian Creek Trail.

0.8 Side path on the left leads a short distance to Indian Creek Falls.

1.2 Junction with Stone Pile Gap Trail on the right. Continue straight on the old roadbed.

1.5 Junction with Loop Trail on the left. Continue straight on the old roadbed.

3.6 Junction with Deeplow Gap Trail. Continue straight on the old roadbed.

4.3 Campsite 46 and junction with Martins Gap Trail and the end of the old road. Continue straight ahead on Martins Gap Trail.

5.8 At Martins Gap turn left (south) onto Sunkota Ridge Trail.

9.6 Junction with Loop Trail. Turn left (east) and follow the trail back to Indian Creek Trail.

10.1 Arrive back at junction of Indian Creek and Loop Trails. Turn right and retrace your steps back to the trailhead.

11.6 Arrive back at trailhead.

Options: From Martins Gap, instead of turning south on Sunkota Ridge Trail, you can continue on Martins Gap Trail for 1.5 miles to Deep Creek Trail. Turn left and follow the trail back to the parking area for a total round-trip distance of 13.4 miles. Another option is to turn right (west) on Loop Trail from Sunkota Ridge Trail and follow it to Deep Creek Trail, again turning left and following the trail back to the parking area. This option makes the total mileage 12.0 miles. The first option replaces the ridge hike with a long walk along Deep Creek, while the second option keeps the ridge hike and adds just a little more to the walk beside Deep Creek.

Numerous other options exist in this section of the park for moderate and long loop hikes. Several campsites make good options for overnighting. Campsite 46 on Indian Creek Trail and Campsite 57 on Deep Creek Trail are two good choices. Study a trail map for possibilities.

Foot log over Indian Creek.

58 Goldmine Loop

At only a little over 3 miles long and offering a fine hiking experience far away from the big crowds in other areas of the park, it's surprising that this hike doesn't get more attention. Beyond the first 0.25 mile there's a good chance that you'll have the hike all to yourself. The 0.2-mile tunnel at the start is a popular destination, however, so expect to meet people when you walk through it. (Don't be surprised if you see them with cans of spray paint in their hands.) The tunnel makes a unique hiking experience. It's long enough that it gets dark and spooky in the middle. Length aside, how many hikes start out with a walk through a tunnel on a road to nowhere?

Start: Lakeshore trailhead at the end of Lakeview Drive
Distance: 3.1-mile loop
Hiking time: About 2 hours—day hike or overnighter
Difficulty: Moderate
Trail surface: Paved road, old forest roads, and forest trails
Best season: June for the mountain laurel bloom

Other trail users: Equestrians
Maps: Noland Creek USGS quad; Trails Illustrated #229 Great Smoky Mountains; Trails Illustrated #317 Clingmans Dome Cataloochee; Trails Illustrated #316 Cades Cove Elkmont
Other: There's plenty of room to park, but there are no facilities. The closest facilities are at Bryson City.

Finding the trailhead: From US 19 in downtown Bryson City, turn north onto Everett Street (the main drag) and follow it out of town. Outside Bryson City the road is called Fontana Road, and when you enter the park, it's called Lakeview Drive. If you just stay on the same road and don't take any turns, you'll get it right. From US 19 it is 8.7 miles to the end of the road at a parking area on the right. GPS: N35 27.533' / W83 32.266'

The Hike

The hike begins on Lakeshore Trail, which is a continuation of the road and passes through the tunnel. Beyond the tunnel the roadbed changes to a trail, and in less than a quarter of a mile, Tunnel Bypass Trail comes in from the left. Horses and claustrophobic hikers use the bypass. Mountain laurel is abundant here, as it is along the entire hike. If you're hiking in May and June, its blooms are a special treat.

Shortly beyond Tunnel Bypass Trail, you come to Goldmine Loop Trail on the left (southwest). You won't find gold on this trail and there is no mine, but the scenery sure is rich. Taking the trail, you descend steeply down the spine of the ridge to a small saddle, where the trail swings off to the right of the ridge and heads down a drainage. You soon cross a tiny stream branch. Look to the right in an open field to see an old chimney. There are walnut trees here too. For the next little while, you roughly parallel Goldmine Branch, and along the way you see other signs of settlement—clearings, wire fencing, broken containers.

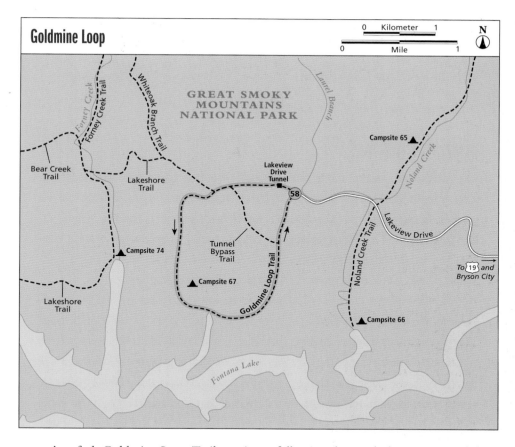

Goldmine Loop

GREAT SMOKY
MOUNTAINS
NATIONAL PARK

At a fork Goldmine Loop Trail continues following the creek downstream, while a side path leads left a few hundred yards to Campsite 67, a very small site beside Hyatt Branch. Back on the main trail, it's a short distance to a small finger of Fontana Lake. After circling the embayment you leave the lake and begin climbing along Tunnel Branch. You soon leave the creek and begin a steep climb up a ridge to meet up with the other end of Tunnel Bypass Trail. This is the official end of Goldmine Loop Trail. A left turn onto Tunnel Bypass Trail takes you to Lakeshore Trail in 1.2 miles (at the point you passed earlier in the hike). A right turn leads in 0.4 mile to Lakeview Drive, just below the parking area. Along the way you pass over a saddle and through good spring wildflower habitat.

Miles and Directions

0.0 Start on Lakeshore Trail as a continuation of Lakeview Drive.

0.2 Enter Lakeview Drive Tunnel.

0.4 Exit Lakeview Drive Tunnel.

0.6 Junction with Tunnel Bypass Trail on the left. Continue straight on Lakeshore Trail.

0.7   Turn left (southwest) onto Goldmine Loop Trail.

1.6   Path on the left fork leads to Campsite 67. Continue to the right on Goldmine Loop Trail.

1.8   Fontana Lake.

2.7   End of Goldmine Loop Trail at the junction with Tunnel Bypass Trail. Turn right on Goldmine Loop Trail.

3.1   Arrive at Lakeview Drive, just below the parking area.

ROAD TO NOWHERE

Why in the world would someone build a thousand-foot-long tunnel, wide enough for two lanes of traffic, and then use it for a hiking trail? Good question. The answer is that the US government reneged on a 1943 agreement to build a road from near Bryson City to near Fontana Dam as part of mitigation for damming Little Tennessee River to create Fontana Lake. The lake flooded sections of NC 288, and a new road would not only provide an access route around the lake, but it would generate needed income for the county from tourism.

The state of North Carolina upheld its end of the bargain by building a road to the park boundary. The National Park Service began its section of the road in the 1960s but stopped after the construction uncovered rocks that, when exposed to air and water, create sulfuric acid runoff that is detrimental to aquatic life and vegetation. The park service's viewpoint was that further construction would be harmful to the environment and to the overall wilderness aspect of the Smokies. Furthermore, the road was no longer as important as it was in the 1940s because NC 28 on the south shore of Fontana Lake provided a suitable route around the lake. Several cemeteries were blocked from road access because of the lake, but the park had always provided boat access for family members.

For decades, many in Swain County fought for completion of the road and many others fought for a cash settlement to the county. The official position of the National Park Service was for the cash settlement. Powerful people on both sides of the fight shook their fists. Finally, through the efforts of Congressman Heath Shuler, a settlement was made. On February 6, 2010, Secretary of the Interior Ken Salazar announced that the US Department of the Interior would pay up to $52 million into a trust fund for Swain County.

The long fight is over, and for most people the hatchet is buried. However, old feelings die hard, especially when the government is involved. As of early 2012, if you want to hike Goldmine Loop Trail, you still have to drive by a particularly opinionated sign, erected many years ago by an obviously disgruntled Swain County resident.

59 Hazel Creek and Bone Valley

All of this hike is on old roads, and the first 5 miles or so aren't much different from walking any of the drivable dirt roads in the park. If you're looking to hike a true trail, this hike will disappoint you. That said, the hike is extremely rewarding for anyone interested in the early settlement and logging history of the park. Also, getting to the trailhead is a special delight as it includes a boat ride across Fontana Lake!

This is a wonderful way to spend a summer day in the Smokies. It's great any time of year, but in summer you can enjoy the stream crossings and take advantage of Fontana Lake. If you get back to your pickup point a little early, you can take a dip in the lake while you're waiting for the boat.

Before you venture into this part of the park, you might want to brush up on the region's history. Get a copy of *Hazel Creek from Then till Now* by Duane Oliver, or *Fontana, A Pocket History of Appalachia* by Lance Holland, both available from park sales outlets.

Start: Boat landing on Fontana Lake at Hazel Creek

Distance: 15.4 miles out and back

Hiking time: About 7 hours—day hike or over-nighter, with options for extended trips

Difficulty: Easy, except for stream crossings

Trail surface: Old forest roads

Other trail users: Equestrians

Maps: Fontana Dam (lake portion only), Tuskeegee, and Thunderhead Mountain USGS quad; Trails Illustrated #229 Great Smoky Mountains; Trails Illustrated #316 Cades Cove Elkmont

Special considerations: Before you can make this trip, you must get to the trailhead on the north side of Fontana Lake. You could hike about 10 miles from Fontana Dam on Lake-shore Trail, but a boat shuttle adds a unique highlight to the trip. Call Fontana Marina at (828) 498-2129 to make reservations. If you plan to day hike, you'll want to leave as early as they'll take you and don't dawdle on the hike in. You can pace yourself on the way back as time allows. If you don't make it back by the pick-up time, they won't leave you overnight, but they may leave for another pickup and come back to get you later. And they may charge you extra for that additional trip. All of the campsites along this hike require a reservation. Four crossings of Bone Valley Creek require wading, which can be dangerous in high water.

Other: Short-term parking is available along the slope leading to Fontana Marina, and there's plenty of parking in the gravel lot back atop the hill. Restrooms are available at the marina entrance. Backcountry camping permits are available at a kiosk near the restroom building.

A special treat for backpackers is the hot showers located at the Fontana Dam Visitor Center. The showers are open all day, every day of the year.

Finding the trailhead: To reach Fontana Marina from the junction of US 19/74 and NC 28 in the southwestern portion of the park, turn west onto NC 28 and drive 21.1 miles to the stop sign at the entrance road for Fontana Dam. Turn right, go a short distance, and turn onto the first road to the right. This road leads 0.2 mile to the marina entrance. GPS: N35 26.469' / W83 47.726'

The Hike

Your adventure begins when you step off the marina dock onto the boat. The boat captain knows the lake and the Smokies well, so ask a lot of questions. The drop-off point varies according to water level, but the captain will make sure you know which direction to hike.

The entire hike is along an old road—you could drive a Winnebago on the first 5.0 miles. Pass by Campsite 86 on the left after about 0.4 mile. The site is popular with boaters since it's so close to the lake. In a kayak or canoe, you can paddle right to it in the summer when the lake levels are high.

A short distance from the campsite, you come to a bridge over Hazel Creek and an interpretive display. If you don't already know a little about Hazel Creek's history, you're in for a surprise. You're standing in the old logging boomtown of Proctor. Today, about all that remains is a frame house (you can see it across the creek), the concrete-and-brick carcass of the large, dry kilns, a few small concrete structures, and a zillion artifacts and foundations scattered about and hidden in the leaf litter. It's hard to imagine that the photograph of Proctor you see on the display was taken here.

If you are familiar with this area but haven't been here in a while, you might be a little confused by the trail signs. Continuing straight ahead, still on the right (east) side of Hazel Creek, is Lakeshore Trail, as always. But after you cross the creek, no longer does Lakeshore Trail go to the right. Now it goes left and follows a new course over Pinnacle Ridge to Eagle Creek. (The old Lakeshore Trail segment that followed Pinnacle Creek is now closed.) The trail on the right, heading upstream, is now Hazel Creek Trail. Locals have always called the trail by this name, but the official park name was Lakeshore Trail. Before taking Hazel Creek Trail, go to the left and explore the Granville Calhoun House. It's open for you to walk through.

Now heading upstream on Hazel Creek Trail, you soon pass a large concrete structure on the left. That was the kiln for the lumber operation. A few yards farther you pass some smaller concrete ruins, and farther on there's a concrete water gauge station beside Hazel Creek. Continuing on, you cross the creek two more times (on auto bridges) and come to Campsite 85, right beside the trail in an open area. If camping, sites 84 and 83, farther along, offer much better options.

Continuing on the road, you come to the fourth bridge over Hazel Creek at a particularly scenic spot with cascades and potholes. Take time to admire the scene, but pay attention to where you lean on the bridge railings in summer. The undersides of the thick railings make choice sites for wasps and hornets. This is the voice of experience speaking!

Just beyond the fifth (and last) bridge over Hazel Creek, the trail forks. On the left is Jenkins Ridge Trail (formerly Lakeshore Trail). You want to go right on Hazel Creek Trail and immediately cross Haw Gap Branch on a bridge. Campsite 84 sits on the right, between Hazel Creek and Haw Gap Branch. It's an attractive site set among

Early morning at Fontana Marina on Fontana Lake.

white pines, with a pine-needle ground cover. This is a good choice for a campsite.

Continue about 0.8 mile from Campsite 84 and reach the junction with Bone Valley Trail, just past the bridge over Bone Valley Creek. On the right, just before the creek crossing, sits Campsite 83. This site is also a fine choice for camping. It's large, with the tent sites spread out, and it's a very attractive site. However, you might have to share it with a party of horse campers.

After crossing Bone Valley Creek, turn left and follow the creek upstream, still using an old road. There are four additional creek crossings, all of which require wading. In normal flows you just need to be careful about walking on the extremely slick rocks in the creek, but in high water you might have to turn back. Just before and after the fourth crossing, look to the left to see a unique sight in the Smokies. Yes, that's a beaver dam. Beavers historically inhabited the Smokies but had been absent in the twentieth century until the 1960s. It's good to have them back.

Just beyond the beaver dam, the trail follows Big Flats Branch a short distance and swings away to an open field. Hall (Kress) Cabin sits here and is open for exploring. An obvious path near the cabin leads a short distance to Hall Cemetery. In the vicinity are the foundation and chimney remains of Kress House, which served as a hunting and fishing lodge for wealthy sportsmen.

The hike ends at the cabin. You have to backtrack from here.

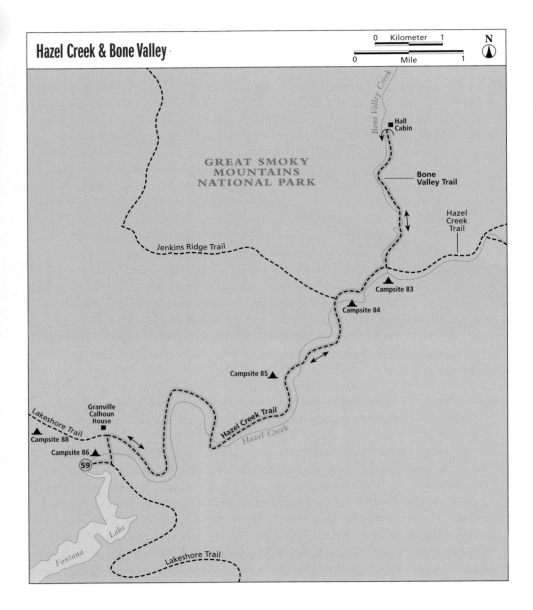

0   Kilometer   1

0   Mile   1

N

GREAT SMOKY
MOUNTAINS
NATIONAL PARK

Bone Valley Creek

Hall
Cabin

Bone
Valley Trail

Hazel
Creek
Trail

Jenkins Ridge Trail

Campsite 83

Campsite 84

Campsite 85

Granville
Calhoun
House

Hazel Creek Trail

Hazel Creek

Lakeshore Trail

Campsite 88

Campsite 86

59

Lake

Fontana

Lakeshore Trail

Miles and Directions

0.0   Start on the lakeshore where the boat drops you off. The exact location will vary according to lake levels.

0.4   Campsite 86.

0.5   Come to a bridge over Hazel Creek and the junction with Lakeshore and Hazel Creek Trails. Cross the creek and follow Hazel Creek Trail upstream.

3.4 Campsite 85.

5.1 Campsite 84 and junction with Jenkins Ridge Trail on the left (formerly the Sugar Fork segment of Lakeshore Trail). Turn right to remain on Hazel Creek Trail.

5.9 At Campsite 83 cross Bone Valley Creek and turn left on Bone Valley Trail, following the creek upstream.

7.7 Arrive at Hall Cabin. Return the way you came.

15.4 Arrive back at the boat landing.

Options: Although the Hazel Creek area is remote and not easily accessed, options for hiking and camping in the area are many and varied. Hike 60 covers some of this region. A terrific two-night backpack would be to take the boat shuttle to Hazel Creek and camp the first night at Campsite 86. The next day you would take Lakeshore Trail to Eagle Creek and stay at Campsite 90. The boat would pick you up from there the next morning. To add more hiking to the trip, have the boat drop you off at Hazel Creek in the morning, then hike to Campsite 90 and overnight there. The next day you would hike 5.5 miles back to Fontana Dam using Lakeshore Trail.

With a canoe or kayak, you have wonderful flexibility. You can paddle into Campsite 86 or 90 and hike as much as you want during the day. Boaters can also use the unique Campsite 87, which lies on an island at the mouth of Eagle Creek.

60 Eagle Creek, Spence Field, and Hazel Creek

For those looking for a kick–butt Smokies adventure, here's your hike. Probably the most strenuous hike in this guidebook, with big elevation gains and enough creek wades to make your feet stay pruny for days. But the rewards go far beyond a good workout. The hike features just about everything the park is famous for: cascading streams, varied plant life, scenic views, and history. As if that weren't enough, you get to take a boat ride across Fontana Lake.

For camp reading, get a copy of *Hazel Creek from Then till Now* by Duane Oliver or *Fontana, A Pocket History of Appalachia* by Lance Holland, both available from park sales outlets.

Start: Campsite 90 on the north side of Fontana Lake

Distance: 27.9-mile loop

Hiking time: About 18 hours—killer overnighter, 2-nighter, 3-nighter, or extended options

Difficulty: Strenuous, due to steep grades and creek wades

Trail surface: Forest trails and old dirt roads

Best season: Summer, to make the creek wades bearable

Other trail users: Equestrians permitted on about half of the hike

Maps: Fontana Dam, Cades Cove, Thunderhead Mountain, and Tuskeegee USGS quads; Trails Illustrated #229 Great Smoky Mountains; Trails Illustrated #316 Cades Cove Elkmont

Special considerations: You have a lot to consider before making this hike. First, you have to get to the trailhead at Campsite 90 on the Eagle Creek embayment. That requires hiking 5.5 miles from Fontana Dam or taking a boat shuttle across Fontana Lake. The boat shuttle is definitely recommended, adding an interesting highlight to the trip. Call Fontana Marina at (828) 498-2129 to make reservations.

A key consideration is the many creek crossings. In all but the lowest water, most of them must be waded. In high water they can be dangerous or impassable. Generally, winter is not a good time to make this trip, but summer is ideal. The water is lower and getting your feet wet is not a problem. Plus, in summer you can take a dip in Fontana Lake at the Hazel Creek and Eagle Creek embayments.

You need to consider your physical abilities honestly before making this hike. The last part of Eagle Creek Trail is a tough climb and most of Jenkins Ridge Trail is a brutal descent that's hard on the knees.

No matter how you plan your campsites, it's likely that you'll want to stay one night at Spence Field Shelter. You need to make a reservation for it, as with all park shelters.

Other: Short-term parking is available along the slope leading to Fontana Marina, and there's plenty of parking in the gravel lot back atop the hill. Restrooms are available at the marina entrance. Backcountry camping permits are available at a kiosk near the restroom building.

A special treat for backpackers is the hot showers located at the Fontana Dam Visitor Center. The showers are open all day, every day of the year.

Finding the trailhead: To reach Fontana Marina from the junction of US 19/74 and NC 28 in the southwestern portion of the park, turn west onto NC 28 and drive 21.1 miles to the stop sign at the entrance road for Fontana Dam. Turn right, go a short distance, and turn onto the first road to the right. This road leads 0.2 mile to the marina entrance. GPS: N35 26.469' / W83 47.726'

The Hike

After the boat drops you off, walk through Campsite 90 and get on Lakeshore Trail, heading upstream along Eagle Creek. After about 0.4 mile you cross the creek on an elaborate metal footbridge. Just beyond the bridge is the junction of Lakeshore Trail and Eagle Creek Trail. Lakeshore Trail turns off right and crosses Pinnacle Ridge on its way to the Hazel Creek embayment. (You'll travel this trail at the end of the hike.) If you are familiar with this area but haven't been here in a while, you might be a little confused by this junction. This segment of Lakeshore Trail opened in 2001. It replaces the segment of Lakeshore Trail that followed Pinnacle Creek, known locally as Pinnacle Creek Trail. That trail, along with its backcountry campsite, is no longer maintained. (Campsite 88 has been moved to the new trail segment, near the Hazel Creek end.)

Take Eagle Creek Trail at the junction. On it, you soon cross the creek a second time on a footbridge. Enjoy this bridge, because it's the last bridged crossing you'll have over Eagle Creek. Coming up are twelve full crossings and three crossings where the creek splits. In all but the lowest water, all could be wades. In high water the crossings are dangerous, if possible at all. If you aren't comfortable with the first one, turn around.

At 1.1 miles you pass the old Lakeshore Trail on the right. Not too far ahead is the first Eagle Creek crossing and shortly afterward, crossing number two. A short way ahead, just before you cross Ekaneetlee Creek, you pass Campsite 89 on the left. Situated in a grove of hemlock and white pine, this site has a soft pine-needle ground cover but no privacy. A couple of old railroad rails remind you that this trail, like many others in the park, follows an old logging railroad grade.

At the sixth ford of Eagle Creek, you cross a split of the stream onto a narrow island. Campsite 96, a very small site, is located here. Conscientious people won't like camping here. Park regulations require that you answer Mother Nature's call at least 100 feet from any streams or trails. That means you have to wade across Eagle Creek every time you have to go. The park puts a lot of trust in people with this one.

Just beyond Campsite 96 are two more fords that take you back to the left side of the creek. After five additional fords you come to Campsite 97 on the left, right beside the creek. A 3-foot-diameter saw blade leans on a tree here. Just beyond the campsite is the final creek crossing. An illegal campsite sits on the left after this crossing. An old bed frame and several other artifacts lie scattered about.

The grade to this point has been a piece of cake—uphill, but almost imperceptibly so. That changes now—gently at first, moderately later on. Pressing on, you pass a huge blowdown of trees off to the right and eventually make two crossings of Gunna Creek. Gunna Creek is the major headwater stream that creates Eagle Creek, and you've been following it for a while. The trail swings away from the creek a couple of times to a switchback and then comes to a fork. Turn left (the right fork ends in a few yards) and climb much more steeply, passing by an interesting rock on the right. It projects out of the ground as a monolith, with rock tripe lichens covering its surface.

Farther up, the trail swings away from Gunna Creek and begins tracing Spence Cabin Branch. The next 0.25 mile or so is insanely steep, very rocky, and overgrown in wood nettle. This is the toughest part of the hike. Once beyond the steep part, the trail dips to cross the creek and continues following it upstream before swinging away to the right and climbing steeply to Spence Field Shelter. Several hundred feet before the shelter, the trail crosses a spring—the shelter's water source.

Continue beyond the shelter about 0.2 mile to the junction with the Appalachian Trail at Spence Field. Turn right (east) and in 100 yards you pass Bote Mountain Trail, which comes in from the left. When you top out on the grassy hump, strike out through the grass a few yards on the right to a rock cairn. There's a great view looking down the Eagle Creek drainage to Fontana Lake. This is probably the only good view you'll find on Spence Field, despite several narratives about the "spectacular panoramic views," even in some recent publications. That's not to say Spence Field isn't scenic. On the contrary, the open, grassy fields are fabulous—a highlight of this hike.

Descend from the hump a few yards and turn right (southeast) onto Jenkins Ridge Trail. The trail starts out heavily overgrown and at first skirts the flanks of Rocky Top, then crosses the headwaters of Gunna Creek and skirts the flanks of Blockhouse Mountain. After 2.8 easy miles and a final steep ascent, you reach Haw Gap, marked by a small clearing overgrown in grass and weeds. Work your way to the other side of the field and reenter the forest.

For the next 3.7 miles, the trail follows on or close to the spine of Jenkins Trail Ridge—a ridge interestingly named after a trail, rather than the other way around. There are a few short ascents, with a couple of them steep—one brutal—but it's mostly downhill. This isn't your average ordinary descent, however. In places, the slope is wicked and there is very little grading—just a clear spot on the ground. With a heavy pack, this stretch is murder on the knees. When it's raining or after the autumn leaves fall, it could be very dangerous. In snow it's suicidal.

Reach Pickens Gap and celebrate the end of the difficult parts of this hike. The remainder is a comparative piece of cake. The old Lakeshore Trail goes to the right here and meets Eagle Creek Trail in about 4 miles. You might be tempted to shorten the hike by taking this route, but remember, this trail is closed and no longer maintained, and there are more than a dozen unbridged creek crossings. Go left instead, and follow Jenkins Ridge Trail (formerly the Sugar Fork segment of Lakeshore Trail) 2.4 easy miles to Hazel Creek Trail. Turn right (south) and follow Hazel Creek downstream.

Once you reach the final Hazel Creek bridge at the horse pasture, continue on the right side of the creek (don't cross the bridge), pass the Granville Calhoun House and yard, and pick up the obvious roadbed. The next 4.4 miles follow along the Lakeshore Trail segment that opened in 2001. About half the route is on an old roadbed, but all of it is wide, well graded, and never overly steep. It climbs alongside Sheehan

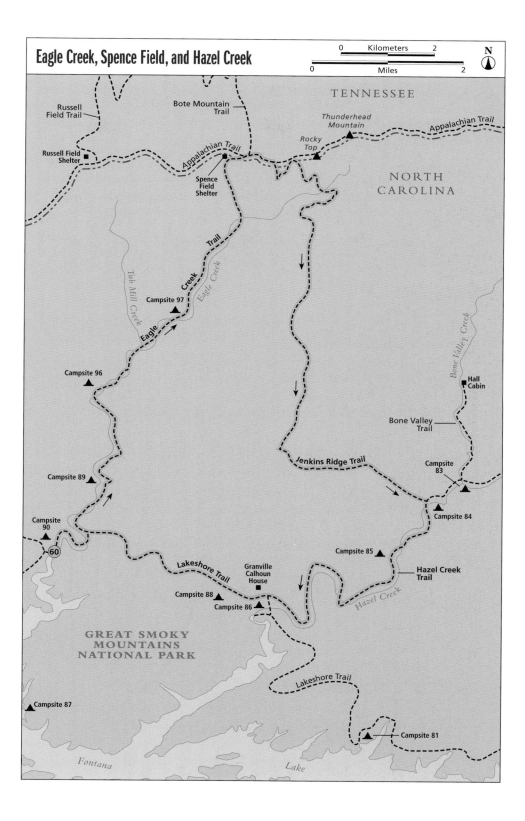

Branch a good distance, swings away and crosses around a ridge, descends to cross a small branch, then makes a long ascent to cross Pinnacle Ridge before descending rather steeply to Eagle Creek. The last section passes through a forest with many dead pines—listen for the jungle call of the pileated woodpecker through here.

Once you get back to the bridge over Eagle Creek, retrace your steps back to Campsite 90. And get some rest—you'll need it!

Miles and Directions

0.0   Start on the lakeshore where the boat drops you off. The exact location will vary according to lake levels. Walk through Campsite 90 and get on Lakeshore Trail, heading upstream along Eagle Creek.

0.5   Cross Eagle Creek on a footbridge and turn left after the crossing onto Eagle Creek Trail.

1.1   Junction with former Lakeshore (Pinnacle Creek) Trail on the right. Continue on Eagle Creek Trail.

2.0   Campsite 89.

3.1   Campsite 96.

4.6   Campsite 97.

9.1   Spence Field Shelter.

9.3   Junction with the Appalachian Trail at Spence Field. Turn right (east) and in a few hundred feet pass by Bote Mountain Trail, which comes in from the left.

9.5   Turn right (southeast) onto Jenkins Ridge Trail.

16.0   Junction with former Lakeshore Trail at Pickens Gap. Turn left to remain on Jenkins Ridge Trail.

18.4   Junction with Hazel Creek Trail at Campsite 84. Turn right and follow Hazel Creek downstream.

20.1   Campsite 85.

23.0   Junction with Lakeshore Trail. Campsite 86 is nearby. Turn right, just before the bridge over Hazel Creek, walk in front of the Calhoun House, and continue west on Lakeshore Trail.

24.4   Side trail on the left leads 0.1 mile to Campsite 88.

27.4   Return to junction of Eagle Creek and Lakeshore Trails. Backtrack to Campsite 90.

27.9   Arrive back at Campsite 90.

Options: A good plan for an extended trip is to take a boat shuttle to Campsite 90 in the afternoon and spend the night there. The next day, hike up to Spence Field and stay at the shelter. The third day, hike down to Campsite 86. Take a dip in the lake and camp there. The fourth day you can laze your way back to Campsite 90 and lounge around the lake the rest of the day. The boat will pick you up on the fifth day. You could trim a day off this plan by having the boat pick you up at Hazel Creek on the fourth morning.

61 Shuckstack

Shuckstack Tower is an old fire tower, one of few remaining in the park. At its base are the old tower-keeper's cistern and the foundation and chimney of the cabin. For such a difficult and remote hike, a surprising number of people make the trek to Shuckstack. Most people backtrack from the tower for a 7.0-mile walk. This hike details a longer loop that experienced hikers can still do in a day. Two campsites provide the opportunity to turn this trip into an overnighter.

Start: Trailhead near Fontana Dam
Distance: 11.9-mile loop
Hiking time: About 6 hours—day hike or overnighter
Difficulty: Strenuous, due to steep grades
Trail surface: Forest trails and old forest roads
Best season: Spring for the wildflowers
Other trail users: Appalachian Trail portion is for hikers only; the rest is open to equestrians
Maps: Fontana Dam USGS quad; Trails

Illustrated #229 Great Smoky Mountains; Trails Illustrated #316 Cades Cove Elkmont
Special considerations: Several creek crossings of Lost Cove Creek require wading in heavy flows and could be dangerous in very high water.
Other: Parking is limited at the trailhead, but it's usually not a problem. Back at the Fontana Dam Visitor Center are restrooms and a special treat for backpackers: hot showers. Fontana Village is nearby with full services.

Finding the trailhead: From the junction of US 19/74 and NC 28 in the southwestern portion of the park, turn west onto NC 28 and drive 21.1 miles to the stop sign at the entrance road for Fontana Dam. Turn right and follow the road 1.1 miles to the dam. Drive over the dam and turn right at the fork. Continue 0.7 mile to the road's end at a trail information board. The Appalachian Trail leads behind the trail board. GPS: N35 27.644' / W83 48.664'

The Hike

Begin at the trail information board and start climbing on the Appalachian Trail immediately. The first mile or so is rather steep, but once you gain the ridge and start following it, the grade lessens and even runs level and downhill in a few places. There is one good view of Fontana Dam off to the right and several leafy views of the lake. As you get close to Shuckstack Tower, the trail passes through an exposed rock face and provides great views on the left toward the Unicoi Mountains. Beyond this view point the trail climbs very steeply to pick up a ridge and continues steeply along the ridge spine. Spring wildflowers are abundant in this section.

A couple hundred yards below the tower, the AT veers off left, while a path continues climbing up the ridge to the base of the tower. Six flights of stairs above you is one of the finest views in the park. The steps are in questionable shape. If you decide it's not safe to climb to the top, at least go high enough to look out over the trees. To the south are Fontana Lake and Dam, with the Snowbird Mountains in the background; to the west are the Unicoi Mountains; and to the north is the crest of

View from inside Shuckstack Tower.

the Smokies. The views make you forget all about the strenuous climb required to get here.

After soaking in the views, backtrack to the AT and turn right, heading in the opposite direction from which you approached. A 0.4-mile easy descent takes you to Sassafras Gap. If you make this trip in mid-April, this stretch is a highlight of the hike. Wildflowers are everywhere—mayapple, several trillium species, purple phacelia, false Solomon's seal—too many to count.

At the gap turn right (northeast) onto Lost Cove Trail and descend through the Lost Cove Creek drainage. The trail is not well graded and in places it is ridiculously steep. You pick up Lost Cove Creek when it's just a small branch and watch it grow to a respectable stream in a couple miles. The three or so crossings above Campsite 91 are easily negotiated. The campsite is small, right beside the trail, and looks rarely used. Below the campsite there are at least seven more creek crossings, some of them easy to rock-hop, some a little dicey. In high water all of them will demand your full attention.

Reach Lakeshore Trail at a nondescript junction. Straight ahead, continuing along Lost Cove Creek, Lakeshore Trail leads 0.3 mile to Fontana Lake at Campsite 90. To the right, and climbing up the bank, the trail leads 5.2 miles to the trailhead. The route to the trailhead is a typical undulating course and rather boring much of the way. A section near the lake obviously follows part of old NC 288, which now lies mostly under Fontana Lake. If there's any doubt in your mind about that, it will be erased when you start seeing the abandoned cars along the trail. Unfortunately, the trail never gets close enough to provide good views of the lake—just the autos.

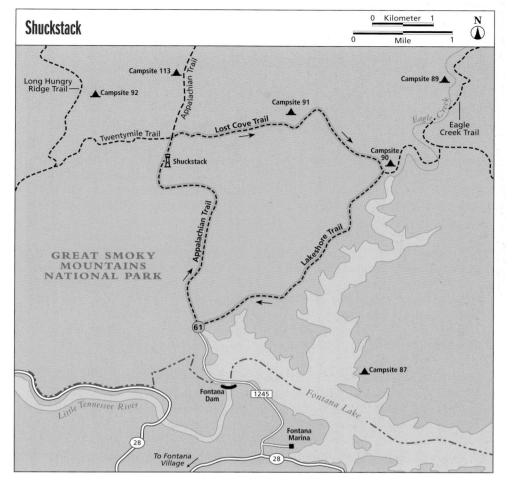

Miles and Directions

0.0 Start at the trail information board on the AT, heading north.

3.4 The AT veers to the left. Continue straight on the spur trail to Shuckstack Tower.

3.5 Arrive at Shuckstack Tower. Return to the AT after enjoying the views.

3.6 Back to junction with AT. Turn right.

4.0 Junction with Twentymile and Lost Cove Trails. Turn right (northeast) onto Lost Cove Trail.

4.7 Campsite 91.

6.7 Junction with Lakeshore Trail. Campsite 90 is straight ahead in 0.3 mile. Turn right on Lakeshore Trail to return to trailhead.

11.9 Arrive back at trailhead.

Options: If you're doing this hike as an overnighter, your two choices for camping are Campsites 91 and 90. Campsite 90 is a good choice. It adds only 0.6 mile to the total distance, and it's a much better site, being right on Fontana Lake. Plus, staying there puts all the creek crossings behind you.

62 Twentymile Loop

Although the Twentymile area is one of the more remote sections of the park, it receives a surprising amount of use. Expect some company on a weekend hike or any day during the busy seasons of summer and autumn.

Start: Twentymile trailhead in the far southwestern end of the park

Distance: 7.6-mile lollipop

Hiking time: About 3.5 hours—day hike or overnighter

Difficulty: Easy

Trail surface: Old forest roads and forest trails

Other trail users: Equestrians permitted on most of the route

Maps: Tapoco and Fontana Dam USGS quads; Trails Illustrated #229 Great Smoky Mountains; Trails Illustrated #316 Cades Cove Elkmont

Special considerations: The park has installed foot logs at the six crossings of Moore Springs Branch and at the Twentymile Creek crossing. As with most foot logs in the park, these foot logs could still wash away in flood conditions, and without them, you'll have to wade.

Other: Parking is limited at the trailhead. On summer weekends you might have to park back at the ranger station. There are no facilities here. Deals Gap Motorcycle Resort, with convenience store, motel, and restaurant, is located about 2.7 miles west on NC 28. It closes in winter. Fontana Village Resort is about 6 miles east on NC 28.

Finding the trailhead: The trailhead is at Twentymile Ranger Station. Drive about 6 miles west from Fontana Dam on NC 28 and turn right at the sign for Twentymile. Pass the ranger station and park at the small gravel lot on the right, just before the gate. The trail is a continuation of the gravel road. GPS: N35 28.033' / W83 52.616'

The Hike

Begin hiking up the gravel road on an old railroad grade. At 0.5 mile you cross Moore Springs Branch on an auto bridge. Turn left onto Wolf Ridge Trail on the other side.

The hike now follows Moore Springs Branch upstream, crossing it six times. After the fifth crossing you soon come to the junction with Twentymile Loop Trail, forking right and continuing to follow the creek upstream. Wolf Ridge Trail turns left and swings away from the creek at this point.

Take Twentymile Loop Trail and cross the creek for the sixth time just below a small cascade. Climb away from the creek on a long, moderate grade before leveling out on a contour run to a small saddle. Descend from the saddle and quickly cross a small branch. Cross a larger stream farther down and follow it downstream to a crossing of Twentymile Creek. Once across, begin a slight ascent and come to a rock-hop of Proctor Branch. Beyond this crossing it's a short, steep climb to the junction with Twentymile Trail.

Paths lead in four directions from the junction. Behind you is Twentymile Loop Trail, which brought you here. Immediately to the left is Long Hungry Ridge Trail,

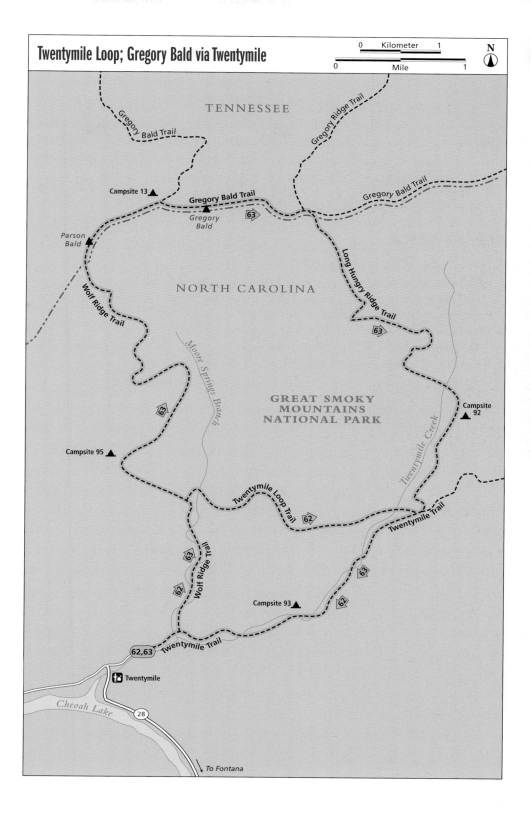

0   Kilometer   1

0   Mile   1

N

TENNESSEE

Gregory Bald Trail

Gregory Ridge Trail

Campsite 13 ▲

Gregory Bald Trail

63

Gregory Bald

Gregory Bald Trail

Parson Bald ▲

Long Hungry Ridge Trail

NORTH CAROLINA

63

Wolf Ridge Trail

Moore Springs Branch

63

GREAT SMOKY
MOUNTAINS
NATIONAL PARK

Campsite
92
▲

Twentymile Creek

Campsite 95 ▲

Twentymile Loop Trail

62

Twentymile Trail

63

Wolf Ridge Trail

62

Campsite 93 ▲

62

63

62,63   *Twentymile Trail*

🏕 Twentymile

Cheoah Lake

28

↓ *To Fontana*

descended in Hike 63. On the well-graded roadbed in front of you, Twentymile Trail goes both ways. You want to go right on this trail and follow Twentymile Creek downstream.

It is 2.6 miles back to the junction with Wolf Ridge Trail, with Twentymile Creek as a constant companion. You cross the creek five times, all on sturdy bridges. Just past the third crossing is Campsite 93, right beside the trail. It's a small site with zero privacy. A few hundred feet before you arrive back at Wolf Ridge Trail, a signed side path to the left leads a few yards to the scenic Twentymile Creek Cascade.

Once back at the lower trail junction, backtrack the remaining 0.5 mile to your car.

Miles and Directions

0.0 Start at the gate on Twentymile Trail.

0.5 Cross Moore Springs Branch on a bridge and turn left onto Wolf Ridge Trail.

1.6 Wolf Ridge Trail swings left and away from the creek. Take the right fork on Twentymile Loop Trail and continue following the creek upstream.

4.5 Arrive at four-way trail junction. Turn right (west) onto Twentymile Trail.

5.8 Campsite 93.

7.0 Pass by Twentymile Creek Cascade.

7.1 Return to junction with Wolf Ridge Trail. Continue following Twentymile Trail back to the trailhead.

7.6 Arrive back at trailhead.

63 Gregory Bald via Twentymile

Gregory Bald is among the finest destinations in the Smokies backcountry. For many hikers, it is *the* finest. Most people access the bald from the Tennessee side by taking either Gregory Ridge Trail or Gregory Bald Trail (see Hike 24). The hike outlined here provides a less-traveled access from the North Carolina side. See the sidebar for Hike 24 for a note about Gregory's wild azaleas.

(See map for Hike 62: Twentymile Loop.)

Start: Twentymile trailhead in the far southwestern end of the park

Distance: 15.5-mile lollipop

Hiking time: About 9 hours—overnighter or tough day hike

Difficulty: Strenuous, due to steep grades

Trail surface: Old forest roads, forest trails, and grassy bald

Best season: Second half of June for the azalea bloom

Other trail users: Equestrians

Maps: Tapoco, Fontana Dam, Calderwood, and Cades Cove USGS quads; Trails Illustrated #229 Great Smoky Mountains; Trails Illustrated #316 Cades Cove Elkmont

Special considerations: The park has installed foot logs at the five crossings of Moore Springs Branch. As with most foot logs in the park, these foot logs could still wash away in flood conditions, and without them, you'll have to wade.

Other: Parking is limited at the trailhead. On summer weekends you might have to park back at the ranger station. Deals Gap Motorcycle Resort, with convenience store, motel, and restaurant, is located about 2.7 miles west on NC 28. It closes in winter. Fontana Village Resort is about 6 miles east on NC 28.

Finding the trailhead: The trailhead is at Twentymile Ranger Station, in the remote southwestern end of the park. Drive about 6 miles west from Fontana Dam on NC 28 and turn right at the sign for Twentymile. Pass the ranger station and park at the small gravel lot on the right, just before the gate. The trail is a continuation of the gravel road. GPS: N35 28.033' / W83 52.616'

The Hike

Begin hiking up the gravel road on an old railroad grade. At 0.5 mile cross Moore Springs Branch on an auto bridge and turn left onto Wolf Ridge Trail on the far side. The hike now follows Moore Springs Branch upstream, crossing it five times on foot logs. After the fifth crossing you soon come to the junction with Twentymile Loop Trail, which follows the creek upstream. Wolf Ridge Trail, which you want to take, turns left and swings away from the creek at this junction. In a little less than a mile from the creek, you come to a sharp right switchback. A side path leads a few hundred yards from the switchback to Campsite 95, a pleasant site in a second-growth mixed-hardwood forest.

Continuing from the switchback, Wolf Ridge Trail begins climbing in earnest and it doesn't let up for the next 3.6 miles. (There's one tiny dip where the trail swings around a saddle, but that's it.) At several points you think you've reached Parson Bald, only to discover that you have to keep climbing. Once on the bald, you know it. It's mostly overgrown, but there are scattered open patches. Blueberries are everywhere, and if you want to see bears, come here in August when the fruit ripens. Parson Bald is an all-you-can-eat buffet for bears.

From Parson Bald, it's an easy and delightful walk through patches of tassel rue to Sheep Pen Gap and Campsite 13. Wolf Ridge Trail ends here at the junction with Gregory Bald Trail. Turn right (southeast) and climb 0.4 mile to Gregory Bald. If you can't make this hike when the azaleas bloom, that's OK. The views alone are more than worth the climb. Cades Cove sprawls out to the northeast; to the southwest lies the Joyce Kilmer–Slickrock Wilderness in the Unicoi Mountains; due south is Fontana Lake, and between the lake and you stands Shuckstack Tower. Trees obscure the view to the west.

It is 0.7 mile from the bald to Rich Gap, heading east. At a four-way junction on the gap, Gregory Ridge Trail goes to the left, while a side path on the right leads a few hundred yards to historic Moore Spring, site of a former herder's cabin and, more recently, a backcountry shelter. The spring is the headwaters for Moore Springs Branch that you crossed several times on the way up here.

Gregory Bald Trail continues straight ahead from the junction and in a few hundred feet comes to the junction with Long Hungry Ridge Trail at a fork. Your hike follows Long Hungry Ridge Trail to the right (south). For nearly a mile the trail loses little elevation and is a joy to hike. Just before the trail drops off the east side of the ridge, you pass through Rye Patch. There may be an old sign marking this tiny clearing. Rye Patch was much more open at one time, and as you would expect, planted in rye.

Upon leaving Rye Patch, the descent increases noticeably and the trail continues uneventfully. After a few creek crossings (some potentially tough in high water), you come to Campsite 92, 3.4 miles from Rich Gap. The site sits in a grove of hemlock and yellow poplar (tulip tree) and appears little used.

Just beyond the campsite you cross a small stream branch, spanned by the rotten remains of an old bridge. The steep grade is behind you now. Now you follow an easy course along an obvious logging grade and cross a few minor branches. A final crossing of Proctor Branch heralds the approach to Twentymile Trail at Proctor Field Gap.

From the gap, head west on Twentymile Trail. (Don't take the immediate right on Twentymile Loop Trail.) It's an easy 2.6-mile walk back to the junction with Wolf Ridge Trail, with Twentymile Creek as a constant companion. You cross the creek five times, all on sturdy bridges. Just past the third crossing is Campsite 93, right beside the trail. It's a small site with zero privacy. A few hundred feet before you arrive back to Wolf Ridge Trail, a signed side path to the left leads a few yards to the scenic Twentymile Creek Cascade.

Once back at the lower trail junction, backtrack the remaining 0.5 mile to your car.

Miles and Directions

0.0 Start at the gate on Twentymile Trail.

0.5 Cross Moore Springs Branch on a bridge and turn left onto Wolf Ridge Trail.

1.6 At the junction with Twentymile Loop Trail, swing to the left to remain on Wolf Ridge Trail and hike away from the creek.

2.5 At a sharp right-hand switchback, a side path goes straight ahead to Campsite 95. Continue on Wolf Ridge Trail.

6.1 Parson Bald.

6.8 Junction with Gregory Bald Trail at Campsite 13. Turn right (southeast) on Gregory Bald Trail.

7.2 Arrive at Gregory Bald. Explore the open bald and continue following Gregory Bald Trail on the other side.

7.9 At Rich Gap pass by Gregory Ridge Trail, which comes up from the left, and in a few hundred feet, bear right (south) at the fork onto Long Hungry Ridge Trail.

11.3 Campsite 92.

12.4 Arrive at four-way trail junction. Head west on Twentymile Trail. (Do not take the immediate right onto Twentymile Loop Trail.)

13.7 Campsite 93.

14.9 Pass by Twentymile Creek Cascade.

15.0 Return to junction with Wolf Ridge Trail. Continue following Twentymile Trail back to the trailhead.

15.5 Arrive back at trailhead.

Option: Although this hike is certainly doable as a day hike, you'd be shortchanging yourself by not staying overnight at Campsite 13, one of the finest in the Smokies. By camping, you can experience Gregory Bald at sunset and sunrise. Campsite 13 is rationed and usually full on weekends and on weekdays in June. Make your reservations early.

Southeast Section

Sunrise at the Mountain Farm Museum and the trailhead for Oconaluftee River Trail.

64 Oconaluftee River

This short, easy walk follows Oconaluftee River Trail from Oconaluftee Visitor Center to Cherokee. The trail is popular among locals as a fitness and dog-walking path. It's one of only two trails in the park that allow dogs (on leash) and one of only four that allow bicycles. (Gatlinburg Trail allows dogs and bikes; Deep Creek Trail and Indian Creek Trail allow bikes on their lower sections.) If you're looking for backcountry solitude, this hike is not for you. It's a good hike for young children because it's flat and provides opportunities for playing at the edge of the river. It also makes a great split-party hike. Have your party drop you off at the visitor center and you can meet them later back in Cherokee.

(See map for Hike 47: Mingus Mill and Newton Bald.)

Start: Oconaluftee Visitor Center
Distance: 3.2 miles out and back
Hiking time: About 1.5 hours—day hike
Difficulty: Easy
Trail surface: Hard-packed dirt
Best season: Apr–May for the wildflowers
Other trail users: Dogs and bicycles

Maps: Smokemont and Whittier USGS quads; Trails Illustrated #229 Great Smoky Mountains; Trails Illustrated #317 Clingmans Dome Cataloochee
Special considerations: Parts of the hike are infested with poison ivy. Watch the kids closely.
Other: The visitor center has ample parking but can fill up on weekends during the summer and fall seasons. Restrooms and drink vending machines are available at the center.

Finding the trailhead: The hike begins at Oconaluftee Visitor Center, located on Newfound Gap Road, 1.3 miles from the park entrance at Cherokee. GPS: N35 30.802' / W83 18.367'

The Hike

Follow the paved walkway to the Mountain Farm Museum, which re-creates an early pioneer farmstead. You can either skirt the museum by walking along the fence to the right of it, or walk through it and pick up the trail on the other side. Once beyond the museum you follow closely along Oconaluftee River for much of the hike. Just before you pass under the Blue Ridge Parkway, there is a little beach area beside the river that is a great place for the kids (and their parents) to splash in the water. Expect to see trout fishers here. Beyond the parkway you pass through a dense forest with a closed canopy and then cross a paved road before finally ending in Cherokee at the footbridge to Chief Saunooke's Trading Post.

Restored cabin at the Mountain Farm Museum.

Miles and Directions

0.0 Start between the visitor center and restroom buildings.

0.7 Pass under the Blue Ridge Parkway.

1.5 Cross over paved road.

1.6 Park boundary at Cherokee. Return the way you came.

3.2 Arrive back at trailhead.

A NEW LANGUAGE

Before the arrival of European settlers and until their forced removal in 1838 along the infamous Trail of Tears, the Cherokee Indians made their home in the Smokies. Until 1825 the tribe had no written language. In that year they adopted the syllabary created by Sequoyah, who had started developing a written language for the Cherokee more than two decades earlier. The syllabary caught on quickly, and in 1828 the tribe began publishing the *Cherokee Phoenix,* the first newspaper published in a Native American language. You'll encounter Sequoyah's heritage often as you explore the Smokies. In the town of Cherokee, the road signs are written in the Cherokee syllabary as well as English and the same is true for the interpretive plaques placed along Oconaluftee River Trail. Mount Sequoyah, Sequoyah Branch, and Sequoyah Cemetery all carry the legendary Cherokee's name.

65 Smokemont Nature Trail

Since it starts from Smokemont Campground, this nature trail is a good choice for families who are camping. For those not staying at Smokemont and planning to drive to the trailhead, most any other short hike would be just as good, especially one of the many Quiet Walkways in the park. The park no longer publishes an interpretive guide for this nature trail.

Start: Smokemont Nature trailhead
Distance: 0.7-mile loop
Hiking time: About 30 minutes—day hike
Difficulty: Moderate
Trail surface: Packed dirt
Other trail users: Hikers only

Maps: Smokemont USGS quad; Trails Illustrated #229 Great Smoky Mountains; Trails Illustrated #317 Clingmans Dome Cataloochee
Other: There is sufficient parking at the trailhead. Restrooms are available at the campground.

Finding the trailhead: Drive 3.1 miles north from Oconaluftee Visitor Center on Newfound Gap Road and turn right (east) at the sign for Smokemont Campground. (From Newfound Gap, drive 12.5 miles south on Newfound Gap Road and turn left at the sign.) Cross Oconaluftee River, turn left, and drive into the campground. The trail begins directly opposite Campsite B31. GPS: N35 33.474' / W83 18.741'

The Hike

Smokemont Nature Trail crosses an overflow of Bradley Fork on a foot log, then crosses Bradley Fork and a split from the main stream. The trail loops just beyond the split. If you're going right, you'll climb rather steeply before descending back to Bradley Fork.

Miles and Directions

0.0 Start at trailhead beside Bradley Fork.

0.1 Come to a fork just after crossing a split off the main stream. Turn right or left for the loop.

0.7 Arrive back at trailhead.

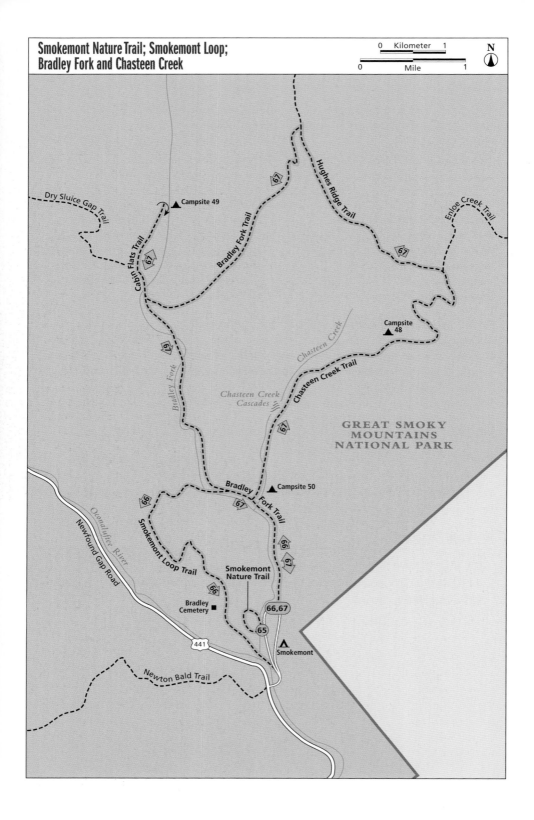

Smokemont Nature Trail; Smokemont Loop; Bradley Fork and Chasteen Creek

0   Kilometer   1

0   Mile   1

N

Dry Sluice Gap Trail

Campsite 49

67

Cabin Flats Trail

67

Bradley Fork Trail

Hughes Ridge Trail

Enloe Creek Trail

67

67

Bradley Fork

Campsite 48

Chasteen Creek

Chasteen Creek Cascades

Chasteen Creek Trail

67

GREAT SMOKY
MOUNTAINS
NATIONAL PARK

Bradley Fork Trail

Campsite 50

66

67

66

67

Oconaluftee River

Newfound Gap Road

Smokemont Loop Trail

Smokemont Nature Trail

66

Bradley Cemetery

66,67

65

441

Smokemont

Newton Bald Trail

66 Smokemont Loop

For people staying at Smokemont Campground, this loop hike is a good way to spend part of the day without having to drive to a trailhead.

(See map for Hike 65: Smokemont Nature Trail.)

Start: Smokemont Campground
Distance: 6.1-mile loop
Approximate hiking time: About 3 hours—day hike
Difficulty: Moderate
Trail surface: Old forest roads and forest trails
Best season: Spring for the wildflowers
Other trail users: Equestrians permitted on Bradley Fork Trail section

Maps: Smokemont USGS quad; Trails Illustrated #229 Great Smoky Mountains; Trails Illustrated #317 Clingmans Dome Cataloochee
Other: Parking is at one of the 3 general-purpose parking areas at Smokemont Campground. The parking area at the trailhead for Bradley Fork Trail can fill up quickly on weekends and during the busy season. The campground has restroom facilities.

Finding the trailhead: From Oconaluftee Visitor Center, drive 3.1 miles north on Newfound Gap Road, and turn right at the sign for Smokemont Campground. (From Newfound Gap, drive 12.5 miles south on Newfound Gap Road and turn left at the campground sign.) Cross Oconaluftee River, turn left, and drive into the campground. Follow the road through the campground all the way to its farthest point at the end of D section and park in one of the spaces around the far end of the loop. During winter D section is closed and you have to park at the end of C section and walk an additional 0.2 mile. You can also continue the loop around the campground and park at the old concrete bridge, just before leaving the campground. Since this is a loop hike, it doesn't matter which you choose. Just be sure not to park in a designated camping space. GPS: N35 33.783' / W83 18.640'

The Hike

Begin on Bradley Fork Trail, which starts at the gate on the north end of the campground. Bradley Fork Trail follows an old road that closely runs alongside Bradley Fork for much of the route. It is an easy and popular walk, lined with wildflowers in early spring. At 1.2 miles Chasteen Creek Trail forks to the right. Stay to the left and continue following Bradley Fork upstream.

At 1.6 miles you reach the junction with Smokemont Loop Trail, heading left (southwest). Take this trail and immediately cross Bradley Fork on a very long, bouncy foot log. On the other side the trail turns south and follows Bradley Fork downstream a few hundred yards to a fork, crossing a side branch along the way. Turn right (southwest) at the fork and begin a climb up Richland Mountain that continues steadily for nearly 2 miles. The varied forest allows many different species of wildflowers to grow. Open areas from downed trees contribute to briar patches and showy summer wildflowers.

After passing through a saddle, you begin climbing the west side of the ridge. You can hear the Oconaluftee River now, but the peacefulness is probably short-lived as you can also hear the cars along Newfound Gap Road. Newton Bald is visible through the trees off to the west.

At 3.4 miles a sharp bend to the left signals the end of the climbing and the beginning of a 2.0-mile downhill stretch. There are fewer wildflowers in this section, but the forest is more scenic. At about 5.1 miles you can catch a glimpse of Bradley Cemetery down the slope to the right. If you want to visit the cemetery, don't take one of the eroded side trails. Instead, continue on to where the trail ends at a service road, about 0.2 mile farther. Turn right, then immediately right again onto another old road. Follow this road a few hundred feet to an obvious path on the right that leads to the cemetery.

To continue the loop hike, turn left (east) on the gravel road and follow it 0.2 mile back to the campground.

Miles and Directions

0.0 Start at the Bradley Fork trailhead at the north end of the campground, or at any point where you can find a suitable parking place.

1.2 Chasteen Creek Trail turns to the right. Continue straight on Bradley Fork Trail.

1.7 Turn left (southwest) onto Smokemont Loop Trail and immediately cross Bradley Fork on a foot log.

5.4 Bradley Cemetery.

5.6 Come to south end of Smokemont Campground. Walk through the campground to your parking place.

6.1 Arrive back at Bradley Fork trailhead, if that's where you parked.

67 Bradley Fork and Chasteen Creek

This is a grand backpacking trip, featuring much of what makes the Smokies famous. It offers several miles of scenic creek-side hiking, old-growth forests, abundant spring wildflowers, a rare shingle (pebble) beach beside Bradley Fork, and a few very nice cascades. One thing it doesn't have, though, is good distinct views. In winter there are some fair views from Hughes Ridge, but this hike is more about getting intimate with the forest all around you.

(See map for Hike 65: Smokemont Nature Trail.)

Start: Bradley Fork trailhead at Smokemont Campground
Distance: 17.2-mile lollipop
Hiking time: About 10 hours—2-night backpack, difficult overnighter, or killer day hike
Difficulty: Moderate
Trail surface: Old forest roads and forest trails, very rocky in places
Best season: Spring for the wildflowers, Oct for autumn foliage

Other trail users: Equestrians
Maps: Smokemont and Mount Guyot USGS quads; Trails Illustrated #229 Great Smoky Mountains; Trails Illustrated #317 Clingmans Dome Cataloochee
Other: Parking is at one of the 3 general-purpose parking areas at Smokemont Campground. The parking area at the trailhead for Bradley Fork Trail can fill up quickly on weekends and during the busy season. The campground has restroom facilities.

Finding the trailhead: From Oconaluftee Visitor Center, drive 3.1 miles north on Newfound Gap Road, and turn right at the sign for Smokemont Campground. (From Newfound Gap, drive 12.5 miles south on Newfound Gap Road and turn left at the campground sign.) Cross Oconaluftee River, turn left, and drive into the campground. Follow the road through the campground all the way to its farthest point at the end of D section, and park in one of the spaces around the far end of the loop (GPS: N35 33.783' / W83 18.640'). During winter D section is closed and you have to park at the end of C section and walk an additional 0.2 mile.

The Hike

The first 1.2 miles follow the gravel road beside Bradley Fork along the same route as Hike 66. At 1.1 miles the road crosses Chasteen Creek on a wide bridge and reaches a fork at 1.2 miles. Turn right (east) onto Chasteen Creek Trail. In less than 0.1 mile, you pass by Campsite 50, one of the nearest sites to a road in the park. It's a good choice for bringing young children on their first backcountry adventure.

Chasteen Creek Trail climbs gradually, loosely following Chasteen Creek, and at 1.9 miles comes to a horse-hitching rack on the left (creek side) of the trail. For a quick side trip, break off at this point and follow the narrow footpath by the hitching post. It leads a few hundred feet to scenic Chasteen Creek Cascades. The footpath

Spring wildflowers grow alongside Bradley Fork Trail.

looks as though it might loop back to the main trail, but it peters out on the hillside, so you have to backtrack from the cascades.

Back on the main trail, the gravel road steepens on its approach to Campsite 48, reached in 3.6 miles. The campsite is scenic, nestled beside the headwaters of Chasteen Creek under a canopy of tall yellow poplars (tulip trees) and small hemlocks. This is a good choice for the first night's stay on a two-nighter.

Beyond the campsite, the trail narrows and steepens as it passes through a headwater cove. Even though logging occurred here, the forest has grown back beautifully and the spring flora display is impressive. In April look for larkspur, an uncommon wildflower with deep-purple flowers.

Once you leave the headwater tributary streams, the trail goes through a series of tough switchbacks and reaches Hughes Ridge and Hughes Ridge Trail at 5.2 miles. The path to the right was once an official trail leading back to Smokemont Campground, but that section of trail is now closed.

Turn left (north) and begin following the crest line of Hughes Ridge. At 5.6 miles you reach the junction with Enloe Creek Trail on the right. Continue along Hughes Ridge Trail for another 2.5 miles of typical ridge hiking—ups, downs, levels—to reach the junction with the upper terminus of Bradley Fork Trail—the same trail on which you started this hike. If hiking in winter, you'll probably notice the views of distant ridges from Hughes Ridge and possibly catch an occasional glimpse of Clingmans Dome.

Turn sharply left (south) on Bradley Fork Trail and descend steeply, passing through several laurel tunnels, and meet up with a finger of Taywa Creek on the left.

The forest through here is similar to the cove forest along Chasteen Creek Trail. The trail remains steep and rocky until it crosses, on a wide bridge, another tributary coming in from the right. Now you're walking on an obvious roadbed and the grade has become a gentle descent. A short distance later, you cross the creek again on a culvert and then again on a wide bridge. After the third crossing you soon bear away from the creek and pass through drier ridges. As soon as you leave earshot of Taywa Creek, you begin to hear Bradley Fork. At 11.4 miles you see Bradley Fork at the junction with Cabin Flats Trail. The wide spot in the trail is the old turnaround for what used to be a motor nature trail.

Turn right (north) onto Cabin Flats Trail and after 200 feet cross Bradley Fork on an out-of-character steel-truss bridge. Just beyond the bridge an ascent takes you through an old-growth forest, with many large trees right beside the trail. You soon cross Tennessee Branch on a foot log above a mossy cascade, and in a few feet you reach the junction with Dry Sluice Gap Trail, on the left. Continue straight (north) for 0.6 mile to reach Campsite 49, your second night's destination on a two-night trip.

Campsite 49 is one of the largest backcountry campsites in the park, situated right beside Bradley Fork in a wide, flat bottomland. There are several tent sites scattered along the flat and a horse-hitching rack at the lower end. Also located here is a real oddity for the Smokies—a good-size shingle (pebble) beach that makes a great picnic and wading spot. Just downstream from the campsite is a huge logjam, the result of heavy flooding in 1994.

From Campsite 49, retrace your steps to the junction of Cabin Flats and Bradley Fork Trails. Continue straight (south) on Bradley Fork Trail, following it and Bradley Fork back to the trailhead.

Miles and Directions

0.0 Start at Bradley Fork trailhead at the north end of the campground, or at any point where you can find a suitable parking place.

1.2 Bear right onto Chasteen Creek Trail.

1.3 Campsite 50.

1.9 Side path to Chasteen Creek Cascades is on the left.

3.6 Campsite 48.

5.2 Junction with Hughes Ridge Trail on Hughes Ridge. Turn left (north) and follow the ridge.

5.6 Enloe Creek Trail turns to the right. Continue following Hughes Ridge Trail.

8.1 Turn sharply left (south) on Bradley Fork Trail.

11.4 At the old traffic turnaround, turn right (north) onto Cabin Flats Trail and in a few hundred feet cross Bradley Fork on an elaborate bridge.

11.7 Junction with Dry Sluice Gap Trail, turning to the left. Continue straight ahead (north) on Cabin Flats Trail.

12.3 Arrive at Campsite 49 beside Bradley Fork. Backtrack to junction with Bradley Fork Trail.

13.2 Return to junction with Bradley Fork and Cabin Flats Trails. Go straight on Bradley Fork Trail, following Bradley Fork downstream.

16.0 Return to junction with Bradley Fork and Chasteen Creek Trails. Retrace your steps back to the trailhead along Bradley Fork Trail.

17.2 Arrive back at trailhead.

Option: Experienced backpackers can do this trip as an overnighter, staying at Campsite 48. If you choose this option, you may want to skip the Cabin Flats Trail extension, but if you have the energy, it's worth it to see the trees.

CARS NO LONGER ALLOWED

Wide and well graded, the lower portion of Bradley Fork Trail seems more like a road than a trail. That's because at one time it *was* a road. The early practices of Great Smoky Mountains National Park were different from those of today. For the first several decades after the park was established, emphasis seemed to be placed on developing visitor services and amenities above resource protection. Several motor roads were built, most following old railroad beds such as the one here at Bradley Fork and some following old wagon traces. At one time there were even plans for damming Abrams Creek and turning Cades Cove into a resort lake.

Today, natural and cultural resource protection plays a principal role in park management. Indeed, the official mandate of the National Park Service states, in part, that the ". . . purpose is to conserve the scenery and the natural and historic objects and the wildlife therein and to provide for the enjoyment of the same in such manner and by such means as will leave them unimpaired for the enjoyment of future generations."

Today's hiking trails that were once partly old motor roads include Deep Creek Trail, Indian Creek Trail, Big Creek Trail, Little River Trail, Porters Creek Trail, Bote Mountain Trail, Hazel Creek Trail, Maddron Bald Trail, and Twentymile Trail. Each of these trails makes for easy hiking along the old roadbeds.

68 Kephart Prong

Kephart Prong is an easy hike that offers a little something for everyone. The hike follows the creek closely for most of the route, crossing it four times on foot logs. You'll pass through historical ruins and artifacts, and good spring and summer wild-flower displays. Kephart Shelter, at the end of the hike, presents a great option for an easy overnighter, with the sedative music of Kephart Prong to put you to sleep. All of these features make this a popular hike, so you might want to avoid it on weekends or during the summer and fall tourist seasons. Or you could begin the trek first thing in the morning and be back at your car before most people even begin their hike.

Start: Kephart Prong trailhead
Distance: 4.0 miles out and back
Hiking time: About 2 hours—day hike or overnighter
Difficulty: Easy, due to gradual elevation gain
Trail surface: Old paved roadbed and forest trail, rocky and rooty toward the end
Other trail users: Horses permitted but not regularly encountered
Maps: Smokemont USGS quad; Trails Illustrated #229 Great Smoky Mountains; Trails Illustrated #317 Clingmans Dome Cataloochee
Other: Parking is usually sufficient at the 2 pullouts. Restrooms are available at Oconaluftee Visitor Center or Collins Creek Picnic Area, south of the trailhead.

Finding the trailhead: From Oconaluftee Visitor Center, drive 6.9 miles north on Newfound Gap Road and park in one of the pullouts on either side of the road. From Newfound Gap, drive 8.7 miles south on Newfound Gap Road and park in one of the pullouts on either side of the road. The trail begins on the east side of the road at the bridge over Oconaluftee River. GPS: N35 35.147' / W83 21.483'

The Hike

The trail begins on the east side of Newfound Gap Road and immediately crosses Oconaluftee River on a wide bridge. Chances are good you'll see a trout fisher on the Oconaluftee and maybe on Kephart Prong as well. The trail is wide and has only a slight grade, owing to its once being a jeep road. You see bits of old asphalt here and there as further testament. At 0.2 mile you pass through the old Civilian Conservation Corps Camp, which operated in the 1930s and early 1940s. Look around and discover old chimneys, foundations, rock walls, a rusty water pump, and other artifacts from the camp.

Beyond the CCC Camp a faint path forks to the right and leads upstream a few yards before petering out. Stay to the left (west) and cross Kephart Prong on a sloping footbridge with a questionable railing. Use caution when the bridge is wet or snow-covered. As you climb the old roadbed alongside Kephart Prong, look for the remains of an old fish hatchery on the left bank. During the next mile you cross Kephart

Kephart Prong; Charlies Bunion and Bradley Fork

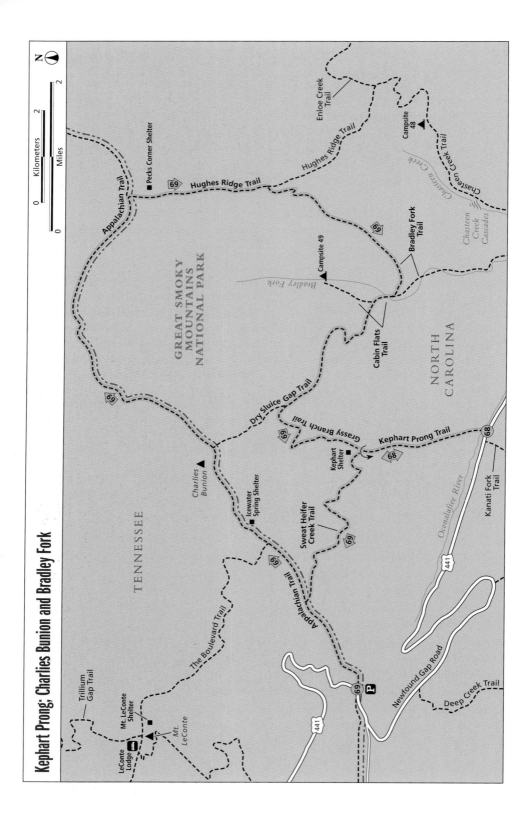

Prong three more times. Each time you can either wade at the ford or follow the trail a few paces and cross on foot logs. You might also see other evidence that humans heavily used this area: old narrow-gauge railroad rails from the logging operations of the 1920s. The final push to the shelter is a little steeper and the trail rockier.

Kephart Shelter sits in a scenic cove beside Kephart Prong. The shelter has a rustic charm, like most in the park, and is a great spot to rest before heading back. It marks the junction with Grassy Branch Trail, which leads northeast behind the shelter, and Sweat Heifer Creek Trail, leading north and passing in front of the shelter. Hike 69 uses these two trails.

Miles and Directions

0.0   Begin the hike by crossing the footbridge over Oconaluftee River.

0.2   Pass through remains of CCC camp.

0.6   Pass by remains of old fish hatchery.

2.0   Arrive at Kephart Shelter. Return the way you came.

4.0   Arrive back at Kephart Prong trailhead.

Option: Kephart Prong Trail provides a good alternative route to Charlies Bunion for those wishing to avoid the overcrowded Appalachian Trail (AT). From Kephart Shelter, take Grassy Branch Trail northeast for 2.5 miles to the junction with Dry Sluice Gap Trail. Turn left (north) and follow the trail for 1.3 miles to the AT. Turn left (west) on the AT and reach Charlies Bunion and its spectacular views in 0.5 mile. Be advised, however, that this route to the Bunion is uphill nearly the entire way.

FRIEND TO THE SMOKIES

Kephart Prong Trail, Kephart Prong, Kephart Shelter, and Mount Kephart, a few thousand feet above the shelter, all carry the name of one of the Smokies' most treasured friends, Horace Kephart. Kephart came to the Smokies in 1904 "to enjoy the thrills of single-handed adventure in a wild country." By 1913 he had written two books, *Camping and Woodcraft* and *Our Southern Highlanders*, both of which are still in print. He was particularly distressed by the massive logging operations in the region and became a staunch advocate for preserving the forests. Kephart's writings, and the images created by a Japanese photographer named George Masa, are largely responsible for the creation of Great Smoky Mountains National Park.

69 Charlies Bunion and Bradley Fork

This is a terrific three-day hike, encompassing much of what the Smokies have to offer. You spend half the time hiking on the high-elevation crest and the other half along headwater streams and through lush forests. With three backcountry shelters and one backcountry campsite, the hike offers several camping options.

Nearly everyone who visits the Smokies spends a little time at Newfound Gap, where this hike begins. Unless you just like hanging out in crowds, you'll want to park and hit the trail quickly. However, don't expect to get away from everyone on this hike. The first 4.0 miles to Charlies Bunion is a classic Smokies hike, and as such, it can be crowded any time of year except winter. Winter hiking along this trail is very rewarding, with great vistas and the opportunity for seeing interesting ice formations, but only experienced hikers should attempt it.

(See map for Hike 68: Kephart Prong.)
Start: Newfound Gap
Distance: 27.3-mile lollipop
Hiking time: About 15 hours—2- or 3-night backpack, with option for overnighter or killer day hike
Difficulty: Strenuous, due to steep grades and very rocky sections
Trail surface: Forest trails and old forest roads, some very rocky
Other trail users: About half of the route is open to equestrians

Maps: Clingmans Dome, Mount Le Conte, Mount Guyot, and Smokemont USGS quads; Trails Illustrated #229 Great Smoky Mountains; Trails Illustrated #317 Clingmans Dome Cataloochee
Special considerations: It is common for snow and ice to cover the trail in winter. Charlies Bunion has dangerous drop-offs.
Other: Newfound Gap has a very large parking lot, but it can fill up on weekends or any day during the summer and autumn seasons. Restrooms are available here.

Finding the trailhead: The trailhead is located at Newfound Gap Overlook on the Smokies crest. Drive 15.5 miles north on Newfound Gap Road from Oconaluftee Visitor Center or 12.7 miles south from Sugarlands Visitor Center. The trailhead is on the northeast end of the parking lot, between the paved path leading to the restrooms and the Rockefeller Memorial. GPS: N35 36.669' / W83.25.495'

The Hike

Begin hiking the Appalachian Trail (AT) from the northeast corner of the parking area. The trail starts out level and wide, but you soon begin a 1.5-mile steady ascent to a grassy knoll. You're walking through a high-elevation spruce-fir forest, with occasional openings providing vistas of Mount LeConte to the north. In late April and early May, spring beauty and trout lily cover the ground.

From the knoll, descend 0.2 mile to a gap and the junction with Sweat Heifer Creek Trail at a huge, gnarled birch tree. You'll come up this trail on your way back;

Bradley Fork Trail passes through a rhododendron tunnel. ▶

for now, continue east on the AT and begin a steep ascent. You soon pass an open view into North Carolina, taking in Clingmans Dome, Newfound Gap Road, and a glimpse of Bryson City. At 2.7 miles you reach the junction with The Boulevard Trail. The Boulevard Trail forks left (north) and leads to Mount LeConte. For a terrific (though difficult) side trip, go about 0.1 mile on this trail to a side path on the right for the Jumpoff. There may be a sign here. It is at a wide spot in the trail created from an uprooted tree on the left. The path goes to the right and climbs the bank on rocks and roots. The rugged path leads about 0.5 mile to an overlook that provides a great view of Charlies Bunion.

Now back on the AT at the junction with The Boulevard Trail, continue heading northeast on the AT. After 0.3 mile a short side path on the right leads to Icewater Spring Shelter, situated in an open, grassy area with good views. You'll probably see other day hikers here, posing for pictures in front of the shelter.

Just beyond the shelter, the trail passes literally over Icewater Spring. A rusty old pipe provides a drop so that you can fill a water bottle, but there's something unappealing about drinking water that comes out of a heavily trodden trail. (Be sure to treat all drinking water in the Smokies, no matter the source.)

Beyond the spring it's an easy hike of about a mile to the side trail for Charlies Bunion, on the left. There's no marker for the side trail, but don't worry, you can't miss it. Charlies Bunion stands out like few other landmarks in the park. The bare, jagged cliffs remind you more of the young Rockies than the old, worn Appalachians. The views are spectacular. To the west is the Jumpoff; to the northwest is the unmistakable Mount LeConte; and northeast is Greenbrier Pinnacle. You'll want to spend some time here, but take extra precaution. Many people have fallen while climbing on the rocks.

The side path circles the knoll and comes back to the AT. Turn left (east) and hike 0.4 mile to the junction with Dry Sluice Gap Trail. (If doing the overnight option, you would take this trail southeast.) Continuing east on the AT, you pass over the Sawteeth, a fitting name for this series of narrow jagged ridges. The views through here are good but nothing like what you experienced at Charlies Bunion. The hiking is typical ridge walking, with ups, downs, and short levels. About 4 miles from Charlies Bunion, and after an arduous ascent, the AT makes a sharp bend to the right (south) and descends along the east side of Laurel Top. Mountain laurel grows densely here, attesting to the mountain's name. Good views of Mounts Chapman, Guyot, and Sequoyah are to the east.

Reach Bradley's View, one of the best of the hike, at 8.9 miles. The view is over the Bradley Fork watershed that you'll traverse tomorrow. At 10.7 miles cut sharply right (south) on Hughes Ridge Trail and hike 0.4 mile farther to Pecks Corner Shelter. The shelter is the best choice for your first night's stay. Water is from a spring about 100 yards in front of the shelter.

From the shelter, continue south on Hughes Ridge Trail. Pass an old park service shack on the left and come to the junction with Bradley Fork Trail. When you hike this section, notice the change in the forest from dense red spruce at the higher elevations to the more open beech forest. Now make a right turn (south) onto Bradley Fork Trail and descend through another forest change, this time to a typical mixed-hardwood forest. The trail is steep and rocky until it meets two joining tributaries of Taywa Creek, and then it becomes a pleasant stroll along an old roadbed lined with abundant spring wildflowers.

At the junction with Bradley Fork Trail and Cabin Flats Trail, turn right (north) onto Cabin Flats Trail and soon cross Bradley Fork on a steel-truss bridge. Just beyond the bridge you enter an old-growth forest with several big trees. After crossing Tennessee Branch on a picturesque foot log, you come to another junction with Dry Sluice Gap Trail. If it's hot and you didn't take advantage of dipping in Bradley Fork back at the steel bridge, you might want to take a side trip straight ahead for 0.6 mile to Campsite 49, which has a neat shingle (pebble) beach beside Bradley Fork. The campsite is also a great place to spend the night if you want to extend the trip.

To continue the hike, turn left (west) onto Dry Sluice Gap Trail and head up the drainage of Tennessee Branch. You cross the small branch or one of its feeders seven times in the next mile or so. This mile is a highlight of the trip as it goes through an old-growth forest with many enormous trees. The foliage is lush and the stream gurgles over and around mossy logs and boulders.

After crossing Tennessee Branch for the last time, the trail begins a series of switchbacks leading to a side ridge that you follow to the east flank of Richland Mountain. After 2.8 miles of climbing, and probably cussing, you reach a gap on Richland Mountain and can now take solace in the thought that all of the uphill hiking is over for the day if you're staying at Kephart Shelter. Grassy Branch Trail heads west from the gap, and Dry Sluice Gap Trail continues north to reach the AT in another 1.3 miles. The gap here is scenic, in a dense stand of rhododendron, but a few open areas look as though they've been used as illegal campsites.

After taking a breather at the gap, follow Grassy Branch Trail down the west flank of Richland Mountain. The trail starts out heavily rutted and soon passes through large, open grassy areas covered in early spring with spring beauty, trout lily, and mayapple. The steady descent continues under rhododendron tunnels, through open forest, over seeps, and finally follows Kephart Prong downstream to Kephart Shelter. The shelter is a good choice for your second night's lodging on a two-night trip.

Begin the third day by heading north on Sweat Heifer Creek Trail, which starts right in front of the shelter and crosses Kephart Prong on a scenic foot log. After the crossing the trail turns left and heads downstream a short distance before switching back to the right and beginning its ascent to the AT. You pass through an open grassy area with old railroad rails beside the trail and spring wildflowers carpeting the ground. The ascent is mostly continuous, with a nice level stretch just before crossing Sweat Heifer Creek, 1.6 miles from Kephart Shelter. The creek tumbles over a long series of cascades and makes a good resting spot on a summer day. Around the next ridge you come to another cascade on a side stream, this one smaller but just as pretty.

Around the next bend is a well-laid rock wall just below the trail, looking out of place this far from the nearest road. You also begin noticing the old logging railroad grades below the trail. A steep section brings you to a flat spot where the trail cuts sharply right. There's a trail sign here directing hikers coming from the other direction to go left instead of straight ahead. It wouldn't matter if they did go straight, because they'd just circle back around to the main trail. This is the site of an old railroad turnaround, and you might notice a few rusty artifacts here from the logging days.

You continue to parallel the old grade for a short distance up the trail. Past the bend the trail keeps up the steady ascent, crossing a few streams (one surprisingly large for this high up), and as it does the forest changes from hardwood to spruce and fir. There are intermittent views south to Clingmans Dome and east to the Plott Balsams in Nantahala National Forest. Just before reaching the AT, you pass through a young stand of American beech trees that provides unobstructed vistas to the south.

Once back on the AT, turn left (west) and retrace your steps to the trailhead.

Miles and Directions

0.0 Start on the AT on the northeast end of the parking lot.

1.7 Sweat Heifer Creek Trail comes in from the right. Continue heading east on the AT.

2.7 The Boulevard Trail forks to the left (north). (See hike description for a side trip from here.) Continue northeast on the AT.

3.0 Short side path on the right leads to Icewater Spring Shelter.

4.0 Turn left on the side path to Charlies Bunion.

4.1 Arrive at Charlies Bunion. Enjoy the views and return to the AT by following the path around the knoll.

4.2 Back on the AT, turn left and head east.

4.6 Dry Sluice Gap Trail turns to the right. Continue on the AT.

10.7 Turn sharply back to the right (south) onto Hughes Ridge Trail.

11.1 Pecks Corner Shelter.

12.9 Turn right (south) on Bradley Fork Trail.

16.2 At an old traffic turnaround, turn right (north) onto Cabin Flats Trail and in a few hundred feet cross Bradley Fork on an elaborate bridge.

16.5 Junction with Dry Sluice Gap Trail, turning to the left. Continue straight ahead (north) on Cabin Flats Trail if spending the night at Campsite 49. Otherwise, turn left (west) onto Dry Sluice Gap Trail.

19.4 At a gap Dry Sluice Gap Trail continues north to reach the AT in 1.3 miles. Turn left (west) instead, onto Grassy Branch Trail.

21.9 Junction with Sweat Heifer Creek and Kephart Prong Trails at Kephart Shelter. Turn right on Sweat Heifer Creek Trail and immediately cross Kephart Prong on a foot log.

25.6 Return to the junction with the AT and Sweat Heifer Creek Trails. Turn left and retrace your steps to Newfound Gap.

27.3 Arrive back at Newfound Gap.

Options: You can do this trip in one night by dropping off the AT onto Dry Sluice Gap Trail, just beyond Charlies Bunion. Follow it down the ridge to the junction with Grassy Branch Trail and take it to the right (west). Spend the night at Kephart Shelter. Experienced hikers could also do this route as a strenuous day hike of 13.6 miles.

Another option for crazy hikers is to stay the first night at Pecks Corner Shelter and finish the rest of the trip the next day. The best option that balances effort with enough time to stop and smell the roses is a two-nighter. Head out early in the morning and spend the first night at Pecks Corner Shelter and the second night at Kephart Shelter. On the third day you can sleep late and still have plenty of time for the hike back.

70 Hemphill Bald

This is one of the best moderate-length loop hikes in the Smokies. The only negative is that some of the views encompass more than you probably wish to see on a
"wilderness" hike. From the high ridges, you can see houses, roads, and, every wilderness lover's favorite—Maggie Valley's Ghost Town in the Sky. Still, the positives far
outweigh the negatives on this hike.

Start: Polls Gap on Heintooga Ridge Road
Distance: 13.6-mile loop
Hiking time: About 7 hours—day hike or
overnighter
Difficulty: Moderate
Trail surface: Old forest roads and forest trails,
some very rocky
Best season: Spring for the wildflowers
Other trail users: Equestrians
Maps: Bunches Bald and Dellwood USGS
quads; Trails Illustrated #229 Great Smoky

Mountains; Trails Illustrated #317 Clingmans
Dome Cataloochee
Special considerations: Heintooga Ridge
Road, which you must drive to reach the trail-
head, is closed in winter.
Other: Parking shouldn't be a problem. Rest-
rooms are available in season at the picnic
area a few miles up Heintooga Ridge Road.
(The section of road to the picnic area remains
closed until mid-May.)

Finding the trailhead: At Wolf Laurel Gap (Milepost 458.2) on the Blue Ridge Parkway, turn
north onto Heintooga Ridge Road and drive 6.0 miles to Polls (Pauls) Gap on the right. The parking
area marks the trailhead for the Hemphill Bald, Rough Fork, and Polls Gap Trails. The hike starts on
far right (east) end of the parking area on Hemphill Bald Trail. GPS: N35 33.798' / W83 09.696'

The Hike

Begin on Hemphill Bald Trail from the east end of the parking lot. The first mile or
so is mostly level and rather unattractive. The trail is overgrown and the surrounding
understory is thick and unappealing. This is definitely not old-growth forest. In fact,
the course you follow is on an old logging grade. The forest becomes more scenic as
you approach Sugartree Licks, a small saddle with good spring wildflower displays and
a split-rail fence. You'll see many more fences over the next few miles.

From the gap, the trail climbs steadily to Whim Knob and then descends to Gar-
retts Gap. For the next 3 miles or so, the trail follows a similar undulating course along
the park boundary. You'll see fences, pastures, roads, and at one point there's an open
view down to Ghost Town, the popular Maggie Valley tourist trap, now shut down.
A solar-energy collection station marks Hemphill Bald. From the bald, you descend
less than 0.75 mile to Double Gap and the junction with Cataloochee Divide Trail.
(Locals refer to the section of Hemphill Bald Trail you just hiked as part of Cataloochee Divide Trail.)

Hemphill Bald

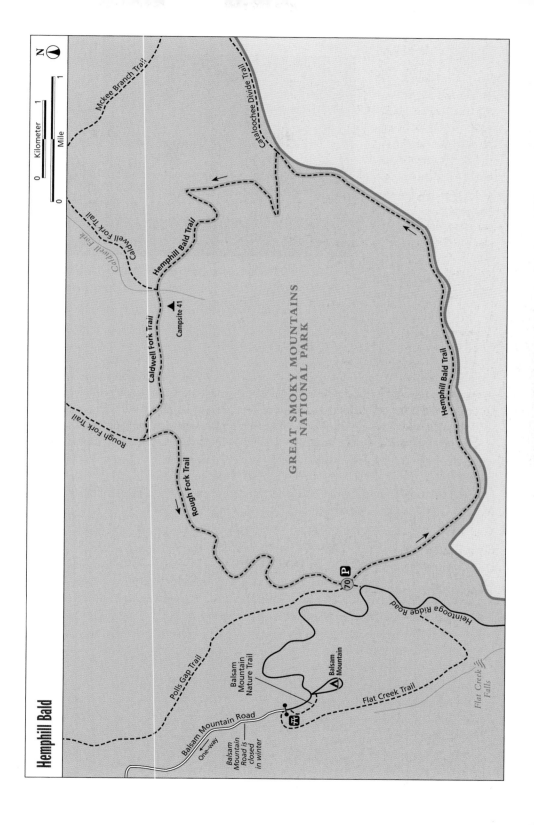

From Double Gap, turn sharply left (west), remaining on Hemphill Bald Trail. The first mile or so is rocky, muddy, and overgrown in wood nettle. On the plus side, this section is good for wildflowers. Farther down, at about 2.5 miles from the gap, you cross Double Gap Branch and soon pass a huge oak tree on the right. With a diameter

*Turks cap lilies (*Lilium superbum*) grow along Heintooga Ridge Road.*

of 6 feet, it must be among the largest northern red oaks in the park. The forest through here is very scenic, with many nice basswoods, yellow poplars (tulip trees), and hemlocks, the latter dying from the adelgid attack. (See the sidebar for Hike 36.)

Reach the junction with Caldwell Fork Trail and turn left (west) onto it. Quickly cross Caldwell Fork on a foot log and enter Campsite 41 on the other side. On an overnighter this is your home tonight. It isn't the most attractive backcountry campsite in the park, but it's more than adequate for a good night's stay.

From the campsite, climb rather steeply and come to a side path on the right. A sign here reads BIG POPLARS, and that's exactly what awaits you a few hundred feet along the path. Back on the main trail, continue climbing and pass through a section of old-growth forest, with many large hemlocks—again, all dying.

Reach Rough Fork Trail at a nondescript spot where the trail climbs Big Fork Ridge. Turn sharply left (south) and climb steeply for about a mile to pick up an old railroad grade. The remainder of the hike follows the railroad grade on a mostly level course all the way back to Polls Gap. Look for a few old railroad crossties along the way, some with spikes still sticking out of them.

Miles and Directions

0.0   Start on Hemphill Bald Trail from the east end of the parking area.

5.5   Junction with Cataloochee Divide Trail, which continues straight. Turn left (west) here, and remain on Hemphill Bald Trail.

8.4   Turn left (west) onto Caldwell Fork Trail.

8.5   Campsite 41.

10.1   Turn sharply left onto Rough Fork Trail.

13.6   Arrive back at trailhead

71 Balsam Mountain Nature Trail

The theme of this self-guided nature hike is nature's reclamation of a logged northern hardwood forest. Use the nature trail brochure available at the trailhead for more details on this theme. While there's no such thing as a bad walk in the woods, some are better than others. If you are camping at Balsam Mountain Campground, particularly if you have kids with you, this hike is a good way to spend an hour or so. Otherwise, it's not worth the long drive, considering the other options available in the park. The trail is often in bad shape—heavily overgrown, many downed trees, and poorly graded.

Start: Balsam Mountain Campground
Distance: 1.0-mile loop
Hiking time: About 1 hour—day hike
Difficulty: Easy
Trail surface: Narrow forest trail and paved road
Other trail users: Hikers only
Maps: Bunches Bald USGS quad; Trails Illustrated #229 Great Smoky Mountains; Trails Illustrated #317 Clingmans Dome Cataloochee

Special considerations: Heintooga Ridge Road, which you must drive to reach the trailhead, is closed in winter, typically from early Nov until mid-May.
Other: There is little parking near the trailhead, but that shouldn't be a problem. Most people who hike this trail are campers. Restrooms are available in season at the picnic area near the end of the hike.

Finding the trailhead: The trail starts at Balsam Mountain Campground. To get there from Wolf Laurel Gap (Milepost 458.2) on the Blue Ridge Parkway, turn north onto Heintooga Ridge Road and drive 8.3 miles to the campground entrance on the left. The trail starts between Campsites 45 and 44. GPS: N35 34.029' / W83 10.522'

The Hike

The trail begins on the right side of the road, just beyond the self-pay station, between Campsites 45 and 44. It follows a poorly graded course through the forest and comes out on Heintooga Ridge Road, just before the picnic area. Turn right and follow the road back to the campground to complete the loop.

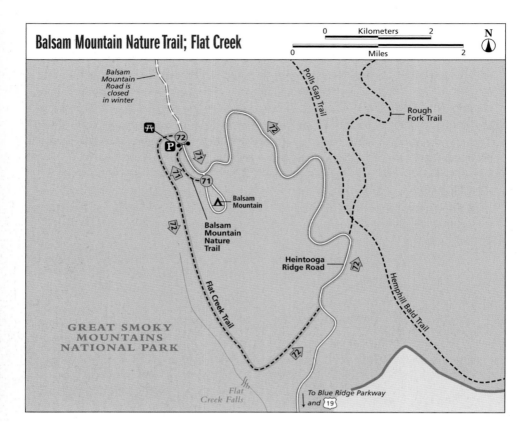

Balsam Mountain Nature Trail; Flat Creek

Balsam Mountain Road is closed in winter

Polls Gap Trail

Rough Fork Trail

72

71

71

71

72

Balsam Mountain

Balsam Mountain Nature Trail

72

Heintooga Ridge Road

72

Hemphill Bald Trail

GREAT SMOKY MOUNTAINS NATIONAL PARK

Flat Creek Trail

72

Flat Creek Falls

To Blue Ridge Parkway and 19

N

0   Kilometers   2

0   Miles   2

Miles and Directions

0.0 Start between Campsites 45 and 44 at the trailhead sign.

0.5 Come out on Heintooga Ridge Road. Turn right and follow the road back to the campground.

1.0 Arrive back at campground.

72 Flat Creek

Flat Creek Trail is an "unknown gem" in the Smokies. Few people know about it, but those who hike it don't soon forget it. Although heavily logged before park establishment, the forest walk is now one of the more scenic higher-elevation hikes in the park.

(See map for Hike 71: Balsam Mountain Nature Trail.)

Start: Balsam Mountain Picnic Area
Distance: 6.2-mile loop
Hiking time: About 3 hours—day hike
Difficulty: Moderate
Trail surface: Forest trail
Other trail users: Hikers only
Maps: Bunches Bald USGS quad; Trails Illustrated #229 Great Smoky Mountains; Trails Illustrated #317 Clingmans Dome Cataloochee
Special considerations: To hike this route as described, you have to walk 3.6 miles on Heintooga Ridge Road. Walking on paved roads in the Smokies is normally discouraged, but this road receives relatively little traffic and there's plenty of space to step off the pavement. It's a rewarding walk as well, with nice views and abundant roadside wildflowers in summer.

Blue Ridge Parkway, which you must drive to get here, is often closed in winter. However, it normally opens much sooner than the last segment of Heintooga Ridge Road above Polls Gap, which remains closed until mid-May. If you find the road gated, just pull away from the gate and park at a safe place on the side of the road. This is a loop hike, so it doesn't matter where you start.

Other: Relatively few people come up here, so parking shouldn't be a problem. Restrooms are available in season at the picnic area.

Finding the trailhead: At Wolf Laurel Gap (Milepost 458.2) on Blue Ridge Parkway, turn north onto Heintooga Ridge Road and drive 8.8 miles to the turnaround at the picnic area. The trail starts to the right of the picnic area at the end of the loop. GPS: N35 34.393' / W83 10.823'

The Hike

Begin at the picnic area at the trail sign on the northwestern end of the parking area. A short walk through a spruce forest takes you to Heintooga Overlook, a little-known view point that provides an open vista toward the west—perfect for sunsets. Becks Bald is prominent in the foreground; Clingmans Dome is far to the left; Mount Guyot is on the extreme right; and Mount LeConte is straight ahead in the distance.

Beyond the overlook the trail forks to the right (the left fork leads back to the picnic area) and soon descends to cross Flat Creek amidst a tangle of rhododendron. The forest is pleasantly open and the ground is carpeted in grass. Although scenic, the grass isn't natural. Grassy forests are usually a good sign of former logging activity. Grouse don't care whether it's been logged or not, and you might flush one out through here.

At 1.9 miles you come to a signed side path on the right that leads a few hundred yards to Flat Creek Falls. There's no good view of the falls from this path and any attempt to find one is dangerous and damaging to the surrounding soil. In spring,

Sunset view from Flat Creek Trail.

right after the road opens and before the leaves come out fully, there's a fair view of the waterfall from Heintooga Ridge Road.

Back on the main trail, you enter a dense forest and descend to cross a fork of Bunches Creek on a foot log. Turn sharply right, climb a small ridge, and descend to another branch crossing on a foot log. Now make a moderate climb of about 0.25 mile to Heintooga Ridge Road.

Once back on the road, turn left and walk 3.6 miles back to the picnic area. In summer you'll have plenty of roadside wildflowers to keep you company along the way.

Miles and Directions

0.0   Start on Flat Creek Trail on the northwestern end of the traffic turnaround.

0.1   Scenic overlook.

1.9   Pass by spur to Flat Creek Falls on the right. There is no good view of the waterfall from this path.

2.6   Junction with Heintooga Ridge Road (GPS: N35 33.251' / W83 09.832'). Turn left and follow the road back to the parking area.

6.2   Arrive back at parking area.

Options: Of course, you can do this trip as a shuttle and eliminate the road portion of the hike. If you have a bicycle, a good option is to leave it at the picnic area (chained, of course), drive back down to the lower trailhead, and hike Flat Creek Trail in reverse. Then you can coast back to your car.

73 Hyatt Ridge

Located in the remote Straight Fork section of the park, this "hidden gem" packs a big punch, especially for wildflower lovers. The best part is that you might have the entire hike to yourself. Relatively few people venture into this part of the park, and most of those who do aren't here for the trails. The scenic Straight Fork runs alongside the access road, providing great opportunities for fishing, sightseeing, and playing.

Start: Beech Gap trailhead in the Straight Fork area
Distance: 9.4-mile loop
Hiking time: About 5 hours—day hike or overnighter
Difficulty: Moderate
Trail surface: Forest trails, some very rocky, and gravel road
Best season: Spring for the wildflowers

Other trail users: Equestrians
Maps: Bunches Bald and Luftee Knob USGS quads; Trails Illustrated #229 Great Smoky Mountains; Trails Illustrated #317 Clingmans Dome Cataloochee
Other: You might have to share parking with a few trout fishers, but there should be plenty of room. The closest facilities are back in Cherokee.

Finding the trailhead: Drive 1.2 miles south from Oconaluftee Visitor Center toward Cherokee and turn left at the sign for Big Cove Road, taking the 0.2-mile connector over Oconaluftee River to the road. Turn left onto Big Cove Road and drive approximately 8.6 miles to a fork, just after crossing Raven Fork. Turn right at the fork onto Straight Fork Road and follow it 0.9 mile to a turnaround at a fish hatchery. Leave the pavement and continue on the gravel road. It's 3.9 miles to a narrow pullout on the right, just before the truss bridge. Beech Gap trailhead is on the opposite side of the road. GPS: N35 37.288' / W83 12.659'

Another option is to take Heintooga Ridge Road from the Blue Ridge Parkway to Balsam Mountain Picnic Area and continue on the one-way Balsam Mountain Road. This gravel road snakes down the mountain, providing good opportunities for viewing forests and wildflowers. The road becomes two-way at the start of this hike. (Blue Ridge Parkway, Heintooga Ridge Road, and Balsam Mountain Road are all closed in winter. The segment of Heintooga Ridge Road above Polls Gap remains closed until mid-May.)

The Hike

Begin on Beech Gap Trail on the west side of the road. Climb steeply through lush spring wildflowers to a point high above Straight Fork, and then swing west and continue a moderate climb in and out of the broad ridges. On the "ins," you cross several branches. Wildflowers abound in the wet spots throughout the year. In summer you can see jewelweed, coneflower, and joe-pye weed.

After a little more than 2 miles, you swing around a spur extending from Hyatt Bald and then go on a short level stretch before climbing the spur flank to the junction with Hyatt Ridge Trail on the ridgetop. Turn right (north) and ascend the flank of Hyatt Bald to the summit. On the bald is an open stand of beech trees that prohibit

View of Straight Fork at the Beech Gap Trailhead.

good views, but the carpet of grass, ferns, and various wildflowers throughout the season makes the bald a scenic spot. Norway spruce grows here, too. Lumber companies introduced this non-native tree after they logged the native red spruce.

Follow the narrow ridge from the bald and reach an open, heavily overgrown stretch. Soon reenter the forest and come to Campsite 44, one of the most delightful sites in the park. The campsite sits in a glade by the head of McGee Spring at an elevation of more than 5,000 feet. Huge red spruce and yellow birch dominate the old-growth forest. McGee Spring, said to be one of the coldest springs in the Smokies, gurgles out of the bank about 200 feet in front of the camp. Lush foliage covers the ground from spring through fall. False hellebore, coneflower, bee balm, and many other wildflowers grow here.

Backtrack from the campsite to the junction with Beech Gap Trail and then continue on Hyatt Ridge Trail. Descend steeply to a saddle and then climb gradually a short distance before descending again to begin a narrow ridge walk through mountain laurel, flame azalea, blueberries, and at one point, lichen-covered trees. The droopy lichens create an eerie sight in the fog.

A steep descent takes you to a gap and the junction with Enloe Creek Trail, which comes up the right side of the ridge. You want to turn left (northeast) and continue on Hyatt Ridge Trail. The trail leaves the ridge and makes a steady and steep descent to Straight Fork Road. This segment is an ankle-turner. It's muddy and covered in loose rocks that twist under your feet. It also has wonderful wildflower displays—foliage literally carpets the slopes.

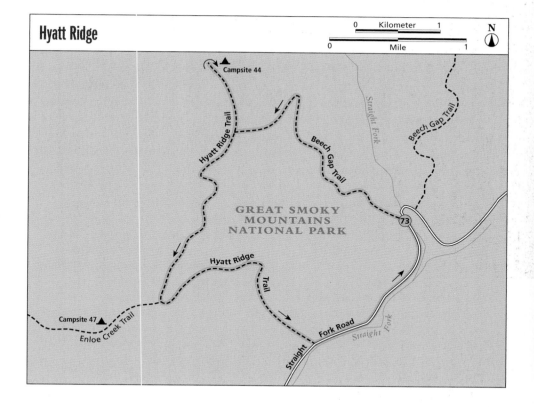

Once you reach the road, turn left and follow it 1.3 miles back to your vehicle.

Miles and Directions

0.0   Start on the west side of the road at the trail sign for Beech Gap Trail.

2.8   At the ridgetop turn right (north) onto Hyatt Ridge Trail.

3.7   Reach the end of the trail at Campsite 44 beside McGee Spring. Backtrack to the junction with Beech Gap Trail.

4.6   Arrive back at junction with Beech Gap Trail. Continue straight along the ridge on Hyatt Ridge Trail.

6.3   Junction with Enloe Creek Trail, coming up from the right. Turn left and descend the ridge, remaining on Hyatt Ridge Trail.

8.1   Arrive at the gravel road. Turn left and follow the road back to your car.

9.4   Arrive back at trailhead.

Option: While this hike is easy to do as a day hike, Campsite 44 is perfectly situated for making the hike an overnighter. There's a good chance you'll have the site, and the trail, to yourself for the entire trip.

74 Boogerman

You might be a little wary of hiking a trail called "Boogerman," but there's no cause for alarm. Robert "Boogerman" Palmer, the former owner of much of the woodland you hike through, supposedly received this nickname in school when he told his teacher he wanted to be the Boogerman when he grew up. (Another version says he told his teacher that his name was Boogerman.) Spooks or not, this hike is among the finest in the park, with prolific spring wildflowers and some impressive trees, although the big hemlocks along the trail are now dead.

Start: Caldwell Fork trailhead near Cataloochee Campground
Distance: 7.4-mile lollipop
Hiking time: About 4 hours—day hike
Difficulty: Moderate
Trail surface: Forest trail
Best season: Spring for the wildflowers
Other trail users: Equestrians are permitted on the Caldwell Fork Trail portion
Maps: Cove Creek Gap and Dellwood USGS quads; Trails Illustrated #229 Great Smoky Mountains; Trails Illustrated #317 Clingmans Dome Cataloochee
Special considerations: During summer you can expect to see many other people on this hike. If you want solitude, try hiking it in winter. You'll probably have it all to yourself, especially on weekdays.
Other: There's room for only a few vehicles at the trailhead. On weekends, you may have to continue on the road a short distance to find a safe place to pull off. Restrooms are available at the campground.

Finding the trailhead: This hike is in remote Cataloochee Cove, in the extreme southeastern section of the park. From exit 20 on I-40, go 0.1 mile south on US 276 and turn right onto Cove Creek Road. Follow this road 5.7 miles to the park boundary (it changes to gravel along the way), and continue 1.7 miles to an intersection with a paved road on the left. Turn left onto this road and drive 3.1 miles to the Caldwell Fork trailhead on the left, just past Cataloochee Campground. GPS: N35 37.896' / W83 05.311'

The Hike

The hike begins with the crossing of Palmer Creek on a long, bouncy foot log, just upstream of its junction with Caldwell Fork to create Cataloochee Creek. The next 0.8 mile follows Caldwell Fork upstream. Cross the creek on a foot log and in a few yards come to the lower junction with Boogerman Trail.

Turn left onto Boogerman Trail and begin ascending moderately. As you climb, you pass some big yellow poplars (tulip trees) and hemlocks. The hemlocks are dead and may have fallen by the time you get here. (See the sidebar for Hike 36.) Upon rounding a ridge the trail levels a bit and then begins descending through a white-pine grove before crossing a small stream branch and ascending again through excellent spring wildflower habitat. Now a quick, moderate ascent takes you over a ridge

Boogerman; Rough Fork and Caldwell Fork

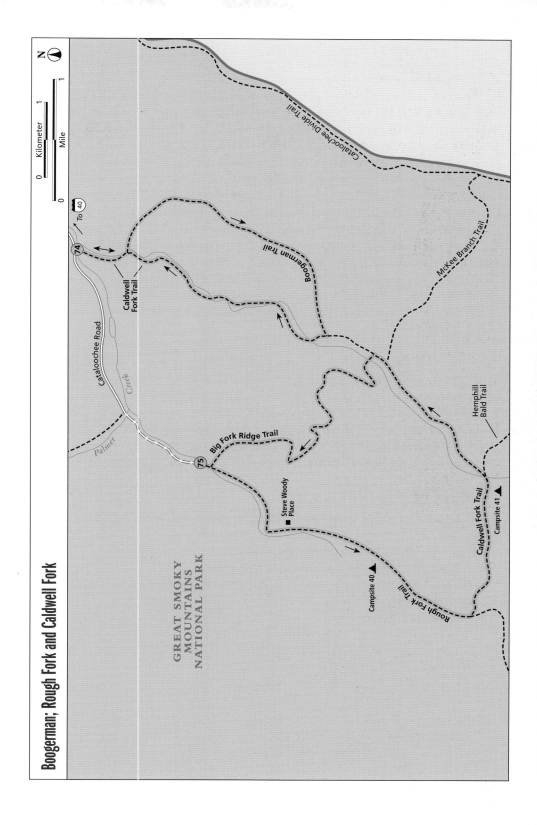

and into a mostly level stretch that crosses several springs, a small branch, and a scenic stand of second-growth yellow poplar.

Now the trail makes a short, steep push up a ridge. As you level out, look to the right to see a huge oak tree, and as you pass through the cove forest, you see many large poplars. This section is the highlight of the hike for many people. At this point you make a short ridgeline walk and begin descending to pick up a small stream. Signs of human settlement start to appear, including a fine rock wall beside the trail. Farther down stands a big poplar on the right that has a hollowed-out base big enough for several people to stand in. If you hike with kids and they run ahead of you like kids do, you can expect to find them standing inside the tree when you get there.

Continue descending along the stream, crossing it several times and passing several more rock walls. Off the trail to the right, you might spot a chunk of metal that seems very out of place. It looks like some sort of lift-gate mechanism, or perhaps an apparatus used in a sawmill. Now pass through a small clearing with walnut trees and yucca, both good indicators of a former homesite. On the left in a depression is the nearly decayed Carson Messer Cabin. A short distance farther you come to the upper junction with Caldwell Fork Trail.

Turn right onto Caldwell Fork Trail, cross Snake Branch (the stream you've been following) on a foot log, and shortly ahead cross Caldwell Fork on a foot log. Before you get back to the lower Boogerman Trail junction, you have to cross Caldwell Fork seven more times, each time on a hefty foot log, and each crossing offering a wonderful view of the creek. The grade is easy but rocky in places, and the trail is very muddy from horse traffic. There is one short section where a landslide washed out a portion of the trail and you have to work your way through carefully.

Once back at the lower junction, retrace your steps to the trailhead.

Miles and Directions

0.0 Start on Caldwell Fork Trail at the trail sign and immediately cross Palmer Creek on a foot log.

0.8 Turn left on Boogerman Trail at the lower trail junction.

4.7 Turn right on Caldwell Fork Trail at the upper trail junction.

6.6 Return to the junction of Caldwell Fork and Boogerman Trails. Retrace your steps from here to the trailhead.

7.4 Arrive back at trailhead.

75 Rough Fork and Caldwell Fork

As with Hike 74, this is a terrific loop hike located in the remote Cataloochee Cove section of the park. While it doesn't have quite as many big trees as Hike 74, it offers several things that Hike 74 doesn't, such as a historical structure to explore, two opportunities for camping, and much more solitude.

(See map for Hike 74: Boogerman.)

Start: Rough Fork trailhead in Cataloochee Cove
Distance: 9.4-mile loop
Hiking time: About 5 hours—day hike or overnighter
Difficulty: Moderate
Trail surface: Old forest roads and forest trails
Other trail users: Equestrians

Maps: Dellwood and Bunches Bald USGS quads; Trails Illustrated #229 Great Smoky Mountains; Trails Illustrated #317 Clingmans Dome Cataloochee
Special considerations: Cataloochee Cove, where this hike begins, is gated at night.
Other: There's plenty of room to park. Pit toilets are located at Pretty Hollow Gap trailhead near the old church.

Finding the trailhead: This hike starts in remote Cataloochee Cove, in the extreme southeastern section of the park. From exit 20 on I-40, go 0.1 mile south on US 276 and turn right onto Cove Creek Road. Follow this road 5.7 miles to the park boundary (it changes to gravel along the way), and continue 1.7 miles to an intersection with a paved road on the left. Turn left onto this road and drive 5.5 miles to the parking area at the road's end, passing through Cataloochee Cove (the road changes to dirt on the way). The trail is a continuation of the dirt road beyond the gate. GPS: N35 36.986' / W83 07.239'

The Hike

The first mile follows the old roadbed along Rough Fork, crossing it three times on narrow foot logs and arriving at a clearing. Here stands Steve Woody Place, a well-preserved homesite open for exploration. The house and springhouse are all that remain of several structures that once stood here.

After exploring the house continue along the roadbed, which narrows and starts to act more like a trail. You probably are alone now, since most people turn around at Steve Woody Place. Pass through a scenic forest with big (dead) hemlocks and cross Hurricane Creek on a foot log. Just past the crossing, situated in the fork between Hurricane Creek and Rough Fork, is Campsite 40. This is a neat site, nestled among hemlock, birch, and a tangle of rhododendron. Although the campsite is close to the trail, the dense vegetation provides seclusion.

Now the trail climbs moderately around ridge after ridge and doesn't stop until it reaches Caldwell Fork Trail, 1.4 miles from the campsite. At the junction take Caldwell Fork Trail to the left and head downhill (Rough Fork Trail continues climbing). Soon you begin passing through a splendid old-growth forest with many tree species. Farther down, in a stand of younger yellow poplars (tulip trees), a side path on the left leads several hundred feet to a few huge poplars known as the Big Poplars. A short distance down from here is Campsite 41, your home tonight if doing this trip as an overnighter. Campsite 41 isn't the most attractive site in the park and it receives a considerable amount of horse use. But it's the only logical choice for camping on this hike. Campsite 40 is too close to the beginning, making for a long second day.

Upon leaving the campsite, cross Caldwell Fork on a foot log and climb a few hundred yards to the junction with Hemphill Bald Trail. Stay left on Caldwell Fork Trail and descend to an easy rock-hop of Double Gap Branch. At this point you go on an easy undulating course, passing through a hemlock forest and then a white-pine forest, and then coming to the junction with McKee Branch Trail, forking off to the right in a clearing. Continue on Caldwell Fork Trail, and in 100 yards come to Big Fork Ridge Trail on the left.

Take Big Fork Ridge Trail and climb steadily to Big Fork Ridge, then descend the other side to Cataloochee Cove. Once back in the cove, turn left on the road and follow it a short distance back to the parking area.

Miles and Directions

0.0   Start on Rough Fork Trail as a continuation of the road.
1.0   Steve Woody Place.
1.5   Campsite 40.
2.9   Turn left onto Caldwell Fork Trail and descend.
4.4   Campsite 41.
4.5   Hemphill Bald Trail comes in from the right. Stay to the left on Caldwell Fork Trail.
6.0   Junction with McKee Branch Trail, forking to the right. Stay to the left on Caldwell Fork Trail.
6.1   Turn left onto Big Fork Ridge Trail.
9.3   Arrive back on the dirt road in Cataloochee Cove. Turn left to return to the parking area.
9.4   Arrive back at parking area.

Option: You can easily do this hike as a day hike, but Campsite 41 makes it a good choice for a lazy overnighter.

BACK AGAIN

Before the arrival of the white man, when the Cherokees lived and hunted in the Smoky Mountains and had only neighboring tribes to fight with, the animals in this region were much different than today. Passenger pigeons darkened the skies with unfathomable numbers, woods bison and elk browsed in meadows and natural clearings, gray (and possibly red) wolves hunted for rodents and deer, peregrine falcons soared overhead, beavers dammed the creeks while otters played in them, fishers hunted for squirrels, mountain lions did whatever they wanted, and the smoky madtom, spotfin chub, duskytail darter, and yellowfin madtom (all species of fish) darted about in some of the streams.

Elk (Cervus canadensis) *in Cataloochee.*

The arrival of the white man signaled the end for many of these species. The bison were gone by 1765, the elk in the mid-1800s, the gray wolf in 1887, and the mountain lion in the 1920s. Martha, the last passenger pigeon remaining on earth, died in captivity at the Cincinnati Zoo in 1914. At one time or another, all of the species mentioned above had been extirpated from the Smokies—every one of them at the hand of man.

In keeping with the National Park Service's mission to "conserve the scenery and the natural and historic objects and the wildlife therein . . . ," Great Smoky Mountains National Park has initiated a number of efforts to reintroduce some of these species. Of course, we will never see another passenger pigeon and it is highly doubtful that people today will tolerate a mountain lion in their neighborhood. But river otters once again play in some of the larger streams, peregrines soar over Alum Cave Bluff, and the smoky madtom, spotfin chub, duskytail darter, and yellowfin madtom ply the waters of Abrams Creek.

In the early 1990s biologists reintroduced the red wolf to the Cades Cove section of the park. Unfortunately, the experimental release proved unsuccessful. Everyone liked the idea of having the wolves in the park, but the wolves themselves had other plans. They kept leaving the park boundary and getting into trouble, so the plan had to be squelched.

Perhaps the most popular reintroduction effort is that of the elk. In 2001 biologists released twenty-five elk in Cataloochee Cove. Another twenty-seven were released the following year. The herd now numbers about 140 and seems to be doing well. The elk release has now moved from what was considered an experimental stage to what is now viewed as a reintroduction. Good places to see the elk are the fields at Oconaluftee Visitor Center and in Cataloochee Cove. The number of visitors to Cataloochee Cove has increased substantially since the elk were released. The cove becomes especially crowded during the autumn season, when the bull elks make their majestic bugling calls.

When viewing elk or any other wildlife in the park, remember that it is illegal to willfully approach within 50 yards or any distance that disturbs or displaces the animal.

76 Little Cataloochee

Few hikes in the Smokies offer a cultural experience as rewarding as this one. In Little Cataloochee you'll find restored cabins, cemeteries, rock walls and foundations, old metal and ceramic artifacts scattered about, and the highlight of the hike for many, Little Cataloochee Church perched on a knoll. It's impossible to walk through the cove without wondering about life before the park was established. Unlike neighboring "Big" Cataloochee Valley, and Cades Cove over on the Tennessee side of the park, the only way to see Little Cataloochee is on foot or horseback, which makes the experience even richer.

Start: Pretty Hollow Gap trailhead in Cataloochee Cove

Distance: 6.0 miles point to point

Hiking time: About 3.5 hours—day hike

Difficulty: Moderate

Trail surface: Rocky forest trail and dirt road

Other trail users: Equestrians

Maps: Cove Creek Gap USGS quad; Trails Illustrated #229 Great Smoky Mountains; Trails Illustrated #317 Clingmans Dome Cataloochee

Special considerations: Cataloochee Valley is gated at night, so you'll want to make sure to complete your hike and shuttle before it gets dark.

Other: The starting trailhead has room for several vehicles, but it fills quickly on summer weekends, particularly when horse trailers are here. The ending trailhead has room on the side of the road for only a couple of vehicles. Pit toilets are located near the start.

Finding the trailhead: This hike starts in remote Cataloochee Valley, in the extreme southeastern section of the park. From exit 20 on I-40, go 0.1 mile south on US 276 and turn right onto Cove Creek Road. Follow this road 5.7 miles to the park boundary (it changes to gravel along the way), and continue 1.7 miles to a four-way intersection, with a paved road on the left and a gravel road to the right and straight ahead. Turn left onto the paved road and drive 2.8 miles to the beginning of Cataloochee Valley, and then continue another 1.8 miles to a parking area on the right, just before the road crosses Palmer Creek. (It's 4.6 miles total along the paved road.) Pretty Hollow Gap Trail begins here as a dirt road. GPS: N35 37.600' / W83 06.742'

If doing this hike as a shuttle, you need to leave a second vehicle at the Little Cataloochee trailhead on NC 284. From the entrance to Cataloochee Valley (1.8 miles before reaching the Pretty Hollow Gap trailhead), turn north onto the gravel road. Drive 1.0 mile, passing the Palmer House on the way, and turn right to cross Cataloochee Creek on a steel bridge. Continue 0.7 mile along the rough road and turn left. (Straight ahead reconnects to the paved road that goes to Cataloochee.) Now drive 1.5 miles to another crossing of Cataloochee Creek and from there another 2.0 miles to the trailhead on the left. GPS: N35 40.571' / W83 05.247'

The Hike

Begin on an easy grade along scenic Palmer Creek. At 0.2 mile you pass to the left of a large horse camp, and at 0.8 mile Little Cataloochee Trail turns to the right (northeast). Take Little Cataloochee Trail and climb moderately, soon picking up Davidson

Dan Cook Place in Little Cataloochee. ▶

Branch and walking in the creek bed for a short distance. The trail becomes very muddy in places and continues to be rocky. You'll cross the creek several times as you climb. After the final crossing the trail swings away to the right, leaving the Davidson Branch drainage but quickly picking up the drainage of a side stream.

Continue climbing along this side stream and soon pass an old homesite on the left. Look for a well-constructed rock wall and the rotten remains of a log building. The logs are American chestnut—most other woods would have decayed long ago. You'll also see yucca plants and, in spring, daffodils—both are good indicators of an old homeplace. Farther ahead, in Little Cataloochee Valley, you'll see lots more of these plants. Beyond the old homeplace the trail dips to cross the branch and then begins the steepest part of the hike. Look for another rock wall on the left as you climb alongside the creek.

You soon reach Davidson Gap after making a sharp switchback to the right. Descend from the gap rather steeply, passing a couple of rock walls on the right. You are entering Little Cataloochee Valley now, and for the next couple of miles, you'll see abundant evidence of the heavy settlement that occurred here. Old homesites are now overgrown with trees, but you can still distinguish many of them. Scattered all about the valley are remnants of rock walls, pieces of metal, shards of glass and ceramics, and homesite indicator plants such as periwinkle and the aforementioned yucca and daffodils.

The steep trail soon moderates and joins an old roadbed for an easy walk. Come to Dan Cook Place on the left at 3.3 miles. This fine cabin is a reconstructed version of an original cabin that was destroyed by vandals in the 1970s. It is among the most picturesque cabins in the park. Across from the cabin is the rock foundation of an apple house.

Continue the gentle descent and then make an easy climb to reach Little Cataloochee Baptist Church, beautifully situated on a grassy knoll overlooking a cemetery. Built in the late 1800s, the church still stands in its original condition and is still the site of occasional services. From the church, the road descends rather steeply and passes a spring on the left side of the road, then goes through the old community of Ola. Ola once boasted several structures, including the finest house in Little Cataloochee, which stood off the right side of the road just before the bridge over Little Cataloochee Creek. In winter you can find scattered artifacts of the community, but the area is now nearly overgrown.

Cross Little Cataloochee Creek and begin ascending. You soon come to a sharp right swing in the road, where a side path on the left leads in a few hundred feet to John Jackson Hannah Cabin. The cabin is open for exploration. Shortly beyond the cabin is the junction with Long Bunk Trail on the left (northeast). About 0.2 mile up this trail is Hannah Cemetery—a nice side trip. Little Cataloochee Trail continues from Long Bunk trailhead another 1.1 miles on a moderate course to NC 284 and the end of the hike. At 0.3 mile before the end, the old road crosses Correll Branch in what used to be a scenic forest with many large eastern hemlock trees. The trees now stand as skeletons, having succumbed to the hemlock woolly adelgid. (See the sidebar for Hike 36.)

When you reach NC 284, you have two choices if you didn't leave a shuttle vehicle. You can return the way you came or walk back to Cataloochee Valley along the road. Most of the park's paved roads are not suitable for pedestrians, but out here in the middle of nowhere, the hike wouldn't be a lot different from walking on a trail. Just be careful as you walk around the blind curves.

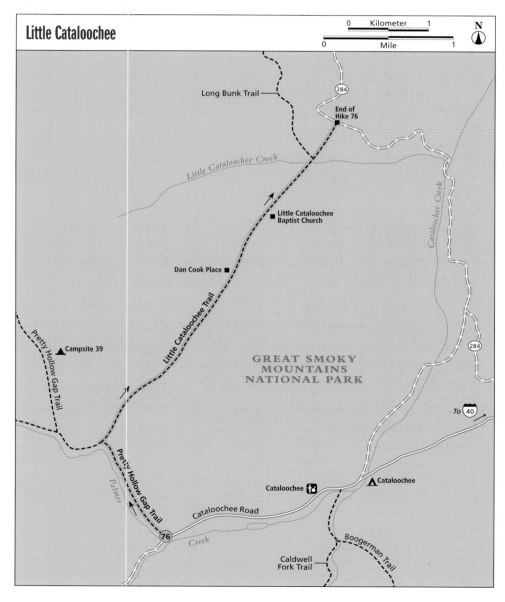

Miles and Directions

0.0 Start on Pretty Hollow Gap Trail, following Palmer Creek upstream.

0.8 Turn right (northeast) onto Little Cataloochee Trail.

2.6 Reach Davidson Gap and begin descent into Little Cataloochee Valley.

4.9 Long Bunk Trail goes to the left (northeast) and leads 0.2 mile to Hannah Cemetery, a recommended side trip. Little Cataloochee Trail continues straight ahead.

6.0 Little Cataloochee Trail ends at NC 284. Return the way you came or hike the road back if you didn't leave a shuttle vehicle.

Options: From Cataloochee Valley, most people hike the trail as described here—a shuttle hike—leaving a vehicle at the other end. Those who are interested only in seeing the historic structures in Little Cataloochee usually hike in from NC 284 and then backtrack. A great option is to leave a bicycle on NC 284 and ride back to the trailhead in Cataloochee.

At the start of the hike, you can cross over Palmer Creek on the bridge and take the path on the right to the old Beech Grove School for a quick side trip. Actually, if you're interested in old schools, churches, and cabins, you should plan to spend a day exploring all of Cataloochee in addition to the hike through Little Cataloochee.

THE BIG HOUSE

From the hilltop church on Little Cataloochee Trail, the old road descends and soon crosses Little Cataloochee Creek in the old community of Ola. Look around here. You'll find some mossy rock walls, a few rusty pieces of tin, and maybe some other artifacts, but the area is mostly overgrown. The scene here was much different before the park came to town. Over on the left (west) side of the road was a blacksmith shop, a gristmill, and a general store, which also housed the Ola post office, all owned by Will Messer. On the opposite side of the road stood Messer's house, the finest in Little Cataloochee, and among the finest anywhere in the region. Built in 1910, the three-story frame house had eleven rooms, hot and cold running water, and acetylene lights.

77 Mount Sterling

Of the three hikes in this guidebook that take you to Mount Sterling, this one is the shortest and the only one suitable for a day hike. It's steep but short enough that you can take all the time you need. Although the trailhead is on the other side of nowhere, a surprising number of people make this steep trek. The elevation of Mount Sterling Gap is 3,888 feet; at the summit of Mount Sterling, it's 5,842 feet. That makes 1,954 feet you have to climb in less than 3 miles. Fortunately, it's a continuous, steady climb, without any severely steep sections.

The summit of Mount Sterling is not pristine. There's the 60-foot steel fire tower, the storage building, the power-line swath, and the clearings for the campsites. However, something about this place makes you feel as though you're in the middle of an enormous wilderness. A chilly one too. The temperature on top is always a good bit cooler than at the gap, and in autumn, winter, and spring, it can be downright frigid. Also, the wind seems to blow harder here than it does anywhere else in the park.

Start: Mount Sterling trailhead at Mount Sterling Gap

Distance: 5.4 miles out and back

Hiking time: About 3 hours—day hike or overnighter

Difficulty: Strenuous, due to elevation gain

Trail surface: Old jeep trail, very rocky in places

Best season: Spring–autumn

Other trail users: Hikers-only for most of the route; horses allowed on a short section near the end

Maps: Cove Creek Gap and Luftee Knob USGS quads; Trails Illustrated #229 Great Smoky Mountains; Trails Illustrated #317 Clingmans Dome Cataloochee

Special considerations: Old NC 284, the access road to Mount Sterling Gap, is closed in winter when there is ice or snow on the road. Because the trailhead is so remote, it isn't the safest place to leave your vehicle. Don't leave any valuables in it.

If you plan to overnight at Campsite 38 on Sterling's summit, don't forget 2 things: a reservation (site 38 is rationed) and warm clothes at any time of year.

Others: There is no parking to speak of at the gap—just a wide spot in the road. You might have to park a little closer to the roadway than you'd prefer on summer weekends. There are no facilities of any kind anywhere nearby.

Finding the trailhead: Getting to the trailhead is as much a part of this adventure as the hike itself. The easiest route is to come in from the north. Take the Waterville exit (exit 457) off I-40 and cross Pigeon River. Stay to the left after the crossing and follow the road 2.0 miles to an intersection, passing the Walters Power Plant on the way. The intersection marks the community of Mount Sterling. Turn left onto Mount Sterling Road and drive 6.7 curvy miles to Mount Sterling Gap. Pull off the road here; the trail starts on the right (west) side of the gap.

From the entrance to Cataloochee on the south side of the gap, turn north onto the gravel road and drive 1.0 mile, then turn right to cross Cataloochee Creek on a steel bridge. Continue 0.7 mile (rough) and turn left. It is 5.8 miles to Mount Sterling Gap. GPS: N35 42.028' / W83 05.843'

View from Mount Sterling Fire Tower.

The Hike

The hike begins rather steeply through an oak forest and doesn't let up until you start approaching the junction with Long Bunk Trail, coming up from Little Cataloochee Cove on the left (south). Beyond the junction the climbing continues, this time not letting up until you reach Mount Sterling Ridge at 2.3 miles. Fortunately, you are climbing on a well-graded trail, owing to its being the old jeep road that once provided access to the fire tower on Mount Sterling's summit. As you ascend, notice how the forest changes from an oak association at the beginning to spruce at the higher elevations, finally turning into a true red spruce–Fraser fir forest on the summit.

Reach the junction with Mount Sterling Ridge Trail at 0.4 mile below the summit. Turn sharply to the right (northeast) and pass a horse-hitching rack just before reaching the top. If overnighting, you have three choices for tent sites, each with a food-suspension cable. Look around—they are well hidden from one another. If you need water, there is a reliable spring on the north side of the mountain. Hike down Baxter Creek Trail (it starts at the tower) about 0.25 mile to the signed side path on the left. Walk a couple hundred yards along this path to the spring.

The hike isn't finished when you reach the summit—you still have 60 vertical feet to go. The 360-degree view from the tower ranks among the finest in the park. If you're camping, give yourself a special treat and climb the tower at sunrise. When the wind is howling, which is often, it's a little unnerving climbing to the top of the tower, but just consider that as part of the adventure.

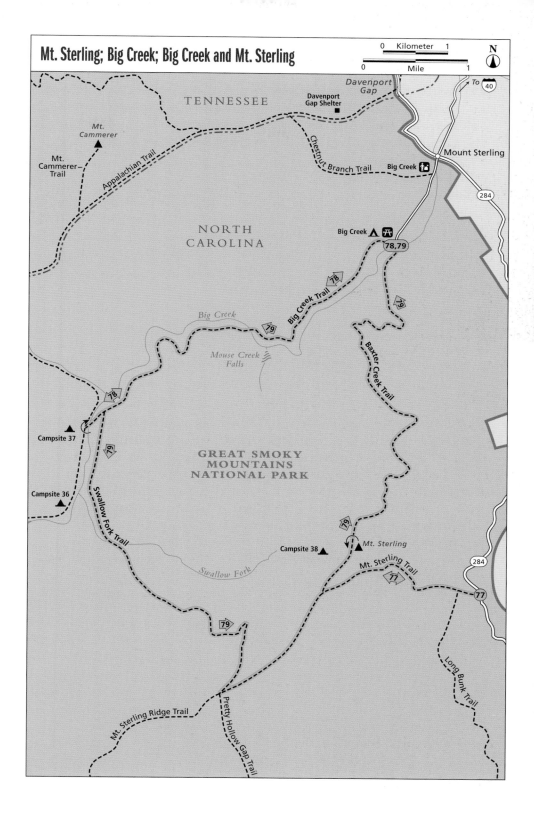

Miles and Directions

0.0 Begin hiking on the west side of the gap.

0.5 Junction with Long Bunk Trail, coming in from the left (south). Continue straight ahead.

2.3 Junction with Mount Sterling Ridge Trail. Bear to the right (northeast).

2.7 Reach the summit of Mount Sterling and Campsite 38. Return the way you came.

5.4 Return to the trailhead.

Options: Two other hikes in this guidebook take you to Sterling's summit: Hike 79 and Hike 80.

78 Big Creek

This may be the perfect hike for inexperienced or first-time backpackers, as well as for day hikers. It's an easy creek-side walk, but long enough to make you feel as though you've done something. It provides wonderful scenery and the campsite is among the finest in the park. But just because the walk to the campsite is easy doesn't mean this hike is for weenies. Several options make it as demanding as you want it to be.

(See map for Hike 77: Mount Sterling.)

Start: Big Creek Picnic Area
Distance: 10.6 miles out and back
Hiking time: About 5 hours—day hike or overnighter, with options for extended trips
Difficulty: Easy
Trail surface: Old forest road
Best season: Early spring for the wildflowers
Other trail users: Equestrians
Maps: Waterville, Cove Creek Gap, and Luftee Knob USGS quads; Trails Illustrated #229

Great Smoky Mountains; Trails Illustrated #317 Clingmans Dome Cataloochee
Special considerations: If planning to camp at Campsite 37, make reservations as early as possible. This is one of the most popular rationed sites in the park.
Other: Parking space is rarely a problem except on weekends during summer and Oct. A restroom building is located at the parking area, but it is closed in winter. Portable toilets are available when the restrooms are closed.

Finding the trailhead: Take the Waterville exit (exit 457) off I-40 and cross Pigeon River. Stay to the left after the crossing and follow the road 2.0 miles to an intersection, passing the Walters Power Plant on the way. The intersection marks the community of Mount Sterling. Go straight, and enter the Big Creek section of the park. Follow the road 0.8 mile to where it ends at the picnic area and campground entrance. Big Creek Trail begins to the right, just before the parking area. GPS: N35 45.073' / W83 06.605'

The Hike

Begin by walking back up the road a few feet and turning left at the gate and trailhead sign. The hike is on an old motor road built by the Civilian Conservation Corps (CCC) in the 1930s. It's wide, well graded, and never steep. Much of it follows the old logging railroad grade. Logging occurred in nearly all of the Big Creek watershed prior to park establishment.

After about 1.0 mile on Big Creek Trail, look to the right to see Rock House, a towering rock cliff a few hundred feet off the trail. Supposedly, the rock overhang served as temporary shelter for loggers and settlers. Less than half a mile beyond Rock House is Midnight Hole on Big Creek. The entire flow of the creek squeezes through a narrow chute and drops 6 feet into a deep, dark-as-midnight pool.

Mouse Creek Falls drops directly into Big Creek.

At 2.0 miles you come to Mouse Creek Falls on the left, indicated by a horse-hitching rack. The 35-foot cascade drops directly into Big Creek, creating a grand scene for hikers and photographers. Shortly beyond the falls, you cross Big Creek on a bridge and keep steady company with the creek for the remainder of the hike.

About 0.75 mile beyond Mouse Creek Falls, you pass a well-known landmark on the left side of the road. Back during the logging days, a logging train engineer placed a brake shoe on the dripping bank to collect the water, similar to the function of pipes you see at many backcountry campsite springs. Brakeshoe Spring, as it became known, was a regular stopping point for loggers and then hikers for more than fifty years until some bonehead stole the shoe in the early 1970s.

From Brakeshoe Spring, you have an enjoyable creek-side walk of 2.5 miles to Walnut Bottoms at Campsite 37. The campsite is one of the best in the park, with secluded tent sites beside Big Creek. If the creek-side sites are taken, you can camp on the other side of the trail under a stand of buckeyes.

Campsite 37 marks the end of the hike if doing it as a day trip. Backtrack from here.

Miles and Directions

0.0 Start on Big Creek Trail on the west side of the road, just before the parking area.

2.0 Mouse Creek Falls.

5.1 Junction with Swallow Fork Trail on the left. Continue on the old road.

5.3 Arrive at Campsite 37. Return the way you came.

10.6 Arrive back at the parking area.

Options: Many people hike to Walnut Bottoms as a day hike, and many others camp at site 37, but few take full advantage of the opportunities available. A great plan is to hike to Walnut Bottoms and camp for two nights. On the second day take a day hike to a scenic cascade. You continue on Big Creek Trail about 0.5 mile to Camel Gap Trail at Campsite 36 (horse campers only). On Camel Gap Trail you go about 0.6 mile and turn left onto Gunter Fork Trail, making a crossing of Big Creek (dangerous or impassable in high water). At about 1.5 miles on Gunter Fork Trail, you pass a pretty cascade on the right. At 1.8 miles you reach a long, sliding cascade known as Gunter Fork Falls. Backtrack to Walnut Bottoms from here for a day hike of about 5.8 miles.

A more ambitious plan is to make a day-hike loop that takes you over Cosby Knob on the Appalachian Trail (AT). For this hike, you climb Low Gap Trail from Campsite 37 to the AT in 2.5 miles. Turn left onto the AT and hike about 2.4 miles to Camel Gap, skirting the summit of Cosby Knob along the way. At Camel Gap turn left onto Camel Gap Trail and follow it 4.7 miles down to Big Creek Trail, 0.5 mile above your campsite. Total round-trip for the hike is 10.1 miles, making for a good workout, considering the grade. (The map for Hike 80 shows the trails for these options.)

Another option is to use Campsite 37 as only the first night's stay on a longer backpacking trip. Hike 79 outlines that option.

CCC BOYS

It's safe to say that had the Great Depression not hit, Great Smoky Mountains National Park would not have much of the infrastructure that it does today. As part of President Franklin D. Roosevelt's New Deal economic program, the Civilian Conservation Corps set up twenty-two camps in the newly formed park. Some 4,000 young men worked in these camps between 1933 and 1942, building roads and trails, constructing visitor centers, picnic areas, and campgrounds, and reclaiming logged forests. The CCC's Big Creek Camp, built on the site of a former logging camp, stood at the current location of the Big Creek Horse Camp, beside the Big Creek Picnic Area. Workers from this camp constructed miles of hiking trails, built several bridges over Big Creek, and constructed the fire towers atop Mount Sterling and Mount Cammerer. It's impossible to hike in the area without seeing the hard work of the Big Creek CCC camp crew. In fact, it's impossible to visit most anywhere in the park without encountering the work conducted by the CCC boys from one of the Smokies' camps.

79 Big Creek and Mount Sterling

Remember that commercial where those guys are sitting around the campfire drinking beer and one of them says, "You know, it just doesn't get any better than this"? Well, he could have been talking about this hike. It may be the best two-night backpacking trip in the park, even without the beer. It offers everything the Smokies are famous for except historical structures, Mount Sterling Fire Tower notwithstanding. And while it's popular among backpackers, the summer crowds thin out after the first few miles. On winter weekdays—a great time to make this trip—it's possible to hike the entire loop without seeing another person.

Two other hikes in this guidebook include sections of the hike described here: Hike 77 and Hike 78.

(See map for Hike 77: Mount Sterling.)

Start: Big Creek Picnic Area
Distance: 17.4-mile loop
Hiking time: About 10 hours—2-night backpack, tough overnighter, or killer day hike
Difficulty: Strenuous, due to steep grades
Trail surface: Old forest road and forest trails, some very rocky
Best season: Early spring for the wildflowers
Other trail users: Equestrians permitted on all parts except the final Baxter Creek Trail section
Maps: Waterville, Luftee Knob and Cove Creek Gap USGS quads; Trails Illustrated #229 Great Smoky Mountains; Trails Illustrated #317

Clingmans Dome Cataloochee
Special considerations: The 2 campsites on this hike are popular. Make your reservation as early as possible, and be prepared with alternative dates when you call.

If hiking between Oct and May, be prepared for cold and windy weather on Mount Sterling. In winter, weather on the summit can be frigid, regardless of the conditions at the trailhead.
Other: Parking space is rarely a problem except on weekends during summer and Oct. A restroom building is located at the parking area, but it is closed in winter. Portable toilets are available when the restrooms are closed.

Finding the trailhead: Take the Waterville exit (exit 457) off I-40 and cross Pigeon River. Stay to the left after the crossing and follow the road 2.0 miles to an intersection, passing the Walters Power Plant on the way. The intersection marks the community of Mount Sterling. Go straight, and enter the Big Creek section of the park. Follow the road 0.8 mile to where it ends at the picnic area and campground entrance. Big Creek Trail begins to the right, just before the parking area. GPS: N35 45.073' / W83 06.605'

The Hike

Begin by walking back up the road a few feet and turning left at the gate. The hike is on an old motor road built by the Civilian Conservation Corps (CCC) in the 1930s. It's wide, well graded, and nowhere very steep. Much of it follows the old logging railroad grade. Logging occurred in nearly all of the Big Creek watershed prior to park establishment.

A hiker fills his water bottle from the spring on Mount Sterling.

After about 1.0 mile on Big Creek Trail, look to the right to see Rock House, a towering rock cliff a few hundred feet off the trail. Supposedly, the rock overhang served as temporary shelter for loggers and settlers. Four-tenths of a mile beyond Rock House is Midnight Hole on Big Creek. The entire flow of the creek squeezes through a narrow chute and drops 6 feet into a deep, dark-as-midnight pool.

At 2.0 miles you come to Mouse Creek Falls on the left, indicated by a horse-hitching rack. The 35-foot cascade drops directly into Big Creek, creating a grand scene for hikers and photographers. Shortly beyond the falls, you cross Big Creek on a bridge and keep steady company with the creek for the remainder of the hike.

About 0.75 mile beyond Mouse Creek Falls, you pass a well-known landmark on the left side of the road. Back during the logging days, a logging train engineer placed a brake shoe on the dripping bank to collect the water, similar to the function of pipes you see at many backcountry campsite springs. Brakeshoe Spring, as it became known, was a regular stopping point for hikers for more than fifty years until some bonehead stole the shoe in the early 1970s.

From Brakeshoe Spring, you have an enjoyable creek-side walk of 2.5 miles to Walnut Bottoms at Campsite 37, located 0.2 mile beyond the junction with Swallow Fork Trail. Campsite 37 is your first night's stay unless you decide to go for Mount Sterling in a day. The campsite is one of the best in the park, with secluded tent sites beside Big Creek. If the creek-side sites are taken, you can camp on the other side of the trail under a stand of buckeyes.

From the campsite, backtrack to the Swallow Fork Trail junction and turn right on it. You climb gradually, crossing a couple of tributaries on the way to Swallow Fork. Cross the fork at 1.0 mile on a foot log over a particularly scenic section of the creek. Soon after this crossing, you cross McGinty Creek and pass several old artifacts on the left side of the trail. There are steel hoops and cables and a metal drum that once served as a belt drive for something—probably a sawmill.

Now you climb alongside the tumbling Swallow Fork. In April this is a great wildflower walk. About a mile above McGinty Creek, you make the final stream crossing and begin a fairly steep push to Pretty Hollow Gap. At the gap Mount Sterling Ridge Trail goes right and left, and Pretty Hollow Gap Trail goes straight ahead, descending to Cataloochee Cove. Pretty Hollow Gap, like many similar areas in the Smokies, often suffers heavy damage from wild hogs.

From the gap, turn left (east) onto Mount Sterling Ridge Trail. The first 0.5 mile ascends steeply to cross a knoll in a particularly beautiful forest of spruce, birch, and beech. You soon begin ascending again and merge into Mount Sterling Trail, coming in from the right. From here, it's 0.4 mile to the summit of Mount Sterling and Campsite 38. This is your second night's stay, and if the weather is typical, this will be a memorable camping experience. It's often very cold and very windy up here. The steel fire tower at the summit is open for climbing and is a highlight of the hike. When the wind howls, it's a little frightening climbing to the top, but you need to get above the trees at least. The panoramic view is among the finest in the park.

Baxter Creek Trail, which you will use to get down the mountain, starts on the summit of Mount Sterling by the base of the tower. The trail descends steadily (sometimes steeply) to the Big Creek Picnic Area in 6.1 miles, with superb forest scenery along most of the trail. About 0.25 mile down from the fire tower, you come to a signed side path on the left that leads in a couple hundred yards to a reliable spring. On the main trail, hike along a ridge and through switchbacks in a boulder field. Lush, thick moss covers every ground surface you see. This stretch is reminiscent of a southeast Alaska rain forest.

About 2 miles from Mount Sterling, you make an extreme left switchback off the ridgeline and enter an enchanted old-growth forest with several species of trees. Look all around through here but especially above the trail toward the ridge, where some gigantic gnarly maples grow. Farther down, you cross a tributary and soon begin paralleling Baxter Creek. Several large yellow poplars (tulip trees) grow in this scenic, open forest. There are some big hemlocks here too, but they are all dead from the adelgid attack (see the sidebar for Hike 36).

After crossing Baxter Creek you pass through a dense stand of second-growth yellow poplar. At the lower end of the poplar grove, the trail makes a sharp right turn and goes a few yards to cross a small stream. At the right turn a side path turns to the left and leads a few hundred yards to one of the tallest standing chimneys in the park. Along the way it passes a stone structure of some sort that has some old metal artifacts piled on top. You can easily see it from the main trail when the leaves are off the trees.

After crossing the small stream, Baxter Creek Trail soon reaches the long footbridge over Big Creek. The picnic area is on the far side.

Miles and Directions

0.0   Start on Big Creek Trail on the west side of the road just before the parking area.

2.0   Mouse Creek Falls.

5.1   Junction with Swallow Fork Trail on the left. Continue on the old road.

5.3   Arrive at Campsite 37. Return to the junction with Swallow Fork Trail.

5.5   Turn right on Swallow Fork Trail.

9.5   On the ridgetop, turn left (east) on Mount Sterling Ridge Trail.

10.9 Junction with Mount Sterling Trail, coming up from the right and continuing straight ahead. Continue straight along the ridge.

11.3 Arrive at summit of Mount Sterling and Campsite 38. Take Baxter Creek Trail, which begins near the base of the fire tower.

17.4 Arrive back at Big Creek Picnic Area.

Option: Experienced and fit hikers can make it to Mount Sterling in a day, but it's a tough hike. Some hikers do the entire route as long day hike, but unless you're in Navy SEAL training, it's a wee bit overkill. It's better to take your time and enjoy the scenery.

THE ROOT OF THE PROBLEM

If you see an area that looks as though a rototiller has gone through it, that's likely the mark of a wild hog. In the early 1900s George Moore established a hunting preserve in North Carolina's Snowbird Mountains, southwest of the park. Among the exotic animals he imported were buffalo, Russian wild boar, and Russian brown bear. Moore's efforts proved fruitless, with many animals poached and others escaping their fenced enclosures. All of the animal species eventually died out except for the wild boar, which flourished and spread, interbreeding with domestic feral pigs and eventually inhabiting forests all over the southwestern mountains of North Carolina and the surrounding region.

The wild hogs have been causing trouble ever since. Their method of feeding by uprooting vegetation causes ecological havoc in the areas where they are most common, particularly in the Smokies. They also carry diseases that can be fatal to native wildlife. The hogs seem to be especially fond of the park's high-elevation beech gaps, like Pretty Hollow Gap, which you hike through on Hike 79. The park removes about 275 wild hogs in an average year through trapping and shooting. You'll see hog traps throughout the park backcountry and you might run across someone carrying a rifle, whose job it is to shoot the hogs. It's a continuous battle, with the hogs holding their own all too well.

80 Big Creek Perimeter Loop

Hike 79 is among the best two-night backpacks in the park. The hike outlined here, which follows a portion of that hike's route, is among the finest three-night backpacks in the park. It follows high mountain crests as it loops around the entire upper Big Creek drainage. The high-elevation forests are dark and mysterious, even with the disheartening death of trees from introduced pests and air pollution. If you're looking for a challenging, grand adventure in the Smokies, this is it.

Start: Chestnut Branch trailhead at Big Creek Ranger Station
Distance: 34.0-mile loop
Hiking time: About 19 hours—3-night backpack, 4-nighter, or killer 2-nighter
Difficulty: Strenuous, due to steep grades and rocky trails
Trail surface: Forest trails and old logging grades, some very rocky
Other trail users: First section on Chestnut Branch Trail and last section on Baxter Creek Trail are for hikers only; the rest is open for equestrians
Maps: Waterville, Hartford, Luftee Knob, Mount Guyot, and Cove Creek Gap USGS quads; Trails Illustrated #229 Great Smoky Mountains; Trails Illustrated #317 Clingmans Dome Cataloochee
Special considerations: The shelters and campsite on this hike are popular. Make your reservation as early as possible and be prepared with alternative dates when you call. Although the first night's stay on this hike is only 8.4 miles from the trailhead, it's a tough climb. Experienced hikers can make it in 4 or 5 hours without pushing themselves, but inexperienced hikers need to head out early in the morning and plan on an all-day hike. Actually, inexperienced hikers probably shouldn't be attempting this trip at all.

Winter is a great time to make this hike. The views are open and you'll meet far fewer hikers on the trail. However, if you do choose a winter hike, you need to make a frank assessment of your backpacking abilities and prepare for snow and frigid conditions. It is not uncommon to leave from the trailhead with clear skies and temperatures in the fifties, only to find yourself plowing through snow and sub-freezing temperatures in the higher elevations. Tricorner Knob Shelter, the most remote shelter in the park, has hosted many a hiker stranded in deep snow.

Other: Parking space is never a problem here. Pit toilets are located here, and the picnic area that is 0.6 mile farther along the road has a restroom building, although it closes in winter. Portable toilets are available in winter.

Finding the trailhead: Take the Waterville exit (exit 457) off I-40 and cross Pigeon River. Stay to the left after the crossing and follow the road 2.0 miles to an intersection, passing the Walters Power Plant on the way. The intersection marks the community of Mount Sterling. Go straight, and enter the Big Creek section of the park. Follow the road 0.2 mile to the ranger station and parking area on the right. Chestnut Branch Trail begins about 200 feet farther up the road, on the right. GPS: N35 45.610' / W83 06.386'

The Hike

Begin ascending Chestnut Branch Trail alongside Chestnut Branch on an old logging grade. Pass a huge oak tree on the left that somehow escaped the logger's ax. Several families once lived along Chestnut Branch; perhaps this tree was part of their holdings. You can see signs of settlement along the lower portion of the hike. Except for one easy stretch, it's a steady climb all the way to the Appalachian Trail (AT).

Reach the AT at a small gap. To the right, it's only 1.9 miles to Davenport Gap and the eastern trailhead for the Smokies portion of the AT. If you had started there, you would have added more than the 0.6 mile of road walking that's included in the route outlined here and you wouldn't have had a good place to leave your vehicle. The hike as described is much more "loop friendly."

Turn left (southwest) onto the AT and make a continuous ascent to Lower Mount Cammerer Trail, on the right. Continue climbing on the AT and pass through a boulder field on switchbacks. Ferns and mosses cover the rocks and varieties of wildflowers grow among them. At an outside switchback around a ridge, you have the first open view, this one toward the northeast. Now the trail becomes even more interesting as it climbs the steep slope of Cammerer Ridge through rhododendron and by rock walls. You soon come to another outside turn at a rock outcrop. From this outcrop are commanding views into Pigeon River Valley and the Big Creek watershed. As good as this view is, it's just a tease for what's ahead.

Continue climbing and reach a tiny gap where Mount Cammerer Trail cuts sharply back to the right (north). If you think you can add 1.2 miles to your hike and still make it to Cosby Knob Shelter before dark, you definitely should take this side trip. The trail leads 0.6 mile along the ridge to Mount Cammerer Lookout (see Hike 45).

The view from the lookout is outstanding in all directions, but study carefully the view from the southwest to the southeast. That ridgeline you see is the one you will follow later in the hike. Look southeast across the Big Creek watershed to the tower rising above the trees. That's Mount Sterling Fire Tower and at its base is Campsite 38, your third night's camp on a three-night backpack. Yep, you've got a long haul ahead of you!

Back on the AT, continue heading south on a mostly downhill stretch to Low Gap and the junction with Low Gap Trail. Low Gap Trail crosses here, having climbed from Cosby Campground to the right and Walnut Bottoms to the left. Continue straight on the AT and climb steadily for 0.8 mile to a side path on the left, leading in a few hundred feet to Cosby Knob Shelter. The shelter is a good choice for your first night's camp.

Pressing on from the shelter, climb through a particularly scenic forest of spruce, hemlock, and rhododendron as you skirt the summit of Cosby Knob. Soon you begin a long descent to Camel Gap and the junction with Camel Gap Trail, forking off to the left. Continue to the right on the AT and begin a long, steady ascent of 2.3 miles

Chestnut Branch cascades through a lush forest. ▶

to another fork. Snake Den Ridge Trail goes to the right here, while your trail goes left and—you guessed it—continues climbing.

As you climb from the junction with Snake Den Ridge Trail, you might spot pieces of wreckage from an Air Force jet that crashed into Inadu Knob on the evening of January 4, 1984. According to the book *Mayday! Mayday!* by Jeff Wadley and Dwight McCarter, the jet was flying at 450 mph when it hit the mountain just 80 feet shy of the summit. The impact created the largest crash site in the Smokies, at nearly 20 acres. You might see pieces of the wreckage along this stretch. At one time there was a heavy chunk of an airplane leaning against the Cosby Knob Shelter, but if it was from this crash site, you have to have sympathy for the person who lugged it that far. (You probably should question their sanity as well.)

Finally, you top out on a grassy ridge with a great view ahead of Mount Guyot and Old Black. Continue through an open area and pass over a helicopter landing pad before entering the forest again. The AT skirts the summit of Old Black (6,370 feet) and then crosses a couple of good springs as it skirts the summit of Mount Guyot. At 6,621 feet, Guyot is the second-highest mountain in the park. As you skirt some 300 feet below the summit, you pass through a tangle of dead and fallen Fraser fir.

After you reach Balsam Mountain Trail on the left, continue on the AT a short distance to the side path on the left that leads to Tricorner Knob Shelter, one of the most remote shelters in the park. This is probably where you'll sleep tonight if doing this hike as a three-nighter. The next morning, walk back up to Balsam Mountain Trail and turn right onto it.

After the hike you just made on the AT, you're going to enjoy the next 9.7 miles. Except for a few short spurts, it's nearly level the entire distance. The first 5.8 miles take you on a heavily overgrown course to Mount Sterling Ridge Trail, on the left. (You pass Gunter Fork Trail at 4.9 miles; go right/southeast to stay on Balsam Mountain Trail.) At the Mount Sterling Ridge Trail junction, Balsam Mountain Trail continues 0.2 mile to Laurel Gap Shelter. If you planned this trip as a four-nighter, the shelter is your third night's stay. Most hikers will want to hike straight through from Tricorner Knob to Mount Sterling in a day, a distance of 11.5 miles.

Now on Mount Sterling Ridge Trail, the level hiking continues. For some 3 miles, you hardly leave the contour line as you pass through a rather uneventful forest. You cross a number of headwater branches in this segment, a few of them surprisingly large for this elevation. Leaving the contour line, you enter a scenic open birch forest and begin an undulating course before descending to Pretty Hollow Gap. The gap marks the junction with Swallow Fork Trail and Pretty Hollow Gap Trail, coming up from the left and right, respectively. Swallow Fork Trail is the route you take in Hike 79 to get to this point.

From the gap, continue straight (east) on Mount Sterling Ridge Trail. The first 0.5 mile from the gap ascends steeply to cross a knoll in a particularly beautiful forest of spruce, birch, and beech. You soon begin ascending again and merge onto Mount Sterling Trail, coming in from the right. From here, it's 0.4 mile to the summit of Mount Sterling and Campsite 38. This is your final night's camp. The steel fire tower

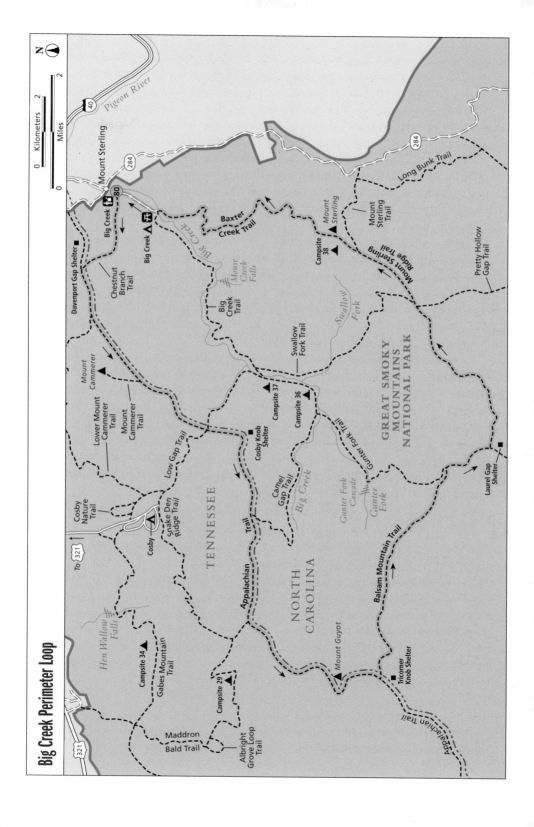

Big Creek Perimeter Loop

N

0 Kilometers 2
0 Miles 2

Pigeon River

40

284

Mount Sterling

80

Big Creek

Big Creek

Davenport Gap Shelter

Chestnut Branch Trail

Baxter Creek Trail

Big Creek

Mouse Creek Falls

Big Creek Trail

Mount Sterling

Campsite 38

Mount Sterling Ridge Trail

Mount Sterling Trail

Long Bunk Trail

Pretty Hollow Gap Trail

Swallow Fork

Swallow Fork Trail

GREAT SMOKY MOUNTAINS NATIONAL PARK

Mount Cammerer

Lower Mount Cammerer Trail

Mount Cammerer Trail

Low Gap Trail

Cosby Nature Trail

To 321

Cosby

Snake Den Ridge Trail

TENNESSEE

Appalachian Trail

Camel Gap Trail

Cosby Knob Shelter

Campsite 37

Campsite 36

Gunter Fork Trail

Big Creek

Gunter Fork Cascade

Gunter Fork

NORTH CAROLINA

Balsam Mountain Trail

Laurel Gap Shelter

Hen Wallow Falls

Campsite 34

Gabes Mountain Trail

321

Campsite 29

Maddron Bald Trail

Albright Grove Loop Trail

Mount Guyot

Tricorner Knob Shelter

Appalachian Trail

at the summit is open for climbing and is a highlight of the hike. When the wind howls, it's a little frightening climbing to the top, but you need to get above the trees at least. The panoramic view is among the finest in the park.

Baxter Creek Trail, which you will use to get down the mountain, starts on the summit of Mount Sterling by the base of the tower. The trail descends steadily (sometimes steeply) to Big Creek Picnic Area in 6.1 miles, with superb forest scenery along most of the trail. About 0.25 mile down from the fire tower, you come to a signed side path on the left that leads in a couple hundred yards to a reliable spring. On the main trail, hike along a ridge and through switchbacks in a boulder field. Lush, thick moss covers every ground surface you see. This stretch is reminiscent of a southeast Alaska rain forest.

About 2 miles from Mount Sterling, you make an extreme left switchback off the ridgeline and enter an enchanted old-growth forest with several species of trees. Look all around through here but especially above the trail toward the ridge, where some gigantic gnarly maples grow. Farther down, you cross a tributary and soon begin paralleling Baxter Creek. Several large yellow poplars (tulip trees) grow in this scenic, open forest. There are some big hemlocks here too, but they are all dead from the adelgid attack (see the sidebar for Hike 36).

After crossing Baxter Creek you pass through a dense stand of second-growth yellow poplar. At the lower end of the poplar grove, the trail makes a sharp right turn and goes a few yards to cross a small stream. At the right turn, a side path turns to the left and leads a few hundred yards to one of the tallest standing chimneys in the park. Along the way it passes a stone structure of some sort that has some old metal artifacts piled on top. You can easily see it from the main trail when the leaves are off the trees.

After crossing the small stream, Baxter Creek Trail soon reaches the long footbridge over Big Creek. The picnic area is on the far side. Walk through the picnic area and then follow the gravel road back to your car.

Miles and Directions

0.0 Start on Chestnut Branch Trail at the parking area beside Big Creek Ranger Station.

2.1 Junction with the AT. Turn left (southwest) on the AT.

3.0 Junction with Lower Mount Cammerer Trail on the right. Continue following the AT.

5.3 Junction with Mount Cammerer Trail, cutting sharply to the right. The trail leads 0.6 mile to the lookout on Mount Cammerer (Hike 45). If not taking this side trip, continue straight ahead on the AT.

7.4 Low Gap Trail crosses the AT at Low Gap. Continue straight ahead on the AT.

8.2 Side path on the left leads to Cosby Knob Shelter.

9.8 Camel Gap Trail forks to the left. Stay to the right on the AT.

12.1 Snake Den Ridge Trail forks to the right. Stay to the left on the AT.

15.8 Turn left on Balsam Mountain Trail. A few hundred feet farther on the AT is a side path on the left leading to Tricorner Knob Shelter. If overnighting at the shelter, return to Balsam Mountain Trail in the morning.

20.7 Junction with Gunter Fork Trail. Stay to the right (southeast) on Balsam Mountain Trail.

21.6 Junction with Mount Sterling Ridge Trail, on the left. Laurel Gap Shelter is 0.2 mile to the right on Balsam Mountain Trail. To continue the hike, turn left onto Mount Sterling Ridge Trail.

25.5 Junction with Pretty Hollow Gap and Swallow Fork Trails on the right and left. Continue straight on Mount Sterling Ridge Trail.

26.9 Junction with Mount Sterling Trail, coming up from the right and continuing straight ahead. Continue straight along the ridge.

27.3 Arrive at summit of Mount Sterling and Campsite 38. Take Baxter Creek Trail, which begins near the base of the fire tower.

33.4 Arrive at Big Creek Picnic Area. Walk through the picnic area and onto the gravel entrance road. Follow the road back to your car.

34.0 Arrive back at the start of the hike.

Options: For most people, the best option for camping is a three-night backpack, staying the first night at Cosby Knob Shelter, the second night at Tricorner Knob Shelter, and the third night at Campsite 38 on Mount Sterling. For a tough two-nighter, you could stay the first night at Cosby Knob Shelter and the second night at Laurel Gap Shelter. If you're like a Navy SEAL in training, you could head out early in the morning and spend one night at Tricorner Knob Shelter. For a "stop and smell the roses" trip, you could do a four-nighter, staying at all three shelters and Campsite 38.

Combining all the trails in the Big Creek and Cosby section of the park offers unlimited backpacking possibilities, especially with the use of shuttles. Study a trail map for possibilities.

HOW DID YOU SAY THAT?

Mystery surrounds the pronunciation of many Smoky Mountain place names, but probably no name in the park is butchered more often than Mount Guyot. The second-highest peak in the park and the fourth highest in the East, at 6,621 feet, Guyot is named after Swiss-born geologist and geographer Arnold Henry Guyot. Guyot surveyed the southern Appalachians in the late 1850s, measuring and mapping the high peaks of the Smokies during this period.

So how do you pronounce Guyot's name? It's gē-ō, with a hard g and emphasis on either syllable. Now when you're sitting around the campfire at Tricorner Knob Shelter in the shadow of Mount Guyot, you can impress your hiking buddies with this bit of trivia. Just remember, however, that blank stares are an occupational hazard for backpackers who know how to pronounce Swiss names.

Appalachian Trail

Silers Bald Shelter on the Appalachian Trail.

Overview of the Appalachian Trail

The Appalachian Trail (AT) needs no introduction to most people in the East. The nearly 2,200-mile trail stretches from Springer Mountain, Georgia, to Mount Katahdin, Maine, passing through myriad natural and modern communities and touching the lives of many people. The 72 miles of the trail that pass through the Smokies are considered by some to be a major highlight of the trail—both the most scenic and the most challenging. The Smokies portion has the highest elevation on the trail (Clingmans Dome, at 6,643 feet), and most of the trail follows high on the Smokies crest, along the state-line divide between North Carolina and Tennessee, where views abound.

It's no wonder that the AT is immensely popular in the park, but it's a shame that more people don't seek out other hiking opportunities. Certain portions of the AT are very crowded. Many people who plan trips to the park start out with the idea that they want to hike the AT no matter what. If they did a little more research, they might find that another trail suited their desires a little better. This is not to discourage you from hiking the AT—just a reminder that of the more than 800 miles of trail in the park, the AT accounts for less than 10 percent.

If you do decide to hike the AT, you need to consider a few things. First, although spring is a great time to hike the trail, it's not a good time to spend the night at an AT shelter because of all the northbound thru-hikers (people who attempt to hike the entire trail from Georgia to Maine). On any given night from March through early May, AT shelters in the park could be crammed with backpackers. You might be tempted to change the name from "Backcountry Shelter" to "Backcountry Snoratorium." And that's not even getting to the issue of trying to crawl over a dozen hikers to make a nature call, or the fact that none of them has had a bath in a while. If the park were located farther north, it wouldn't be as big of a problem. As it is, the park is so close to the southern terminus of the AT that most of the people who attempt a thru-hike haven't yet given up.

Reservations, which you must obtain to camp at any park shelter, don't help much during this time of year. AT thru-hikers aren't required to make specific shelter reservations because it's so difficult to determine exact schedules. (See thru-hiker regulations below.) Park rules state that thru-hikers must give up bunk space to reservation holders, but who is going to wave a little piece of paper at a group of exhausted backpackers and tell them they have to get out? Furthermore, the park issues limited permits for AT shelters during April and May, so the likelihood of obtaining a permit in the first place is diminished. Your best bet is to plan overnight hikes on the AT for another season.

Another consideration for hiking the AT in the Smokies is the weather. Many parts of the trail are in high elevations, including some 34 continuous miles above 5,000 feet. You can leave warm, sunny skies in Cherokee or Gatlinburg and arrive at Newfound Gap in a snowstorm. Winter hiking on the AT, especially overnight hiking, requires a lot of planning and a frank evaluation of your abilities.

This guidebook doesn't follow the route that thru-hikers use. Northbound thru-hikers start at Fontana Dam in spring and hike straight through to Davenport Gap, while southbound thru-hikers hike straight through from the opposite direction. Rather than beginning at the low elevations outside the park and hiking in, the two AT hikes in this guidebook start at Newfound Gap, at 5,046 feet, and head east and west to the park borders. Truth is, neither of these hikes is highly recommended. Unless your goal is simply to complete all of the AT within the park, you'll probably have a better hiking experience by utilizing sections of the AT along with other park trails. Thirteen hikes in this book do just that.

The AT is the only trail in the park that has consistent blazes marking the route. Along its entire length, the official blaze for the AT is a white vertical stripe. Two vertical stripes indicate a trail junction or other situation that could cause confusion. You might see an occasional blue stripe, which indicates some feature of interest, such as a nearby spring. If you bring a good map, such as the Trails Illustrated maps, you'd have to work hard to get lost on the AT in the Smokies. Like all official park trails, signs mark all the trail junctions. Even when the bears chew them up, it's a simple matter to determine the route. In most cases, simply remaining on the ridge-line will keep you on the AT, but there are a few junctions where that isn't the case. In nearly all official trail junctions, however, the adjoining trails *descend* from the AT, either right away or after a short, level stretch. Confusion can come from some of the many side paths that lead to view points or other features. Bring a good map and use it.

The AT follows the Smokies crest line for most of its length through the park and, except for the section from Fontana Dam to Doe Knob, it roughly follows the boundary between North Carolina and Tennessee. Because it follows the crest line, it does not cross any creeks in the park and in only a few places does the trail cross or come within a few feet of a spring. However, there are numerous springs located a short walk down from the ridge. All of the shelters and Campsite 113 (the only backcountry campsite—not shelter—along the AT in the park) have water sources, although some of them are unreliable during dry periods. Before setting out it's a good idea to call the park backcountry office at (865) 436-1231 and inquire about the current conditions of the springs. The rangers might not know whether a specific spring is running, but they can give you an idea of the general conditions. It's also a good idea to ask the hikers you meet along the trail.

Regulations for Appalachian Trail Thru-Hikers in the Smokies

Thru-hiker regulations apply to anyone who attempts to hike the entire length of the AT in a single trip, or anyone who begins hiking at least 50 miles from outside the park, hikes the entire AT through the park, and continues to hike at least 50 additional miles outside the park. Thru-hiker regulations do not apply to *any* hikes included in this book, including both Hikes 81 and 82.

- Thru-hikers are required to obtain backcountry camping permits, the same as with any other person camping in the backcountry. However, instead of designating specific campsites or shelters, they should write "Thru-Hiker" in the space for the campsite name.
- Thru-hikers must complete their journeys through the park in 7 nights, or else they must designate where they will spend the night.
- Thru-hikers must sleep in the bunks at shelters if there is space, and in the immediate vicinity if the shelter is full. Hikers who have reservations for a shelter are supposed to have priority over bunk space.
- Thru-hikers who camp at backcountry campsites or shelters that are not located along the AT forfeit their status as thru-hikers and must obtain permits the same as everyone else.
- The general hiking regulations listed in the introduction apply to thru-hikers as well as everyone else.
- Northbound thru-hikers can obtain permits at the self-registration station located at the restroom building at the top of the ramp leading to Fontana Marina. Southbound thru-hikers can obtain permits from the US Forest Service ranger station at Hot Springs.

81 Appalachian Trail West

Sections of this hike are covered in other hikes in this guidebook and there is no shortage of literature about the Appalachian Trail (AT). The intent here is simply to provide a concise outline of key points and alert you to any potential concerns along the way.

A good time to make this trip is in October or November, when the crowds have thinned. In October there will be crowds from Clingmans Dome to Silers Bald and in the Spence Field area, but most of the "leaf peepers" don't get far from their cars. In autumn you also avoid the heat of summer, which is good on a hike that has no streams to dip into. However, you have to prepare for cold weather. Snow is common in November, and you should come prepared for it in October.

Obviously, for this hike, you want to remain on the AT at all trail junctions, so this isn't necessarily specified in the directions.

Start: Newfound Gap
Distance: 40.3 miles point to point
Hiking time: About 23 hours—3-night backpack, killer 2-nighter, relaxed 4-nighter, or insane overnighter
Difficulty: Strenuous, due to steep grades and very rocky trail
Trail surface: Forest trails and hard-packed dirt paths, some very rocky and rooty
Other trail users: Equestrians permitted on about a third of the route
Maps: Clingmans Dome, Silers Bald, Thunderhead Mountain, Cades Cove, and Fontana Dam USGS quads; Trails Illustrated #229 Great Smoky Mountains; Trails Illustrated #317 Clingmans Dome Cataloochee; Trails Illustrated #316 Cades Cove Elkmont (does not show most of the section from Newfound Gap to Clingmans Dome)

Special considerations: Read the introduction to the AT at the beginning of this section for general considerations. In very dry periods the springs at Russell Field and Mollies Ridge Shelters can dry up. The implications of making extended winter hikes at these elevations can't be overstated. If you are not experienced in winter backpacking, this is not the place to learn.

Other: Newfound Gap has a very large parking lot, but it can fill up on weekends or any day during the summer and autumn seasons. Restrooms are located here.

The Fontana Dam Visitor Center, near where you end this hike, has free hot showers that are open 24 hours a day. That's something to think about as you sweat along the trail.

Finding the trailhead: The trailhead is located at Newfound Gap Overlook on the Smokies crest. Drive 15.5 miles north on Newfound Gap Road from Oconaluftee Visitor Center or 12.7 miles south from Sugarlands Visitor Center. The AT runs across Newfound Gap at the painted crosswalk. You want to head northwest, on the opposite side of the road from the parking area. GPS: N35 36.669' / W83.25.495'

You need to leave a second vehicle or arrange for a shuttle to pick you up at Fontana Dam. From the junction of US 19/74 and NC 28 in the southwestern portion of the park, turn west onto NC 28 and drive 21.1 miles to the stop sign at the entrance road for Fontana Dam. Turn right and follow the road 1.1 miles to the dam. Drive over the dam and turn right at the fork. Continue 0.7 mile to the road's end at a trail information board. GPS: N35 27.644' / W83 48.664'

An autumn view along the southern portion of the Appalachian Trail.

The Hike

Walk across Newfound Gap Road on the painted crosswalk and enter a different world. Within a few yards the crowds will be gone and you'll have relative solitude along most of the trail. You'll encounter plenty of other hikers, to be sure, but except for a few short stretches, you'll feel like you left the tourist crowd behind and entered a different realm of the Smokies. And in fact, you did.

The 8.0 miles from Newfound Gap to Clingmans Dome follow the road closely, with the grumbling of loud mufflers rarely out of earshot. The first part of this section is relatively easy. Come to a hog exclosure with a unique ramp system allowing hikers to pass through. Hog hoofs can't make it up the ramp; hiking boots have no trouble unless it's icy. Descend to Indian Gap and the junction with Road Prong Trail and a parking area. The Clingmans Dome USGS quad does not give a name for this gap and names the previous gap you hiked through "Indian Gap." Old editions of the Trails Illustrated map call the gap here "Little Indian Gap" and it has also been referred to as "Luftee Gap." However, most references, including park literature, refer to the gap here at the parking area as Indian Gap.

Regardless of what you call it, continue straight from the gap and climb steeply. Crest out in a dark forest of young spruce and fir. This spot provides a hint of what the great spruce-fir forests must have looked like before the arrival of the balsam woolly adelgid and acid precipitation (see the sidebar for Hike 49). Imagine what this forest would look like with all the trees being 2 to 3 feet in diameter.

Now go on a long and very scenic stretch where the trail passes through a dense and lush closed-in forest. There are ups and downs typical of the AT, but the grade is not too bad. A spur path on the left leads in a short distance to Clingmans Dome Road and the Fork Ridge trailhead. Notice the uprooted trees here. Life is hard in the cold and wind of these elevations—hard enough without the extra burden of introduced pests and air pollution.

From the spur path, continue southwest on the AT and reach the junction with Sugarland Mountain Trail, on the right. A 0.4-mile easy walk on this trail takes you to Mount Collins Shelter. The AT continues south on a typical undulating course. In summer look for Turk's cap lily growing in patches beside the trail. A long, steady ascent heralds the approach to Clingmans Dome. The trail passes within a few yards of the lookout tower. On a clear day a side trip up the tower is a must. Fortunately, you don't have to walk on the paved path that leads from the Forney Ridge Parking Area to the tower. Scoot up the tower, soak in the views, and get back to your dirt and rocks.

Just beyond the tower you come to another spur on the left, this one connecting with the paved path. Stay to the right (west) on the AT and soon reach the junction with Clingmans Dome Bypass Trail, coming in from the left. Continue on the AT, but take time to admire the view off the north side of the trail toward Mount LeConte. The next 2.5 miles on the AT to Double Spring Gap Shelter are relatively easy and provide numerous open vistas. (About 0.6 mile before reaching the shelter, you pass the junction with Goshen Prong Trail.) Not surprisingly, Double Spring Gap has two springs, one on each side of the gap and only a few yards from the shelter. If you're getting water, the spring on the south side is much better; the northern spring seeps through a boggy area.

Pressing on from the gap, the AT goes on its typical roller-coaster grade through a forest of beech, buckeye, and mountain ash. At one point the trail opens in a grassy spot with fair views on the left toward High Rocks. At this point you come to the Narrows—a knife-edge ridge with good views off both sides. The trail soon forks at the junction with Welch Ridge Trail, which goes to the left. A 0.2-mile steep climb from here brings you to the 5,607-foot summit of Silers Bald at a small clearing. There's only one fair view from the clearing, looking back toward Clingmans Dome. On a sunny day you can see the light reflecting from the cars at Forney Ridge Parking Area. An obvious path leads north from the summit a few hundred feet to a rock outcrop with wonderful open views to the north, as well as leafy views to the east and west.

From the summit, descend on the AT to Silers Bald Shelter. If you're camping here and the weather is clear, you can take in a show after dinner. Hike back up on Silers Bald and watch the sunset from the rock outcrop.

The trail from Silers Bald Shelter to the junction with Miry Ridge Trail is the typical undulating ridge-walking characteristic of the AT. By now you've surely noticed that you left the spruce and fir trees back at the higher elevations and are hiking in a mixed-hardwood forest. At the Miry Ridge Trail junction, continue straight on the AT and climb steeply up Cold Spring Knob. After topping out it's a relatively easy hike to the Greenbrier Ridge Trail junction. From Greenbrier Ridge Trail, continue straight (as usual) on the AT and climb Big Chestnut Bald before leveling out to Derrick Knob Shelter. This shelter has one of the most scenic settings of any in the park. In summer coneflower and snakeroot cover the open field in front of the shelter.

From the shelter, it's a short and easy climb over a knoll and then a nearly continuous descent to Sugartree Gap, marked by sugar maples and an American chestnut log that makes a great seat. Climb steeply from Sugartree Gap and then descend to Starkey Gap, also featuring a chestnut sitting log.

From Starkey Gap, you make a brutal ascent up Brier Knob, perhaps the most strenuous segment on the Smokies portion of the AT. The elevation of Starkey Gap is 4,527 feet. On the peak of Brier Knob, a little more than 0.5 mile farther, it's 5,215 feet. Beyond Brier Knob, you soon come to an open area with views and then descend dangerously over rocks. From here, you go on a fairly easy stretch, a steep descent, a short climb, and then an easy ridgeline walk to a gap. A small sign on a cherry tree reads WATER, indicating that a small spring lies a short distance down the north side of the gap.

From the gap, proceed on a long (but not too steep) climb to the summit of Thunderhead Mountain (5,527 feet). Thunderhead is the highest peak in the western portion of the park and dominates views from all directions. Unfortunately, there are no good views from the mountain itself. From the top of a small pile of rocks, there's a fair view to the south and west, but that's it.

A short distance from the summit of Thunderhead, the trail opens into a grassy clearing with great views to the south and west. A good portion of Cades Cove is plainly visible. After a quick descent you climb on a rocky knoll and enjoy more great views. The view straight down is of graffiti-covered rocks. The graffiti does have historical value in that some of the markings were made by early livestock herders in the late nineteenth and early twentieth centuries. It's a shame that modern hikers sometimes add their marks as well. Continuing along the rocky ridge, you reach the official Rocky Top (according to the USGS map) and its nearly panoramic views. What a special place this is!

From Rocky Top, descend steeply to a gap and then climb steeply over a knoll and to the junction with Jenkins Ridge Trail, cutting sharply to the left. You're in Spence Field now, and you will be for the next 0.75 mile or so. Cross a small knoll and descend a short distance to the junction with Bote Mountain Trail on the right, and a few hundred feet farther, Eagle Creek Trail on the left. A 0.2-mile hike down Eagle Creek Trail takes you to Spence Field Shelter.

Continuing on the AT, the 2.6-mile stretch from Spence Field to Russell Field Shelter is a cakewalk compared to some of the hiking you've done to get here. There are a few slight humps, but mostly it's a pleasant downhill grade. Russell Field Shelter sits at the junction with the AT and Russell Field Trail. The setting is attractive, and the rustic shelter, like most in the park, is charming.

On leaving Russell Field Shelter, the AT goes through rerouted sections that take a lot of the steepness out of the old route. The trail makes an easy descent to Little Abrams Gap, and then it begins a long climb before making a short descent to Mollies Ridge Shelter. The shelter sits on a ridge—imagine that—in a pleasant open forest of maple, buckeye, and black cherry.

From Mollies Ridge Shelter, you go on a long descent to Ekaneetlee Gap. A side path leads off the right (north) side of the gap to a small spring. From the gap, you make a long, moderate ascent up Doe Knob, skirting just short of the summit. A quick dip leads to the junction with Gregory Bald Trail. This time you don't continue straight—Gregory Bald Trail does that, continuing to follow the state-line ridge, as did the AT at one time before a reroute took it across Fontana Dam. You need to turn left (south) to stay on the AT.

The 2.2-mile segment from Doe Knob to Birch Spring Gap is downhill, with just enough bumps to keep you from getting lazy. At the gap a sign directs you to Birch Spring Campsite 113, off the right side of the trail. Walk 0.1 mile down the path to the most unique backcountry campsite in the Smokies. At other campsites you find a place for your tent in the clearings wherever you can. At Birch Spring the spots are carefully chosen for you. Scattered along the paths that lead on both sides of the drainage are level tent pads carved into the slope, with timbers from the old shelter

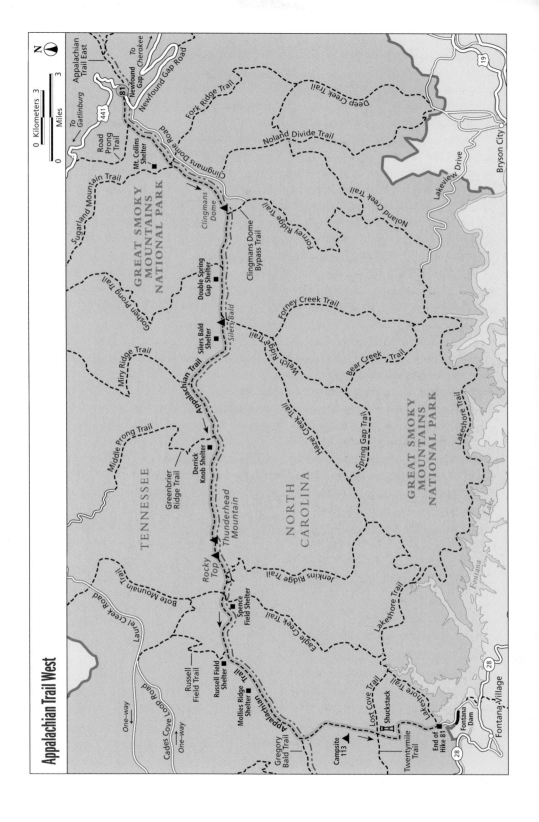

Appalachian Trail West

(no longer standing) used as retaining walls. Each site is far enough away from the others to offer privacy, but close to the central spring and campfire ring. Individual campfires are prohibited. Most of the stone from the old shelter now creates a network of terraces. If you want a souvenir from the shelter, grab a chunk of concrete from the pile, but leave the stones.

From Birch Spring Gap, you follow a typical undulating course to reach Sassafras Gap and the junction with Lost Cove Trail and Twentymile Trail. An easy 0.4-mile ascent from the gap brings you to a side path on the left that leads to the old Shuckstack Fire Tower. Do yourself a favor and hike the short trail to the tower and climb the steps at least above the tree line. No matter how tired you are, you won't regret it. The views are among the best in the Smokies. To the south are Fontana Lake and Dam, with the Snowbird Mountains in the background; to the west are the Unicoi Mountains; and to the north is the crest of the Smokies.

After soaking in the views from Shuckstack, backtrack to the AT and descend steeply for 3.5 miles to the trailhead parking area near Fontana Dam. Now, do everyone else a favor and visit those hot showers at the Fontana Dam Visitor Center!

Miles and Directions

0.0 Start from the northwest side of Newfound Gap Parking Area and cross Newfound Gap Road at the painted crosswalk.

1.7 Junction, right, with Road Prong Trail at Indian Gap.

4.2 Side trail on the left leads to Clingmans Dome Road and Fork Ridge trailhead.

4.5 Junction with Sugarland Mountain Trail on the right. Mount Collins Shelter is 0.4 mile on Sugarland Mountain Trail.

8.0 Summit of Clingmans Dome. Short spur leads to observation tower.

8.3 Junction with Clingmans Dome Bypass Trail on the left.

10.2 Junction with Goshen Prong Trail on the right.

10.8 Double Spring Gap Shelter.

12.1 Junction with Welch Ridge Trail on the left.

12.3 Silers Bald.

12.5 Silers Bald Shelter.

15.3 Junction with Miry Ridge Trail on the right.

17.7 Junction with Greenbrier Ridge Trail on the right.

18.1 Derrick Knob Shelter.

22.5 Summit of Thunderhead Mountain.

23.2 Rocky Top.

23.9 Junction with Jenkins Ridge Trail on the left.

24.3 Junction with Bote Mountain Trail on the right.

24.4 Junction with Eagle Creek Trail on the left. Spence Field Shelter is 0.2 mile on Eagle Creek Trail.

26.9 Junction with Russell Field Trail, right, at Russell Field Shelter.

30.3 Mollies Ridge Shelter.

33.5 Junction with Gregory Bald Trail on the right.

35.7 Birch Spring Backcountry Campsite (the shelter no longer stands).

36.6 Junction with Lost Cove Trail (left) and Twentymile Trail (right) at Sassafras Gap.

36.8 Side trail on the left leads to Shuckstack Tower.

40.3 Parking at end of road from Fontana Dam. Lakeshore Trail starts here.

Options: Most people probably will want to do this hike as a three-nighter. You can stretch it out as far as you want, but four nights is the most that you can take and not start feeling lazy. Of course, if a lazy outing is what you want, go for it. A two-nighter is certainly doable, but you'll miss smelling some of the roses along the way.

Experienced hard-core hikers can make the trip as an overnighter if they leave early in the morning from Newfound Gap. Some AT thru-hikers do this stretch as an overnighter, having rested and fattened up in Fontana Village before entering the park. The shelters are spaced well enough that you should have no trouble planning a trip to suit your needs. Study a trail map for possibilities.

Appalachian Trail East

Sections of this hike are covered in other hikes in this guidebook and there is no short-age of literature about the Appalachian Trail (AT). The intent here is simply to provide a concise outline of key points and alert you to any potential concerns along the way.

A good time to make this trip is in October or November, when the crowds have thinned. In October there will be crowds from Newfound Gap to Charlies Bunion, but most of the "leaf peepers" don't get far from their cars. In autumn you also avoid the heat of summer, which is good on a hike that has no streams to dip into. However, you have to prepare for cold weather. Snow is common in November, and you should come prepared for it in October.

Obviously, for this hike you want to remain on the AT at all trail junctions, so this isn't necessarily specified in the directions.

Start: Newfound Gap
Distance: 31.5 miles point to point
Hiking time: About 17 hours—2-night back-pack, 3-nighter, or tough overnighter
Difficulty: Strenuous, due to steep grades and very rocky trail
Trail surface: Forest trails and hard-packed dirt paths, some very rocky and rooty
Other trail users: Equestrians permitted on about two-thirds of the route
Maps: Clingmans Dome, Mount LeConte, Mount Guyot, Luftee Knob, Hartford, and Waterville USGS quads; Trails Illustrated #229 Great Smoky Mountains; Trails Illustrated #317 Clingmans Dome Cataloochee
Special considerations: Read the introduc-tion to the AT at the beginning of this section for general considerations. The implications of making extended winter hikes at these elevations can't be overstated. If you are not experienced in winter backpacking, this is not the place to learn.

This hike outlines the entire eastern stretch of the AT from Newfound Gap to Davenport Gap, but you may want to consider ending at Big Creek Ranger Station instead of Davenport Gap. If you're leaving a shuttle vehicle, it will be much safer at the ranger station than at the gap. Dropping off the AT 1.9 miles short of the gap and hiking 2.1 miles down Chestnut Branch Trail adds only 0.2 mile to the total distance. If you're determined to hike all of this section of the AT, you could still leave your car at the ranger station and walk an extra 1.3 miles along the road.

Other: Newfound Gap has a very large park-ing lot, but it can fill up on weekends or any day during the summer and autumn season. Restrooms are located here.

There is very limited parking and no facili-ties at Davenport Gap at the end of the hike. Ample parking is available at Big Creek Ranger Station. Pit toilets are available here.

Finding the trailhead: The trailhead is located at Newfound Gap Overlook on the Smokies crest. Drive 15.5 miles north on Newfound Gap Road from Oconaluftee Visitor Center or 12.7 miles south from Sugarlands Visitor Center. The trailhead is on the northeast end of the parking lot, between the paved path leading to the restrooms and the Rockefeller Memorial. GPS: N35 36.669' / W83.25.495'

You need to leave a second vehicle or arrange for a shuttle to pick you up at Davenport Gap or Big Creek Ranger Station. Take the Waterville exit (exit 457) off I-40 and cross Pigeon River. Stay to the left after the crossing and follow the road 2.0 miles to an intersection, passing the Walters Power Plant on the way. The intersection marks the community of Mount Sterling. For the ranger station, go straight and enter the Big Creek section of the park. Follow the road 0.2 mile to the ranger station and parking area on the right (GPS: N35 45.610' / W83 06.386'). For Davenport Gap, turn right at the intersection and drive 1.1 miles. There is no parking lot here, just a narrow pull-out a short distance from the gap. GPS: N35 46.243' / W83 06.669'

The Hike

Begin hiking from the northeast corner of the parking area. The trail starts out level and wide, but you soon begin a 1.5-mile steady ascent to a grassy knoll. You're walking through a high-elevation spruce-fir forest, with occasional openings providing vistas of Mount LeConte to the north. In late April and early May, spring beauty and trout lily cover the ground.

From the knoll, descend 0.2 mile to a gap and the junction with Sweat Heifer Creek Trail at a huge, gnarled birch tree. Continue east on the AT and begin a steep ascent. You soon pass an open view into North Carolina, taking in Clingmans Dome, Newfound Gap Road, and a glimpse of Bryson City. At 2.7 miles you reach the junction with The Boulevard Trail. The Boulevard Trail forks left (north) and leads to Mount LeConte. For a terrific side trip, follow The Boulevard Trail about 0.1 mile to a side path on the right for the Jumpoff. There may be a sign here. It is at a wide spot in the trail created by an uprooted tree on the left. The path goes to the right and climbs the bank on rocks and roots. The rugged path leads about 0.5 mile to an overlook that provides a great view of Charlies Bunion.

Now back on AT at the junction with The Boulevard Trail, continue heading northeast on the AT. After 0.3 mile a short side path on the right leads to Icewater Spring Shelter, situated in an open grassy area with good views. You'll probably see day hikers here, posing for pictures in front of the shelter.

Just beyond the shelter the trail passes literally over Icewater Spring. A rusty old pipe provides a drop so that you can fill a water bottle, but there's something unappealing about drinking water that comes out of a heavily trodden trail. (Be sure to treat all drinking water in the Smokies, no matter the source.)

Beyond the spring it's an easy hike of about a mile to the side trail for Charlies Bunion, on the left. Do yourself a favor and take this side path. The bare, jagged cliffs of Charlies Bunion remind you more of the young Rockies than the old, worn Appalachians. The views are spectacular. To the west is the Jumpoff; to the northwest is the unmistakable Mount LeConte; and to the northeast is Greenbrier Pinnacle. You'll want to spend some time here, but take extra precaution. Many people have fallen while climbing on the rocks.

Back on the AT it's 0.4 mile to the junction with Dry Sluice Gap Trail. Beyond the junction you pass over the Sawteeth, a fitting name for this series of narrow jagged ridges. The views through here are good, but nothing like what you experienced at Charlies Bunion. The hiking is typical AT ridge walking, with ups, downs, and short levels. About 4 miles from Charlies Bunion, and after an arduous ascent, the AT makes a sharp bend to the right (south) and descends along the east side of Laurel Top. Mountain laurel grows densely here, attesting to the mountain's name. Good views of Mounts Chapman, Guyot, and Sequoyah are to the east.

Reach Bradley's View, one of the best of the hike, at 8.9 miles. At 10.5 miles Hughes Ridge Trail cuts sharply right. A 0.4-mile hike down this trail brings you to Pecks Corner Shelter.

Beyond the junction with Hughes Ridge Trail, you hike along perhaps the least-traveled and most remote stretch of the AT in the park. That doesn't mean you won't see other hikers, but you'll probably see fewer here than elsewhere on the trail. Less than a mile from Hughes Ridge Trail, you come to a rock outcrop called Eagle Rocks. The view from here into the Middle Prong watershed is spectacular. Descend from Eagle Rocks to a gap and climb again to cross over Mount Sequoyah, just below the summit. Now make a long, gradual descent before climbing again to swing around Mount Chapman. Top out a good distance below the summit of Mount Chapman and descend to a gap. A short climb from the gap takes you to Tricorner Knob Shelter, on the right.

Balsam Mountain Trail turns to the right a short distance beyond Tricorner Knob Shelter. As you swing around Mount Guyot, some 300 feet below the summit, you pass through a tangle of dead and fallen Fraser firs. You'll cross a couple of good springs along this section—the water from them eventually flows over Ramsey Cascades. At 6,621 feet, Guyot is the second-highest mountain in the park. After skirting Guyot you swing around the summit of Old Black and then enter an open grassy area with a helicopter landing pad. As you top out on a grassy ridge, look behind you for a great view of Old Black and Mount Guyot.

As you descend to the Junction with Snake Den Ridge Trail, you might spot pieces of wreckage from an Air Force jet that crashed into Inadu Knob on the evening of January 4, 1984. According to the book *Mayday! Mayday!* by Jeff Wadley and Dwight McCarter, the jet was flying at 450 mph when it hit the mountain just 80 feet shy of the summit. The impact created the largest crash site in the Smokies, at nearly 20 acres. You might see pieces of the wreckage along this stretch. At one time there was a heavy chunk of an airplane leaning against the Cosby Knob Shelter, some 4 miles away, but if it was from this crash site, you have to have sympathy for the person who lugged it that far.

An Appalachian Trail hiker takes a break at Icewater Spring Shelter.

Beyond the junction with Snake Den Ridge Trail, you continue on a long steady descent of 2.3 miles to the junction with Camel Gap Trail at Camel Gap. Now you start climbing again and skirt the summit of Ross Knob and then Cosby Knob, before descending to a side path on the right leading to Cosby Knob Shelter. Continue descending for 0.8 mile to Low Gap and the junction with Low Gap Trail.

From Low Gap, begin a steady climb for about a mile before leveling out on an easier grade. At 2.1 miles from Low Gap, you reach the junction with Mount Cammerer Trail, forking to the left. No matter how exhausted you may be, do yourself a favor and follow the path for 0.6 mile to the lookout on Mount Cammerer. It's a highlight of the AT hike.

Continuing on the AT, make a long steady descent, passing a couple of good views at rock outcrops. Reach the junction with Lower Mount Cammerer Trail in 2.3 miles from the side path to Mount Cammerer. From the junction, continue descending another 0.9 mile to the junction with Chestnut Branch Trail.

If you left your vehicle at Big Creek Ranger Station, from the junction with Chestnut Branch Trail, you can turn right onto the trail and hike 2.1 miles to the ranger station. If you left your vehicle at Davenport Gap or if you want to complete the AT, continue on a short, level stretch and then descend steeply to a side path on the left leading to Davenport Gap Shelter. From the shelter, continue

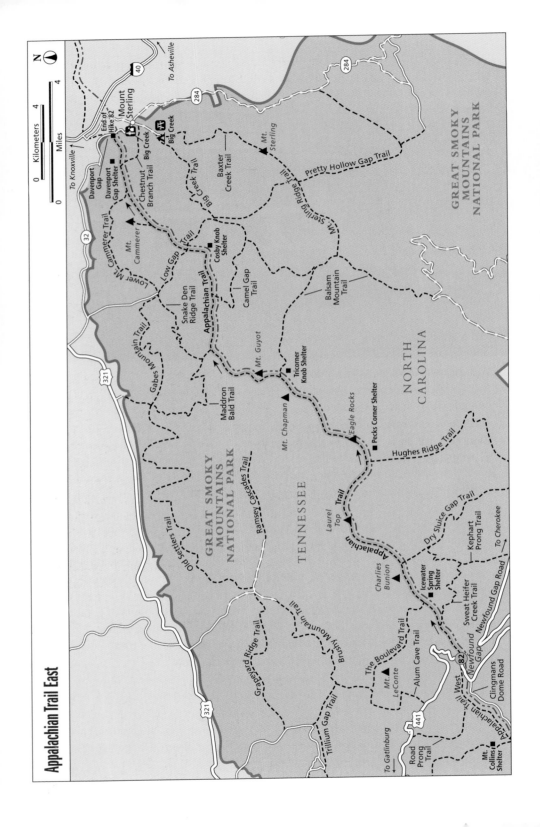

Appalachian Trail East

N

Kilometers 0 4

Miles 0 4

To Knoxville

40

To Asheville

32

321

284

Mount Sterling

End of Hike 82

Davenport Gap

Davenport Gap Shelter

Chestnut Branch Trail

Big Creek

Mt. Cammerer Trail

Lower Mt. Cammerer Trail

Mt. Cammerer

Low Gap Trail

Big Creek Trail

Baxter Creek Trail

Mt. Sterling

Pretty Hollow Gap Trail

Mt. Sterling Ridge Trail

Gabes Mountain Trail

Snake Den Ridge Trail

Appalachian Trail

Cosby Knob Shelter

Camel Gap Trail

Balsam Mountain Trail

Old Settlers Trail

Maddron Bald Trail

Mt. Guyot

Tricorner Knob Shelter

GREAT SMOKY MOUNTAINS NATIONAL PARK

GREAT SMOKY MOUNTAINS NATIONAL PARK

NORTH CAROLINA

TENNESSEE

Ramsey Cascades Trail

Mt. Chapman

Eagle Rocks

Pecks Corner Shelter

Hughes Ridge Trail

Laurel Top Trail

Dry Sluice Gap Trail

Kephart Prong Trail

To Cherokee

Brushy Mountain Trail

Grapeyard Ridge Trail

Appalachian Trail

Charlies Bunion

Icewater Spring Shelter

Sweat Heifer Creek Trail

Newfound Gap

Newfound Gap Road

Trillium Gap Trail

The Boulevard Trail

Mt. LeConte

Alum Cave Trail

West

82

441

To Gatlinburg

Road Prong Trail

Clingmans Dome Road

Appalachian Trail

Mt. Collins Shelter

descending nearly a mile to Davenport Gap. If you left your vehicle at the ranger station, turn right onto NC 284 and walk 1.1 miles to the intersection in the community of Mount Sterling. Turn right to reenter the park, and walk 0.2 mile to the ranger station.

Miles and Directions

0.0   Start on the northeast end of the parking lot.

1.7   Sweat Heifer Creek Trail comes in from the right.

2.7   The Boulevard Trail forks to the left (north). See hike text for a side trip from here.

3.0   Short path on the right leads to Icewater Spring Shelter.

4.0   Side path on the left to Charlies Bunion.

4.4   Junction with Dry Sluice Gap Trail, on the right.

10.5   Junction with Hughes Ridge Trail on the right. Pecks Corner Shelter is 0.4 on Hughes Ridge Trail.

15.8   Tricorner Knob Shelter and junction with Balsam Mountain Trail, on the right.

19.6   Junction with Snake Den Ridge Trail on the left.

21.9   Junction with Camel Gap Trail on the right.

23.5   Side path on the right to Cosby Knob Shelter.

24.3   Junction with Low Gap Trail on both sides.

26.4   Junction with Mount Cammerer Trail on the left.

28.7   Junction with Lower Mount Cammerer Trail on the left.

29.6   Junction with Chestnut Branch Trail on the right.

30.6   Side path on the left to Davenport Gap Shelter.

31.5   Davenport Gap.

Options: If you're doing this hike as a two-nighter, a good plan is to leave early in the morning from Newfound Gap and hike to Pecks Corner Shelter for the first night's stay. The next day you'd hike to Cosby Knob Shelter and stay there. This is certainly doable for experienced hikers, but if you haven't been on a trail in a while, you probably should do the trip as three-nighter, staying at Icewater Spring, Pecks Corner, and Cosby Knob Shelters. On a four-nighter, you'd add Tricorner Knob Shelter.

Appendix A: For More Information

The best sources for up-to-date and accurate information about Great Smoky Mountains National Park are the official park website at www.nps.gov/grsm and the site for Great Smoky Mountains Association at www.smokiesinformation.org. A plethora of other websites provides information about the park, but these official park sites are by far the most comprehensive and the only sites whose information you can trust to be accurate. In addition to useful online information about the Smokies, the GSMA website features the official park store, where you can buy everything that is sold in park visitor centers, including a large selection of books and maps. In conjunction with this guidebook, these two websites provide everything you need for planning your adventure in the Smokies.

You might consider becoming a member of Great Smoky Mountains Association. Membership entitles you to a 15 percent discount on books and other items at park visitor centers; a subscription to *Smokies Guide;* the association's newsletter, *The Bearpaw; Smokies Life* magazine; and many other benefits. There is an annual membership fee. You can join through the GSMA website.

Appendix B: Commercial Shuttle Services

Utilizing a shuttle service increases your hiking options greatly. Even if you live close enough to bring two vehicles, the convenience of a commercial shuttle is often worth the cost, not to mention the fuel savings from leaving that second car behind. If you plan to hike in the Eagle Creek and Hazel Creek region on the north shore of Fontana Lake, a boat shuttle saves you from a long hike in and also adds an exciting component to the hike.

The drawback to commercial shuttles, besides the cost, is that you must plan ahead. While it's possible that you'll catch the shuttle available on a last-minute call, in most cases you'll need to call ahead and make reservations.

AAA Hiker Service: (423) 487-3112 or (865) 322-0691

A Walk in the Woods: (865) 436-8283

Fontana Marina (for boat shuttles to the Eagle Creek and Hazel Creek embayments): (828) 498-2129

Fontana Village (for shuttles between Fontana Village and the Appalachian Trail or Fontana Marina): (828) 498-2211

The Hike Inn (service for the entire southwestern portion of the park and surrounding area): (828) 479-3677

Appendix C: Park Contact Information

Great Smoky Mountains National Park
107 Park Headquarters Rd.
Gatlinburg, TN 37738

Website: www.nps.gov/grsm

Main park number: (865) 436-1200
General backcountry information: (865) 436-1297
Backcountry campsite reservations: (865) 436-1231
Updated road information: (865) 436-1200, ext. 631
Updated weather information: (865) 436-1200, ext. 630

Hike Index

About the Author

Kevin Adams has had a lifelong love affair with nature, particularly in his home state of North Carolina. In the mid-1980s he received a camera as a birthday present. That gift set the stage for Kevin's total immersion into the outdoors and for his extensive traveling to photograph it. Kevin is author of seven other books, including *North Carolina Waterfalls, Backroads of North Carolina,* and *Waterfalls of Virginia and West Virginia.* An accomplished photography instructor, Kevin leads photo tours and teaches numerous workshops and seminars throughout the year. In addition, he has produced a series of eBooks and instructional videos about photography.

When he can get out of the office, Kevin enjoys hiking, of course, but also kayaking and just gazing at the night sky. Kevin lives in the shadow of the Great Smokies with his wife, Patricia, their two cats, Lucy and Titan, and a groundhog that lives under the house and eats Patricia's flowers.

For more about Kevin, visit his website at www.kadamsphoto.com.

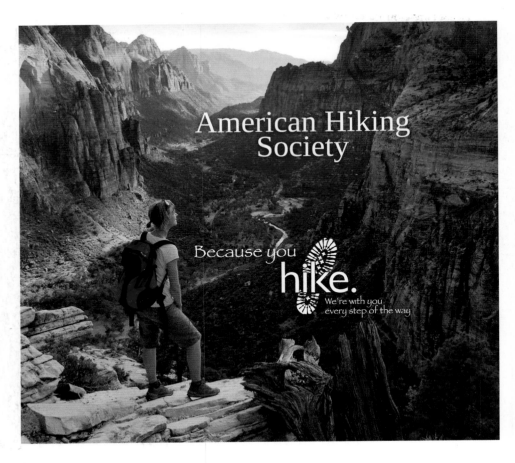

American Hiking Society

Because you hike.
We're with you every step of the way

As a national voice for hikers, **American Hiking Society** works every day:

- Building and maintaining hiking trails
- Educating and supporting hikers by providing information and resources
- Supporting hiking and trail organizations nationwide
- Speaking for hikers in the halls of Congress and with federal land managers

Whether you're a casual hiker or a seasoned backpacker, become a member of American Hiking Society and join the national hiking community! You'll enjoy great member benefits and help preserve the nation's hiking trails, so tomorrow's hike is even better than today's. We invite you to join us now!

American Hiking Society